FREEDOM FROM FEAR

How to Step Beyond Your Illusory Fears and Realize Your Dreams

VERA CULKOFF

FREEDOM FROM FEAR
How to Step Beyond Your Illusory Fears
and Realize Your Dreams

Limit of Liability/Disclaimer of Warranty: The information given in this book should not be treated as substitute for professional medical advice; always consult a medical practitioner. Any use of information in this book is at the reader's discretion and risk. Neither the author nor the publisher can be held responsible for any loss, claim or damage arising out of the use, or misuse, of the suggestions made in this book or the failure to take medical advice. The publisher and author make no representations or warranties with respect to the accuracy or completeness of the contents of this book and specifically disclaim any implied warranties or merchantability or fitness for a particular purpose. The recommendations and strategies contained herein are intended for a general audience and do not purport to be, nor should they be construed as, specific advice tailored to any individual and may not be suitable for your situation. You should consult with a professional adviser where appropriate.

Neither the publisher nor the author shall be liable for any loss of profit or any other commercial damages, including but not limited to special, incidental, consequential, or other damages.

Published by Celebrity Publishers
www.CelebrityPublishers.com
USA +1 702 997 2229
Australia +61 2 8005 4878

In Praise of This Book

Vera Culkoff has penned an extraordinary book on the challenging issue of Fear.

The theme often aligns with Emotional Intelligence discourse that suggests emotions like 'fear' can be framed as data, inviting the individual to optimize it, rather than avoiding it and triggering negative health outcomes.

Her book is both a treatise and a manual and will liberate, educate and inspire the reader to say 'Yes' to life when confronted by fearful self-limiting and lopsided perceptions of what is possible.

She discloses autobiographical milestones to profile how both disadvantage and privilege might challenge us to successfully convert perceived adversity into opportunity.

The book will undoubtedly be a transformative engagement for many readers and given it is being published in the time of Covid19 it is extraordinarily topical as humanity wrestles with fear, real and illusory.

In 1975 the reviewer worked with a group of Jewish barristers in Hampstead, London. They can be a tough group. Vera will certainly raise some eyebrows in Sydney. Good.

This reviewer can't help thinking that this book signals the end of one life stage and the beginning of a new chapter. I wonder if this new chapter may see Vera's extraordinary awareness, power to manifest intention and expertise in Law call her to contribute in some extraordinary transformative humanitarian endeavor to equilibrate collective fear.

Robert Gordon BEd M Coun GAICD CCG (INSEAD) FSID
CEO Board Accord
ww.boardaccord.com.au

Freedom from Fear by Vera Culkoff is not just a book on freedom from fear, it's surprisingly more. This book puts you in a state of adventure and every journey Vera takes you on it's like you are walking side by side with her. An easy read where you don't want to put this book down till you get to the end.

Vera is raw, and strips away every aspect of what is going on in everything that is shown in this book. Having the courage to show her real self is so refreshing. Yes: there are amazing exercises and practical tips, but it's more than that.

Her book has ignited a spark inside of me that has been sitting dormant for a while. We all have choices, fears, excuses that hold us back in life. By doing nothing that becomes a choice. Vera's life journey is inspirational and her drive to move forward whenever she was faced with challenges is a great lesson to all of us. She has now shown us a door we can walk into to create a life we all deserve.

I challenge you to read this amazing book. I highly recommend it. Can't wait to see what happens to her and her future journey in this lifetime.

Michael Malacos, Author and Speaker

In sharing her own personal journey, Vera Culkoff explores both the neuroscience and the philosophy of fear. She lucidly explains the role fear had in keeping us alive during the dangerous and uncertain eons of our prehistoric existence. At the same time, she challenges readers to examine and reflect on the beliefs that were formed during childhood, but that continue to hold us back as adults. As Vera so succinctly explains, we all have these fears, unarguably instinctive but also individually cultivated, based on our reactions to the personal experiences we encounter over our lifetime. We can all benefit from accepting Vera's challenge to expel the dysfunctional beliefs that are holding us back from manifesting our dreams.

**Elizabeth Noske: Neuro-Educator, Author,
Presenter and Trainer in
Brain-based Living and Learning. Author of *Mindfull Parent***

I have been privileged to read Vera's book, Freedom From Fear. Vera is one of the strongest women I have ever met. Yet, her book reveals – with honesty and openness - that even the strongest of us experience many fears that are the universal negatives that prevent us from realizing our dreams. I got a real insight into how a fear for one person could look ridiculous to another. I got in touch with some of my own ridiculous fears and chuckled at some of Vera's "illusory" fears. Her book is an easy, light-hearted read that will inspire you to transcend your fears and open the door to a true freedom. It worked for me. Thank you, Vera, for enlightening me about some of my fears.

**Natasha Lukin: Scientist and Positive
Psychology Practitioner and author –
*"The Lukin Longevity System"***

In sharing her deeply personal story, Vera Culkoff has provided a simple road map for anyone wanting to confront their fears and self-imposed limits. It's a fantastic how-to guide with short, sharp tools that support personal growth and help you discover the mindset to succeed at anything.

**Dr Rochelle Hammond: Dr of Traditional Chinese Medicine/
Acupuncturist & Educator, Sydney, Australia – promoting balance and
harmony of the body (that in turn has a positive effect on the mind)**

From the conditioned, illusory fears of childhood…

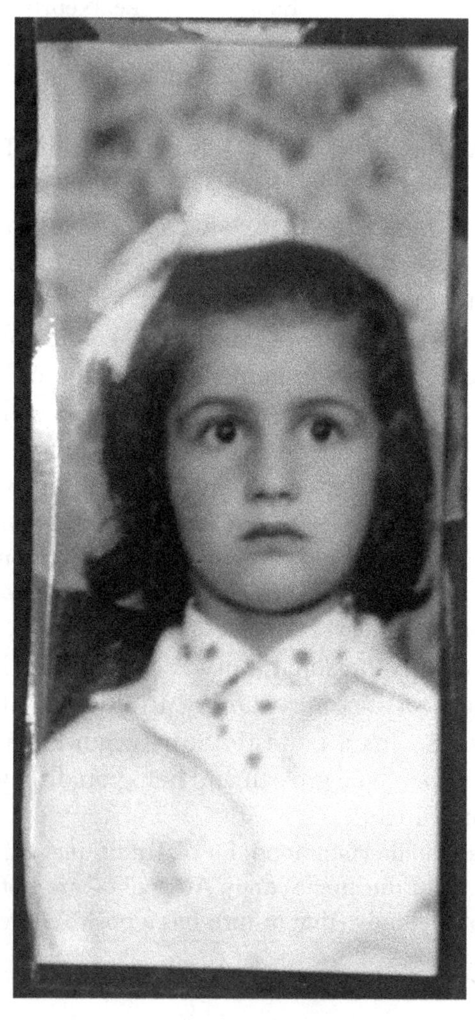

...to the freedom of today!

I invite you to read Freedom From Fear with an open mind and an open heart
Let your own intuition and wisdom connect the dots of your own unique life.

Let it open the door to a life you know you were meant to live.

About the Author

Vera Culkoff was a migrant of Macedonian heritage, having arrived in Australia from the former Yugoslavia, at the age of seven. She was an incredibly shy child, with a deep-rooted fear of not belonging that led her onto a path of academic excellence. Driven by that survival instinct that many migrants are confronted with, she ended up top of her class throughout high school and college. But she still left school at the age of 16, married at the age of 20 and became a mother at 23 - because that is what was expected of her. That was her cultural conditioning. Vera took up law as a hobby and ended up graduating with First Class Honours and the University Medal. Still driven by that deep-rooted fear of not belonging, she even considered doing a PhD to have "Dr" in front of her name - surely with this exalted qualification under her belt, she would then belong and be relevant in her new country.

Vera was confronted with a major life challenge at the age of 30 which set her on a path of self-questioning, discovery and growth. She finally woke up to the illusory nature of her fears, and to the conditioned nature of all our fears, which are instilled and inculcated in all of us by our cultures, our schooling, our parents, our friends and our very societies. She discovered that it is those conditioned fears that evolve into our belief systems and identities that prevent us from fulfilling our dreams. She discovered that what is conditioned in us can be unconditioned.

Vera shares her life's journey and the discoveries made along the way so that her readers can awaken to this reality and manifest their dreams – without having to undertake the decades of growth that she experienced.

Vera is now in her sixties and lives in the Eastern Suburbs of Sydney, Australia. She is a mother, daughter, sister, friend, practicing barrister...and hopefully an inspirational writer! Her life's journey opened the door to many new learnings and insights, over several decades. During her search, she travelled many roads, with many potholes that caused much pain.

She is passionate about sharing her life's lessons so that your potholes and your pain may be lessened; so that you can realize your dreams in a much shorter timeframe and with far less pain; so that you become aware of the many illusory fears that are preventing you from experiencing your true freedom and living your dreams.

That is the aim of her book: to inspire you to manifest your wildest dreams in the shortest time possible by learning how to step beyond your conditioned fears.

Acknowledgements

To my parents, Stefan and Milica: thank you for your unconditional love and support throughout my life's journey.

To my children, Sandy and Michael: thank you for being my triggers for growth and teaching me to love unconditionally.

To my brother, Kris and his methodical, analytical, structured mindset: thank you for editing FFF and for all your support.

I have been truly blessed.

What is your number one most
heartfelt passion?
What is that itch you have that refuses to be
scratched away?
That yearning deep within your
heart and soul?

Is Freedom From Fear the catalyst to inspire
you towards that passion and yearning?

Contemplate these questions as you read on.

Foreword

*"Our deepest fear is not that we are inadequate.
Our deepest fear is that we are all
powerful beyond measure"
— Marianne Williamson*

The aim of this book is to inspire you to manifest YOUR heartfelt dreams; to awaken you to the TRUTH that the only thing stopping you is your illusionary fears.

It is to inspire you to step onto that precipice of illusory fear and use it as a springboard to launch yourself into the unknown, so that you can experience your true FREEDOM.

It is an invitation to explore your own journey, just as I embarked upon my own exploration. That exploration led me on a quest of understanding who we truly are. This book is a tool, an aid to you exploring, contemplating and hopefully answering the age-old question: "Who am I?"- or more precisely: "Who am I NOT"?

You are not your mind. You are not your thoughts. You are not your body. You are eternal consciousness; the eternal witness, the observer, the all there is, was and ever will be. This pure, eternal consciousness has many names: your essence, your soul, God, Spirit, Higher Self, Inner Sharman – to name but a few.

Still the mind and you will capture that essence. Still your thoughts and you will step into the realm of consciousness, and be the witness who is ever present:

- observing your thoughts, your judgements, your fears;
- observing your incessant mind chatter;
- observing how you unconsciously (for the most part) create your very reality;
- observing how you – and by you, I mean your conditioned mind, your conditioned personality, your conditioned ego – is captive to all the countless conditioned fears that are an illusion.

Lao Tzu (the ancient Chinese philosopher, writer and reputed author of Taoist teachings), Mahatma Gandhi and Margaret Thatcher (amongst others) have all been credited with the following words:

> Watch your thoughts: They become your words
> Watch your words: They become your actions
> Watch your actions: They become your habits
> Watch your habits: They become your character
> Watch your character: It becomes your destiny

My bottom line is: as you think so shall you be! If you feed your thoughts and words with fear and fear-based words, they will become your actions. You will develop fearful habits and you will become a person who is feared or is fearful. Neither will support a destiny of love and peace and grace, which is your true essence. The late Wayne Dyer's best-selling book, *Change Your Thoughts – Change Your Life: Living the Wisdom of the Tao,* encapsulates this wisdom.

So, I invite you to join me on this exploration.

Contents

Introduction

I begin with the partial quote shared in the foreword that is commonly mis-attributed to Nelson Mandela and cited as being part of his 1994 Inaugural Address. It rings so very true for me:

> Our deepest fear is not that we are inadequate
> Our deepest fear is that we are all powerful beyond measure
> It is our light not our darkness that most frightens us
> We ask ourselves: Who am I to be brilliant, gorgeous, talented, fabulous?
> Actually, who are we not to be?

(The passage actually comes from the book "A Return to Love" (1992) by Marianne Williamson).

Nelson Mandela's story is one of sheer inspiration. Despite his circumstances, he emerged without bitterness, or a desire for any revenge. Instead, he fearlessly pursued freedom at a very grand scale: a dream of freeing his people; freeing his Nation. He understood there was a greater plan, a bigger picture.

What stops us from playing full-out and realizing our wildest dreams? What are *your* deepest, wildest dreams? Do you have any? Or have you buried them so deep, that even the question is an unexpected surprise? What keeps us playing small?

Fear.

Fear of what, we ask: fear of failure; of being judged; who am I to be great; who am I to have such wild dreams; who am I to seek such massive success? Quoting the above passage, I also ask: who are you not to?

What stops us from chasing our dreams; from fulfilling our life's purpose?

Fear.

Fear infects every aspect of your life, from the smallest to the grandest. From walking in a room full of strangers and making small talk, to standing in front of thousands and publicly engaging them in who you are and what you are all about.

We were all born with unique talents that no one else on the planet possesses. Unique stories. Unique life experiences. Unique journeys. And a unique purpose to fulfill that is YOUR life's purpose and no one else's.

We stop at the door of fear: I'm not good enough. I'm not worthy enough. I'm a loser. It's not safe. What will people think...and a myriad of similar excuses, all grounded in fear.

What is it that causes this monumental lack of belief in ourselves that we are capable and worthy of achieving mammoth success? What is the difference between you, me and Mandela or Ghandi or Martin Luther King or – traversing into the realm of religion – Buddha?

What is it about the human condition that keeps us stuck, that prevents us from experiencing our magnificent potential? How do we stop that incessant negative mind chatter (some call it the monkey mind) from sabotaging our success and our dreams?

One of the main problems, if not *the* main problem with our society is our conditioned fear. That conditioned fear stops us dead in our tracks from being, realizing and knowing our magnificent self. We are bombarded on a daily basis with our "what ifs"; our "couldn'ts/shouldn'ts"; our "can'ts"; our "won'ts"; our "that's impossibles". We are constantly sabotaged by our internal voice that lives through that prism of fear; that internal voice that shuts down our greatness, our innate essence, our purpose and our ability to impact our loved ones, our family and friends – and yes, humanity itself.

You, yes – YOU – stripped of that conditioned fear, have a unique contribution to make to the evolution of our human race on this planet Earth. Now. You know, deep down, at your very core and essence, there is a yearning – a knowing – that you were meant for something far greater than what you are doing with your life now.

Fear can shut down that yearning. Fear can shut down that knowing.

Fear can have us playing life as a small, insignificant being. Unimportant and unheard. Fear can stop us from switching on that global light we call the Sun on our unique greatness, our innate wisdom, our reason and purpose in having this human experience. It can stop us from imparting that wisdom to create a cosmic shift in the evolution of our planet. Fear has you thinking, even as you read this...who I am to dream so big?

What do you think is the cause of all the unrest and upheaval on our planet? Fear. Fear of our perceived differences: religious, social, cultural. That fear affects us globally. It affects the whole of humanity, from the terrorist jihadist, to the democratic governments running the biggest nations in the West. It shapes political policies and reinforces fears at the grass roots of society. Fear causes us to act in ways we know in our heart are wrong and unjustified.

What are the motivators? Fear of being different; fear of not belonging; fear of being judged; fear of not being good enough; fear of failure; fear of being rejected; fear of being shamed; fear of being unlovable; fear of appearing stupid and unintelligent; fear of being perceived as ignorant; fear of being seen as ugly, or too old, or too fat. Fear of being ridiculed...

The list is endless.

How many more fears can you add to it? Go on, list a few. Unleash that voice of fear. Become aware of how it has limited your life – or has it, in fact, stopped you dead in your tracks?

List how many opportunities and crossroads you have dismissed because of fear. Consider, for a moment, how different and how much more empowered your life may have been if you had but taken *one, just one,* of those opportunities, instead of being blinded and sidelined by your fear.

Reflect on just one such opportunity. Do you hear the whispering voice of greatness, of what may have been if you had transcended that fear? Do you hear the echoes of an inspired and courageous life, if only you had taken that crossroad, despite all the "what ifs"?

Let me tell you, you are not alone. This is the human condition. I say "condition" because it is what we are taught. It is a learned behavior. Every learned behavior can be unlearned.

When I reflect back on my life, I can see each crossroad where fear could have stopped me dead in my own tracks and prevented me from experiencing a fuller life. I am at that crossroad now. Fear has again raised its ugly head. Oh, it's saying: this vision, this so-called purpose, this quest that you think you are here to fulfill, is *way toooo big!!* Who do you think you are to fulfill such an epic mission?

Well, I say again to that voice of fear...I am the same person who said yes to climbing to Base Camp, Mt Everest – without any training, without any preparation. Just a massive vision of reaching Base Camp in glowing health, feeling elated and heroic. I allowed myself to believe that I could spread my wings and soar like never before. I dismissed the fear of altitude sickness; the fear of diarrhea; the fear of not being strong enough; the fear of having to be airlifted out; and yes, even the fear of death. But more on that later.

How do we transcend our fears that prevent us from having such wild and crazy experiences that expand our horizons and feed our souls? How do we transcend our fears so that we can forever expand on what is possible?

The first key is awareness. Know your fears. Identify them. Feel them. Be aware of what that voice is saying. Be aware of all your what ifs. Bring consciousness to that negative, conditioned voice that will put barrier after barrier up to prevent you from being your magnificent self.

And then, hang up on it!

Or tell it to "shut up, no more".

Then fill your mind with your vision. Visualize the successful fulfillment of that vision. Feel it deep within you. Feel the reasons you have embarked on such an adventure. Feel the empowerment and exhilaration. Be inspired by your courage. Know that your dream will manifest. When all of this is far bigger and grander than your fears, know that you will shift to a state of absolute possibility and do-ability.

You will enter the realm of manifestation from a space of empowerment.

And always remember that 99.9% of our fears are not real. They are an illusion conjured up by our active mind, supported by our cultural conditioning and upbringing. There is no saber-tooth tiger chasing you. You are not in fear of your life. All your fears are imagined. They are all learned. You are not your fears.

Stepping into that realm of fearlessness will open the door to a freedom that you rarely experience in your day-to-day life. It will open the door to your very essence; to the sheer enormity of your courage. You get to experience your magnificence at a scale that seemed unimaginable. You can soar like the eagle that embodies freedom.

The embodiment of that freedom, in each and every one of us, will become a domino effect which will eventually reach a critical mass that will one day transform the whole of humanity. Individually, every single one of us, is a part of that transformation: one individual; one experience at a time. Be bold. Be brave. And, above all be YOU.

This is the aim of this book – to inspire you to rise above your constrained conditioning and experience your very essence so that you too can realize YOUR dreams.

Part 1

My Life's Journey – My Awakening: where it all began

What is your number one greatest fear?

How has that affected your life choices?
Are you still on that treadmill?

Contemplate these questions as you read the next chapter.

Chapter 1

My Greatest Fear – My Greatest Teacher

"To conquer fear is the beginning of wisdom."
— Bertrand Russell

Know that our greatest challenges in life, which give rise to our greatest fears, are our greatest teachers:

- for understanding and experiencing unconditional love;
- for building resilience;
- for bringing awareness and an awakening to who we truly are; and
- above all, for fostering our evolutionary growth.

My greatest challenge and one of the biggest curveballs in my life, which gave rise to a huge well of fears, concerned my son. That is when my journey began. That is when my greatest growth began. That is when I learned to surrender to that which was outside of my realm to "fix". That is when our greatest growth begins.

I was 30 years-old when my son, aged three, was diagnosed with a hearing loss, in both ears. The hearing aids he was given to wear at the time were almost as big as his ears. I cried oceans of tears.

That was the beginning of my greatest fears.

All of the learnings and teachings in this book have grown and evolved over the last 35 years of my life from this beginning.

The day that he was diagnosed still lives deep in my memory. First the shock. Then the outrage. If there was a merciful God, how could that God inflict a young, innocent child with such an impediment? Take away my hearing, not my son's – I screamed on so many occasions! But no agreement could be negotiated. All faith in a God, preached by all Christian religions, faded into obscurity.

I first looked for medical answers. I came across Professor Graeme Clark, who refuses to give up on finding some way to help the profoundly hearing impaired to hear. His determination is a result of the struggles he witnessed with his profoundly impaired father. He saw his father suffering, as his father lived in silence. He saw the pain, the anguish and the isolation, and the difficulty in forming easy connections. These were the very fears that resonated at the core of my being.

In 1981, the company, Cochlear Ltd, was established in Sydney with finance from the Australian government, in order to commercialise the implants pioneered by Dr. Graeme Clark. Today, the company accounts for over two-thirds of the worldwide hearing implant market, with more than 250,000 people receiving one of the company's implants since 1982.

The company was established to promote Professor Clark's invention around the world, ahead of the first successful cochlear implant in 1982. This was all amazing news at the time.

So, I went straight to the top – to Professor Clark. I thought I had found the answer. Hope had finally replaced all my fears – only to be told that my son was not a candidate for a cochlear implant. The technology was too new. They would not even touch anyone unless they were so profoundly deaf that hearing aids could not assist in any way. I came away with my fears reinforced. My son was doomed to wear hearing aids. He was doomed to suffer the stigma; doomed to the partial silence that would breed isolation.

I could not face the reality that there was no cure for my son's hearing loss. I then began my search for the meaning of my life, his life, our very existence.

I did not want him to feel different. I did not want him to feel as if he didn't belong. His language skills at the age of three were already below those of my daughter at the same age. That is what caused me to investigate. I was originally told by our family Doctor...don't worry, everything is fine. Boys are slower than girls. Then the diagnosis confirmed my fears.

How would this affect his learning? Would he be bullied at school when other children noticed his hearing aids? Kids were used to seeing other children wear glasses, but how many wore hearing aids that stuck out so prominently? Would he be left behind? Would he have trouble making friends? Could he play sport? Could he take swimming lessons if he couldn't hear and couldn't wear his hearing aids? How silent was his world? How would placing a microphone in each ear help at school and in life when all the two microphones did was to pick up the nearest and loudest noise? The movement of a chair against the floor would drown out the teacher's voice if the chair was nearer to him. There was no natural filtering of sounds and distractions that we grow to master with 'normal' hearing. Would he find love as he grew up? Teenage years are so difficult. Would girls shy away from him? Would he feel isolated and outcast? They were my deeply ingrained fears.

And, yes, every single one of the above fears was experienced by my son, to one degree or another. But that's another story.

I did not want to meet other mothers with children with similar problems. His world was not going to be restricted by that type of mindset. Not for a moment did I see such an approach as one that would provide support and a feeling that my son was not alone; I was not alone. Instead, I viewed engaging in such a circle as being detrimental. He would not go to any 'special' school for hearing impaired children. He would grow up in mainstream schooling and even go to a private high school. I wanted him to feel privileged. I wanted him to feel as 'normal' as all other children. To this day, I use the statements 'hearing impaired' or 'hearing deficient', instead of the word 'deaf'. I rejected that word outright. It would not define my son. He was so much more than that.

I, once again, immediately got into action. He would be starting kindergarten in two years' time. His speech had to improve so that it matched the speech of a five-year-old by the time he started at the local school. I was adamant - my son was not going to go to any special needs school. And so, it came to be.

I enrolled him with a speech therapist. We attended diligently every single week and I supervised his daily speech exercises, recordings, and the listening of recordings. I was on a mission. My daughter was seven years old at the time. I now look back and see how all that uncompromising attention on my son would have, and indeed did, adversely impact on her. She saw her brother getting so much attention, but never at that tender age, appreciating why. She was the center of my Universe for the first four years of her life, and until my son's diagnosis, my time was shared with both. Our family dynamic was experiencing a massive shift, which was not consciously acknowledged by any of us until much, much later.

By the age of five, my son was indeed ready to attend the local school. His language skills had improved significantly and equaled those of other children of the same age. However, many years later, I learnt that he would always sit in the back of the classroom and would often turn off his hearing aids, as he could not hear the teacher in any event. He did, however, excel at sport, much to my amazement. Any sport that he participated in, he would end up coming home with ribbons or trophies. This included swimming races where he would have to intuitively dive in after seeing others next to him making their move, as he could not otherwise hear anything. Yet he still came home with ribbons. Cricket turned out to be his real passion. He played 1st XI at the private high school he attended and U/16 Green Shield at his local Club in the Sutherland Shire. He was opening batsman for one and opening bowler for the other. Each one told him - no you can't bowl as you are a batsman, and, no you can't go up in the batting order, as you are a bowler! Go work that one out. He ended up playing 1st Grade for Sydney University.

My son did eventually finish an Arts Degree, in Communications! Yes, in Communications. But there were trials and tribulations along the way as he battled with his own demons; his own negative chatter; his own conditioning; his own meanings that he derived from his hearing loss. There were a lot of "why me's?"; a lot of victim mentality; why am I such an outcast?; why am I so different?; why do I not belong?; and a lot of guilt and blame and shame on my part. All fear-based.

This is the power of fear, until we awaken and realize we are the masters of our reality. When we choose to break through that fear, doors open up magically. That is what started happening with my son as he stepped through his many fears. Was there pain? Yes, mountains of it. But if you keep pressing forward then success will meet you at the other end. As it did with my son. His journey is indeed inspirational, filled with much anguish, suffering and heartache at one end – and then such peace, love and success at the other.

As for me, it took many, many years before I could see the gifts that sprang forth from my greatest fears. Decades in fact.

In the meantime, I sought escape and captured moments of freedom in creativity. With very little, if any, conscious awareness, I began to open the door to my essence.

What do you love doing?
What causes you to literally
lose track of time:
Cooking
Knitting
Painting
Writing
Playing music
Dancing …

Contemplate these questions and notice how you can step into that realm of freedom, just by contemplating.

Chapter 2

Freedom in Creativity

"Without creativity there is no life"
— Benjamin Spock

Writing and painting helped me on the path to find my true self. To connect with my essence. When we connect with our creative side, with that part of us that ignites fun and joy, our fears begin to melt away. And so, it was that my greatest fears around my son indeed began to slowly melt away, once I connected with this side of myself. My mind's negative conditioned chatter began to be slowly replaced with positive thoughts, reflected in the "My World" poem below.

Delving into my creativity helped me in my search for the meaning of my life. What was my life's purpose? How could I best serve my family's needs? How could I be the best mother to my two beautiful children? How could I be a good wife to my husband, who was also struggling and really checking out? What did I need to ignite inside myself to dissolve the pain and the fears that were driving my life?

Initially, these types of actions and choices were a means of escape. When the pain and fear were too great, the mind sought an escape. Delving into something creative and taking action, rather than locking myself in my room and inviting depression, was the only way forward.

Writing poetry was the first time that I released my inner world. It was always there inside me, but was lying dormant until I indulged in the romance of pen on paper. It all began serendipitously. A friend I met at one of the seminars I was attending at the time – a surfer – challenged me to write a poem on surfing. Something that was never in my experience. Here is what I wrote:

SURFER

Sand, surf, sea
Wrapped in the arms of a whispering breeze
Turquoise skies, puffy white clouds
Catch the rising sun on that glassy sea
Dawn is breaking   All is still …

Surfer, board emerge from the sand
Where does one start, and the other end?

Sand, Surfer, Sea
All is still

Waves pound against the shore
They beckon the Surfer
Today, tomorrow and forever more

Waves, Surfer, Sea –
A symphony of pure ecstasy.

I wrote to my friend: How is the above, coming from a non-surfer, riding the crest of a wave for the very first time? I wanted to know if I had stepped into a surfer's shoes. I certainly glimpsed a vision of what it must feel like – from my own conditioned perspective.

Let me share "My World" poem that I also wrote around the same time. As I was beginning to let go of some of my many fears around my son, and as my more dismal days finally began to evaporate, I found myself scribbling these words:

MY WORLD

My world is a bird, a feather in flight
in all its grace, glory and might

My world is a ray of sunshine shedding its warmth
in a world where there are no longer storms

My world is a brook lazily meandering and whispering by
a baby eaglet attempting to fly

Oh, how could I express feelings that unfold
So deep, so clear and yet so old

You are truly a wonderful, beautiful world
Filled with joy, love and miracles that do daily unfold

A world that is now filled with peace
Not my sorrow, my tears that did so sadly weep

As I sit here and revel in glee
I realize you were always deep within me

Many years later, and well after my divorce, I was inspired to scribble the following words so that the door would open to the kind of partner in life that my heart was yearning for:

INSPIRATION

I am not inspired by your godly good looks,
your physique, your eyes, your lips
But, I am inspired by the words you write,

the words you speak that expose the
purity of your soul and the bigness of your heart.

I am not inspired by your success, the
influence you wield, the fear and power you command
But, I am moved by the lives you touch
and change and shape.

I am not inspired by the obscenity of your wealth,
your mansions, your cars, your jets
But, I am touched by the generosity of
your spirit, the difference you make.

As I gently stretch and slowly yawn
And as another night of slumber welcomes a new dawn
I see the sun rise in your eyes, golden and bright
I am embraced by its warmth
Reflected in its light
On the wings of Angels, I see birds flutter, chirp and sing
As the morning bells of heaven do softly ring

I gaze upon your gentle face
And I recall all the things – great and small – you have done and still do

And I know I am inspired by the essence of you.

I also took up oil painting during the same decade. I had always loved art, but had never considered it, even as a hobby, until my hairdresser invited me to attend an art class. We are always called towards our healing and growth.

I recall finishing my first painting during my very first art class and bringing it home, late in the evening, already framed! As I walked up the stairs of our home, I held it in my arms and asked my husband: "What do you think?" His response was: "I thought you were going to do painting, not buy artwork". He was dead serious. He wanted to know how much it cost. That was and has remained the best compliment I have ever received on my painting. I still have that very first "piece of artwork" hanging on a wall in my home. It is a good reminder of what we can be inspired to do.

I bought numerous canvases, paintbrushes, paints and an easel. I set myself up in the garage of our home. It became my way of experiencing the peace and serenity that often evaded me in my everyday life. I worked three days a week. I cooked. I washed. I ironed. I looked after my whole family. My artwork, as was my poetry, was a world I entered after my two children were fed and bathed and their homework done; after the dishes were put away and family discussions about finances or anything else dealt with.

I would then enter my sacred little cave in the garage and start painting. It was truly meditative. I would become totally engrossed in what I was seeking to paint. As my mind became still and transfixed, as the silence pervaded my whole cave, there was simply no door open for any of my fears to surface. There were a few nights when time did cease to exist for me, so much so that I recall on one occasion looking at my watch and discovering that it was 4am! Wow! It felt like I was only painting for a couple of hours; time had ceased to exist. I quickly went to bed and promised myself that I would be a little more conscious and conscientious next time.

In case you were wondering how good or bad my painting is, I have included below a few samples of the artwork that I still have at home. I did exhibit a few times locally, and did sell a few paintings. I recall that when I sold my first painting, I was so sad (yes sad) that I went home that night and painted it again. This version was on a different sized canvas and was never going to be identical to the one sold, but it was my way of capturing what I had sold. I was also very excited. Someone actually liked it enough to buy it ? Wow!

The subject was a happy clown. Clowns for me depicted the joy and laughter that they embody, often masking the deep sadness and fears below the surface. This was my 'clown period'. I then had my 'horse period'. Horses, for me, are magnificent animals that personify freedom. Visions of horses galloping through the wilderness encapsulates my notion of freedom to this day.

And I also had my 'blue mountain period'. What is beyond that mountain? (Indeed, years later I had that very conversation with my husband when I decided to end our marriage). What is behind that mystical blue haze??

I was certainly no Van Gogh or Monet. (I was, however, lucky enough to visit Monet's Gardens at Giverny, France. Simply beautiful). Here are some samples (I gifted another clown painting as a wedding present to a very dear friend):

My clown period:

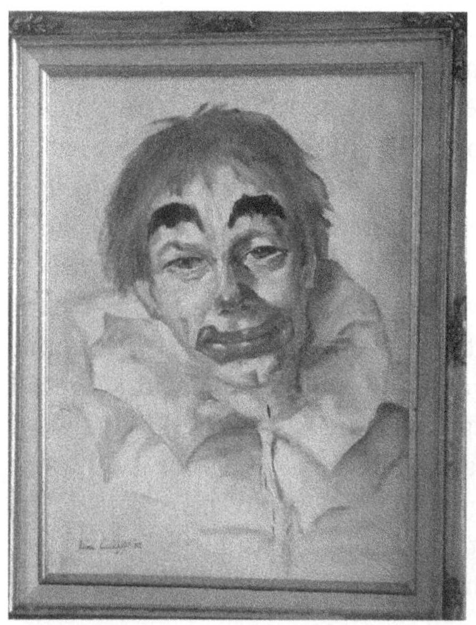

My horse period:

My misty, blue mountain period:

My freedom period: sail the seas or fly like an eagle

Painting was unquestionably meditative for me.

Meditating, cross-legged in a lotus position with spine upright and hands on your thighs, with palms facing up, is not the only way to still the mind and bring an inner calm to the moment. It is, however, an excellent ritual to start and end your day, which I encourage. I am still working on improving my flexibility, which will enable me to fully enjoy the lotus position.

Writing also was (and is) meditative. As I said, both painting and writing would often keep me occupied well into the early hours of the morning, as I would literally lose track of time. That is precisely what happens when you still the mind and immerse yourself in the present moment. Both are meditative as they shut out the external world and still the constant mind chatter. They shut down all of your illusory fears. But they are more than this.

As I reflect now on that period, both painting and writing were more than meditative, they were restorative. They were healing. They were my coping mechanisms, my escape. They allowed me to enter the door of hope and freedom. A much safer escape than drugs (even prescription drugs) and alcohol. I have never been an advocate of either. Our fears can lead to anxiety and depression which, in turn, can lead to addictions, including to prescription drugs. A dear friend once said to me: how could you have grown up in the same era as me and never even tried a single bong?? Have you ever been drunk? I smiled and responded: "well, I did grow up without trying a single bong and, no, I have never been drunk. But I do enjoy a glass or two of champagne."

This is what the road of creativity opens up for us. This is the type of magical experience I invite you to explore. It is the type of experience that can free you from your fears and insecurities. It flings open the door to the life we were meant to have. A life that is filled with bliss and peace and conscious awareness. A life that brings a smile to your face. A life that fills your heart with joy.

I was certainly not conscious of this truth at the time. Let it be a light bulb moment for you.

What is it that you love to do? It might be, like me, writing poetry, or painting, or taking up law as a hobby! It may be hitting the tennis court; or cooking up a storm; or playing music; or designing beautiful clothing or furniture? Are you perhaps a crazy dancer? Can you get on the dance floor and lose yourself completely in the moment and the music, not giving a damn about who is looking at you, or how good or bad you might be dancing? We all have a creative soul within us that is yearning to be recognized and acknowledged.

Did I know all of the above at the time? Certainly not. All I knew and experienced whilst I was embroiled in the thick of it was love and fear. I oscillated between the two, as we all do. It was indeed a long bittersweet journey. Love, if you will let it, will always emerge victorious. It will always open doors for you and lead you to the next chapter in your life.

In order to walk though those doors, we have to conquer our existing fears by bringing conscious awareness to their illusory nature.

Chapter 3

Many Ways to Conquer Illusory Fears

"Nothing in life is to be feared.
It is only to be understood."
— Marie Curie

The deep-rooted fears around my son during this period ensured that I commenced my journey on a road of discovery that I am still on. I searched for solutions. I searched for spiritual healing – emotional and physical. I searched for anything and everything that would allay my fears. I undertook so many courses and seminars and retreats. I read so many books and attended so many talks by the authors that inspired me. The list below is a snippet of all that I pursued:

- Alpha Dynamics course where I questioned my fears and my negative, limiting beliefs that my mind was throwing up; where I questioned emotional healing;
- A series of Insight Seminars where I explored the opening of my heart and seeing a different reality;
- A series of Landmark Forum seminars where I again pursued freedom from my fears and peace of mind (using the intellect rather than the heart, was how I viewed these seminars);

- Anthony Robbins Seminar (his very first in Sydney) to Unleash the Power Within – searching to further free myself from my fears. I attended this with my daughter. We both walked on hot coals as a metaphor for the power of the mind. I read his book. It still sits on my bookshelf at home. More recently, my son has attended a number of his seminars and found them very inspirational. My son's own research led him full circle. There are no coincidences;

- Meditation courses, including a ten-day Vipassana silent retreat in the Blue Mountains outside Sydney. Vipassana means to see things as they really are. It is an ancient Indian technique taught more than 2,500 years ago. The course is conducted solely on a donation basis – all over the world – and includes food and accommodation. More recently, I have conducted an online meditation course with Craig Hamilton, Evolving Wisdom and Enlightenment, which provides tools for the practice of direct awakening. My daughter has done Kundalini and other meditation courses. I attended a Kundalini meditation retreat in the Blue Mountains with her. My son has participated in Mindfulness meditations. Again, no coincidences. The acorns do not fall far from the tree;

- A five-day seminar at the Oneness University in India (with my son) headed at the time by Sri Bhagavan and Amma, avatars of enlightenment and ending human suffering by recognizing that we are all One. Freedom was at the heart of the teachings. My daughter had previously undertaken a much longer course there;

- NLP course with the Tad James Company;

- Dr John Demartini course (a renowned human behavioral specialist);

- Dr Joe Dispenza courses, blending quantum physics with the science of the mind-body connection, and exploring our capacity to rewire our brain for self-healing and manifestation;

- Dr Brian Weiss seminar on past-life regressions. Weiss is the author of "Many Lives, Many Masters";

- Mike Dooley TUT "Playing the Matrix Workshop";

- A St John of God healing seminar which I believe was his first in Sydney, having reached international fame through Oprah Winfrey, by allegedly performing healing rituals on her and the former US President, Bill Clinton;

- Reading the many books and/or listening to recordings of Deepak Chopra; Louise Hay; Wayne Dyer; Dr Brian Weiss; Marianne Williamson, Nick Ortner, Abraham Hicks; Neal Walsh;

- Hoffman course in Byron Bay. Hoffman was a US psychotherapist who developed the practice of incorporating all four parts of the self: spiritual, physical, emotional and intellectual. The course helps you identify negative behaviors and belief systems (i.e. fears) that develop unconsciously and are conditioned in us from childhood (interestingly my daughter is studying for her Masters in psychotherapy in London as I write this);

- Martin Brofman healing process in Greece (attended with my daughter). He was diagnosed with terminal cancer in 1975 and was told he had only one to two months to live. He healed himself and passed away in 2014. His belief: cancer begins in your mind and that's where you can get rid of it. His wife, Annick Brofman continues his legacy of healing with the Brofman Foundation in Switzerland. Read his books;

- Yoga – i.e. meditation on the mat that has so many benefits.
- And so much more.

Each course, seminar, book helped in its own way.

I hope that the above list inspires you to take action in your life, NOW, to conquer your fears that stop you from pursuing your dreams.

The aim of candidly and vulnerably sharing the lessons from my life's journey is to give you a little head start in reaching that space that I refer to as 'The Intersection of Fearlessness and Freedom'.

Chapter 4

The Intersection of Fearlessness and Freedom

"Too many of us are not living our dreams because we are living our fears"
— Les Brown

I believe that there is an incredible power at the intersection of fearlessness and freedom.

I have embraced fearlessness all of my life as a powerful tool to live an empowered life. It is nothing to do with any reckless act. Fearlessness comes from the essence of who we are. It is a part of our DNA to empower us to achieve our life purpose and uplift others to be the best that they can be. It is at the heart of our evolutionary growth. Our progress.

Any fear that stops you dipping into the unknown, into something new, keeps your life stagnant. It hinders your growth. It produces a mundane life of repetition and boredom, lacking in fulfillment. Let me repeat that: repetition and boredom, repetition and boredom; repetition and boredom. Are you on that treadmill?

Conversely, at the intersection of fearlessness and freedom, we can experience a life filled with adventure, bliss and joy. We can live our purpose in the glorious way we were all meant and designed to.

Fearlessness and freedom go hand-in-hand. One rarely exists without the other. Once we step into that state, where the two intersect, we are uplifted and energized. We experience our true essence. Bliss. Freedom.

The day I reached Base Camp in Nepal (which I discuss in more detail in a later chapter) I felt I had sprouted wings. The climb became effortless. I soared. The freedom was exhilarating. If I were an eagle in flight, I could not have felt greater freedom.

When my daughter and I reached the peak of Mt Kilimanjaro (also discussed in a later chapter), the joy in the mother-daughter experience of conquering a mountain together lives at the core of me to this day.

Our true essence is to follow our passion; to take risks; to fulfill our purpose. To be. To experience the magic and majesty of life. Each of the major decisions in my life have catapulted me into that realm of freedom.

The flaws or brakes we place on both freedom and fearlessness are eliminated when they both intersect.

Fearlessness will always bring you to the door of freedom. And freedom can only occur when you step into the realm of fearlessness. When you let go of the limiting fears that are conditioned in us by society and our cultural upbringings.

I have been placed on this planet, at this time in history, to help you come to this intersection and be the unique individual you know yourself to be. Are you ready? Yes, you are! You are reading this book. Read on to discover how!

Part 2

Uncovering the Truth - Lessons from My Life's Journey

Who are you??
Have you ever had moments of sheer bliss
when you personified love?
Did you feel your energy rise dramatically
in those moments?

Contemplate these questions and
those moments.
See if you can spot the "observer" –
observing the mind chatter.

Lesson 1

Who you are not

What are your three to five fears that repeatedly surface?

List them:

Public speaking

Heights

A mouse ...

Contemplate how those fears have impacted your life as you read on.

CHAPTER 1

You are not Your Conditioned Fears

"Of all the liars in the world, sometimes the worst are our own fears."
— Rudyard Kipling

"Fears are educated into us, and can, if we wish, be educated out."
— Karl Augustus Menninger

Our fears are indeed our greatest liars and we have succumbed to them as the truth.

Those massive lies can only be expunged with conscious awareness to the real truth.

The design of a human being is to ensure that we experience safety. It is built into our DNA and it is a big part of our conditioning. However, this innate survival instinct does not serve us when most of our fears are self-created and illusory. We gave birth to our fears in order to keep us alive. But how many of our fears are actually necessary today to keep us alive? Very, very few.

So, I guarantee you that most of your fears are:

1. self-created; and
2. illusory, that is, not real.

I say self-created because the mind has been conditioned from our Neanderthal days (and beyond) to 'protect' us from danger. Back then it was from the saber tooth tiger. Staring potential death in the face caused adrenalin to pump through our bodies; the pounding and racing of our heart; sweating and shaking uncontrollably – the fight-or-flight response. It is the first stage of a general adaptation syndrome. This was first described by Walter Bradford Cannon, M.D., who was an American physiologist, professor and chairman of the Department of Physiology at Harvard Medical School. He first coined the term, 'fight-or-flight' in 1915, and expanded on his theories in his book, "The Wisdom of the Body", first published in 1932.

The fight-or-flight response is an automatic physiological reaction that occurs in response to a perceived fear of a threat to survival. The autonomic nervous system is a control system that acts largely unconsciously and regulates heart rate, digestion, respiratory rate, pupillary response, urination, and sexual arousal. This system is the primary mechanism in control of the fight-or-flight response. The science associated with this system is now well-established. The physiological changes that occur during the fight-or-flight response are activated in order to give the body increased strength and speed, in anticipation of fighting or running. We have all experienced these physiological changes at some stage(s) of our lives.

Hormones, such as adrenalin and cortisol, are released during this process, speeding the heart rate, slowing digestion, and stunting blood flow to major muscle groups, causing them to become tense. You may become sweaty and your hearing may become more sensitive, all of which is intended to provide the body with a burst of energy and strength. When our life, or the life of a loved one, is threatened, our strength can be magnified tenfold, and suddenly we're capable of superhuman actions. Later, we look back and wonder 'how did I do that?'

All of these changes are adaptive bodily responses essentially designed to keep us alive, and because these responses are important to our survival, they occur quickly and without thought. They come automatically, and are essential when there is real danger.

But our mind cannot tell the difference between real and imagined fear.

For example, the imagined fear of speaking publicly to a large audience can trigger the exact same fight-or-flight responses. Public speaking is listed as America's number one fear, before death at number five and loneliness at number seven. Many studies have confirmed this. It seems that most of us are far more afraid of being judged and appearing stupid before our peers than dying or going to our grave alone! Or as Jerry Seinfeld noted: that means to the average person, if you have to go to a funeral, you're better off in the casket than doing the eulogy!

So a fear of public speaking has been repeatedly found to be a far greater concern than death itself. Think about that. Is that one of your fears?

Have a look at some of the well-known phobias our society is confronted with:

Claustrophobia: the fear of small enclosed spaces
Agoraphobia: the fear of open or crowded spaces
Acrophobia: the fear of heights.
Pteromerhanophobia: the fear of flying
Astraphobia: the fear of thunder and lightning
Cynophobia: the fear of dogs
Ophidiophobia: the fear of snakes

Arachnophobia: the fear of spiders
Entomophobia: the fear of insects
Trypanophobia: the fear of needles
Mysophobia: even the fear of germs

How many of these fears do you have? How real are they? Are you kidding? How real – very, very real, you would say, for they can stop you dead in your tracks. I have a friend who has such a fear of enclosed spaces and flying that she found the superhuman strength of literally scaling and jumping over all the seats in the plane to escape, immediately after the plane had landed. The fear was so potent that she could not control her actions. The fight-or-flight response had certainly kicked in. To those that do not have such fears, the vision that this may conjure up could also bring a grin to their faces. Really??? But to my friend, there was nothing funny going on. Her response was 100% on auto drive.

I recall, as a teenager, on one occasion I witnessed a mouse scurrying across the front foyer of our home. In a state of absolute panic, I picked up a plastic-backed broom with a long handle and trapped the little mouse behind it, screaming and calling out "dad, dad, where are you, come down quickly, hurry, hurry, dad where are you, DAD?!! D A D WHERE ARE YOU?!!". My screams got louder and louder as my fear intensified.

My father came running down the stairs like a thunderstorm, yelling in reply: "I'm coming, what's happening?", terrified himself that my life was in danger. He stopped dead in his tracks as he saw me with a broom in my hand, screaming uncontrollably. Shaking his head, he said: "What's going on?" Still screaming, I yelled back: "There's a mouse behind that broom, there's a mouse". He knelt down near the broom, whilst I remained shaking and panicked. He picked up the mouse by its tail and hung it from his hand: "Is this what you're afraid of? Really?" At that moment, I threw my hands up in the air, screamed loudly, and ran to the family room, firmly slamming the door shut behind me.

By the time my father came back, I had contained myself. "Are you OK now? It was only a little mouse. It couldn't harm you," he said. All I could do was just shake my head. I felt so very stupid. To this day, I do not know what my father did with that mouse.

That was the end of that episode. I reflected that it was a one-off. That was not how I would react to any other mouse in the future – or so I thought. Some years later, my daughter's little friend, who lived across the road from us, came into our foyer. She approached me, and as proud as could be said: "Look, Mrs C, look at my new pet. Where's ....", at which point I noticed - yes, she was holding a little white mouse, cupped gently into her little hands. I screamed: "Megan get that mouse out of my home, now, go, go, just go, please, now!" Megan immediately ran out the door and ran all the way back to her home, still cupping her little white mouse in between her two hands. She had never seen me in this state.

My daughter heard all the commotion and came running into the foyer: "mummy, what's going on? Why did you send Megan away, why is she running home?"

Again, I took a very deep breath and tried to contain myself. I sat down on the stairs and took another deep breath. When I told my very young daughter that the commotion was all about the little white mouse, her response: "That's so silly, mummy. He's so cute. He has this little cage and he spins around in this little circle, going round and round and round. Why didn't you like him, mummy?"

Why indeed? I told my daughter to go to Megan's home and tell Megan how sorry I was for yelling, but to make sure that Megan did not bring the mouse back to our home. They could play with the mouse as much as they liked, but at Megan's home, not ours. And so it was. That mouse never entered our home again. No mouse has (to my knowledge).

How would I respond now? There is a tiny doubt, however I believe I am aware enough now that I would be able to avoid going into auto-drive and reacting excessively from that fight-or-flight response. In fact, a smile is creeping across my face as I write this and reflect on how "silly" (as my young daughter described it) my whole reaction was. I was an adult, after all. Right?

Could I cup that little white mouse in my hands today? The smile just disappeared and the word that immediately popped into my head was "gross". So, the answer is still no. The crazy fear may be gone today, but how I relate to mice is still entrenched. It is a far cry from a cute little duckling or a fluffy little chick that I can gently hold in my hand and pat lovingly. Why? Because of the irrational conditioning of my mind that I have unwittingly and unconsciously allowed.

Sitting, sipping a Soy decaf cappuccino at the iconic Bondi Beach, I recently noticed a young girl in her twenties walk past. Tattooed on her back, in between her two shoulders was a tiny mouse, with its face down, sniffing, as mice do. Oh my God!! The love of a mouse can be that deep. I laughed – certainly not my experience.

Yet, I recall when I was in Kathmandu, I allowed a total stranger, in a third world country, to wrap and wind a big snake around my neck. Go figure?? This is the power of our conditioned mind. This is how irrational it can be. What irrational fears do you have?

What thoughts spring to your mind as you view the below images? Are you in awe of the insanity of those thoughts?

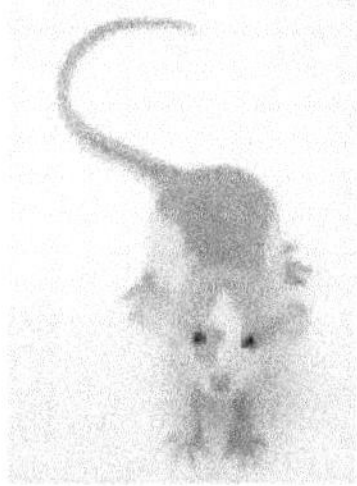

Let's explore these self-created and illusory fears further by examining two of our most common fears.

Our Conditioned Body Image – fear of being seen in all our glory!

The first that springs to mind based on my personal experience relates to my relationship with my body. How many of us have fears related to our body image? To this day, I cannot fully parade nakedly around the privacy of my own bedroom/bathroom. I cannot confidently walk around naked in search of my clothes or blow dry my hair (naked), whilst my partner is there. I routinely come out of the shower with a towel wrapped around me. I also recall that at the age of about 18 there was only one part of my body that I really loved. That was my nails. Yes, my nails. To this day, my nails are always impeccably kept. I have a ritual where I routinely do my nails every Saturday or Sunday evening and, from time to time, I have them done professionally. But they are always well manicured.

My partner, on the other hand, has absolutely zero reservations in this regard. He happily walks about – stark naked – unperturbed about my presence. Does he have a great body? Not according to our conventional conditioned standards. Using his own words, he has skinny arms and legs, a big stomach and fairly white skin. Not an ab muscle in site!! Nor any other kind of muscle. Does he care? Not a hoot! I have often thought, how liberating must that be.

I recall many years ago we were on a fairly secluded beach on an island in Greece. As we spread out our towels on the sand, there in front of me, parading up and down the beach, was this magnificent, Greek God. Stark naked; looking resplendent and majestic. He was glistening and bronzed. Muscles galore. The only hair on him was the hair on his head. No pubic hair. He was parading confidently up and down the beach as the waves came in and out. Dangling in his full glory. I watched him, mesmerized. What a body! What a handsome man! In that moment, we realized we must have landed on a nudist beach. I could not keep my eyes off him.

Until I heard my partner say: "Oh well, when in Greece, do as the Greeks do". I watched him as he then pulled down his board shorts and strolled nonchalantly towards the Greek Demigod, looking back over his shoulder at me, with a cheeky grin. The vision makes me laugh, even as I write this. There was my partner, as white as a ghost, not a muscle in sight, skinny legs and arms and hairy – parading next to this perfectly opposite vision of himself. Again, he simply did not give a hoot!

He took a dip in the ocean and returned, asking with a sheepish grin: "Did you enjoy that?" We laughed as I told him that he completely destroyed the vision. Oh, how liberating, I thought.

I, on the other hand, kept my swimmers on. I did not dare show my 'imperfect' body to that 'perfect' Greek Demigod!

I recall a few years later we were holidaying in Budapest. We stayed at one of Budapest's iconic landmarks – the Gellert Hotel, on the banks of the Danube River and home to the Gellert Baths. The architecture is simply stunning and has featured in many Hollywood movies, including Cocoon. In fact, when I first stepped in, I thought I was having a past-life experience, until the concierge asked if I had seen that movie (which I had).

To cut a long story short, we both visited the baths, wearing our swimming costumes, even though we were aware you could go in with your bathrobe and go from one bath to the other, completely naked. The women were separated from the men. As I approached one of the hot baths, I noticed this huge woman, sitting on a bench, legs wide apart, with one leg propped up against the bench – reading the paper! Wow, I thought, how bold is that!! She does not give a damn about how she looks, or how big or fat she is. There she was reading the paper, completely comfortable in her skin.

I was so inspired. I told my partner that I was going in naked the next day. He asked: "What if there's an Australian Judge there?" My response: "Her problem, not mine". I slipped my bathrobe off and walked slowly into the hot bath – stark naked. It was so freeing. I then walked across to the other bath to cool down. The baths had naturally different temperatures. It was so amazingly liberating. In fact, even the word 'liberating' does not come close to how I felt. In those moments, my fear of being seen naked completely vanished. I felt this incredible lightness in my being that I can even feel now, as I write this. European women did not appear to have the same hang-ups about their bodies as I was obviously conditioned to have about my own body.

Our experience on another holiday in Cuba was very similar. A woman, at least 15-20 years older than me, took my partner onto the dance floor and to the beat of the palpable Cuban drums, I watched her sexy moves. Boy, could she dance! Her body weaved and waved to a combination of mambo and salsa. In the language of the Africans who were brought to Cuba, mambo apparently means "conversations with the gods". She was definitely in deep conversation with those gods. Her moves were amazing and her smile and laughter were infectious, as she tried to teach my partner a few of the moves. He sadly has two left feet. He says it is all part of his Jewish heritage. Apparently, no Jew can dance?? That's according to my partner and his conditioned belief systems. I have a very different view. He says he could not dance to save his life. By our conditioned standards, she was quite overweight.

Her pink lycra outfit covered rolls upon rolls of fat – all of which she magically displayed with such wonderful grace as she moved around the dance floor. Again, I thought, how liberating is that? How crazy am I not to love my body with that same freedom and grace? How crazy am I not to embark upon my own 'conversations with the gods' and revel in the very essence of who I truly am? I swore that I would take up Cuban dance lessons. I am currently exploring doing so. The vision of that beautiful woman has never left me.

I have, over the years, broken free from many of the fears around my body image, but not all. I am still working on it. This fear still has a hook or two deeply embedded in me. The photos below are aimed at eliminating that hook or two. And, no, you are not getting a near naked photo of me. That hook is still embedded!

The first two photos are the only photos I could find of me, in a bikini. I was 20 years-old at the time, so they were taken 45 years ago, by my husband. As is self-evident, I was a very reluctant subject. I had strong fears around being photographed in my swimwear. I deliberately avoided letting any friend walk behind me, for obvious reasons. Looking at these very old photos now, I was somewhat astounded by my reactions. I recalled all my old beliefs, but that internal voice inside me is so much kinder and less judgmental now:

- my boobs were too big – really? They don't look too big now;
- my hips and stomach were too fat – they don't look that huge today;
- my legs were awful for a whole range of reasons – they also look OK.

With my decades of growth and wisdom, I could at last laugh at the insanity of my fears around my body image. Wow, I thought, I wouldn't mind having that body now.

But it was a very different era. My fears and conditioning around my body image were obviously as a result of the unhealthy body ideals that were ridiculously promoted at the time. I recalled that Twiggy was *the* fashion icon of the 1960's. She was revered for her stick thin figure. Today, some might even call it anorexic looking. I hated the fact that I could not wear braless t-shirts. I hated my curves. I had locked myself in the 'Twiggy cage' and my conditioned mindset could see no escape for at least two decades. As I awakened to the illusion of my fears around my body, and to my absurdly conditioned mindset, the bars from that cage began to slowly melt away. New neural pathways began to emerge as the old ones faded away. The science of change was in action, and was no longer a concept that I merely understood.

Today, the cultural shift could not be more dramatic. Women are no longer having breast reduction surgery. On the contrary, breast implants are the new rage, along with Kardashian hips and bums! The pendulum has fully swung the other way. The fears around body image are now very different: my breasts are too small; my hips and bum need enhancement, as do my lips and cheeks and abs and, and, and .... There are no judgments here. The only question to explore is this: is your choice a truly conscious one that is not seeking to mask some deep-rooted fear, or 'filling' some deep void (pun intended)?

Sadly, for many of us, the nature and context of the fears may have changed, but the fears still remain.

I remember one of my old sayings: when I come back in the next life, I am coming back with the body of Elle McPherson and the voice of Whitney Houston. It was always said in jest and with laughter, but the sting was there. We often mask our deepest hurts and fears with humor.

Writing this segment of the book, and unearthing the old photos shown below, was somewhat cathartic for me. The reactions from any members of the legal profession that may read the book could be very brutal. The analytical mind that is so powerfully effective in presenting legal arguments and demolishing the opposition, can surface here. Did I really want to expose myself in this very intimate way to my professional peers? I could not believe the range of fears that were still surfacing for me!

That is the power of our mind and our thoughts. I seriously considered removing this whole segment, or watering it down significantly, in order to eliminate my exposure. I once again stood on that precipice of fear as that voice repeated: how childish; is she for real; what a nutter; whoever feels that way about their bodies?; she wasn't even grossly fat; what a joke; no credibility; all total nonsense; how did she ever become a lawyer?; who thinks like that? ..... on and on and on.

I again looked at the two photos of me at 20. That is certainly not what I expected to find. But I was now looking at them through the lens of decades of growth and inner wisdom. When I uncovered those two photos I was indeed in a state of shock. My fears around my body were all illusory. Ridiculously illusory. I had punished myself all those years – for nothing. I finally had my 'AHA' moment. This is the very real power of our unconscious thoughts. This is the very real power of our illusory fears. I had finally exposed my own 'naked' truth.

I was, at last, free.

The third photo is me today. And yes, I went from a brunette to a "platinum blonde".

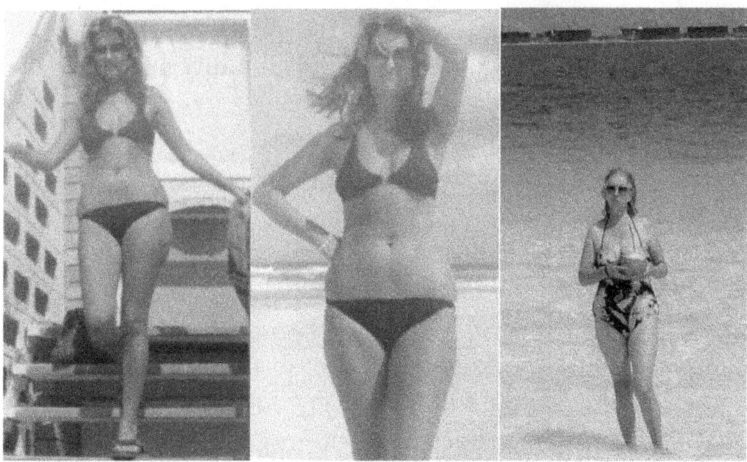

What is your mantra around your body? Are you as free around your body as the beautiful Cuban woman or my partner? If not, why not? Equally importantly: if so, why so?

Many beautiful women (and men) have no fears around their body image because their bodies are "beautiful" and perceived to be so by our conditioned cultural standards – of the day. The Greek Demigod springs to mind! But is it a chicken and egg scenario: do they have 'beautiful' bodies because they are not hampered by conditioned shame? What comes first? Irrespective, I have seen people with 'average' bodies that prance around as if they were the most 'beautiful' person on the planet. My Cuban experience is but one. Very liberating indeed.

Beauty is in the eye of the beholder, as the saying goes. How liberated or hampered we feel around our body image is entirely up to us. It is only more recently that women of all sizes are coming out and celebrating their bodies. It is only more recently that the modelling world has begun to even acknowledge the existence of such beauty.

I eventually mustered enough courage to include the above pictures of my 'beautiful' body. Something my 'old' me would never have considered. Something even my 'new' me labored over, as new fears sprang forth. So, I asked myself this question - will I die of any shame, embarrassment or judgment? No. So I dived in yet again and 'exposed' myself.

Now that's a breakthrough of mammoth proportions for me!! I encourage you to try it.

Our Conditioned Fears of Public Speaking

Let's look at public speaking as another example. If public speaking is one of your fears, you will find that your mouth can become so dry that you can barely open it to utter a single word. Your voice will quiver, and your whole body can begin to shake. Some people in extreme cases will even blank out. Once you have triggered that fight-or-flight mode, the production of gastric juices and saliva decreases because blood flow to the digestive system is decreased. Our bodies can literally interrupt the digestion of a Big Mac until after the threat has been eliminated, or deemed by the mind to have been eliminated.

When such fears kick in, our prehistoric DNA forces our bodies to automatically prioritise the thing that we fear. In other words, dealing with our perceived fear and threat is far more important to our body than digesting that Big Mac. That's the very basic science of our makeup.

My fear of public speaking can be traced back to my kindergarten days, which is outlined in the next chapter.

My job today involves appearances before Courts and Judges, and attempts to persuade in favour of my clients. Is there some apprehension and even excitement in the lead up? Yes. Do unexpected curveballs fly from the Bench from time-to-time? Yes, they certainly do. And, with time, I have learnt to not only accept that this will happen, but often revel in the mind's capacity to step into that 'zone' and deal with the questions. The result is not only a growth in confidence, but a glimpse into our true magnificent essence.

Put yourself out there. Next time there is an opportunity or an invitation for you to speak, even for a few minutes, put your hand up. Write out what it is you wish to say – from the heart. Bring integrity to your message. It is YOUR message. As such, it will resonate. When a close friend asks you to speak at their 30th or 50th (as one of my good friends did) say a big YES, despite your fear. And, as I said, speak from the heart. I could not imagine not speaking at my daughter's wedding. Expressing our deep love can be emotional and uplifting – for all.

We obviously do not go about consciously conditioning illusory fears into our minds. Such fears arise unconsciously from our childhoods and develop into patterns that, in turn, begin to run our lives.

The trick is to bring awareness to their illusory, conditioned nature so that we can obliterate them from our lives. We are not our conditioned patterns. We always have choice in all that we do. But we are far too often blind to these choices.

What patterns do you keep repeating?

Can you identify how you keep reinforcing the pattern(s) to further entrench it as a belief and eventually your personality?

Eg: I am a shy person – always have been (really?)
I am an introvert
I am not confident, clever, smart, attractive ...
I could never do xyz (why?)

Contemplate a life without your patterns?
Contemplate choosing another reality as you read on.

CHAPTER 2

You are not Your Childhood Patterns

"We are our choices."
— Jean-Paul Sartre

Tracing our childhood patterns is a very useful exploration and I encourage you not to skip it.

Our education system is based on competition; achieving good marks; degrees; medals – all results based. Competition fosters and encourages comparisons. It reinforces and ingrains limiting belief systems that are simply not true. Johnny got 100% in math. He's smart. I'm not. I'll never do well. I'm dumb. I will never succeed in life. This is how self-beliefs are born.

But none of that is true.

Johnny may have done well because he had extra training; or he worked extra hard and spent more hours; or simply had a greater natural interest and aspiration to do well in math; or he may have come from a family of mathematicians, where, from the day he was born, it was an integral part of his life. Or a million other reasons.

We are all naturally gifted, and hence driven to do well and leave our mark on the world in our own unique, specific areas.

But we are never taught to explore, from a young age, what those areas are.

We are conditioned to constantly compare ourselves to others. Social media has exacerbated this conditioning and further eroded our self-belief in many realms. We tend to look to external forces, to someone else's experiences of what may make us happy and successful, rather than focusing internally on who we are.

If the math teacher praised Johnny, but then asked him: Johnny why do you think you did so well in your math exam? The response may shed light and put to rest a lot of the self-doubt experienced by some of the other students in the class. Johnny might say for example: I've been doing Kumon since I was 4; or my mum's a math teacher, she's been training me; or I just love math and I can spend hours doing problems and equations, or a raft of other explanations. The math teacher may then turn around to the rest of the class and ask: what is it that you love doing and are good at? I guarantee each student will have some response, some love for some particular learning that excites and inspires them. She or he could take a little more time to explore and reinforce that unique talent and, at the same time, engender a self-belief in all of his or her students.

But this is not what happens. Instead, we take away our 50/100 in that math exam and start forming a belief that, unlike Johnny, we are not intelligent. I think you get the gist of the example and what causes us to make decisions about ourselves. Those decisions create patterns that reinforce our self-beliefs. That same old vicious cycle.

If you were to map out your life, outlining the key significant decisions or 'non-decisions' that have led you to where you are now, I guarantee that you will discern a clear pattern that touches at the very core of who you believe yourself to be and why. If you then delve deeper, with a conscious awareness of how you got there, you will also begin to discern what your real life purpose is.

This exploration will also provide you with valuable insight, and some understanding, of what is driving your behaviors and why. Just by shining a light into that unknown darkness, a change will be triggered.

Critically, it will bring about an awareness. That awareness is the first step towards affecting a change in your belief system. That change in your belief system will change your behavior. From awareness springs choice. It will help you move away from unconsciously repeating the same behavior over and over again, thereby reinforcing the belief that there is no other way. Which is not true. There is always another way.

We are always at choice in relation to every aspect of our lives.

Without awareness, your mind will constantly seek reinforcement of your belief system that will, in turn, repeatedly attract other circumstances into your life that prove to you that your belief system is real and unshakeable. It is driving who you are, which is not true. Your mind will continue to create an ever-expanding folder of similar experiences that you will keep adding to and enlarging to demonstrate the veracity of your belief system. This reinforcement will have you repeat: see I told you that's what always happens to me; you see, that's just who I am. I repeat, and with respect, that is all a load of nonsense.

Let me demonstrate. My first life experience (that I consciously recall) happened at kindergarten. I started school a very, very, very shy, timid and withdrawn child. No! You say. Not possible. Yes, very possible. The teacher would ask us to all read little snippets from the books we were given. At a parent/teacher interview, and in front of all the other parents and children in the class, my teacher told my mother that when I was asked to read, not only could he and the whole class not hear a word I was reading, but I could not even hear myself reading!

My mother thereafter embarked on a fierce agenda of forcing me to read – ALOUD – every single night, to her and to my younger brother (if he was paying attention). The repetition resulted in my learning the texts and the stories all off by heart. My mother then repeatedly caused me to pause at every comma; stop at every full stop; raise my voice in surprise or in a loud tone at every exclamation mark. I began to read with passion and meaning and context. As I did so, I stood taller. My head lifted a little higher. I 'grew' an inch or two – just through being forced to find my voice and cultivate some confidence in my ability to read aloud.

The final test was my teacher's public request for me to read aloud. Was I ready? My teacher was staggered, surprised and thrilled. He asked my mother: "What have you done? She is now reading, not like a kindergarten child, but has surpassed the children in 3rd and 4th grade primary school." He shook his head in disbelief and smiled frequently at me. My mother's pride was written all over her face.

As for me, my debilitating fear of failure; of being humiliated in public; of not feeling good enough or worthy enough; and fearing I would be judged as being hopeless – transformed into a massive 'can do' attitude. They were not words that a seven year old could articulate or understand. But the experience was embedded into my brain and formed the beginning of a neural pathway that would springboard me into my future.

Looking back now, with the wisdom and knowledge of hindsight and half a century of personal growth, I can see how I transcended my fear of publicly reading with all of the preparation forced on me by my mother. The nightly repetition that I was required to conduct liberated me from my deep-rooted fears. I could, at last, hear myself. And be heard by my class!

Many of you may have had similar experiences as children, albeit in a different context. Others may have had very different experiences, where your fears may have been sheltered, maybe causing them to be instilled even deeper by parents or carers who took a very different approach to your life's challenges. There is no right or wrong here. No judgments. As parents we all try to do our best to protect our children.

One parent, like my mother, may feel the best for her child is to do what she did. Maybe even acting out of addressing the deep embarrassment my mother must have felt at the time; or even feeling that she had somehow failed her child in some way. Other parents, faced with the same situation, may feel that the best thing for their children is to protect them, to shield them from the embarrassment of having to engage in the task at such a delicate age. That parent may even tell the teacher not to force her daughter or son to read; that they are too young; or too shy; or not ready yet.

You can see that both actions spring from a space of love.

Tracing your history will shed light on what has been driving you in many areas of your life. It will shed light on how your belief systems are conditioned. That knowledge and awareness will, in itself, open the door to a freedom of choice you may not have contemplated as possible.

How many of you say: "I am a shy person. I have always been shy" and hence you do nothing about that. You accept, unconditionally and without question, that this is who you innately are. But that, with respect, is also a nonsense. An absolute fiction. That is merely a choice you made at age six to seven – from a multitude of choices you did not even know you had. You begin to see now that such a choice was a cop out that prevented you from experiencing yourself as the more powerful being that you are. It sheltered you from any risk taking. It sheltered you from any failure. If you do not try, how can you fail? All fear-based.

If my mother had instead sheltered me, and told the teacher to leave me alone as I was a very shy person and she didn't want me to be further stressed or distressed, what patterns do you think I would have developed? What reinforcement of future experiences do you think I would have sought and attracted to validate that belief system that I was a shy person; that that is simply who I was? You can see how, in such an instance, my pattern of shyness could have been cemented and entrenched; so much so, that it may have formed an intractable belief system that prevented me from exploring the career that I am in now. Think of all the fears that shy people have around being a voice for others. Would I have been able to embark on a career as a barrister who seeks to persuade judges about the merits of her clients' cases? Certainly not. If I continued to hold that illusory belief system that I was a shy person and I would die a shy person, such a career would have been worse than death for me. Do you think I would have even considered embarking on such a course?

Shedding a light on how our belief systems are formed frees us from our fears. My experience could have gone either way. I was never a 'shy' person, as a defining, indelible feature of my being. None of us are. I was full of unlimited potential and possibility that could have been stripped from me by an early experience that I had little control over. As we all are. It could have gone either way, as I said - the flipside of the same coin.

Now as you reflect on my experience, did my childhood recollections jolt any first-time experience for you of fear at a young age? Have you allowed the word 'shy' to define you? And if you were to trace that experience through to today, I guarantee there will be a discernible pattern that can be recognized. You will have a multitude of experiences - reinforcement upon reinforcement upon reinforcement that the mind has attracted to validate and confirm to you that you really are a shy person. That is how our so-called identities are formed. Even your friends, family and society have all accepted that, yes, John/Jenny is a very, very shy person. He/she has been that way all his/her life. That's just who they are. More reinforcement.

All a massive illusion.

In the process, we have forgotten that we are always at choice. We have forgotten that we are the sole creators of our lives. We have forgotten that those ingrained thoughts and beliefs were created by us in the first place. They are not the truth of who we are. When we awaken to *that* Truth and that reality, our lives shift miraculously.

As I said, if I had a different experience, I could well have decided that I was just born shy; that shyness was somehow embedded in my DNA. I would certainly have had difficulty with a career as a barrister. If I were to describe myself as being a shy person to my friends today, they would laugh loudly, waiting for some joke to spring forth. However, very deep down, and from time-to-time, I still do sense some remnants of that early shyness that have not fully been obliterated. The fear may arise, but it will not stop me from engaging fully in life and making choices, despite the presence of fear.

I now know that the fear is a symptom of our illusory belief systems.

How long have your identity patterns been driving your life choices?
When did they become entrenched beliefs about yourself?
How long have they been your identity/personality?

Contemplate discarding at least one of those patterns and creating a new one.
I AM ... (fill in the new you!)

Chapter 3

You are not Your Illusory Belief Systems

"The illusory reality tends to become whatever you are prepared to accept."
— Steven Redhead

My next childhood experience took place the same year as my kindergarten experience discussed in the previous chapter. I found myself on a huge ship, migrating from Europe to Australia. The ship caught on fire and I found myself on the deck, holding mum's hand with my brother on the other side. I do not recall any fear. My sense was one of alertness, excitement and curiosity. I have little doubt, looking back, that my original fear of reading aloud to a class of my peers was far greater than a ship on fire, where I was in the safety of my mother's loving care.

Can you see how much of an illusion our fears are? Caught in a fire on a ship versus reading publicly – all too ridiculous when viewed through the eyes of an adult.

I arrived in Australia with my hair in funny plaits, with my two front teeth missing and with not a word of English. My father literally enrolled me into the local school the following day. I had an overwhelming sense of not belonging; of being different. In that moment I decided (unconsciously) that my road to validation was academic achievement. I had already experienced success in that arena. At least there was some familiar territory there, in this otherwise strange, new country. I fell back on what I already knew. I fell back on my prior experience of myself. My early belief system and pattern had begun to take form and I was now looking for more validation and reinforcement. The road to perceived success or failure is exactly the same.

This is precisely how belief systems are conditioned and formed. This is precisely how patterns are conditioned and formed. So much so that we, and those around us, i.e. society, relate to them as truths, and not choices. Johnny is such a great academic! Jenny is so smart, so intelligent. Or the converse.

All are false labels that keep us boxed in until we awaken to the real truth.

Did I excel academically, you are wondering? Of course. That belief system came with so much at stake. That's how I was going to belong in this strange, new country.

Can you see how critically relevant that was to me at the time? It was a core challenge to my very existence. Belong...or become invisible and lost. I chose to belong. And my belief system gave me the only pathway I knew at the time. The wiser version of me that exists today would know that such a choice can just be made.

At the end of my first year, not only had I mastered speaking English, but I was in the top 5 in my class. I finished DUX of my High School. I finished DUX of the college I attended. And I finished with First Class Honours and the University Medal from the University I attended. I am not bragging here. I am merely seeking to highlight how our belief systems can sometimes drive us to insane 'choices'. What we believe to be choices. I was compelled to achieve out of a need to belong, and to be validated in an environment that felt foreign to me. I was not at choice. I was driven, but my drive was on auto-mode. It became my automatic way of being that arguably protected me from the very threat to my survival. I will say it again: all an illusion that I created.

That discernible pattern followed me throughout my academic life. It defined me for a very long time. I recall considering doing a PHD, not for the learning and not for any deep interest in the subject. I wanted to do a PHD so that I could have the label 'Dr' in front of my name. Maybe then I would truly belong in this strange, new country. Maybe then I would not feel so different. It had become my automatic way of being. My belief system had become so entrenched that I did not even know I was at choice in this area of my life, until that moment.

I felt an enormous freedom when I realized I did not need to do a PHD. I finally let myself off the hook. I finally shone the torch of awareness on that automatic way of being, that gave me my actual freedom to choose. Did it take a long time? Yes, much much longer than it should have. But I was part of a society that showered me with such "success" and positive reinforcement. She must be really intelligent. How smart is she? More positive reinforcement that kept enlarging and entrenching my belief system.

Every single belief system we hold has a pattern. It has a beginning. And it has ongoing reinforcements that the mind attracts subconsciously, that cement it as a truth, until we awaken. It is not a truth. I could have just as easily chosen to believe that, with such a perceived disadvantage, I could never be academically successful and instead focused my attention in other areas to give me my sense of belonging. I could have decided to be a joker or a funny storyteller. Who are the jokers out there? Or an all-round pleaser who always said "yes" to my peers. I could have decided to excel in some sport. Or I could have decided to accentuate the funny clothes I originally wore to school in order to stand out and belong that way. That may have led me into a career of fashion and design. I could have decided to seek to protect other young, shy, 'disadvantaged' children and built up a belief system that I was fundamentally a compassionate, caring individual. That, in turn, may have driven me into a career in medicine. These are all decisions we make, driven by our fears of not belonging, of failing, of being ridiculed. These are, more often than not, the choices of our ego.

What decisions did you make that have formed some of your core belief systems? If you reflect on those, I guarantee that you will quickly see the patterns that have evolved, and the ongoing reinforcements that your subconscious mind has attracted, in order to keep those belief systems in place.

Look at your belief systems around your 'shoulds'; your should nots; your cant's. What do you identify with? What have you conditioned yourself to believe you are, which you are not, of course? What did you condition yourself to believe about who you are, and from when, most probably from when you were a very young child?

We have all heard about how baby elephants are conditioned to believe that a tiny, insignificant rope around its foot or neck will prevent the massive, adult elephant from claiming its freedom. Can that adult elephant break that tiny piece of rope? Without any doubt. But as long as that adult elephant maintains its conditioned belief that it cannot, it will not even try. As a baby elephant it tried and tried to break free and could not. The rope was enough of a constraint at that time. It now accepts, as an adult elephant, that the same rope remains enough of a constraint, which is simply not true.

Human beings experience the same childhood conditioning. Where in your life are you mimicking that elephant?

What do you say about yourself: I'm a hopeless athlete (I can't run, swim, play sport, ski etc.); I'm not creative, I can't even draw a pencil to save my life; I can't string two sentences together; I'm not a logical thinker; I'm airy/fairy; I'm always last in every competition; I'm a shy person, always have been, always will be. Really?? Again, the list is endless. Add yours. Then ask yourself, where did all that come from?

I guarantee if you take the time and effort you will be able to trace that belief back to an incident when you were young. Like the elephant you have conditioned yourself to believe that is your reality. It is not.

You have unconsciously and unwittingly defined yourself. Know that you are not that definition. You are not that identity. You are not that personality. You have infinite potential to be as great as any being on the planet. And even greater!

Until a world record is broken, no one believes it is possible to run that fast, or to climb that high, or to swim that fast. Once broken, the floodgates open as the belief systems shift as to what is, in fact, possible.

We can all break through our belief systems and break through that conditioned glass ceiling in our minds. Look at your 'limitations' and know they are self-imposed. They are not who you really are.

We have all experienced exhilarating joy when we have transcended a particular belief system that has been limiting our way of being, and have instead chosen to do something spontaneously. We feel alive. Free.

I repeat, you are not who you believe yourself to be. Know that every belief system – whether it is sabotaging or uplifting you – is not who you truly are. You are far greater, far more powerful.

As an example, if you believe yourself to be athletic and fit and vibrant, what action do you think you would take that feeds that belief system and ultimately creates a very different identity? Yes, you would be taking actions consistent with that. You would be exercising regularly, eating healthily, training with professionals. You would be operating from an entirely different mindset. Shift your mindset and you shift your belief systems and your whole identity. You will be the creator of a very different reality.

As you begin to operate more and more from that altered mindset, it will progressively become your automatic way of being. No more willpower needed; no more striving and failing. That is how we manifest our visions and goals and our very life's purpose. It all eventually becomes possible with effortless ease and grace. And it works at every level and for every situation: finance; relationships; career; your weight; your spiritual awareness; your life's purpose.

Aim to eliminate all the fears, the what ifs', the should and should nots; the cant's; and know that lasting change is an inner game. It is an inner state of being. That inner state of being will manifest your outer reality. Learn to visualize and feel (deep in your body) where you want to be and what you want to experience and manifest. Then watch magic happen. Be witness to fears melting away. They will no longer even be on your radar.

You are always at choice. That is the realm of freedom. And you are always in that realm, if you bring your awareness to the situation.

Conscious choice is the only road to freedom. So, who are we – really? Do you describe yourself as a powerful being, always at choice? Do you believe it? Do you live it? Put simply: that is who you are.

Lesson 2

Who you are

What "mountain" have you not climbed?
If you could manifest your dream self,
what would that be?
Write the various connotations,
again using the I AM …

Contemplate a life lived from that
context as you read on.
Contemplate: YOU are the
creator of your life.
No one else.

CHAPTER 4

You are a Powerful Being: Believe it; Live it

"It is not the mountain we conquer, but ourselves."
--Sir Edmund Hillary

Let me illustrate this by sharing with you my experience of climbing two mountains. I am by no means a mountain climber. I have never before undertaken any mountain climbs or any treks whatsoever. It was never even a long-held vision or dream of mine. Actually, I can honestly say, hand on heart, that not in my wildest dreams did I ever envisage such adventures. So, how did they happen?

When such an opportunity (or *any* opportunity) or invitation presents itself, I have a habit of responding intuitively. I had some time ago attended seminars on the awakening of our heart. An invitation hit my email from one of the speakers who had previously trekked to Base Camp, Nepal and found it such an amazing experience, he was inspired to organize another. Nepal was not even on my bucket list and I am a very seasoned traveler. I was immediately and intuitively called to go. And did so.

All I did beforehand was a quick search to see what Nepal had to offer. I was immediately awe struck. If you, like me, do nothing other than look at the pictures of the Himalaya Mountains, Namche Bazaar and the Tengboche Monastery, you will also be awe struck by the sheer majesty and magnificence of what I was about to embark on. My whole heart screamed a big YES! It would be a magical, once-in-a-lifetime adventure. And it was.

Since my two climbs, I have often said, in jest: climbing two mountains in one lifetime is two too many… These were heroic, Herculean adventures, at a truly grand scale. I am forever grateful for my heart's wisdom.

Let me start with Mt Everest.

To Base Camp - Mt Everest

If someone asked you to go hiking up to Base Camp Mt Everest in Nepal, altitude 5,380 meters, and said to you: you will need insurance that includes a helicopter lift out of the mountain range; pills to stop you getting altitude sickness which could kill you; other pills to stop you getting diarrhea; headache medication – what's the first thing that comes up? Fear of dying on the mountain. Fear of suffering illnesses and pain. Do you immediately give up even the thought of climbing and think to yourself: are you mad?

Or, like me, do you not hear any of that? Do you merely see a vision of yourself reaching Base Camp, exhilarated and triumphant? No headache. No diarrhea. No altitude sickness. No pills. Instead, you see yourself beaming and glowing with good health and vitality and excited by the sheer challenge and adventure of hiking through Nepal, meeting the locals and reveling in the extraordinary magnificence of the place.

Both are true. Which would you rather experience? Which do you think you would experience? What is your conditioned mind saying to you now, as you read this?

Bring awareness to your very thoughts, right now. They are the indicator of how and why you choose your life experiences. Jot down your awarenesses. Stop reading and do it now.

As you continue to do this, you will see a very clear and discernible pattern emerge that has shaped your life to this day and will continue to do so in a similar fashion, unless you choose to create a very different reality.

All I heard was: footsteps to the Roof of the World. My first purchase from Nepal was a little green covered book - "Hand Made Paper NEPAL" – with two footprints on the front, in which I recorded my mystical experiences.

There were roughly 30 of us that went trekking through Nepal, up to Base Camp. Roughly 15 females and 15 males. Four made it to Base Camp. Three males and one female. That female was me.

I recall a very close friend/colleague warning me that I had no idea what I was letting myself in for, telling me: "You will be confronted by your body in ways you have never known. Physical exhaustion will happen and you deserve it; you have done nothing to prepare yourself for it". I told him I could and would handle it. He did not have to worry about me. I was so bold as to suggest to him that I would be dancing with the locals. He shook his head in disbelief and restated that I really had no idea whatsoever what I had signed up for; and I would certainly not be dancing with the locals!! He even wrote: "You are leaving with visions of dancing on tables with the Sherpas. They do not exist for your amusement".

Well, guess what – I did dance with the local Sherpas one evening, tucked away in one of the tea houses in a tiny Sherpa village. I can still hear the Nepalese music. I can still visualize the gentle movements of the Nepalese as I tried to emulate them. And yes, there was much fun and laughter, connectedness and freedom.

Despite my colleague's very severe warnings, it is true, I didn't embark on any fitness regime. I didn't exercise. I didn't subject myself to any similar mountain altitudes to acclimatize. In fact, I did nothing outside my normal routine. I didn't even break in my new hiking boots.

As I recorded in my little green book, even the fittest in the group, and despite their extensive training, struggled more than me and were afflicted with altitude sickness.

Mind over matter (as I said to my friend). That is indeed the power of the mind and the power of the language we use. The power of that voice inside our mind that rarely stops.

I had also recorded that at the end of our climb to Base Camp, Dumche, our lead Sherpa came to me and said: "I have been looking at you. You are 100%. Most people are 80%, some are 70% some are sick, some get altitude symptoms. But you are perfect, 100%."

That is the power of the mind.

Just as an aside, Dumche also played the guitar and taught us a Nepalese song. So, not only did I dance at the Roof of the World, but I also sang – and in Nepalese. I recorded: "The atmosphere was warm and magical. I danced in the Himalayas. I sang in the Himalayas. Life is good".

I have a very vivid recollection of arriving at Namche Bazaar. There, smack bang in the middle of the road were two huge, hairy Yaks – making out!! By the time I pulled the cover off my camera, they were done. Yes, it was very quick indeed. Damn. A golden opportunity for a photoshoot gone.

My experience at the Tengboche/Thyangboche Monastery, one very early morning, still brings tears of joy to my heart. I sat at the back of the Monastery, alone on the floor, perched up against the wall. Legs crossed. There was a peace and a stillness that no words can describe. I felt as if I had merged with all before me.

I heard the bells ringing. The sun began to hit the peaks of the mountains, starting with Mt Everest which was literally set on fire. It was as if somebody was putting a match to the top of a white peak, creating a golden hue. The sun went from peak to peak as it set alight all the other mountains surrounding the Monastery. No words could describe the majesty before my eyes.

I sat quietly in the Monastery in a meditative state that I had not experienced before. I then observed the monks coming in, sitting, cross-legged, on their benches, reciting their teachings and performing their rituals. They began to sing and chant. One monk, dressed in full monk robes, could not have been more than eight to nine years old. I was truly transfixed. A much deeper peace and love I have never felt before, a love that knew no reason, permeated my whole body. Tears began to roll down my cheeks. My vision of that experience remains very vivid to this day. I have difficulty in finding the words to fully describe it. Thankfully the below two paragraphs are a direct record of what I wrote in my little green book:

> *The mystical sound of the monks resonated deep within the Monastery and deep within my being. I was hypnotized. Tears kept streaming down my face. I was overwhelmed with such love, peace and compassion. I have always known, at an intellectual level, how very much I love my children, my parents, my brother, close friends.*
>
> *I now sat in the experience of that love. It gushed over me and through me in such waves and with such depth that it was almost overpowering. I felt expansive. I felt bliss. I felt enormous gratitude.*

These were not only footsteps to the Roof of the World. These were footsteps into my heart; into my very soul.

I treasure every moment of that morning, with immense gratitude.

Oddly, no other group member came. Maybe it was too early for them.

The Monastery is a very sacred Tibetan Buddhist Monastery, sitting at a height of 3,867 meters, said to have been originally built on the footprint of its founding Lama. It is a UNESCO World Heritage site, with the Himalayan Mountains as a backdrop - a truly rare beauty.

As I wrote and reflected on the above memories, I recalled a somewhat odd experience I had at a Dr Brian Weiss seminar that I attended (along with my two adult children), in Melbourne. It was at the invitation of my son. I had never heard of Dr Weiss. He was a very traditional psychotherapist, having graduated from Columbia University and Yale Medical School. He was (and maybe still is) Chairman Emeritus of Psychiatry at the Mount Sinai Medical Centre in Miami. With serious skepticism and astonishment, he finally worked up enough courage to publish "Many Lives Many Masters" when he recorded one of his patient's experiences of past-life traumas that held the key to her recovery in the present life.

This catapulted him in a completely new direction as he embarked upon international seminars and experiential workshops that engaged participants in past-life regressions therapy. At the workshop we attended in Melbourne, one of my hypnotic experiences revealed a past-life to me where I was an ancient Buddhist monk myself !!

I have only now (as I write this), sought to connect the dots. Maybe my very deep, mystical experience at the Tengboche Monastery had something to do with that past-life? I wonder what Dr Weiss would have to say about that? Life is indeed intriguing. Back to my climb/ trek to Mt Everest Base Camp ...

Were there challenges along the way? Of course. I learned to listen to my body. On many days the trekking itself was meditative. Some days I would feel as though I had sprouted wings and was about to soar. The day we trekked to Base Camp, passed the glaciers, in the freezing cold - was one such day! I felt so blessed. Other days, I could barely put one foot after the next, particularly when we hit the high altitude. As I told my buddy: "I will get fit on the trek". And yes, my fitness level improved daily. That is what I told my mind and my body. Not once did I doubt that.

When an opportunity like trekking to Mt Everest was presented to me, I saw it as an adventure; an amazing experience. I had no idea what doors would open for me. All I knew was that my heart and my intuition were aligned. My decision to go never wavered. Not once.

So, what is it exactly that impacted on the experiences outlined above? My 'yes' brought me unimaginable growth and adventure. My 'no' would have waited for another opportunity that may have materialized in a very different way. I may have never seen or experienced Nepal, in all its glory.

I reiterate, it is your mindset. It is the very belief systems that you have in place that will determine and attract and manifest your external experiences. What is it the Bible says (and I am not religious)? As you think, so shall you become.

Bringing awareness to your belief systems is the starting point. Ask yourself: what are my beliefs around climbing a mountain if the opportunity came up? Then ask where did those belief systems come from? Or, better still, identify one burning desire you have harbored for ages but have never pursued. Then ask yourself, what entrenched beliefs have I held around that desire that have prevented me from even exploring its potential?

Again, catch yourself. What are you thinking now? Are you saying to yourself that is the biggest BS I have ever heard?? That thinking will only keep you rooted to the same life reality that you have manifested to date. Do you want to create some positive shift in your life in one area or more? If the answer is 'yes', then the answer to doing so is your mindset. Change your beliefs and your thoughts and you are on the way to creating whatever wild dreams you are afraid to give voice to.

Put your hand on your heart and ask yourself: what do I feel about this opportunity? What resistance is coming up, if any? Why? If I put that resistance aside, what possibilities are likely to manifest? What great things are likely to happen? And then be surprised when something ten times greater begins to emerge. That was my experience when I decided to walk through the Nepalese "Door". In fact, it has been my experience every time I have followed my heart and embarked on a new journey.

You are powerful beyond measure. Believe in yourself. Dare to be great. Dare to dream big. Dare to live the life you deserve.

At the end of our trek, I gave away my hiking boots and my other gear to a beautiful young Sherpa girl who was part of our support team on the climb. I have small feet and my hiking boots fitted her perfectly. She cried. I recall my hiking buddy saying: "Don't give away all your stuff. You may go climb another mountain, or you could use it back in Sydney". Climb another mountain? Do this again? That was simply not a possibility – or so I thought.

Mt Kilimanjaro

That was 1999. Wind the clock forward to 2012. By society's conditioned standards, I was certainly no spring chicken. But that did not even enter my thinking.

It was the year my parents celebrated their 60th wedding anniversary and their 80th birthdays. It prompted a conversation between my daughter and I, with my daughter, Sandy, posing this question: "Mum, what memories do we want to create as mother and daughter that we can look back on in twenty years' time?"

Sandy then proceeded to flippantly blurt out that: “we should climb Mt Kilimanjaro”. I said: “Really????? But I’ve already climbed my mountain”. “It can be a fund-raising climb and we could raise money for the Wayside Chapel”, she said. “Really ???? What about shopping and shows in New York? That would be a great mother-daughter experience”, was my response. “Mum … seriously, I always saw us climbing a mountain together”.

I did not take much convincing. I thought about it for all of 10 minutes before declaring: “OK. Let’s do it. I’m in!” In that moment I saw a clear vision of us reaching the peak and capturing that special moment in a photo that would hang in my home. Her response: “Are you sure? Don’t you want some more time to think about it? Don’t you want some more information”. “No, I’ve already climbed a mountain. I know what to expect”.

We had no difficulty in raising our target. We did not even need to put on a single function or event. The dollars just poured in on announcing our mission. Sandy’s vision had certainly inspired our family, friends and our wider circle.

I recall thinking to myself as I was entertaining my daughter’s vision: “are you mad? One mountain in one lifetime is one too many. Two mountains is just plain crazy.”

However, in that moment my projected vision of us reaching the peak of Mt Kili and having our photo taken lit up my face and brought an instant smile to it. I could literally feel the excitement of that moment! What a journey this would be with my daughter. What a legacy to leave my grandchildren (yet to come). I said “yes”, despite knowing what that entailed and despite all the fears for my daughter. And I was 12 years older than when I climbed my last mountain?? What are you encouraging your daughter to do - that inner voice shouted in my ears? What if she becomes really ill? What about her knee problems? More fears. More what ifs. I hung up on that voice with a very decisive “no more, none of that will ever happen”.

I looked at my daughter's face and saw her warm, inquisitive eyes gazing back at me and I repeated and declared my unequivocal: "yes, I'm in. Let's do it. I mean it". The decision was made. If she had any fears or even considered bailing out, that option had just vanished. We were committed.

The excitement then really took over. Wow, how many mother/daughter experiences include climbing a mountain together? I knew of none personally. Nor did my daughter. This was going to be epic. And, if I had to carry her up that mountain I would somehow do it. Again, there was no preparation; no training; no pills; no altitude sickness; no diarrhea; no real headaches; no medications.

In short, I did the same zero preparation - except, this time, I broke in my new hiking boots a week before departure doing the Bondi to Bronte walk. Sandy asked if I wanted to climb a smaller mountain around Sydney, for training. My response: "Are you mad? I will climb one mountain and that is Mt Kili. Why put myself through a dummy trial?" My only fear and reservation that kept popping up was not knowing how Sandy would go? How resilient was she? Would her knee (that was slashed by a glass pane when she walked through the glass door of our home at age 16) cause any problems?

The word 'epic' does not even come close to describing our journey to the peak of Mt Kilimanjaro. I discovered that not knowing anything much about such climbs is far less stressful than the anticipation and expectation of the arduous task ahead. Mt Kilimanjaro felt harder than Base Camp, Nepal. Viewed objectively, it was not. I once more reflected on the power of the mind.

Sandy's word to describe our climb was 'brutal'. Mine was 'grueling'. But we made it. And we took the obligatory photo at the peak Summit of Mt Kili, an epic 5.895 meters high. Sandy said that the air was so thin she could hear her lungs crackling with each gasp of air. The sun was out in its full glory trying to fool everyone: it was a freezing minus 15-20 celsius!

The climb to the summit was truly an incredible feat. We woke at 11.30pm to hike six hours to the rim of the crater - Killi's first summit at Gilman's Point. It was pitch black. We were guided by the small head torches on our foreheads. That was our only light. The mountain was steep with rocks falling beneath our feet. Seeing the sign at the top filled me with false relief.

Somehow, I gained the impression that reaching Gilman's Point was it. This was the peak. How crazy for the group to get the timing so wrong. The victory shots would have to be taken in the dark.

Sandy saw my confusion and hugged me saying: "No mum. This is not THE peak, only the first one. We have another three hours before we reach the TOP peak. But, if you are exhausted, please head back. There are others that aren't going further. It's OK. It really is". My response: "what are you going to do, continue to the top?" She nodded a big yes. "OK – which way is up? Let's go".

God, I thought, it would be another three hours in freezing temperatures and heart-breaking thin air before we reached the ultimate summit. Why would they even put a dummy peak here?

Finally, we arrived. The darkness gave way to the morning light, as the sun rose to greet us. Tears of joy and exhilaration and disbelief came flooding down our cheeks. We made it! We stood at THE peak, hands flung in the air, for the photo that would capture this unforgettable moment of glory. A glory shared by a mother and daughter.

But that glorious sense of achievement was short-lived. We had to now turn around and head back. We had to keep moving. It was too freezing to remain still for any length of time.

Sandy found the descent even harder, as our bodies and minds battled dehydration and exhaustion. I was shown how to 'ski' through the dirt on my heels. Unbelievably, I found myself in that 'zone' again. Freedom!! When I finally stopped and looked up at the mountain slope, I could not believe how far down I had come and how quick it was. I watched others struggle, unprepared or afraid to try to "ski" down the massive mountain slope. Fear stopped them even trying. How do you ever know success if you do not even try? The worst that could happen was a harmless fall on soft dirt. The best was the exhilarating freedom of soaring down effortlessly. I recall I had one fall in my attempt to maneuver around a rock. My heels could not turn around to miss the rock in time, so I just caused myself to fall and drop to the soft dirt below. I got up, walked around the rock, and started my 'skiing' again. Knowing what to expect this time round brought a confident smile to my face. This was actually fun and easy. Far, far easier than trying to 'walk' down the slope of the mountain.

I looked up and saw many 'walk' down on their backsides. I saw others being airlifted by two of our local support team, holding a bent elbow on each side. I saw yet others walking sideways with so much care and caution that I wondered if they would be back at the base for dinner?? The 'heel skiers' soared to the bottom. As I looked up, I saw all of this and smiled. Humanity .... in all its diversity and wonder. All resplendent and determined and magnificent. How inspiring, I thought. What a glorious journey we all shared.

At the end of that massive journey together, my beautiful daughter said she wasn't at all surprised, knowing me as well as she did. But she said she had grown a newfound respect for my determination and will; my refusal to take any altitude medicine, or other medication; and my sheer tenacity to reach the peak. Thinking I had already done so three hours earlier! Yes, Sandy ... we were indeed a mirror image of each other.

We made it to the peak with a glowing newfound respect and admiration for each other. That vision of us reaching the peak and taking the photograph with our arms in the air, hangs in my loungeroom. It floods my computer screen at work. The shared memories are indelible. The shared victory at the peak leaves me speechless to this day. It engendered a sense of indescribable freedom and achievement. What stories I have to impart to my grandchildren one day. What a legacy we leave behind for future generations. To this day I often shake my head at the enormity of what we set out to achieve and did achieve.

Two crazy girls wanting to experience a glorious adventure together as a mother and a daughter. It still brings tears to my eyes – even as I write this.

Now let me tell you about the most challenging aspect for me. It was the camping. Yes, you read that correctly: the camping! I have never camped in my life. I am not a camper. And I will never be a camper. But camp, we did, in tiny bubbles. I was expecting the big African tents that we enjoyed during our safari through the Serengeti. When I saw the little tents, I assumed they were for our hiking gear and bags. "No," my daughter informed me. "You and I are sleeping in that tent". Shock, horror. "What, both of us? In that tiny little tent, what about all our stuff?" "That's going in with us", was the response. One of our group members obviously overheard the conversation. The expression on my face must have been one of sheer disbelief. I was stunned. It was all incomprehensible to me. He came over, smiled, and gave me a hug and reassured me it would all be OK….

I began to quieten my mind. It's all OK, OK … I caused my internal voice to say: yes, you can do camping. Yes, I can do camping.

Any campers out there? I bet your mind is racing now, in stunned disbelief. She said "yes" to climbing the mountain, but is questioning and feeling challenged by camping? You've got to be kidding! But that's because in your world, you have conquered the challenges of camping and probably enjoy it. Your mind conjures up positive thoughts around camping. That was certainly not my experience and it was coming on top of my decision to do the climb. This is the power of the mind. This is exactly how ridiculous it can get. This is how our belief systems and conditioning can impact us – from the smallest decision, to the grandest.

I can guarantee that this madness will not afflict me again. As I said, two mountains in a lifetime is two too many. As for camping, I need add nothing further. It never occurred to me that people camped and slept in these tiny, yellow 'bubbles'. Yes, to my conditioned mind, that was a mammoth challenge. More so, given that I was expecting the full upright tents, with proper beds, with the little table and chairs, the glass of champagne ... that we had experienced in Africa during our safari! That's how you do Africa. It's irrelevant whether you are on a safari, exploring the grandeur of the animals or on a mountain climb exploring the breathtaking splendor of the scenery. Nepal had the tea houses. We didn't tent. This was too ridiculous, taking us on a trip that required such massive commitment and expecting us to sleep, on top of each other, with our equipment, in these silly tiny bubbles .... On and on and on my mind argued. All to no avail.

I again saw the power of (mostly) unconscious belief systems that are etched in our minds. My beliefs around camping are not pleasant ones. Yet, I have a brother who goes camping often and talks about the freedom he experiences sleeping under the open sky; lighting a fire; putting up the tent; cozying up inside when it starts raining, or there are thunderstorms. Glorious. That's his conditioned mindset.

I see none of that. My mind conjures up rain and wind; mud and dirt; flapping tents; discomfort; strain and effort in putting up the tent; confinement; lugging equipment; toileting in prickly bushes, and a whole lot more. My sense of freedom is very different from that of a happy camper.

But once again, the bigger vision of our mother/daughter adventure sprang to mind. No yellow bubble of a so-called tent was going to jeopardize that. And camp I did. I told myself it was a sideshow, irrelevant to the real mission at hand. My mind jettisoned it to one side and, instead, focused on turning Sandy's dream into a reality.

Success? Failure? The mind does not care. It will give you whatever you choose and perceive and believe in. The vision I projected was one of absolute, unquestioned success. This was our mother/daughter adventure. One that I would hand down to my grandchildren. There was simply no room for a single doubt. If I had to carry Sandy up that mountain myself, I would have done it. That was my only persistent question mark – was she going to be OK? Yes, she was. The little bubbles were discarded to the bottom of the list, irrelevant against that bigger picture.

As I said, the photo of the two of us at the Summit is hanging, framed, in my loungeroom – just as I had visualized it. I projected talking about it to my grandchildren. I await that experience with knowing excitement.

I learned, on that mother-daughter climb, that the acorn does not fall far from the tree. Sandy's resilience and determination were inspiring. She too only saw success. Whatever fears were there were submerged and overcome by our shared vision. I learned what a truly amazing human being she is. Not a bad or harsh word between us. Only tears of joy. And tears of disbelief at the enormity of the task.

We now have the legacy that was Sandy's vision.

I was definite then as I am now that our next mother-daughter exposé will be Broadway shows and shopping in New York! I also have little doubt that Sandy will find something more adventurous and inspiring!

Did we have to overcome our many fears to boldly embark on our adventure? You bet. The joint vision of reaching the Summit together could not be realized with too much doubt. Our very core was challenged (and I am not talking about our stomachs, although they too were challenged). The vision remained and prevailed. There was enormous release and exhilaration and pride in having reached the peak and reached it together. There was freedom. There was a tranquil peace. There was a massive sense of accomplishment. And not a single injury.

So, what is the difference between success and failure; fear and freedom? Your mindset. And what is your mindset? Your conditioned belief system. It's that simple. By visualizing myself at the mountain peak and believing I would achieve it – in glowing health and exhilaration – I caused a shift to a higher vibration that manifested that outcome. I did not worry about the how. I had an unquestionable belief that my vision would take me to that mountain peak. I was already living my reality, in my mind. I felt the sheer magnitude of my achievement. There was no room for failure. Our subconscious mind cannot perceive the difference between what is real and what is imagined. It will give you what you, at a deep level, believe you deserve. And what you believe you deserve or are capable of achieving is a conditioned belief. Know that the only limits on you climbing *your* mountain are the limits that you impose and inflict on yourself.

The same sports psychology is used by elite sports people to get them to achieve their end goal – by speaking (including their internal dialogue), thinking, visualizing the mental image and feeling the victory at the end. This creates a fundamental shift in our belief systems. It is a mental performance, a mental rehearsal that can be as powerful, if not more powerful, than going in the field. This is how I climbed my two mountains.

Again, I ask what is going through your mind this very moment? Catch your thoughts, right now. Having digested all this, what are you saying to yourself? Wow, that's inspiring. I can do that. It's exactly the kind of experience I will have with my mother, with my daughter, with my son, with my partner, with my best friend. Are your energy levels up in just visualizing such an adventure?

Or are you saying: "crazy, I could never do that; I would never take that risk, let alone allow a child or a mother to take that risk; the altitude sickness could kill me; I am not fit enough; I am not strong enough; I am not brave enough; I am not crazy enough!" …?

If the mind chatter is negative, then again, I encourage you to take the time to write down all the negative belief systems that are coming up. Stop reading and do it now. Then, against each negative belief, write down its positive connotation. This is the beginning of creating a new belief system that will propel you into the freedom you deserve.

Be in no doubt that whatever you are saying to yourself now is creating your reality. That language and those belief systems will determine your life experiences. Fears will spring up. But it is how you deal with those fears and the language that you use that will create your belief systems about who you are and what you can do. In turn, those ingrained and conditioned belief systems will manifest your reality (usually unconsciously). I repeat, you are the creator of your life. Be in no doubt about that.

And the language you use is one of the most powerful tools for manifesting – or not.

If, like me, you have a vision: then see it; think it; feel it; declare it; cast all doubt aside – and it will manifest. That is exactly how I climbed not one, but two mountains. These were not small visions, but you can start experimenting with smaller visions. Then work your way up to the grandest vision you have.

In both instances, the vision my mind captured and imprinted was one of undoubtedly reaching the peak. The end goal. My mind did this, not quietly and nonchalantly, but with the excitement I knew that the accomplishment would and did generate.

Let me demonstrate further. After my divorce, I had this vision of living near the ocean. I loved the thought of hearing the waves lapping against the shore; waking up to the smell of the ocean; feeling the fresh ocean breeze against my face. Your vision may be the rolling hills of a peaceful countryside.

This internal vision that we think about often, that we feel and internalize at our core, has a magical way of manifesting. If you bring conscious awareness to how it is you are where you are today, you can easily track your internal processes that got you there.

You guessed it. For the last 16 years I have been living at Tamarama (some call it Glamarama), a five-minute walk to Tamarama Beach and a fifteen-minute walk to either Bronte Beach or the iconic Bondi Beach.

How did I get here? With that vision as my driving force, about a year after my divorce, I embarked on a casual search, on the spur-of-the moment, one weekend. In hindsight, there is little doubt I was being guided that morning, albeit not consciously so. It was all spontaneous, with no serious intention (so I thought). We drove around the Bondi Beach area, and had a look at one property, then another. No good, too expensive. I felt deflated.

I then noticed there was a little house for sale on another Street in the area. It was in its "original state" (meaning barely livable).

As we drove into the Street, it was as if my vision was manifesting before my eyes. The house was in a terrible state of disrepair, but I saw none of that. I saw the fabulous location. I saw the beach. I heard the lapping of the waves. I smelt the freshness of the ocean. I felt the ocean breeze.

In that moment, I declared to my partner: "That's my home!" His response: "What are you talking about? You haven't really seen anything. We just came out on the spur of the moment. You can't be serious?" I re-declared: "That's my home!" I staked it in that moment. It was going on auction. We tried to secure its purchase before auction by making an offer and indicating we would not be around for the auction. The couple that owned it were going through their own divorce and the wife was particularly attached to the home, as I discovered after I bought it.

I turned up at the auction without even the deposit. That's how spontaneous the purchase was. I took my business partner along, with his cheque book. I told him he would bid and I would watch the other bidders carefully. Towards the end I told him to go up by $5,000 increments. I was already $185,000 over my budget; i.e. what I thought I would have to pay. It was a record for the Street. But all I could hear was the voice in my head: "that's my home".

Two bidders were finally left standing: me and another couple. The woman was heavily pregnant. I could see she was also stressed. They were at their limit, as was I.

I turned to my business partner and said: "And Five". He whispered: "you are well over your limit". I whispered back - with a smile – to indicate I was there to the end: "And Five". He bid the last $5,000. I waited. The silent minutes felt like hours. Were they going to bid again? The final call and the final fall of the hammer seemed to take an eternity. I watched the pregnant woman and her husband shaking their heads. They were done. The hammer fell. It was my home.

I then had to convince the bank to lend me the money. But when you bring this type of conviction to creating your reality, the rest all falls into place.

I now wake up every morning to the sound of the ocean. I meditate. I go to the gym and then we walk along the coastal walk to Bronte. Every morning. There are times when I stare out in awe at the magnificence of the vast ocean. Many mornings its stillness is mesmerizing as it flattens out like a lake. I gaze at the beauty of the sunrise emerging from the ocean. I still marvel at our only sight of half a dozen or so dolphins surfing the waves, in unison. Pure magic.

In that whole process my conviction was crystal clear. Would the bank lend me the money? Of course. Would I build my dream home there? Of course. Any hurdles along the way can and will be managed.

This is the power of the mind and the language we use. Never, ever underestimate it. It is creating our lives and our life experiences. Our very thoughts create our reality. I cannot say that often enough. I have to keep repeating this truth to make sure it hits its mark. If you take nothing from this book but that truth, I will be filled with gratitude.

Chapter 5

You Create Your Own Reality

"You can have anything you want
if you are willing to give up the belief
that you can't have it."
— Dr. Robert Anthony

You are not your mind. You are a spiritual being. Your mind is no more than a significant resource. It is not who you really are. The only problem is that, as a result of our conditioning, our upbringing, our education – we grow up believing we are our mind; that the mind has control over us and our actions.

Pay heed to Eastern philosophy that acknowledges our mind is a wonderful servant, but an abysmal master. Do not allow it to run your life – mostly unconsciously. Bring awareness to that inner voice that is preaching negativity. Replace it with conscious, positive thinking. As I said earlier, our mind has been conditioned to protect us. That conditioning has necessarily focused on danger, on a fear of being harmed in some way – physically, mentally, emotionally, spiritually. It is little wonder then that the mind constantly conjures up such negative thinking. That has been its programming. And it will continue to be its programming unless, and until, you consciously retrain it. It is no different to training any other muscle in your body, except that it is far more powerful.

I certainly recall all the fears my mind conjured up when my son was very young. I used to call him "Houdini". Harry Houdini was an American illusionist, revered for his jaw-dropping escape stunts. Well, my son was capable of escaping – wherever I placed him. My over-protective maternal instincts kicked in big time. I was literally run by my mind's fear of what could happen to my son, and all the steps that I needed to take in order to protect him.

Even where there was no problem, my conditioned protective mind created one. I've placed that lock on the door so high, but what if he climbs on a chair and unlocks it and escapes? He was still in nappies!

That is the power of the mind. Until we bring our consciousness to all it is saying and thinking, it will run your life. Just as you are not your body, not your hands or fingers, not your eyes or ears, not your hair – so it is, you are not your mind. You are always at choice. Bring consciousness to your thoughts. Monitor what the mind is saying and thinking every time it voices a negative fear. Reclaim your power. Know that you and you alone can control your mind; you and you alone can eliminate all the negative patterns that are running wild inside your mind; you and you alone can replace those negative patterns with a new, positive mindset – in every area of your life.

Know that those thoughts - mostly unconscious – affect your physical and emotional well-being. There are studies that demonstrate that up to 95% of all illnesses that afflict us today are as a direct result of our thoughts. Yes, our thoughts. The Institute of Heartmath (Glen Rein PhD and Rollin McCraty PhD) undertook an experiment headed "Local and nonlocal effects of coherent heart frequencies on Conformational Changes of DNA". Long heading, but the study made a very clear finding. Fear, that is, thinking and feeling fear, can cause DNA changes, causing our DNA to tighten up, become shorter and switch off/on many gene expressions that can be harmful to our health. However, this shut down by negative thoughts/feelings is reversed when we begin to express love and joy and gratitude.

What was it the Apostle Paul wrote over 2,000 years ago? "You'll do best by filling your minds and meditating on things true, noble, reputable, authentic, compelling, gracious – the best, not the worst; the beautiful, not the ugly; things to praise, not things to curse" (*Phil 4:8 The Message Bible*).

The power of our thoughts is literally creating our lives and our life experiences. It is that simple. Sad thoughts create sad people and sad experiences. Sad thoughts attract and manifest sad circumstances in our lives. Fearful thoughts attract and manifest a life filled with fearful events and people. What we are repeatedly thinking and feeling is what is manifesting our reality – daily!

This is what, in turn, reinforces our belief systems. It is a vicious cycle - until we bring awareness to the whole process, and a knowledge that we can make different choices. Those different choices can create positive belief systems that will support the blissful, amazing lives we were all meant to live.

We have over 60,000 thoughts a day. About 90% are the same, reinforcing the same belief systems and creating the same reality until we are so conditioned that they become our identity. We need to take conscious control over what those thoughts are and not allow our mind to run havoc, based on its unconscious conditioning. We need to still the mind by meditating on the best and not the worst; on the beautiful and not the ugly, to quote the Apostle Paul.

Next time you are walking (as I often do) along a beautiful coastal beach, do you actually see the beauty of your surroundings; the clear blue sky; the fluffy white clouds; the blazing red sunset; the waves cascading against the shore; the surfers riding the waves with elegant ease; the children playing in the sand? Or are you caught up in your negative thoughts of what happened yesterday, last week, last year, a decade ago? Or what MAY happen tomorrow, next week, next year, a decade from now? Do you finish your walk and see and feel nothing in that present moment? Catch your thoughts next time.

Stop. Look around. Be present. Any stress, fear or upset will vanish in that moment.

Change your thinking and you will change your reality.

Recent discoveries in the fields of Quantum Physics and Neuroscience have created a massive paradigm shift that is yet to filter through into our daily lives. There is no fixed objective reality out there. It is all in here, in our minds. It is our mind and our thoughts that create our reality from an infinite range of possibilities. Go, do your own research. Go and watch "What the Bleep Do We Know", as a starter.

We are not the victims of our life. Circumstances do not just happen to us. We are the creators. Consciously or unconsciously we create our reality in every moment of every day. Quantum physics now confirms what all the old mystics and religions have espoused over the centuries: that is, we are all interconnected, interdependent and part of the unified Oneness. Everything is energy. And we choose what energy we attract. We choose (usually unconsciously for the most part) our life; our stories; our experiences. There is no pre-determined fate out there that we are a victim of. We decide. We choose.

Do you have a belief that says that's all nonsensical, unintelligible – in short, a "load of hogwash"?

I have a cousin with exactly such a view. She has a deeply entrenched victim mindset. Her constant complaint is that no one understands what this person or that person; or this circumstance has done to her. In short, no one understands how the whole world is conspiring against her and creating her unhappiness. She seeks out and attracts experiences that feed her suffering and persecution, and ensure that she avoids taking any responsibility for her non-actions. After all, it is not her non-actions that are the cause of her suffering. It is the actions of all those people out there and, indeed, the world at large. Life for her is not only well beyond any personal control or responsibility

– it is out to deliberately hurt her. And is doing so. For years, she keeps repeating the same pattern over and over and wonders why she keeps getting the same result. She keeps refusing to open the door to another possibility. To explore – maybe I am wrong?? Maybe there is another way of looking at the world. Maybe I should at least entertain the possibility and see if there is a change.

Albert Einstein is credited with saying: "the definition of insanity is doing the same thing over and over again, but expecting different results". Can you identify with any repeat patterns that you are stubbornly, and with much justification, refusing to shed light on? Are you now saying: "but you don't understand. It's simply not my fault. I had nothing to do with it. He said … she did …. they hurt me in this way …"?

What deep fears do you harbor if you stepped out of that mindset and took full responsibility for your current state? If you were to openly declare that you are the cause of all your unhappiness; of all that is negative in your life – what fears surface that prevent you from taking any action to effect change in your life? List them. Be honest. Try on something different.

The fact that you are reading this book means you have had enough of swimming around in that same old fishpond. You are ready to dive into the vastness of the ocean and explore a new way of being.

We are only limited by our conditioning and belief systems. Remember when Magellan's fleet sailed around the tip of South America and he stopped at Tierra del Fuego. The ship's historian documented that when Magellan went ashore and pointed to the sailing ships at anchor off the coast, none of the natives could see the ships. Their brains had no reference point. How much are we still limited by our own conditioning, our own reference points? There have also been other reports of natives not being able to see any images of photographs taken by cameras for the same reason. This all plays an essential role in our perception of what we call reality.

Let me illustrate this further by looking at my experience of walking on hot coals – literally. Several decades ago, I attended an Anthony Robbins seminar: Unleash the Power Within or Awaken the Giant Within (can't recall what it was actually called back then). It was his first time in Australia. My teenage daughter and her best friend wanted to attend. I knew the power of my mind, but I wasn't sure about my daughter and her friend. So I told her she could go if I went along as her chaperone. Walking on hot coals was advertised as a highlight of the seminar. My fear was my young daughter would burn her feet and, as a parent, I would be held responsible.

Our conditioned and cultural belief system around hot coals is: if I walk on them, I will burn my feet. Some participants actually received minor burns. They obviously needed the proof of having walked on the hot coals. I came away squeaky clean and elated. I then waited anxiously whilst my daughter kept being sent to the back of the line on a few occasions until she reached the necessary state of mind to allow her to walk across the hot coals. Leaving aside whatever your scientific views are around this issue, there is no doubt that breaking through our cultural beliefs and walking across hot coals is a very strong and effective metaphor in helping you break through other perceived fears. If I can do that, what else is possible? That 'significant' hurdle that you perceived was preventing you from moving forward in another area of your life, now becomes a non-issue.

There are still islanders who are revered for their ability to walk on hot coals and perceived by other islanders as possessing some mystical, magical powers. The only mystical, magical powers are in their ability to determine their mindset; an ability that we all possess.

I have little doubt that our reality will shift dramatically as new neural pathways open up, and we begin to really accept and apply the emerging truth that we are the creators of all that is unfolding in our lives.

So-called 'successful' people are successful because the majority of their thinking is around success and whatever that means to them. Colonel Sanders no doubt continued to think and see his vision of KFC selling nationally and internationally, otherwise he would have given up. But he held onto that vision until it manifested. There is no failure. However, if your predominant, on-going thoughts are "I can't succeed, how can I make this happen; it's not possible; I keep getting told no; it will never work; I'm doomed to fail" etc. – then that will be the reality you create. You will simply give up and add that to your list of reinforcements, entrenching that same belief even further.

The truth is that you cannot fail. Nothing can stop you from achieving your goal. Let's explore that reality.

List at least two pursuits you have jettisoned or not even attempted?
Was that because of a fear of failure?
Not trying is guaranteed failure!
Giving up is guaranteed failure!

Contemplate these words as you read on.

Chapter 6

You Cannot Fail

"Nothing can stop the man (or woman) with the right mental attitude from achieving his goal"
— Thomas Jefferson

In my world, there is no failure. It is a belief that I strongly commend to you! Try it on. What do you have to lose?

There is only a different way of doing something. All you have to do is keep bringing your creative talents to the task. No failure. You either reach your goal, or you give up. As I said, who doesn't know the story of Colonel Sanders and KFC? At 65 years of age he got 1,009 negative responses to his fried chicken recipe before he got a yes. Now that's perseverance. And who doesn't know the story of Thomas Edison who made 1,000 unsuccessful attempts before inventing the light bulb – leaving aside the fact he was told by one of his teachers that he was too stupid to learn anything. Can you imagine the affect that would have had on him, growing up? The negative belief that he had to reject of himself in order to realize his vision?

Or, more recently, Oprah Winfrey, who was fired from her job as a reporter and told she was unfit for TV. She ended up hosting her own very successful TV program and now her own TV Network, making billions in the process. Elvis Presley was told by the Grand Ole Opry

Manager, Jimmy Denny: "you ain't going nowhere. You ought to go back to driving a truck". He became the singing legend and icon of the 20th century. JK Rowling was sacked as a secretary and rejected by 12 publishers for Harry Potter. The Harry Potter series of novels is a worldwide phenomenon. Fred Astaire was told and described by a director at MGM: "he can't act, can't sing, slightly bald, can dance a little". He made 31 musicals and the Fred Astaire and Ginger Rogers dancing duo are revered to this day. Steven Spielberg was turned down three times by the University at Southern California School of Theatre, Film & Television. He won best director for Schindler's List in 1993, not to mention achieving box office records for Jaws, ET and Jurassic Park.

Where have you been rejected and made to feel worthless? What action did you take or NOT take? How many times did you persist in realizing your dream?

Know that any such rejection of a deeply held passion is no more than a call to your greatness. It requires you to step outside your fear of failure. It requires you to point blank refuse to believe you are hopeless or worthless or not good enough to manifest that dream. It requires you to press on with that vision which is etched deep within you.

One of my biggest fears involved my decision to end my marriage of 24 years. I was married at 20. Just a child by today's standards. We had two teenage children at the time. My son was due to study for his Higher School Certificate. The timing could not have been worse for him. He declared that he would chain himself to the house and it would have to be sold with him in it. My fears of having failed my children; failed my husband; failed my parents; failed our close-knit circle of friends - were mammoth. I would hurt so many people that I loved so deeply.

The question that repeatedly challenged me was: is my freedom worth all that pain I am about to inflict? I would wallow in my 'what ifs?' and my 'shouldn'ts' and 'couldn'ts' endlessly. I was bombarded by a ceaseless stream of fears.

I wanted to separate with my husband before any deep resentments set in; whilst I still cared for him and was able to acknowledge that he was a good man and a good father.

Was my price for freedom too high?

But there was this deep, profound inner voice that knew beyond a doubt that this was the right path for me – and if it was the right path for me, then it would be the right path for our children and for him. It was a knowing I could not deny. I felt like I had to get off the treadmill of married life whilst there was still love and compassion between us. At the heart of who I was, I harbored this strong desire to sprout some wings and experience freedom.

The battle between fear and freedom could not have been more intense.

Somehow, I mustered the courage to tip the scales towards freedom. Endings are always hard in the beginning. They are messy in the middle – and transformational in the end. Mine was no different.

I distinctly recall a pivotal conversation with my husband who could not understand what more I could possibly want. We had two beautiful children, a lovely home, a great weekender on a lake. "What more do you want?" was his repeated question.

My response: "I feel there is this river of life running by and I am sitting on the riverbank, watching, observing – all the while, life is passing me by." I could not explain it better.

"What", he said: "you want to jump in that river and drown?"

No. I wanted to jump in that river and swim towards adventure, excitement, exhilaration – and freedom. I wanted to feel alive again. I wanted the euphoria that comes with freedom. I wanted to expand my experience of who I was. I wanted to explore.

He would shake his head and ask: "I don't understand, I just don't understand".

Therein lay the problem.

I told him: "You are like the shepherd, herding his sheep, content with your family, your surroundings, with a quiet life, looking after your family. You don't want to venture outside your little world.

Me, I am the shepherd who looks at the mountains in the distance and says, I wonder what's over that mountain? I want to explore all that life has to offer, not sit still and do nothing."

I often wonder how many married couples walk this path and never take another. How many are stopped by their conditioned fears. How many are stopped by that cultural conditioning that unless your husband is a gambler, an alcoholic, a womanizer, a bad financial provider – there is simply no reason or justification to leave him. That is the very sentiment my loving, caring father expressed to me. How many are stopped from ever exploring the depth of who they truly are?

I am by no means advocating that this is the only way. It was the path that was right for me. Many can, no doubt, expand and grow together as a couple. I genuinely salute those couples. But they too will experience their individual and combined fears. They too will be confronted by their conditioned 'what ifs?'. They too will need to move forward with courage and awareness if they are to experience themselves fully as the vibrant, dynamic beings we all are. They too will need to make truly *conscious* decisions.

A union based on conscious, fearless choices is indeed a blissful one.

Did I leave or abandon my husband; did I destroy our marriage? This is the negative language we are taught to unconsciously use in such situations.

Or did I release and free myself and him and create a space for something bigger and better to come into our lives?

To this day I can tap into the exhilarating freedom I felt on a business flight from Sydney to the US, soon after the decision was made. I felt a lightness of being that was so powerful, I thought I had sprouted wings and was flying the plane. It was like I had created this vortex of energy that was swirling around me, uplifting me with every breath. The 15-hour plus flight seemed like a blink. I was at the back of the plane chatting to a colleague about how amazing life was, when we were directed to our seats for the landing. We are landing?! It felt like we had just taken off.

Were there practical things to sort yet? Yes. Was there pain? Yes. Were there oceans of tears? Yes. There were many heart-wrenching moments and many moments of pure joy. Life's potholes had to be maneuvered as we all travel on our path to liberation and greater connection. Looking forward to our family unit today, we have all emerged stronger, wiser, more aware and more deeply connected. A connection that is at the soul level. My children know who I truly am. They know me at my core. They can laugh at me and with me and together we can and do reflect on our individual growth. My two children have formed a sibling bond that is anchored at their very essence. And, yes, their father, after almost 15 years, found the strength and courage to forgive me and come back into the fold of the family. So much so, that he discussed and sought my legal guidance on estate issues. So much so, that I could jokingly ask him whether he wanted to leave his worldly goods to me. So much so, that I could lend him a large sum of money through my own line of credit to minimize his hassle of obtaining a loan, pending the sale of his unit. So much so, that he could open up about family matters involving his own siblings, in the safety only of his own family unit. We could finally share many lunches together. We could finally be our true selves, unhindered by the conditioning of our society that often leads to superficial relatedness in family units. Stripped of the pretenses. Stripped of all vindictiveness. And finally, basking in the glow of true love and acceptance.

That growth is ongoing. In fact, it never ends. If we ever think there is no more room for improvement – in any area of our life – it is a sure sign that we are on that treadmill of life and some force is about to knock us off, if we do not take conscious action ourselves.

A common saying is "if you are the smartest one in the room, you are definitely in the wrong room". It is our ego that wants us in the dumbest room so that we can 'shine'. That is not a room of growth. Wallowing in complacency and back pats stunts our growth. If you believe yourself to be at your absolute best, and your mind keeps attracting that reinforcement that has you repeatedly coming back to that dumb' room; saying you do not need to get better; saying you do not need to grow; saying you do not need to take further risks - beware. Red lights should be flashing.

Know that it is your ego and your subconscious mind protecting you from any fear of future failure. That same ego and that same subconscious mind, in turn, will stop your growth if you do not bring awareness to it. Your potential is limitless. For as long as we live, we have the potential to grow. We have the potential to shed all of our fears that have kept us locked in one cage or another.

As we begin to peel away one conditioned belief system after another, and as we begin to shed one illusory fear after another, we begin to see the essence of who we truly are. We see glimpses of our limitless nature. As those glimpses grow stronger and expand, we begin to live from our essence, unconstrained by our conditioned fears. We are at the door of freedom.

Following my divorce, when I now reflect upon my family, I can see that through our individual and collective growth we have learned the power of language and the power of our mind. We have learnt to exercise free choice and to bring awareness to our subconscious ways of being. In the process, we have shared many experiences both together and separately, based on our own individual guidance systems. We have shed many of our conditioned belief systems, and replaced them with new ways and approaches that honor our true essence.

My son is a master practitioner in neuro-linguistic programming (NLP). But he is yet to put this training to effective use. He has articulated his fears. Maybe this book will give him further guidance and inspiration. He went through his own heart-wrenching challenges, but that's another story for another book (maybe by him). My daughter is studying a double Masters in psychotherapy and in writing. She had to massively shed her conditioned and limiting belief systems about having to work in the corporate world in a job that she disliked, but which earned her a huge salary. She confronted that fear of the unknown and, in the process, entered the realm of freedom and true choice.

I often revel in how blessed I am to have two children that understand me at a very deep level. They understand the power of language. They understand the power of the mind. And they understand that these are mere tools that, when used consciously, can transcend our illusory fears and attract and manifest a life of incredible freedom and abundance in all areas.

Know that once you step beyond your illusory fears and take action, your will achieve your dream.

If you could jettison your illusory fear in one of the above pursuits, what action could you take (no matter how small)?
What are you saying to yourself now?

Contemplate: Is my fear real? Will I die? Could I manage my life's circumstances and still move in that direction?

Lesson 3

How to achieve your dream by stepping beyond your fears

Do you have a belief: "I'm too old for xyz now?"
Do you have a belief: "It's too late for me now?"

Can you for a moment put that belief aside?
Can you be inspired by the many who have achieved goals in their eighties and beyond?

If not – contemplate why not, as you read on.

Chapter 7

It is never too late – the "Ship has not Sailed" – Age is another Conditioned Illusion

Would you ever consider embarking on a new, risky career at age 47? Or, would you say: "no, I'm way too old". Would you then give birth to all your illusory fears as to why not?

The first thing you need to realize when you look at how to achieve your dream by stepping beyond your fears is that 'it's never too late!' It is never too late to scratch that itch that refuses to go away. The ship has not sailed. There is always a ship on the shore, waiting for you to embark on your life's journey.

Our conditioned mind, however, will throw up fear after fear and countless 'what if's?' and excuses as to why you should remain safe and not embark on that ship. After all, aren't we supposed to finish our schooling in our twenties; start our careers in our thirties; peak in our forties and fifties (having worked really hard); then bask in our success in our sixties, awaiting that glorious retirement that we have been conditioned to believe is the pinnacle of success? The earlier the retirement we have been able to secure, the more successful we are perceived to be??

All conditioned, cultural nonsense!

It is never too early or too late to start. Have a look at my life. I became a barrister at 47. By writing this book I became a writer/ author at the age of 65. My daughter did her Masters in writing at age 42. She will complete her Masters in psychotherapy aged 43. Does that inspire you? It should. There are far greater inspirational stories of people peaking in all areas of life, at much 'older' ages. What is age anyway, but a number.

Colonel Sanders launched his Kentucky Fried Chicken franchise at age 65 and went on to become a multimillionaire. God apparently spoke to Abraham, when Abraham was 75 years-old, and instructed him to leave his country and go to a land that would become a great nation, blessed by God. And so it came to pass. Look at Dame Judi Dench. An actress in her prime – at age 84! And opening up about active sex in her eighties. Now that's inspirational.

Look at Susan Boyle. Her singing career started in the most dramatic and amazing way at 47 years of age. Her first audition on Britain's Got Talent still gives me goosebumps when I listen to it. She was relieved, yes relieved, when she was diagnosed with Asperger's. Laura Ingalls Wilder published her first book (Little House in the Big Woods) aged 65, her last in the series aged 76! Harry Bernstein started writing his book at 93 and published (The Invisible Wall: A Love Story that Broke Barriers) at 96! Yes, he was a magazine editor and freelance writer, but he was inspired to write about his family struggles during WWI and his personal struggles and experiences as a child. At age 101, Sarah Yerkes published her first book of poetry, "Days of Blue and Flame" (published by Passager Books at the University of Baltimore, USA). She was invited by a friend to try something new at the age of 90 and she had the courage to do so. Look her up.

Life's curveballs are meant to challenge us, not stop us dead in our tracks. Age is another conditioned illusion. Let it be replaced with new thoughts that savor all the wisdom you have acquired and can now share. Let age make you more powerful. Let it make you more courageous to share your unique wisdom. Let it make you more passionate to leave your own personal legacy, your own footprint on humanity. Risk? What do you have to lose at age 96 or 101? Really.

It is never too late to become the powerhouse you were born to be. Believe it and you will live it.

I share my story below in the hope that it will inspire you to take action so that you too can live and share your own inspirational story.

It is a story of how I ended up at the Bar, the legal term for becoming a barrister (Oh, are you a barista, as some would say? No, but I don't make a bad coffee, although I like to think I am a better barrister than barista!).

The legal firm in which I was a partner had a very strong policy of encouraging the partners to conduct their own advocacy, as much as possible, but short of running full blown trials, which required a barrister to be retained. The firm was at the forefront of many novel legal arguments. It prided itself in pioneering such bold new legal arguments. One such legal argument resulted in an appeal to the High Court of Australia for special leave to run the substantive argument before a full bench of the High Court. The argument necessitated persuading three of the High Court's best legal minds to grant special leave.

I was presented with a choice of either briefing a very Senior Counsel (known as an SC or a QC in the profession), who later became and remains a Judge of the Court of Appeal of the Supreme Court of New South Wales. Alternatively, I could run the special leave application myself. What a choice, I have often reflected? Me or this pre-eminent SC? Many would not have even seen themselves as part of the "choice".

Know, we are *always* at choice!

I had the weekend to choose, as time was running out if the SC was to be retained. During that weekend, I was confronted with every *imaginable* fear that my mind could conjure up:

- are you mad?
- you are a five year out solicitor, you are not even a barrister;
- what makes you think you can do this?
- you have not even seen a special leave application being run and you want to run one yourself!
- you will be addressing three of the best legal minds in the country, what makes you think you can step up to that, without any prior experience?'
- why do you think SC's always run these applications?
- the Court doesn't even know who you are; they've never heard of you;
- what if you freeze?
- what if your mind goes blank?
- what if; what if; what if ....

The list went on and on and on.

I then countered those fears and negativity with:

- but I may never have such an opportunity again; the opportunity to actually run a matter in the High Court – myself;
- solicitors and barristers go through their entire 30, 40, even 50 years at the Bar, without ever having a matter in the High Court, let alone running it themselves;
- how can you allow such an opportunity to slip by?
- you know the legal principles; you can prepare; you can seek guidance from other SC's.

Then the negativity would creep in again:

- you have got to be joking!
- you are not seriously considering doing this are you?
- what if your mind seriously goes blank and you can't utter a single word?

- what if the Judges throw questions at you that you can't answer?
- what if? what if? what if? what if? ...

I finally hung up on my mind and all its incessant 'what ifs?'. Enough.

Not one of these countless fears was real. They were all imagined possibilities of what might (or might not) happen, some time in the future, if I decided to take on the challenge.

The decision was made. Yes. I would be running the special leave application. Yes, I would be putting my arguments forward to three of the best legal minds in the country. And yes, if I was successful, I would take full responsibility. That's what I told my other partners. Jokingly I uttered that if I was unsuccessful, then clearly the Judges had made up their minds before I even opened my mouth. The response was – this was no joking matter. And it wasn't. My innate nervousness was attempting to use humor to deal with my fears.

The wheels were set in motion. The SC was not retained. I would be addressing the High Court. I would be presenting this novel argument to the High Court. I would be making an appearance before the High Court, as a five year out female solicitor. I painted a magnificent picture of me appearing before the High Court - greater than all the imagined fears put together. All I had to do was step into that reality. That's all!!

Feeling all the imagined fears; being aware that they were, in fact, imagined; and then not allowing them to make the decision, is the first and biggest step. Was my life in danger? Certainly not. Was my safety and well-being threatened in any way? Certainly not. Would I 'die of embarrassment'? Certainly not. It's just another bad saying that we have been conditioned to use. I might be embarrassed. But that embarrassment would not cause me to die. Do you know anyone that has died of being embarrassed? I don't. Would this affect my reputation? Maybe, but hey I was a female solicitor with five years of experience, how badly could it affect my reputation? That's assuming the worst. But what about the flipside of that coin? What if I was successful and was granted special leave? I was literally jumping out of my skin with excitement at that very thought.

That is precisely what our thoughts do to us. They either cripple us with imagined fears. Or they inspire us with imagined success. We choose (assuming the choice is a conscious one).

My whole being screamed out: we are not geared for failure; we are geared for success. Greatness and success are just a decision, a choice. Once we make this choice the Universe will help us sprout wings and soar to victory. We will become inspired by our very own courage to rise to such a challenge; to overcome our imagined fears and to exalt in the freedom and exhilaration that will inevitably follow.

I was at choice and the choice had been made. I refused to allow the opinions and fears of others to dictate *my* choice. I would not be stifled by the opinions of others. What will the Judges think? What will my colleagues think? Osho, the great Indian guru (who died in 1990) used these words:

> *The greatest fear in the world is of the opinion of others.*
> *And the moment you are unafraid of the crowd you are no longer a sheep, you become a lion. A great roar arises in your heart, the roar of freedom.*

I had become the lion. The roar had risen in my heart and I honored it. Did the roar of freedom follow? Without a doubt. Whenever we honor our heart's greatest desires; whenever we transcend our greatest fears; we are catapulted into an unimaginable freedom.

The preparation then began. The one mistake I made was seeking advice from a learned Senior Counsel who had made many such applications before the High Court. His advice to me was: "Prepare your written script carefully. Being a female and a solicitor with little experience, the Judges will allow you to go through your written script with little interruption".

The only problem was that no one told the three Judges.

I had no sooner opened my mouth to put forward the arguments that I had so carefully scripted, when grenades started to fly from the three Judges! Each had their different issues that they wanted to be addressed. My written script sat on the lectern absorbing the perspiration from my hands.

When I was finally allowed to return to it, I was forced to quickly collect my thoughts and determine what additional areas of argument I needed to cover that had not been the subject of the rigorous questioning from the bench of three.

It was soon the lunchtime break. I had assumed that the Judges would discuss the submissions during the luncheon break and return to the bench with their decision. That appeared to be their normal modus operandi in relation to earlier applications. They would have a short break and then return to the bench, with their decision.

I was elated. It was all over. A media reporter was also in the Court room and came over to congratulate me. The novel argument was certainly news-worthy. My assistant solicitor also congratulated me on a job well done. We left the Court room smiling and in high spirits as we went to level 14 of the Court building, for our lunch break. I could not eat. I barely touched my coffee. The excitement of awaiting a decision from the High Court was etched in every cell of my being.

I did it!

Yes, I did it!

I seized the opportunity! I mustered the courage! And I appeared before the High Court! I didn't die. I didn't freeze. I stepped into that magic 'zone' that sportspeople talk about, and I delivered.

That is what happens every time we choose and decide to transcend our imagined fears. We step into the realm of freedom and exhilaration and fearlessness. We become a truer version of who we really are and what we are really capable of being.

We returned to the Court room at 2pm. I stood behind the lectern, waiting for the presiding Judge to hand down the decision. What fell from His Honour's mouth was like a sledgehammer: "Yes, Ms Culkoff", his Honour said.

What? I thought. You want more submissions. I haven't prepared any more. My script is done. As I gathered my thoughts, my young instructing solicitor later told me that I, in fact, lifted the lectern slightly. I then gazed across to one of the Judges and commenced to recall the questions from the bench before the break, from one Judge. Then I moved to another of the Judges. I once again found myself embroiled in a debate I had not scripted. Where those submissions came from, I have no conscious idea. How those questions were recalled, I did not consciously know. How I dealt with the bench being fully engaged again, with further questions and arguments, I had absolutely no recollection of, until I subsequently read the Transcript.

Our deepest fear is indeed, not that we are inadequate.
Our deepest fear is that we are all powerful beyond measure …

The words echoed in my mind. We are indeed far greater than we can ever imagine.

The words of that reporter also echo in my mind to this day: "you kicked arse in reply". I "kicked arse in reply", really? My response: "Did I? Wow, I'll have to read what I said."

And yes, special leave was granted. I could now take full responsibility!

I described my experience to a colleague as the "best orgasmic experience of my life!!" I was told I really did need to get a life.

I was elated and energized beyond imagination. Every cell in my being was vibrating at a crazy frequency. I felt like an electric charge. I was certain that if anyone touched me, they would be electrocuted.

The lesson from that one experience was a mammoth one. I had put myself out on the edge of a legal precipice and I had soared to victory. Even if I had lost, the victory would still have been massive. The lessons of breaking through my imagined fears would still have been edged deep within me. Victory or loss – I would still have been the winner in the game.

Every time we transcend our illusory fears, that type of experience awaits us at the other end. It is a freedom that can only be experienced and felt in its full glory – at the opposite end of the fears we have decided to transcend.

It was that experience that planted the seed for me to become a barrister.

It is that type of experience that will catapult you to the next phase of your life; to the next glorious chapter of experiencing who you truly will know yourself to be. Dare to be a grander version of you. Of who you know yourself to be. When that opportunity comes knocking, all you have to do is dare to take the plunge. You are already being guided by your Higher Self.

So how do you begin? You begin by throwing out the conditioned rule book that you have been carrying around since childhood.

If there were no barriers, what would you love to try on?
Writing; climbing a mountain;
sailing the seven seas …

What do/did you dream about doing "one day"?

Contemplate that day is here.
Contemplate you can still choose, regardless of your age.

Contemplate transcending your self-imposed limiting beliefs.
Write down a few "I can't do/be xyz"
And then contemplate deleting the "t" in can't.

Contemplate there is still joy
in the journey …
with or without the end result.

Chapter 8

Throw out the Conditioned Rule Book – Gender, Age, Body Image are not Barriers to Success – nor is anything else

"It is confidence in our bodies, minds, and spirits that allows us to keep looking for new adventures."
— Oprah Winfrey

To continue my story from the previous chapter, I was an equity partner in a law firm that had a significant presence in the legal sphere. I was engaged in interesting work. I was secure financially, with significant windfalls on the horizon. All very comfortable. Some would say – I had arrived.

Yet, I sat the Bar Exams. That experience before the High Court would not leave me. Other circumstances manifested that reinforced my place was at the Bar. The itch was there and it could not be scratched away.

I was then confronted with three fears. At the time I called them "My three F's" – female, forty plus and fat:

- *I was a* ***f****emale* (the Bar was and remains pretty much a boy's playing field, but it is improving – slowly, very slowly);

- *I was* ***f****orty plus, approaching* ***f****ifty* (nobody, not even males go to the Bar that late in life, that was my thinking back then); and

- *I was* ***f****at* (for some reason this was an important negative for me at the time, looking at the young law graduates, all of them with gorgeous size 10 figures!)

If you are a female, has that in itself stopped you from pursuing your passion? If you are 40 plus, approaching 50, has that in itself stopped you from manifesting your dream and life purpose? If you perceive yourself to be fat, has that stopped you? It is only more recently that we are seeing more and more 'plus size' models. It will, no doubt, be sometime before we view 'plus size' as 'normal size' and then as irrelevant.

I had a whole raft of different 'what ifs?' that my mind also threw up. These were now more of a financial nature. What if no one briefed me? How would I pay my mortgage? How would I support myself? How would I help my children? What if I made less money than I am making now, would I feel I had made a huge mistake? What if I found preparing endlessly for hearings and appearing before Judges really stressful rather than exhilarating? What if my experience in the High Court was a one-off? What if I found it lonely at the Bar, not really knowing anyone (there was certainly an element of this experience in the beginning)? What if I was briefed in matters I knew nothing about, and yet was still expected to give advice on them? (This also certainly happened and continues to happen, but I have learnt to revel in exploring different factual and legal scenarios and thinking outside the square – even considering novel legal arguments). What if I was forced to work really long hours and on weekends – something I deliberately avoided my entire working life? I was told this was the 'norm' at the Bar. (It has not been my norm. I am highly organized and well prepared.)

My persistent question was: should I take the risk? It was so much easier to just play it safe. It wasn't as if I hated the work I was doing. But don't all amazingly great experiences come from taking that risk; from pursuing that deeper passion?

Throwing that old caution to the wind once again, I committed to practicing as a barrister. I sat the Bar exams. I was not changing my mind. I threw out the old conditioned rule book.

I recall I was in London at the time, a month or so before the Bar exam results were due to be announced. I was trying on a wig and gown, with a view to buying them when my partner said: "But you don't even know if you are going to pass the Bar exams yet. Don't you want to wait? You may change your mind". No. Not an option. I am going to the Bar. I am going to be a Barrister. I will pass the exams. I told him I didn't recall having failed any exam in my life, but if I had failed one of the subjects, then I would re-sit it. The decision was made. And there was power in having made it. The fears were cast aside, yet again.

I bought my wig and gown in London, and wear them to this day.

For those of you who have never seen a wigged and gowned barrister, I include this photo taken by a colleague as I was about to head to Court for a hearing, with my trolley.

What has been coming up for you as you read the above? What has been your automatic mantra? Catch yourself. What have you said to yourself when such choices have presented themselves?

I CAN'T.

I can't possibly do that.

Yes, you CAN.

How different would your life experiences be if you simply eliminated the 'T' in that word? How much more powerfully would you approach life's challenges if you cultivated an 'I CAN' attitude?

So, you can see that in the face of all my fears of going to the Bar, I mustered the courage to become the fearless being we all are. I recall one of my business partners was actually concerned for my well-being, absolutely convinced I was making a disastrous choice that would destroy me emotionally and financially. I suspect many others were of the same view, but feared expressing it. I suspect my own father was among them.

As for me, I again found myself knocking on the door of freedom.

I stepped out of my self-imposed limitations (not to mention those imposed by our society and my friends and family) and into that magical realm of freedom. It is at that very intersection where our innate essence springs to life. I felt alive. I felt invigorated. And I felt a little apprehensive. That fear never fully goes away. Wow! Look at what I just did! I just gave up my well-paying partnership in a high-profile legal firm to pursue yet another dream.

I am now in my nineteenth year at the Bar. I have often said that I will never understand how solicitors come to the Bar, practice as a barrister for a number of years, and then return to being solicitors. The freedom at the Bar is phenomenal. I cannot even recall the number of times I have taken impulsive overseas trips, just because I could. Or the number of times that I have taken an 'early mark', just because I could. I can come in early and leave early, if it suits me. Or I can come in late and leave early. I am in command of my time and how I spend it.

I have since transformed my then 'Three F's' into my three very different F's' – Freedom From Fear.

We have all come into this time-space illusion, into this human experience, on this glorious planet we call Earth, to experience the ever-expanding realm of our freedom. To know that we are infinite. To experience the true joy and bliss that comes from the laughter, the fun, the exuberance that springs from that realm of freedom.

The desire within to be free to express who we truly are is an itch that can only be scratched away when you give yourself the permission to boldly go forth and fulfill the purpose you, and only you, came here to fulfill, this time round. Otherwise that itch will continue to surface.

No matter how many tons of negativity you try to drown it with or pour over it, the itch will continue to scratch. And if you do not satisfy it now, it will be there on your final day, when you depart this human experience. Do not be someone who, on their final day, says "my big regret" was:

- not pursuing my love of baking;
- not giving my love of art a go;
- not opening up that business;
- not writing that book;
- not getting that teaching degree; that law degree; accounting;
- not pursuing a singing career; music;
- not going all out for my cricket career, my football career.

You can fill in the gaps. Again, the list is endless. Are you on that conditioned treadmill of life that your parents, your teachers, your culture, your society has ordained for you? Has your life been mapped out automatically, fulfilling expectations that are not your own?

Are you courageous enough to step off that treadmill and explore your own heart's yearning? What is stopping you from playing the true game of life? That's what we came here to do. To play. To laugh. To love. To revel in the mysteries of who we are and to discover our essence.

I love the freedom of working for myself. The freedom to hop on a plane. Travel has been one of my life's great passions. The instant I enter an airport I am in a state of anticipation and adventure. I step into the exhilaration of the moment. I cannot tell you how many times I have said "yes" to weekend adventures to Hong Kong. Or a week to Bali. I cannot even recall the number of occasions I have hopped on a plane on a spontaneous impulse, including to Sicily for a wedding. I had a full calendar the week before and a full calendar the week after, but the week of that wedding my diary was completely free. I have always viewed that kind of synchronicity as a sign from the Universe that it was time to play and have fun. Yes, I did have to manage my work before and after. Not too difficult if approached with the right mindset. After all, 'work' is just another form of play. Right? If it's not, it should be. Right??

I certainly had fun in beautiful Milano where I was dazzled by the tall, gorgeous beautifully dressed men (and women). Then to magnificent Taormina in Sicily, with its secluded coves and sandy beaches; its cliffs and the Greek/Roman theatre, not to mention the beautiful food, people and shopping. Oh, yes, and we did attend the grand wedding, in true Italian style.

When an opportunity knocks on your door, such as a wedding in Italy or a mountain climb in Africa/Nepal, or a work project in Zimbabwe, do you embrace it fearlessly, with gratitude and enthusiasm? Or do you shy away and retreat into your shell of safety?

One way of bringing awareness to your conditioned response is to look closely at the language you use, especially your internal chatter, how you frame things and the intentions your set for yourself. All of these collectively can intensify the result – whether that is success or failure.

Write down the most repeated
language you use –
internally and externally –
I'm hopeless doing xyz
I'm an insomniac
I always get headaches

Contemplate how that language has
become a belief?
Contemplate how that language has
become your personality?
Contemplate how that language has
become your identity?

Read on and do the exercises to
shift those beliefs
and transform yourself.

Chapter 9

Bring Awareness to the Power of Language, Framing and Intention

"Language is the armory of the human mind and contains… the weapons of its future conquests"
— Samuel Taylor Coleridge

Power of Language

The power of language (whether internal thoughts or the spoken word) cannot be overestimated. Self-talk can be one of the most destructive forces in our life; or one of the most powerfully positive. All experience is a duality.

Not only do our thoughts and the language we use (internally and externally) affect our life experiences, but they affect our very health and wellbeing. Depression, anxiety and yes, fear, are all self-generated. I have a mother who has had two standard sayings for as long as I can remember:

- I always get headaches; and
- I can never sleep at night.

And guess what, both are very true, for her. She does get a lot of on-going headaches. And she does have mostly sleepless nights. I remind her incessantly to be aware of her language and to take steps to actively change it. But she has a very strong belief system that it is who she is. She has made it who she is. She was not born that way. She has unwittingly allowed those two negative patterns to define her. Knowing my mum's history and her stories, I can actually trace the patterns that have reinforced her belief that she can never sleep at night. She has, until recently, believed it is in her DNA, and that nothing could affect any change. My mother is set in her ways. Very set in her ways. Some may say stubborn.

Finally, she has indicated a preparedness to undertake NLP training with her grandson (my son) to create a shift in her conditioned sleeping pattern. She has – at last - opened the door to a different possibility. That, in turn, will create a very different reality for her. She is yet to schedule her sessions.

My two sayings in that area are: I never get headaches! Never leaves no door open. A good thing in this instance. And, I'm a very good sleeper. If anyone engages in a conversation with me and complains about the headache they are suffering, my automatic response is always: Gee, I never get any headaches, how bad is it?

Neuroscience and neuropsychology now recognize that negative, toxic thoughts are the cause of up to 95% of the illnesses that afflict our society.

Fear alone triggers more than 1,400 known physical, emotional and chemical responses. It alone activates more than 30 different hormones. Minimize or eliminate fear from your life and you will minimize and eliminate most of your physical and emotional illnesses.

Depression, anxiety, panic attacks, diabetes, asthma, skin conditions, nervousness, allergies and, yes, even cancer, are all the by-products of our toxic thoughts. Just to name a few. Detox your thoughts and you will detox your physical and emotional well-being. These toxic thoughts create physical and emotional blocks in our bodies that, once released, will generate a freedom and a lightness that will cast away all doubt as to the power of our thoughts and the language we use.

We all have the power to heal ourselves or harm ourselves. And the internal and external language we use is the key culprit.

Let's look at the power of language a little further.

How many of us focus on what we don't want rather than what we do want?

- I don't want to be fat;
- I don't want to be embarrassed;
- I don't want to get it wrong;
- I don't want to make a mistake;
- I don't want to fail;
- I don't want to look stupid;
- I don't want to be unhappy;
- I don't want to be sad;
- I don't want to be ridiculed …

What this language forces the mind to focus on is the 'fat', the 'embarrassed', the 'wrong', the 'mistake', the 'fail', the 'stupid', the 'unhappy', the 'sad', and the 'ridiculed'. Add your list.

The end result is – you remain fat; you draw circumstances that cause you to feel embarrassed; you make wrong decisions; you make mistakes; you give up and 'fail' in the goals you set; you cause yourself to feel stupid and unhappy and sad, and attract situations that cause you to feel ridiculed.

In short, the mind is giving you exactly what you are focusing your attention on. And that is exactly what you will manifest, so that you can turn around and validate your life's experiences by confirming: I knew I'd fail; I always do stupid things; no matter what I do, I can't lose weight and I'm still fat. More reinforcement for the mind that keeps you stuck in exactly what you do not want.

By focusing on what you do **not** want, you keep attracting the same experiences so that you can continue with the same mantra. It is a vicious cycle. How many times have you repeated the same negative experience and at the end confirmed it by saying something like: "I knew that would happen. It always does"?

And it always will until you change your language which, in turn, will change your belief system which, in turn, will change your reality. You have to stop telling your mind (and the Universe) what it is you don't want and start telling it what it is you do want. Taking the above list as an example, you want to be:

- slim and gorgeous and vibrantly healthy and radiantly beautiful;
- confident and empowering;
- you want to make clear and correct decisions;
- you want to succeed;
- you want to be clever and insightful;
- blissfully happy;
- you want to be praised and acknowledged for who you are.

Does this second list light you up? Notice the change in your demeanor in just reading the two lists. Notice the different feelings the two lists enliven in you. Start to choose your daily mantras consciously and be witness to a very different reality that will spring forth and change your life.

It's simple: keep your mind OFF what you don't want and ON what you do want.

Yes, you might get stuck in the beginning. If you have been overweight for 10 years and your constant mantra has been "I don't want to be fat but no matter what I do, I never lose the weight; and even if I do, it just keeps coming back ...", then it will take a little time for you to believe that you deserve to be slim and gorgeous and vibrantly healthy. There is much in the old adage: fake it till you make it. The mind does not judge. You will be drawn to better eating plans and good exercise regimes that will ultimately manifest what you want.

Then there are the 'I can't' lists; the 'I should' lists; the 'I'm not going to do that again' lists. The instant you declare: "I can't do xyz" is the instant that you place yourself behind bars on that aspect in your life. Such a declaration is a command to your brain and to the Universe that you can't do 'xyz'. That is precisely what you will manifest until you start believing otherwise; until you start voicing and expressing the exact opposite.

Until you turn all your should's and cant's into "I can" or "I will" or better still into positive I AMs, your life experiences will see little, if any change. You will keep repeating the same old patterns. As noted above, Albert Einstein is credited with the statement: "the definition of insanity is **doing the same thing** over and over again, but **expecting different results**".

Our conditioning has indeed made us all insane.

Let's take public speaking again, as an example. How many of you have this mantra: I can't get up and speak in front of an audience? I would be too embarrassed. I'd make a fool of myself. That's just not who I am.

Yet deep down...is there a longing to break free from that fear? If there is, you will keep attracting opportunities that are aimed at helping you break through those fears and enter the realm of freedom. All of a sudden you will find yourself in a situation where you have to address an audience; where you have to give a presentation at work; or reinforce an ideology that you may be passionate about with a particular group. If you remain unconscious, you will view those opportunities as adversities and setbacks. You will see all these opportunities as strokes of bad luck that keep bringing all your fears to the fore. That is what they are meant to do, the ultimate goal being, to set you free. You will go from being fearful, to engaging in public speaking - to feeling excited and exhilarated at the prospect of doing so. That's freedom. You will then wonder why there was any fear in the first place.

Be in no doubt that these deeper, innate knowings that are at the core of every individual will attract circumstances in our lives aimed at releasing the negative patterns that are preventing us from actioning and manifesting our wildest dreams and our life's purpose.

Let's stay with the fear of public speaking (as I said some would rather die than address a large audience). It is guaranteed that if this is a major fear of yours, you will find yourself in a job or situation that requires you to take action that will ultimately free you from that fear. The more you hide and resist taking that action, the greater the fear. Remember that what you resist will always persist. This is not the road to freedom. It is the old, worn out road that will continue to have you behind bars, living a restrictive life. Those bars that prevent you from escaping all the cages in your life are self-created. Be in no doubt about that.

For example, you may choose careers where it would be unimaginable for you to be called upon to speak publicly. A librarian perhaps. Now that's a good cage. The bars should be fairly solid. An assistant in a morgue! An even better cage, with stronger bars. A backroom admin role collating data and preparing reports. Yet another cage.

But what is your real calling? What is that deeper knowing you have of who you really want to be?

If, despite creating all these cages with solid bars, you have a deep yearning to be heard, to speak publicly – even these occupations will bring about circumstances that will force you to confront your fears. You may find that your boss has booked you in for a lecture to teachers and students as to the special workings of that particular library. Or, you are doing such a great job as an assistant in the morgue, your boss has arranged a seminar for you to address the precise workings of the morgue relevant to the many funeral companies who charge big fees to bury our loved ones.

If public speaking is one of your life's purposes and you have a voice deep within you that demands to be heard, then all you have done is attempted to bury it within you. But you can rest assured that it will continue to surface and challenge you. The deeper you go into your cage or your internal cave, the greater the challenges that will present themselves. Until you awake and allow yourself to break free from your self-imposed constraints and limiting belief systems. It is then that you will begin to grow and fulfill your life's purpose. The small steps you initially take will soon expand into giant leaps into a life that you always dreamed of. This is how our dreams manifest. And there is no greater freedom than living your dream!

The aim and the challenge is to master the best way to consciously direct our sub-conscious mind to play ball with our visions, our goals and our true life's purpose. We start by bringing the power of positive language to all we do and say. We start to re-program our language until it becomes our norm. It is then that we step into the realm of boundless freedom and magical joy. It is then that we begin to truly live from the heart. It is then that negative thought patterns fall away and no longer imprison us.

Raise your expectations of who you are and what you can experience, and play to win. Know that the only person you are competing with is yourself. You always want to become a better version of yourself. Not anyone else. Stop comparing yourself to anyone else. You are unique.

Conscious Framing

The effect of conscious framing ties in with the power of language; with our ingrained belief systems; and with the role of the mind. How you frame your dream or a goal may determine the ease with which its success manifests – or alternatively, the many programmed hurdles you are automatically expecting to experience. Your intention can add laser sharp clarity to that ultimate goal.

Sports people may often start playing tennis, rugby, basketball, etc. as a pure hobby that ends up as a mind-blowing career. They love it, they want to master it, they want to have fun with it and then realize that it has moved far beyond that. Or, like Serena Williams, a parent may have started the child's intensive training at age three, with the very clear intention instilled in that child from that early age of becoming a Grand Slam champion - resulting in 23 Grand Slams. Serena's conditioning towards those 23 Grand Slams was a deliberate and conscious decision made, not by Serena Williams, but by her father who was determined to teach and train both his daughters to become great tennis players.

As is evident, conscious framing can operate in different ways.

We have mental filters as a result of our cultural influences, which can be positive or negative. In journalism, for example, the framing used to deal with a key issue can totally change the reader's perspective, despite the facts. Likewise, with the marketing/advertising sphere. There is, for example, a deliberate intention to frame or label news items to create sensationalism in order to sell papers. Ditto with respect to marketing/advertising strategies.

The "glass is always half full" is one of my key frames (dealt with below). If I am presented with any situation, no matter how dire, and no matter how negative the consequences, the cup is still half full. I look to see what further positive action I can take; what positive steps I can put in place to bring the situation into a happier state. If it is affecting someone that I deeply love and care about, I do not know how to give up.

I am a type A personality is another. I take on a hobby, but I only persevere with it if I love it, otherwise I let it go and try something else. None of these need any explanation as to what is automatically expected.

That is how my study of law started.

Let me explain.

Taking up the study of Law and 'framing' it as a 'hobby', directly and powerfully impacted my experience of my six years at University, while working three days a week and looking after my three and seven year old children. How does the mind think of a 'hobby'? How are we conditioned to act around a 'hobby'? How do we feel about our hobbies? Aren't they meant to be fun, uplifting, enjoyable – something we love and enjoy doing, even though there may be some challenges thrown our way?

What do you think was the standard reaction from friends and family: are you mad? Who takes up Law as a hobby? Macramé maybe, according to one friend, but not Law. It's too hard. It's too long – SIX years, are you crazy?. You have two children. You will never finish it. Why put yourself through it?

I did give myself an out: if I didn't enjoy it and didn't love it, I would simply pull out. What's all the fuss about? After all, I am only taking it on as a hobby.

There were also many judgments expressed about that view, rest assured!

How I signed up to do Law is also a story in itself. We don't normally think too hard and too long about embarking on a hobby do we? I was working with a colleague at the time. Her very long dream was to study law and become a lawyer. But she never expressed this, not even to me. After many years, she finally worked up the courage to obtain the necessary application forms and put everything in train. We were casually having lunch that day. I enquired what all the paperwork was, sitting on her desk. She finally came clean and said it was something she had been thinking about for many years, and had eventually worked up enough courage to make the application. That was the paperwork, sitting on her desk.

Wow. That could be interesting, I thought. I then immediately asked her if she had another application form. She was bewildered. Speechless. She went into all the barriers, all the beliefs she had held onto that prevented her from making the application for so many years. Even now she was not sure she could do it. There were still more barriers to overcome.

I saw it as no different to my taking up art (another hobby I had). If I liked it, I would continue. If not, I would simply bail out. I filled out the application form - with the supporting material (that my friend told me would be impossible to obtain) - that very week. I think it encouraged her to follow my "madness"!

In hindsight, there is little doubt that there was a calling, an intuitive desire (unconscious at the time) that led me to choose Law over anything else. The 6 years had their challenges, but they were met with inspiration, zest and fun. As that same close friend said to me during our studies together: "Kid, I swear, you must have been a Judge in a past life. How can you otherwise pick up all the concepts so quickly?"

I don't know about being a Judge in a past life (maybe, who knows – Dr Weiss?), but I do know that, as with any hobby, there is a drive to master the art and that drive is accompanied by high energy, generated from the notion of 'fun' and from the sheer love of what you are doing. My mind had accepted this was a hobby for me, and a hobby, according to my mind, was to be enjoyed and mastered – in short, I would be good at it and it would be a lot of fun. If not, I would just stop. No big deal, really.

Totally unexpectedly, I ended up getting the University Medal. The SCREAM of joy and surprise that morning, as I read the letter from the University, is etched in my mind, and could be heard across the suburb of Kingsgrove, where we were living at the time!

What repeated framing do you use?

With the benefit of hindsight and wisdom, in my case, I now realize that I embarked on doing law as a hobby. However, once I made the decision to graduate, my unconscious patterns to excel academically also kicked in big time. It was not until a few semesters down the track that I actually decided I wanted to finish the degree. I recall that it was a relief to my father, who thought it would be embarrassing for the family if I pulled out. More judgments to contend with.

I also recall that when I was well past my third year, a good friend I met in semester one said to me: "you must be in line for honours with your marks". I actually had no idea about what that entailed. Nor had I given any thought to *consciously* pursuing such a course. He advised me to ring the university office and find out, which I did. I was told that I was certainly in line for honours; that it did entail doing a research paper and continuing to get the same or similar marks. Research papers, I was told, would take a minimum of an extra six months, and often occupied a longer period than this. The only problem was that I was considering accelerating the course and doing the last two years in one year. Could I also fit in a research paper, not even fully appreciating what that would actually involve? This was no longer a hobby.

That's when all of the familiar fears surfaced:

- this hobby was now turning into a real academic quest and with it came the fear of being judged: who does she think she is anyway? And, boy, was I judged;
- fear of failing: what if I failed a semester? There was now pressure as more was at stake. What would people say?;
- fear of being too old: I would be 36 if I finished it within the 6-year period, older if it took longer. I never really thought of practicing law. Everyone would expect me to become a lawyer. At the time, 36 felt ancient, who would employ me? (given I was married at 20. It was a different era!);
- fear of failing my children: up until now, the study did not really impact my family life. But if I accelerated and did the research paper, how would that affect my two young children and my husband?

My 'hobby' was now conjuring up all these fears – just by renaming it in my mind. Nothing else had really changed. Whether I called it a hobby or not, the workload was the same. This is the power of the mind. This is the power that fear can conjure up. Clearly, all an illusion.

I did accelerate the course. I studied the last two years in one year. And I completed the research paper. In order to achieve this, I reduced my three days at work to two days, and I had to manage my time quite diligently. Most of my university work happened after I cooked the family meal, washed up and helped my children with their homework, before putting them to bed.

I recall finishing the first draft of my research paper. I did all my typing on an old manual typewriter. Computers were just coming in and I didn't have one. I also recall that my old typewriter had a 't' that would fly across the room every now and then. Many pages of my draft research paper had words with a missing 't' in them! And I had lots of inserts that would require manual manipulation. Did I really want to finish with Honours? That was a dangerous question, given that it triggered (unconsciously at the time) my very old and entrenched pattern, going back to my kindergarten experience. Who was I kidding? Of course, I wanted an Honours degree. And we were talking here about First Class Honours. But I was still looking at cutting whatever corners I could so it did not impact my family.

I figured I had at least a pass in that first draft. Did I need more to not lose my First Class Honours? I phoned the University office again. I was told with my marks I did not need anything more than a pass, but the Research Paper had to count, even if it replaced a distinction. I was reassured all I needed was a 50% pass. That was it for me. I paid someone to properly type up that first draft and I submitted it. My supervisor was extremely disappointed and gave me two marks short of a credit. She made her point. She told me the heart of the paper was 'brilliant', but it needed a lot more work to properly finesse it and make it fit for publication. What publication?? I had not even thought of a publication. I'm glad that wasn't raised before I handed in the draft! But the 63% mark was well over the 50% pass I needed. I was home and hosed.

Then my old pattern kicked in and for quite a few weeks, I viciously hammered myself for submitting something that I knew required more work. That critical voice repeatedly stated that I had failed my own standards and the standards and expectations of my supervisor. I would then try and exonerate myself by thinking it would have been unfair to my family for me to extend my study for another six months to make that happen. The dialogue went backwards and forwards over and over again. Once again, the power of the unconscious mind was hard at work. At no time, however, was I even remotely aware that the University Medal was hovering in the background. And I thank my lucky stars for that lack of awareness.

As I reflect back now, I shake my head at how I ended up with a law degree, without much thought as to what I wanted to do with it, given I had taken it all on as a hobby.

Let me briefly trace back for you how I ended up practicing as a solicitor.

I recall that I missed all of the graduate interviews. This was a catastrophe for someone wanting to practice law, after completing their law degree. More so for an older graduate – and I was around 15 years older than most graduates. To this day, I do not even know how I missed the graduate interviews. Obviously, my focus was simply not there.

Did I really want to practice law? Initially, I didn't think so. I thought maybe academia and lecturing a few nights a week would give me more freedom to be with my children, and to raise them in the process.

But I was told by some of my lecturers that would involve a lot of research and a lot of time spent in the library. This was far from ideal, as I hadn't spent a lot of time in the library during my entire period of study. Instead, I had a colleague who loved spending time in the library, turning up papers and cases that we were meant to read and printing them off for me. I exchanged my typed-up lecture notes for his time in the library. All he had to do was copy what he had obtained for himself. He was often over-zealous and I would say: "Just give me copies of what's on the list". He was very grateful for my typed-up lecture notes. So academia was looking very unattractive for me.

Having missed all of the job interviews, I was now even more uncertain what to do next. I certainly had no desire to spend years in a library researching legal cases. So, on a whim, I prepared three job applications, and sent them to three of the top firms that I thought would be great to work at as a solicitor. With the first on the list, I was merely going for the interview experience. I had won that firm's

Commercial Transactions Prize and I was advised that getting an interview and a job there was very much on the cards – even with a very late application. Apparently, big firms always have room for one more job offer if the applicant was a standout candidate. More so, if the applicant has won their university prize. So, I added the firm to the short list. As I said, the applications were all sent after the firms had already had their graduate interviews and had made their graduate offers. None of my university friends could believe how I had missed the graduate intake. The common response from the Law Faculty was: what were you thinking, not to apply at that time? What was happening? You should have been at the front of the lineup?

Anyway, to cut a long story short, two of the firms offered me a position. I chose one and accepted the offer. Some four years later, I left that firm and shortly after ended up an equity partner in a successful law firm that was involved in class actions and (following a successful merger) remains the leader in that field to this day.

The attraction: not only would this class action firm secure a terrific income and lifestyle for the partners and employees of the firm, but it would also address corporate wrongs and bring accountability and transparency to the corporate world. And the icing on the cake was that it would involve travel to the US. The firm had a New York office at the time. I thought I had hit the jackpot. My love of travel and adventure was about to manifest, and not even at my expense! And my sense of justice could impact the broader community by not only addressing individual harm, but also corporate conduct aimed at protecting the broader community. The combined appeal jumped out at me.

Soon I was taking a couple of trips to the US each year. I had always had a passion for travel. Here I was in a job that was paying for me to travel to New York, to Chicago, Washington, Dallas, Texas, Boston, Los Angeles, San Francisco and more. Even to Zimbabwe.

Was this a coincidence? No. Our thoughts create our reality.

If you take away nothing from this book, take away that one truth – our thoughts, your thoughts, create your reality. If you are thinking this could not and would not ever happen to you. You are right. Your very thoughts, as dogmatic as they are, will ensure you get that very result.

How you *frame* those thoughts can significantly amplify your result – for good or bad.

I remember at one point thinking how much I wanted to one day explore Africa and Egypt and how great it would be if my work took me there. In the whole history of the firm, all travel was restricted to the US. All of my friends and colleagues, including my partners at the firm, said it was a pipe dream. They laughed. Well, be aware of your pipe dreams because they too can turn into reality.

My frame around my job and its attraction was 'travel for work'.

I attracted a client who was involved in a dispute in Australia arising from a mining venture. While preparation for the case was taking place in Sydney, the client moved on to his next mining venture. You guessed it. In Zimbabwe. I had to prepare the client's evidence in readiness for the hearing in Sydney. There were two options: either the client could travel to Sydney, or I could travel to Zimbabwe. My business partner at the time was adamant: this firm is not paying for you to travel to Africa. OK, I thought. Not a problem. I can work with that. Following some candid conversations with the client, it became apparent that the client's preference was that I travel to Zimbabwe to take his evidence, rather than him wasting time travelling to Sydney. I could certainly accommodate that.

I landed in Bulawayo full of excitement. The road trip to the client's mine was a further two hours away. I saw that as part of my adventure. We arrived at a big, sprawling house. Lunch was waiting for us. The client wrongly assumed I would need some time to get over my jet lag. What jet lag? That's another belief system I have never fostered.

I do not get jet lag. My body adjusts as I travel. The preparation of the evidence would start early the next morning and would be completed by the end of the following day.

I had already commenced my interrogation during the two-hour trip from the airport. I also had a safari booked and I was hoping to spend a night at Victoria Falls. Providence stepped in again. The client 'coincidentally' (the Universe is a magical wizard that meets all of our desires) had two visitors, one from Australia and the other from the UK, who were co-venturers, but who also had a desire to see Victoria Falls. So the three of us drove down with much chatter and anticipation. The Falls were spectacular. The safari was more than I had even imagined. To see these beautiful, majestic animals in their natural environment was mind-blowing. I swore that I would never go to another zoo. And I swore that I would come back for a much longer visit.

If you are wondering whether my return to Africa manifested, I can assure you that it did. But this book is not about those glorious travels. It is about how miraculously life orchestrates itself around our belief systems; it is about how we can transcend our conditioned fears to manifest our boldest and wildest dreams; and, in the process, awaken to the truly powerful beings that we all are.

I left the safari to catch an evening flight to Cairo – still in my shorts and t-shirt. Little did I realize back then (and this is going back some 20 years or more) that showing up in Cairo in shorts and a t-shirt was like walking around the airport, naked. The mistake was not repeated. That journey is another book in itself.

I was in awe. I had manifested a trip to Africa and a trip to Egypt, that was in large part met by a paying client. The power of the mind; the power of the language we use; and the power of our deep belief systems was reinforced and etched even more deeply. All a lucky 'coincidence' you might say? No.

Power of Intention

Let me now share with you the power of our intention, especially when it is laser-focused on something.

We were travelling in India, walking through Buddha Jayanti Park, one of the most beautiful parks in New Delhi with lovely green spaces, lots of flowers and lakes. Over the last week, we had been travelling through Rajasthan, and I had been searching for a traditional white tunic and pants with some sparkling embroidery, along with a matching scarf. But it had to be white! And it had to be a certain design. My intention refused to diverge, even slightly. Not on color. Not on the style I wanted. Everything I came across was in vibrant colors. After all, this was India. I only wanted the all-white look. The search continued in New Delhi – unsuccessfully (or so I thought).

It was then that we bumped into a local couple in the Park. He was a businessman importing and exporting various goods. She was a Senior Registrar in the High Court. There was an instant connection as we chatted and exchanged experiences of the court system. We were invited to their home to see where and how they lived. As we sipped our tea and chatted on about our families and their son, the Registrar called me to her bedroom. (Not a single word had been spoken about my search for a white outfit).

Laid out beautifully on her bed was the very white outfit I had been searching long and hard for!!!

What I had been visualizing in my mind over the last few weeks had just manifested before my very eyes! I was stunned.

She told me she had only worn it once, but wished to gift it to me as a memory of our visit to their home and New Delhi. I was gobsmacked!

That is the pure power of the mind. That is how we create our reality. That is how we *manifest thoughts into actual things*!

I was asked to try it on. I did. And it fitted perfectly. No surprise there, either.

My daughter wore that outfit many years later at a three-week course she did in Southern India, at the Oneness University in Chennai. Everyone had to wear white. A few years later I wore that same outfit at a truncated one-week course I attended at the Oneness University with my son. An amazing experience all round of my beautiful white Indian outfit that had 'miraculously' manifested and that I still own, neatly packed in one of my drawers, awaiting the next experience.

With these three lessons in mind, let's now look at what you can do to start realizing your dream. Right now.

Take just one area in your life you want to transform –
And ask what action can I take – now?

Try on a few of the exercises

Contemplate what illusory fear is stopping you?
Contemplate what judgments/beliefs are surfacing that stop you taking action?
Contemplate: What do I have to lose?

Chapter 10

Start Now

You don't have to be great to start,
but you have to start to be great
— Zig Ziglar

Do you want to know who you are?
DON'T ASK. ACT!
Action will delineate and define you
— Thomas Jefferson

If you can't fly, then run
If you can't run, then walk
If you can't walk, then crawl
But by all means, keep moving
— Martin Luther King Jr

Hopefully this book has inspired you to take action. You might be now thinking, where do I begin?

There is no one correct way or place to begin. The most important thing is simply that you do begin! Run, walk, crawl ... so that you can eventually fly and soar to your heart's quest. Just start.

To help you with that beginning, this chapter outlines a series of exercises / actions that you can take now. Have a look at the table below. See which outcome/action speaks to you first. Trust your intuition – you cannot fail. The chapter reference for each exercise is also listed. If you need to, you can go back and review the background to the recommended action / exercise.

Ask yourself first: which story resonated most for me?. Use that as a guide.

Alternatively, try out each exercise, one at a time, for a week before moving to the next. There is no right or wrong here.

Action/Exercise To:	Chapter Reference
1. Bring Awareness to your Conditioned Fear	Part 2 Ch 1
2. Shift a Negative Body Image	Part 2 Ch 1
3. Identify Your Belief System and Be at Choice	Part 2 Ch 3
4. Achieve your Vision	Part 2 Ch 4
5. Shift your Mindset	Part 2 Ch 5
6. Step Beyond Your Fear of Failure	Part 2 Ch 6
7. Identify and Change Your Negative Language	Part 2 Ch 9
8. Manifest a new you – I AM	Part 2 Ch 10
9. Eliminate fears - The 22x11 Exercise	Part 2 Ch 10
10. Release Negative Thoughts	Part 2 Ch 10
11. Identify Your Priority List	Part 2 Ch 10
12. Start a Journal	Part 2 Ch 10
13. Do a Daily Gratitude List	Part 2 Ch 10
14. Develop a Daily Affirmations Practice	Part 2 Ch 10
15. Start a daily meditative practice	Part 2 Ch 10
16. Start a regular exercise routine	Part 2 Ch 10

1. Exercise/Action – Bring Awareness to your Conditioned Fear

Take a moment to identify one fear you have. One of your repeating fears. Now ask yourself: how irrational is that fear? Stand outside yourself and observe your reaction. Bring awareness to your conditioned fear. What is your adult, rational voice saying to you about that fear? For me, when I did that with the mouse, I could see, for the first time, how truly absurd my conditioned reaction was to a helpless little mouse that could do no harm whatsoever to me. I could, once and for all, step outside that automatic fight-or-flight response and react in a sensible, measured way. I could giggle and see (as an observer) how silly my fear was (to use my daughter's word).

Could I go so far as to fall in love with a mouse? No! But that's OK. You don't have to fall in love with whatever you fear. You just need to release it so that it no longer has any control over you, or any adverse impact on your life. It is a conditioned block, a conditioned way of reacting that you are releasing that will no longer disempower you. Try it.

2. Exercise/Action – Shift a Negative Body Image

So, do you have a fear around your body? Are you so ashamed that you chastise yourself every time you are alone, naked, looking into a mirror? Then I encourage you to develop a mantra that you can sing every morning and evening – in the shower and when getting dressed, and when staring at yourself, deep into your eyes, when looking into the mirror. It goes something like this:

I AM ENOUGH
I AM BEAUTIFUL
I LOVE MY BODY
I LOVE ME

Develop a catchy beat that resonates with you. You will soon experience just how powerful your singing can be, with each phrase. The mantra will also often pop into your head even during the day. It will routinely bring a smile to your face. Or cultivate your own voice through your own words and let that voice be heard – loud and clear. Try it. And look deep into your eyes as you gaze into the mirror. Feel your body. Place post it notes on the mirror or wall where they cannot go unnoticed. Read them – and smile to yourself. I guarantee within a matter of days, you will begin to experience a magical shift. Love and acceptance create change, not resistance. If you resist your body, it will only persist.

3. Exercise/Action – Identify Your Belief System and Be at Choice

Take a moment to identify your greatest success – it may be in your career, sport, music. Write it down. Now, identify your belief system around that success. What is the first sentence or two that springs to mind immediately after jotting down your big success in life.

Then start to jot down your unique path to that success that you are experiencing now; the crossroads; the beliefs; the fears that you had to overcome. How far back can you go? Were you able to discern the very patterns and reinforcements that landed you to your pedestal today?

Is there a deeper passion, a deeper yearning, an innate purpose that keeps springing forth in your mind? Jot down your big dream. Is it something that you even fear sharing with friends and family? If so, jot down why?

Write down all the reasons that have stopped you from stepping onto that road of manifestation. Against each reason, ask yourself how true that reason is; where did that belief come from; what patterns of reinforcement did you attract to validate your belief system?

Are you bold enough to now step onto that road to manifest your big dream? If yes, BOLDLY GO FORTH! If not, write down why. What is the mind saying to you? Repeat the process of identifying your ingrained belief systems until a new awareness opens up where you can see that each hurdle you have put forward is self-imposed. It is not true.

4. Exercise/Action – Achieve your Vision

What is your biggest vision at present? What is that something that you would love to,do, but keep on the side lines with a multitude of false, fake excuses? The vision simply won't go away. But neither will all your conjured-up excuses. So, you find yourself treading water and doing nothing. Does this sound familiar? Many of us can tread water for years, even decades, until the pain becomes so great that we plunge in – and succeed! We then wonder why we 'procrastinated' for so long.

Now picture the end goal of your vision being achieved. Don't worry about the how and the why and the when. Just bring to mind the complete, unadulterated success of your vision. What are you saying to yourself and others around you? Feel the success. Feel the magic and the pride. Feel how liberating it is to achieve such a momentous, pivotal moment in your life. Journal those feelings. Journal what you see and say in that moment of victory. This will give you the courage to leap forward and create that reality.

5. Exercise/Action – Shift your Mindset

As a start, write down your top five limiting, negative beliefs – i.e. the ones that routinely pop into your head. The ones that the mind constantly repeats that stop you from pursuing any dream, small or large.

Now beside each negative belief, write down its positive configuration.

As an example:

- I hate my life; nothing ever works out for me = I LOVE my life; everything always works out for me, in perfect timing;
- I can never speak publicly; how fearful and embarrassing = I now have the courage and eloquence to speak publicly, with passion and brilliance.

Read your positive list aloud every night before going to bed and every morning upon awakening. Add new beliefs that you want to change as the old fall away. This will clear old negative patterns. Observe how your life shifts to a more positive reality. How much better you begin to feel in the process.

At the same time develop a daily practice (morning or evening as your time permits) to journal a gratitude list for all the positive things that are already in your life – large and small. For example: I am grateful for the great sleep I had last night; for my comfortable bed; for my delicious breakfast; for my beautiful son/daughter. I think you get the gist.

You will again observe a shift towards a greater freedom and happiness just by taking a few moments every evening and morning to record the above. You will not believe the mind shift that will happen over time. You will witness yourself transforming into the REAL YOU. Be in no doubt. And stop that negative mind chatter, right now, by doing the above exercise on whatever just came up for you! You are indeed a powerful being. If you believe it, you will live it. You and only you can and will create that reality.

6. Exercise/Action – Step Beyond Your Fear of Failure

What unfulfilled dream keeps wrenching at your heart? Write it down, in bold capital letters, using positive language, as if it has already manifested. Put expression to it, despite your negative belief systems that you are repeating in your mind, even as you write. What always lurks in the background of who you know yourself to be, but are too fearful to put voice to? Elaborate on what that looks like into the future. Describe it. Write the key details that make it real. Notice, again, the old patterns and belief systems that spring to mind, even as you write.

Finally, what baby steps can you take initially that would propel you on the road of your greatest dream? Write them down and include the dates by which you will take the action. Feel, really feel, the joy and pride and freedom in having plunged forward towards your passion. See and feel your ultimate goal manifesting. If you hit a pothole, know that it is only a sign there is a better way of getting to your ultimate goal. It is not a sign of failure. Or your goal may have shifted to something even more amazing. Be open to that intuitive guidance that has sheltered your dream all those years. Not giving up can only lead to your success. And the role of your mind is pivotal in consciously reaching your goal. It is not in the driver's seat. You are. Be aware of that. Do not let your conditioned mind sabotage your dream.

7. Exercise/Action – Identify and Change Your Negative Language

Take the time now to write down at least half a dozen limiting 'shoulds'; half a dozen limiting 'should nots' and half a dozen limiting 'can'ts'. This will begin to give you an idea of your automatic way of being that is creating your reality. If you are stuck, ask your family members and best friends what it is they hear you saying repeatedly. You may be surprised.

The awareness that this exercise will bring to your conscious mind is the beginning of a vital and necessary shift.

Go back to the lists you created and add against each negative belief/ mantra its equivalent positive statement, preferably with an "I AM" prefacing it.

Let it become your automatic way of being. As your beliefs shift, the negativity will fall away and you will experience yourself in a very different light.

8. Exercise/Action – Manifest a new you - The Power of the – I AM

At a deeper, truer level we have a very strong desire not to be limited by perceived fears and negative thoughts. This is where the "I AM" exercise can assist to break through our conditioned barriers.

There is not a day that goes by that I do not, either before going to bed or upon waking up and during my meditation sessions, repeat these words:

> I AM confident: meaning I can and will succeed
> I AM competent: meaning it will be done with effortless ease
> I AM clear thinking: reinforcing a clear path to the end result
> I AM creative: i.e. I will think outside the square for the best solution
> I AM courageous: I will be fearless and daring; obstacles will not deter me
> I AM carefree: it will be fun and adventurous
> I AM calm: it will all go smoothly and harmoniously
> I AM captivating and charismatic: needs no explanation
> I AM compassionate and caring: i.e. not hurting anyone in the process

I deliberately chose my 'c' words to generate the type of daily experiences I wanted to project, irrespective of the challenges thrown my way. This has been my mind's automatic mantra.

If the above speaks to you, by all means take it and adopt it. Use it. We do not have to re-invent the wheel. Make it your daily mantra and see how your life will transform.

The power of the "I AM" needs to be taught in our schools. It is a simple tool that can create a massive shift in who we believe ourselves to be. It is transforming.

How many 'I AMs' do you repeat to yourself daily? How many of them focus on negatives?

I AM:

- too fat; too thin
- ugly
- stupid; unintelligent; not smart like him/her/them
- full of shame for x, y, z
- unlovable
- unworthy
- never good enough
- never able to get things right
- always putting my foot in it
- always making mistakes
- always needing to be bailed out; to be helped; to be rescued
- shy
- an introvert
- unimportant; irrelevant; insignificant
- afraid of speaking in public
- afraid of the dark; afraid of heights; spiders
- a fearful person
- a cautious person

Add your list. There are also the endless "I AM NOTs" – all to the same effect:

- I AM NOT intelligent
- I AM NOT smart enough, clever enough
- I AM NOT courageous, bold, adventurous
- I AM NOT articulate; creative ...

Delete the "NOT" and experience the beginnings of a life-changing shift. I AM intelligent, smart, clever, courageous, bold, adventurous, articulate, creative .... What are the words that spring forth from your wishing well that best describe you in those moments you dare to think you are indeed great?

The damage that these negative I AMs cause is reversible and transformative.

Stop – and prepare your list now. Read it until it becomes an automatic mantra.

Try focusing on those positive statements daily. Develop a routine, preferably a morning ritual to start your day on a positive note. Over time, those mantras will become your automatic way of being. As your beliefs shift, the negativity will fall away and you will experience yourself in a very different light.

9. Exercise/Action Eliminate fears – The 22x11 Exercise

There is a '22x11' exercise that I once taught my young son that transformed his batting in cricket. Try this out for those beliefs that are stubbornly resisting to shift; those that are very deeply ingrained; so much so that when you utter your positive affirmation, the mind bounces back with an ever stronger negative.

You will find the exercise is deliberately bringing to the fore all of the negative mind chatter that keeps you stuck in believing that your goal is not possible. But, with the exercise, you now keep telling your mind, "No! I am discarding that belief system and I am reinforcing, ongoingly, a new belief system that 'I will now score 100 runs'" (just to explain briefly for those who don't know – a run is essentially a point in cricket!). Some of your stronger negative beliefs will repeat themselves. Just write them down, followed by your positive statement. It is imperative that you keep your positive statement in the language of it having already manifested. It should not be, for example, a statement that says: "I will score 100 runs". That projects it as sometime in the future, as in "I will one day, someday score that". No. Your statement needs to be in the NOW, as if you have already achieved it.

Through this process, the exercise will consciously and ongoingly program and reinforce the new belief systems while, at the same time, clearing out the old negative thought patterns that are preventing you from realizing your goal. I cannot even recall how or when I came across this exercise, but it has been a part of my arsenal for decades.

Take an exercise book. Label it Day 1, Day 2 etc., right up to Day 11. Then number each page 1 down to 22. Start by writing the actual outcome that you want. It has to be in the present tense, as if it has manifested already. For my son it was: "I now score 100 runs". Then immediately following this write down the negative response that comes up. For example, at number 1 you might write: "I now score 100 runs". Immediately following the mind says: "No way, you're not that good". Then at No 2: write again: "I now score 100 runs". The mind might say: "Are you mad, only professionals score those sorts of runs?". Write it down. Keep going. The mind will come up with reason after reason as to why you believe you cannot do that. Write it all down. Continue the process until you reach the end of the 22 times for this day. The next day do the same. The sequence must be consecutive, that is, you cannot do 5 days, then a gap of a few days and then think you can complete the remaining 6 days. If you have a break, you need to start afresh.

You will also note that the mind may wonder off with a nonsensical response like: "I hope I'm not late for work tomorrow". Or..."I wonder what my friends would think if they knew I was doing this crazy exercise?!" Write it all down. Do not double-guess your mind or try to correct it. Just write down your positive statement (i.e.. "I now score 100 runs") and then immediately following, write down whatever the mind comes up with. No judgment. No double guessing. No correcting. Even if the mind goes into some form of repetition, write it all down. This is a mind game and your mind is trying to win. Follow the rules. The results will amaze you.

The 22x11 must also all be done in one go. As I told my son, he could not do 1-5 in a one-sitting batch, go up have something to eat, and then come back down and do another batch. If he distracted himself for any reason, he had to start again until the 22x11 was completed that day. He chose to write his much-desired outcome, every night, after school. He stuck to it religiously. Cricket was a real passion for him at the time. You may be shocked at some of the nonsense your mind will put forward.

Did my son score his 100? He sure did. He became opening batsman. His response at the time was: "Gee this stuff really works, mum!!" And it does.

10. Exercise/Action Release Negative Thoughts

An exercise that might also assist is for you to write out all that negativity; list it, exactly as the mind is speaking it, and then tear it up into tiny pieces and throw it in the bin. Gone!

Now, create what it is you truly want to manifest if you could control those crazy fears and anxieties. Write it down.

You will never succeed
I AM successful in all that I do. If one way does not work, I will try another. The right way will show itself to me. My intuition will guide me on the right path. Every obstacle, every challenge is no more than a process of learning how better to approach it

Your kids and family will suffer
My children and family will be my greatest supporters. We will grow and flourish.

At the end of your positive list, write: this or something better manifests for me, in perfect timing.

11. Exercise/Action Identify Your Priority List

Try also listing everything you LOVE to do, or would love to do, but have failed to put into practice. List it in priority of your strongest desires.

Read it daily before bed each night and again every morning, on awakening.

Remember, fake it till you make it. The mind does not know the difference.

12. Start a Journal

You can also start to journal, each morning and/or evening. Journaling can be very effective, particularly when the mind is too active and cluttered with too many thoughts. Confusion swirling round and round that prevents you from sleeping, eating and taking any action.

Take an exercise book, date it, and then start writing, for 15 minutes or so (or until you have exhausted the mind) everything that the mind is conjuring up. Don't stop. Don't analyze. Whatever criticism comes up, write it down. Whatever nonsense the mind dreams up, write it down.

Repeat the exercise for 3-5 days, or longer, if necessary.

You will marvel at the freedom and lightness this will bring you. It is an exercise that actually declutters the mind by acknowledging the thought (no matter how crazy it may be) and eliminating its force.

13. Exercise/Action Do a Daily Gratitude List

Or you may choose to start each day by listing three or more things you are truly grateful for in a gratitude book.

Or you may choose to do what my son does – keep a "Gratitude Jar". It used to be my M&M jar as my children were growing up. I used to have one in my office and later in my chambers. Hand-fulls of chocolate M&Ms became too regular so I had to stop filling it. He has yellow post-it notes that he writes the date on and what he is grateful for on that day, before placing the note in the jar.

Here is a picture of my son's Gratitude Jar that was once my chocolate M&M jar. Sweet?? One type of sweetness turned into another, although this was a far more powerful one!

14. Develop a Daily Affirmations Practice

Again, use post-it notes on walls and mirrors that you cannot miss during your morning routine.

And remember to always follow your intuition – that internal voice that can guide you…if you let it.

Never take "no" for an answer if that internal voice is shouting otherwise. And remember that modern science has uncovered the "SNAG" effect. Stimulating Neural Activity Growth of your mind, *with repeated positive focus,* will eventually dissolve all of the negative conditioning and all of the negative belief systems that we have grown up with. Yes, we can rewire our brains until we reach a point where they are our automatic way of being. Where every problem that presents itself, every curveball, has a solution, and we can see that solution. It is no different to how a baby re-wires its brain in order to start walking.

15. Exercise/Action Develop a daily meditative practice.

It does not have to be for long periods initially. Do a meditation course (online or in person). Consider Vipassana or a mindfulness meditation course. Look up Chakra Dhyana online and see if that speaks to you and your seven chakras. There are so many options. Commit to the daily practice. Any new practice after six weeks becomes a habit. Your negative chatter about why you don't have the time or how hard it is to still the mind or whatever – will begin to evaporate. None of that comes up for me anymore. But it certainly did in the beginning.

There are also recordings to activate the SNAG effect; recordings that also help your brain move away from our normal Beta state and into the Alpha, Delta and even Theta state; that generate brainwave frequencies that can put you in a deeper meditative state and suspend your external reality to give you greater access to your true essence. The very first Alpha Dynamics course I did (over 36 years ago now) exposed me to the magic of this type of 'music'.

The aim is to expunge your negative patterns and replace them with your heart's yearnings and desires that you were designed to manifest. Start creating your new neural pathways now by eliminating your conditioned fears. Use all that you have read here to inspire you to springboard into the life you know you were meant to live.

16. Exercise/Action Start a regular exercise routine

I recall when I first started going to the gym, the minute my feet hit the floor as I got out of bed, I used to say to myself: "Ohhh, how I hate this, it's so early, it's so cold (in winter), it's so hot (in summer)! When will I start loving it, how much longer can I do this for? There must be another way!" .... That voice went on and on ... But persevere I did. I now bounce out of bed without a single one of those thoughts.

Instead, I am happy and grateful to be able to go to the gym and keep my body fit. I often smile to myself as I pass the mirror whilst putting my gym gear on. That too can be your experience. My coastal walks in the morning are blissful. In fact, if I have to very occasionally miss one, due to whatever else is happening in my life, I complain. I actually miss my walk if I can't do it. Same with my yoga and my gym.

Take care of your body by starting some regime of walking, or going to the gym, or joining a tennis group, or doing laps in a heated pool. You know what calls to you. Commit to a daily or weekly regime and stick to it. Promise yourself that you will go well beyond that six-week threshold. Tell your partner or buddy of your commitment so they can call you on it. And if you fall off the bandwagon, just jump back on again. You will only 'fail' if you give up. Remember what you read above about this.

17. Exercise/Action Give birth to that inner creative voice

What is it that puts a smile on your face? What excites you? What are you passionate about doing 'one day'? Is it writing or painting, like me? Is it dancing? Is it cooking or practicing / teaching yoga? Is it playing an instrument? One of the barristers on my floor plays the violin (often in his chambers) which, no doubt, significantly reduces his stress levels and opens his heart to the peace and freedom that music can bring. What intense longing do you continually hunger for that is yet to be satisfied?

Give birth to that inner creative voice that you have stifled all your life. Give birth to it NOW. Scratch that itch. If you are not sure what you should try first, try one and then another. Let your intuition / Higher Self guide you. Trust it. As you do this, like any muscle, it will strengthen and reach a point where you will no longer doubt yourself. It will become your joyful, automatic way of being.

18. You have Enough time

There is enough time in your life to explore all that excites and inspires you. To scratch that itch. Remember, for the last 29 years I have been fully and actively involved in the practice of law, with the last 19 years as a Barrister. Successfully so.

I hope the above list inspires you to take action in your life. NOW. Let me share with you my daily practices. Not to boast but to embolden you to take that action; to show you what is possible if you break through your conditioned fears. Small steps will lead to massive leaps that will, in turn, see you soar to your highest potential.

Monday to Friday:
I wake up at 4.45 am. Yes, you read that correctly! I meditate for around one hour. I then head to the local gym and do exercises for half an hour. I head back home and then walk for 20 minutes along the coastal walk to Bronte Beach (the iconic Bondi Beach is the same distance at the opposite end, but busier). I sit in one of the local cafes, have a "soy, decaf cappuccino, with no chocolate on top" (the 'why bother'); read the paper and return home. I shower and head to work. I am generally in by 8.30 am.

On Wednesdays and Thursdays I also attend evening Yoga classes that are 1 hour 15 minutes long. I literally chill out on the mat with the mind fully occupied with the poses.

Saturday-Sunday
I wake up at 6am (a big sleep in, you would agree!) and do my hour's meditation, then head to Bronte Beach for my walk. This is a truly magnificent way to start the day. I have experienced amazing sun rises with flaming balls emerging from the ocean. I have watched surfers play on the ocean waves with such ease and grace, often accompanied by dolphins – on that one occasion surfing in unison. Magical.

I have a coffee and a chat with my parents and then head off to do my 1 hour 15 minutes yoga, on both mornings. I am back by 10.15 am with the full weekend ahead of me.

Are any of the above activities on your 'should do' list? What has stopped you from actioning them? What is beneath those reasons that are popping in your mind now? How can I fit that in my busy routine? I don't have enough time?? Yes you can, and you do. Or are you saying: I'll do it when X or Y happens? I guarantee if you delve below the surface of your excuses there will be some deep-rooted fear that is stopping you. So delve in the inquiry and be brutally honest with yourself.

What creative ventures are also constantly popping up for you that you repeatedly shut down with: I'd love to write a book; I'd love to do a painting course; I'd love to do a cooking course; I'd love to teach yoga – BUT I can't (there's that word again that needs the 't' deleted) right now BECAUSE …… (you fill in the reasons)? Creativity breeds freedom. It can shine a light of hope in some of our darkest hours. It can also inspire us to leap forward in our most glorious hours.

Start NOW. Start somewhere and allow it to evolve organically. Choose just one thing you have been putting off. Use this book to inspire yourself to break free from just one of your conditioned fears.

Fling open the door of your conditioned cage.

What inspires you – truly – from the heart?
What is your immediate, intuitive response?

Contemplate why you have stopped yourself
from following that passion?

Part 3

Live an Inspired Life

If you could identify one unique gift what would that be?
How is your "mind chatter" sabotaging that – even now?

Trust your heart
Trust your intuition

Do one or more of the exercises in the previous chapter
Try it on – like a new pair of shoes

Contemplate: What do you have to lose – nothing !
What do you have to gain – everything !

Chapter 1

What is your Unique Gift to the World; your Life Purpose

"Never dim your light because others are too afraid to come out of the dark."
— Matshona Dhliwayo

Once you learn to step beyond your illusory fears, you will experience the freedom on the other side. The inevitable question that will then spring forth is: what is my life's purpose; what is my unique gift to the world?

In my experience you can only get in touch with this gift by trusting your heart, your intuition – getting in touch with your essence. We are spiritual beings having a human experience; not human beings awaiting to have some spiritual experience when we die and ascend to heaven. We need to silence the overactive, analytical mind; to bring it to stillness; so that we can hear our essence speak in that silence. One tool that will assist is cultivating a meditation practice. There are many others. As I have noted, I meditate every night before going to bed and each morning before going to the gym. I initially followed the teachings of the 10-day Vipassana meditation retreat I did many years ago in the Blue Mountains, outside of Sydney. There are also Mindfulness meditation courses, like the one my son has done. Both are highly recommended. There are many others. Explore and find the one that resonates most with you.

Meditation stills the mind and awakens us to our essence.

Identifying who we truly are and why we are here is all part of our awakening.

Begin to activate some or all of the above positive habits that will magically become your automatic way of living. Start by actioning one or more of the many options in this book that have marked my life's journey. Feel the fear that comes up and take the action anyway.

I have travelled on three very distinct roads during my own life's journey: the first being, what I call, my intellectual road - analyzing, evaluating, reasoning, assessing. The second, my creative road; and the third my spiritual road. Add to that my motherhood road. I can honestly say, hand on heart, that my most challenging and rewarding road has been my motherhood road which has crisscrossed all of my three key roads from the age of 23. It has inspired me to seek justice wherever I saw injustice. so that my children and all other children can grow up and experience a more equitable and non-discriminatory planet.

I stepped onto the creative road, mostly seeking escape and refuge and stillness and reflection (albeit mostly unconsciously in the earlier days).

In the face of my most dire fears, my innate spirit (our innate spirit) drew me on the spiritual road. I was certainly guided on how to release those deep fears. But so much more - as I then began to question my higher purpose. Why am I here? What is my real calling? Who am I, really? What does this human vessel really hold?

Fearlessness. Trust. Awareness. Acceptance. Non-judgment. Surrender. These are the words that we should be uttering incessantly to ourselves and others. These are the words that will fling open the door to our freedom.

Deep down you and only you know your calling. What is etched so deep in your heart that you can't stop thinking about it? Or what massive dream do you have deep within you that you are afraid to even voice to anyone. Fear of judgment??

Step out of your conditioned cage and give voice to that dream. You can make it happen.

Consider where you thought you "failed"
in a pursuit you still hold in your heart.
Identify your "curveball".
What did you actually do?
What could you do differently?
What lesson(s) did that "curveball"
teach you?

Contemplate: What if that "curveball"
was a springboard
to my next step?
What would that be?

Contemplate: Whether the "limitations"
that stopped you are all
Self-imposed and live in your mind??

Contemplate a new version of you! Be it!

Chapter 2

Life's Curveballs and Challenges are a Springboard

When life throws curve balls at you,
don't try to dodge them.
They are meant to hit you, to mould
you and to shape you to become the
person you were meant to be.
Enjoy the impact, smile and move on
— Legion L

Life never stops teaching us.

Life always steers us in the direction towards our ongoing growth. Every 'curveball', every perceived 'disaster', every 'challenge' is an opportunity for growth. An opportunity to free ourselves from the shackles of our conditioning. If only we viewed life's curveballs in this way, much of our pain and fear would be eliminated. Many years and decades wasted wallowing in that pain and fear would be eliminated if only we consciously bring this truth to mind and reinforce it on an ongoing basis.

Life's curveballs are but springboards into the next chapter of our life.

My partner of almost 20 years was diagnosed with Parkinson's some eight years ago. What do we do when such a curveball hits us? Do we wallow in a sea of sadness and helplessness? I had to learn to surrender, to accept what was not within my power to change. I learnt to trust, to let go of the fear and emptiness that often engulfed us both. Above all, I learnt to bring a deep compassion to his inability or unwillingness to not succumb to the condition. You are not that condition. You are far greater, far more powerful. These were words that fell on deaf ears as he delved deeper into the 'poor me' syndrome. The victim that we can all play, unconsciously. I had to accept that I had no power to change him. Only he could do that. Our powers revolve around ourselves. We can actively change ourselves only. The only power I had was acceptance. Trust. Everything happens for a reason.

We were once a dynamic duo: two lawyers that worked together and played together. We still laugh at the many odd and interesting legal cases we ran together in the various courts, he as my instructing solicitor and me as the barrister putting the arguments forward. What fun we had!

We were also two bold, adventurous spirits, constantly embracing and creating amazing experiences. Two spirits that soared from one fun-filled adventure to another; that travelled the globe, immersed in the wonders of all that life offered on this glorious planet. We sunbaked with seals on Galapagos Island. We danced to the rhythms of the drum with the locals in Cuba, and swam with the dolphins in the wild. We searched for the Northern Lights, and slept in an ice hotel in Norway. We got lost (literally) amongst the Moai on Easter Island. We went on magical safaris in Africa, celebrating my partner's birthday with the Masai Mara, including a surprise birthday treat that had him dressed and dancing as a Masai. The only problem was his two Jewish feet again! That same heritage that had him believe he was not a dancer and would never be a dancer! What a myth. But watching him try to copy the Masai as they jumped sky high still brings a massive grin to my face.

We trekked in search of the Gorillas in the mist in Uganda. I still get goosebumps thinking about my eye-to-eye contact with the big Silverback, less than a couple of feet away. I looked into the soul of another being and felt our Oneness.

I bravely ate bull's balls in Argentina – a so-called delicacy. They looked so small, I asked the waiter whether they were, in fact, the matadors! Don't ask me about the taste. It is an experience I invite you to try. Have no fear. You will not die.

We played with the penguins in Antarctica. We went in search of my partner's family home in the Czech Republic in the middle of winter, with the snow knee-high. A solitary man with his dog was walking along the path in a tiny village called Vodu Radi. We asked whether he knew my partner's family, or had heard of them. He knew nothing, but said his father, who was still alive, was the eldest person in the village and if anyone knew, he would. We were invited to have a warm drink at his home, near an open fire. His father not only knew my partner's family, but he was a playmate of my partner's father! And the family home was just behind us. We went and explored. How grand it must have been in its heyday. Another magical experience where the universal forces collided to bring forth what we, as humans, describe as a 'coincidence'. There are no coincidences. This was a completion for my partner and he attracted exactly what was needed in that moment (albeit unconsciously).

We did an Ayurvedic retreat in Kerala, India. That's a whole new story in itself that makes us laugh to this day. We visited the Taj Mahal where my partner got down on one knee and proposed. We travelled to South America, explored the wonders of Machu Picchu and Cuzco in Peru. We climbed up and down a mountain slope, watching the men knitting (I kid you not), then explored Lake Titicaca and visited the local indigenous people in all their colorful costumes. We saw the Inca ruins and played with the Alpacas in Lima. Iguazu Falls. Rio de Janeiro. Buenos Aires. The magnificent Gaudi landmarks in Barcelona. We visited the Hermitage Museum in St. Petersburg and wondered whether the sleeping little old lady, sitting on a chair, next to an open window, would notice if we removed one of the Monet or Van Gogh paintings from the wall! We went dog sledding in the very surreal wilderness of Quebec in Canada. We were amazed at how all of the stories in the Bible came to life as we travelled through Israel and the West Bank.

All this is just a snippet. We explored so, so much more together.

I could write endless books on all of our adventures. Legal and travel.

A part of my life that is no more, as I have learnt to accept my partner's succumbing to his condition. Sri Lanka and the Maldives would be his last trip. His vision: retirement in Bali. And when that didn't work out, retirement in a retirement village on the upper North Shore of Sydney. He could see no alternative for himself and his condition.

My internal voice screamed: I am not ready for retirement! There is still so much more I want to be and do. I want to inspire people and be inspired. I still want to move mountains. I am not ready for a life on the treadmill of 'retirement'.

I observed as fear after fear sprang forth: fear of being alone; fear of starting afresh, doing and exploring I know not what; fear of what my life's new chapter will bring; fear of abandonment (both in feeling abandoned and the guilt in feeling I am abandoning my partner in his time of need); fear of being judged; fear of not doing the right thing ....on and on and on. The mind chatter is endless and very powerful when life's curveballs are so fiercely flung at us.

All I can do is what I have always done.

Every major decision in my life was as a result of, primarily, 'hanging up' on my mind's constant chatter and listening to that inner wisdom.

Every past choice has brought me to the intersection of fearlessness and freedom. This book was the result. I await with anticipation and excitement as I step into the next chapter of my life. I know my next choice will present itself in perfect timing. And I know that I will have to choose with the same conscious boldness that this book has espoused.

I hope it inspires that spark in you, that will ignite into the magnificent fireball you know yourself to be. I already feel that spark within me, yet again. I trust it. And I know it will, once again, launch me into the realm of freedom. And it will do so with greater wisdom, compassion and understanding. For that is my path. It is your path. It is the path of all of us, as we grow and free ourselves from our illusory fears to experience ourselves as the true, magnificent beings we all are.

I hope *you* trust *you*. I hope you follow your unique bliss. Now and always. That is my heartfelt wish for you.

I hope this book has opened up at least one door for you into a freedom that you were born to experience. The fact that you have read this book, means that you are ready, willing and able to launch yourself off that conditioned treadmill (we all experience) into the truly blessed life you were meant to live. As your conditioned fears begin to subside, one by one, and eventually dissolve completely, you will live a conscious life, filled with true joy. You will deal with life's curveballs (and they will keep coming) from a conscious position of strength and inner knowing.

You will remember that every curveball is no more than another opportunity for your growth. You will embrace it and grow and grow and grow …

With much love and gratitude.

And finally, let me finish with the wisdom of Buddha:

> *We are what we think.*
> *All that we are arises with our thoughts.*
> *With our thoughts, we make the world.*
>
> *The mind is everything. What you think you become.*

www.ingramcontent.com/pod-product-compliance
Lightning Source LLC
Chambersburg PA
CBHW051829090426
42736CB00011B/1723
* 9 7 8 1 9 2 2 0 9 3 7 1 4 *

MAKING THE MODERN SOUTH

David Goldfield, Series Editor

RESIDENT STRANGERS

IMMIGRANT LABORERS IN NEW SOUTH ALABAMA

JENNIFER E. BROOKS

Louisiana State University Press
Baton Rouge

Published by Louisiana State University Press
lsupress.org

Designer: Barbara Neely Bourgoyne
Typeface: Sentinel

Portions of chapter 2 first appeared, in somewhat different form, in "'John Chinaman' in Alabama: Immigration, Race, and Empire in the New South, 1870–1920," *Journal of American Ethnic History,* 37.2 (Winter 2018): 5–36, and are reproduced with permission of the editor.

Cover photo: An Italian "floating gang" crew of miners. *Birmingfind Collection, 829.3.28, Birmingham, Ala. Public Library Archives.*

Library of Congress Cataloging-in-Publication Data
Names: Brooks, Jennifer E., author.
Title: Resident strangers : immigrant laborers in new South Alabama / Jennifer E. Brooks.
Description: Baton Rouge : Louisiana State University Press, [2022] | Series: Making the modern South | Includes bibliographical references and index.
Identifiers: LCCN 2021032574 (print) | LCCN 2021032575 (ebook) | ISBN 978-0-8071-7665-8 (cloth) | ISBN 978-0-8071-7758-7 (pdf) | ISBN 978-0-8071-7757-0 (epub)
Subjects: LCSH: Foreign workers—Alabama—History. | Immigrants—Alabama—History. | Alabama—Social conditions. | Alabama—Race relations.
Classification: LCC HD8083.A48 B76 2022 (print) | LCC HD8083.A48 (ebook) | DDC 331.6/209761—dc23
LC record available at https://lccn.loc.gov/2021032574
LC ebook record available at https://lccn.loc.gov/2021032575

And if a stranger sojourn with thee in your land, you shall not vex him. But the stranger that dwelleth with you shall be unto you as one born among you, and thou shalt love him as thyself; for ye were strangers in the land of Egypt.

—Leviticus 19:33–34 (KJV)

CONTENTS

ILLUSTRATIONS

ACKNOWLEDGMENTS

Throughout the course of this project, I have been lucky to be embedded in a community of scholars and like-minded individuals who both supported and shaped what *Resident Strangers* turned out to be. The College of Liberal Arts at Auburn University twice provided Competitive Summer Grants that allowed me to continue research and writing without the distraction of summer teaching. My history colleagues at Auburn listened to me, and sometimes read portions and offered critiques of the manuscript, no matter how busy they were. I am especially grateful for the conversations and critiques provided by Keith Hebert, Ken Noe, David Carter, Sarah Hamilton, Christopher Ferguson, Eden Mclean, Melissa Blair, and Charles Israel. Big thanks as well go to the scholars and friends who reviewed the work at different stages or indulged me with a supportive ear over the years as this work developed: Moon-Ho Jung, Jim Cobb, Cindy Hahamovitch, Scott Nelson, and Jessica Jackson. I am especially thankful for Series Editor David Goldfield and Editor-in-Chief Rand Dotson at Louisiana State University Press, for believing in this project and sticking with it for the long haul. Thank you to Todd Manza and Catherine L. Kadair for their careful editing of the manuscript for the Press. Thanks as well to the anonymous reviewer for LSU Press who offered a detailed review that proved enormously helpful in shaping the final manuscript. Thank you as well to the students in my New South graduate seminar, Brucie, Emily, Ben, Luke, Kyle, Laura, Coty, and Amberly, who read the chapter on the Chinese in Alabama and helped me think through the good and bad of various book titles. Thank you also to the descendant of Dolphina Lesko, Ceara Comeau-Rosello, who provided insight to Dolphina's story and the family photographs included here. Her generosity is much appreciated.

This project would never have reached completion without the support, forbearance, and crucial comic relief provided by my spouse, John Ellisor, and our daughter, An-Mei. This project spanned years that have traversed a rocky road, but we have always navigated the journey better together. Finally, I am deeply grateful for the time I spent with local immigrant communities fighting in 2011 and 2012 to overturn Alabama's hateful anti-immigrant law, HB-56. Both the pain and the dedication I witnessed in that fight were the genesis of this project.

RESIDENT STRANGERS

Counties of Alabama. *Map by Mary Lee Eggart, based on Contemporary Maps, Cartographic Research Laboratory, College of Arts and Sciences, University of Alabama.*

INTRODUCTION

When sixteen-year-old Dolphina Lesko prepared to disembark from the passenger ship *Victoria* at Ellis Island in the late summer of 1897, she discovered to her great horror that her Austro-Hungarian passport was missing.[1] After traveling with distant relatives from her small village of Spiska, just south of the Polish border in Hungary, Dolphina now lacked the requisite documents that would allow her to leave Ellis Island to join her sister in Brookside, Alabama. Intent on reaching their own destinations, her fellow travelers abandoned her to immigration officials, who would not allow her to leave. Dolphina could not understand or speak English, nor was she familiar with the most common languages and dialects heard among the ships, docks, and queues of Ellis Island, whether German, French, Italian, Greek, or Russian. She had no way to alert her sister in Brookside, who expected her to arrive on the train from New York within days.[2]

Born in 1881, and orphaned by the time she was fourteen, Dolphina departed the Austro-Hungarian Empire in 1897 on a wing and a prayer, with the hope that crossing the Atlantic would set her on a new path in the United States.[3] By 1910, around 5 million emigrants such as Dolphina had left the Austro-Hungarian Empire, particularly from the eastern regions of Hungary. The "Magyarization" policies of the Hungarian state intensified in the nineteenth century, suppressing minority languages and cultures and obstructing the "social and economic advancement" of Slovaks such as the Leskos.[4] The Hungarian government worked to prevent emigration of ethnic Magyars in the late nineteenth century, but it facilitated the departure of ethnic minorities, including Slovaks, Croatians, and Germans. From 1900 to 1910, almost one-quarter of all immigrants who arrived in the United States came from the Austro-Hungarian Empire.[5] Several hundred Slo-

Dolphina Lesko, age sixty-six, in 1946. *Birmingfind Collection, 829.4.15, Birmingham, Ala. Public Library Archives.*

vakian immigrants, including Dolphina's family, eventually landed in Alabama's Birmingham District, beginning mostly in the 1890s and continuing approximately until World War I.

Dolphina's daughter, Annie Latenosky Patchen, later explained why her mother and many other Slovakians came to Brookside: "The people in the old country was poor and couldn't find no work and couldn't make ends meet, and they all started coming to the United States." Searching for work and possibly a place to call home, "they went from town to town and finally landed here in Brookside." Having opened its Brookside mining operations in 1894, the Sloss-Sheffield Company soon had a few hundred Slovakian families residing in the town, where the men typically worked in the coal mines. By 1897, immigrants arrived at Brookside almost every day, and Dolphina's family kept close watch for her arrival. In fact, soon every Slovak in Brookside, as well as other residents, regularly surveilled the depot. Still trapped on the *Victoria* in New York, however, Dolphina failed to show.[6]

An inability to communicate with anyone on the ship left Dolphina increasingly frightened as the days slipped by. Some fellow German passengers grew concerned for the often-crying young woman, attempting to distract her with kitchen work or by trying to direct her to a church down the wharf. A Jewish mail carrier, however, eventually found that they could communicate. "There was one Jew who spoke Mama's language," her daughter recalled, and after almost three weeks, he was able to tell her, "Your passport has arrived." Shortly thereafter, immigration officials informed Dolphina that she finally could leave for her destination.

If the time on the ship had been frustrating and lonely, the streets of New York around Ellis Island were no improvement. "While Mama was in New

John, Mike, and George Bensko, Slovakian miners and brothers, pictured in a 1937 newspaper article as "returning home after a day's work in Brookside mine." *Birmingfind Collection, 829.6.4.21, Birmingham, Ala. Public Library Archives.*

York, she didn't know nothing. All she knew was that somebody was hollering at her in one language and telling her to 'change the money' [as] they gave her a handful of cash." An official then put Dolphina "somewheres" and "told her to wait . . . for a train that was going to leave." But Dolphina could not even understand what time the train departed. At the station, a man kept pointing at his watch, "telling her the time the train was coming," but when it actually arrived, he had to physically drag her to the train platform. Stumbling along, Dolphina finally boarded the railcar. Fortunately, it was indeed a train bound for Birmingham. Profoundly alone, Dolphina set out for the long journey southward from New York, down the Atlantic Seaboard to Birmingham. To find her sister, she ultimately would need to switch lines at Birmingham and catch a connecting train to Brookside.

Dolphina finally arrived at the Brookside depot at night, and three weeks late. Spying a young woman dressed in a traditional long skirt with a shawl over her head on the Georgia Pacific railcar, an officer familiar with the family recognized her as the long-lost sister.[7] Dolphina, however, felt far from certain that she was in the right place, nor was she confident about what might happen next. The policeman, whom Dolphina remembered as a "tall man with long hair," approached her.

> [He] tried to make her come [off the train]. He took the shawl off and put it in her lap. Mama takes it and puts it back on her head. She wasn't going to have nothing to do with this man. . . . She didn't know what he was saying and he didn't know what she was saying. He tried to help her out of the train, but she wouldn't have anything to do with him. He kept calling her to follow. She finally got off the train, and she wouldn't have anything to do with him. Nobody was there but her. They had a footlog and he was trying to help her across it. She wouldn't go. He just kept motioning her to follow him, and she [finally] followed him.[8]

With no better option, Dolphina reluctantly followed the officer down the street to a house near the city hall. When the officer hailed a Mr. Perunko to come out, Dolphina finally recognized a name. He informed Mr. Perunko that Mrs. Petras's sister had finally arrived, and the man then told Dolphina in her own language to trust the officer and go with him. For the first time since that awful moment on the ship three weeks earlier, Dolphina started to relax. "That made Mama feel good." The officer then escorted the young woman to another house, where they pelted the side with rocks to roust the sleeping inhabitants. Eventually, Dolphina heard her sister call out "I think Dolphina is here!," and the front door opened.[9] An exhausted, dirty, and undoubtedly greatly relieved teenager had finally found her family.

To obtain the thirty-five dollars needed for passage to America, Dolphina had promised her sister that she would marry a Slovakian man chosen by her brother-in-law, once she arrived in Brookside.[10] From among three possible men in Brookside proffered to her, Dolphina chose Mike Dziak. They married on May 12, 1900, in the newly built Catholic church in Brookside. Soon, they were joined by a son, Johnny, born on February 27, 1901. Within months, however, typhoid claimed first her five-month-old infant and then her husband, just a few weeks later, leaving Dolphina alone again. The grieving young widow lived with her sister for a while but soon left Brookside to join a brother in Illinois. She married and divorced Slovakian Stephen Ogursak in Illinois, then returned to Brookside and married fellow Slovakian immigrant Joseph Latenosky. Dolphina ultimately had eight sons and three daughters, including three children who died in infancy, all in Brookside. Although some Slovakian families eventually left Birmingham for work in Ohio and elsewhere, Dolphina remained, as did many others. Her husband Joe also died tragically, in a mine accident in 1937. Dolphina died in Brookside in 1958.[11]

By all accounts, Dolphina Lesko found a fulfilling life in Alabama. She established a family and a home in a community far away from the village of Spiska. She chose to remain in Birmingham for the rest of her life, in the place where she had buried two husbands and a son. Many in her family stayed in Alabama as well. But the Leskos' story, like that of thousands of other immigrant laborers, has played little role in popular conceptions of Alabama's history and has only recently influenced academic interpretations of the New South and its labor history.

For that reason, and others, I seek to restore immigrant laborers from around the world to their place in the New South project, considering not only the campaigns to recruit them to Alabama but especially how various immigrant groups and individuals experienced their sojourns in Alabama. As used here, the term "immigrant laborers" refers to people who arrived to work as wage laborers (or shifted to that from farming), typically in the

Dolphina Lesko, Brookside, Alabama, with the stuffed toy bears she apparently loved. Along with her husband, Joseph Latenosky, Dolphina raised a large family in Alabama. Her grandchildren and great-grandchildren called her "Babka."
Photo and details courtesy of Lesko descendant Ceara Comeau-Rosello.

urban or rural industries of the New South (such as coal mining, railroad construction, or timber industries), but also as farmhands, peddlers, small market grocers, or laundry workers. The term "sojourners" identifies immigrant laborers who traveled within the New South and/or back and forth to their home countries or to other locales within or outside the United States.[12]

The immigrant groups examined here are those who appeared most often as laborers in the records consulted, including the Chinese, southern Italians, and the diverse nationals of the Austro-Hungarian Empire, along with a sprinkling of others.[13] I am focusing on Alabama to explore immigrant laborers for two reasons. First, the post–Civil War industrial boom that spawned the Birmingham District generated sufficient pressure on the state's labor supply to inspire consistent recruitment campaigns by New South employers and officials. Such campaigns in Alabama appear to be similar to those carried out in other southern states. Although these crusades typically failed to bring in the great numbers that recruiters had envisioned, significant immigrant populations did arrive in the Birmingham District and in industries and communities sprinkled across the state.

Second, Birmingham's industrial employers, particularly the Tennessee Coal, Iron and Railroad Company (TCI) and the Sloss-Sheffield Company, relied extensively on convict labor, most often in the coal and ore mines. The lease system, which lasted well into the twentieth century in Alabama, generated a database of convict records, now digitized and accessible online. The availability of Alabama's convict records, along with digitized manuscript census records, immigration documents, and local newspapers, provides a unique opportunity both to identify national groups of immigrant laborers in New South Alabama and to trace individual immigrant experiences, including as convicts leased to industrial employers.

Until the post–World War II period, most African Americans in the United States clustered in the sweep of counties from North Carolina to east Texas, along that fertile crescent of tobacco, cotton, and sugarcane agriculture.[14] In the New South, immigrant recruitment campaigns aimed to suppress Black agency and mobility. If that failed, both planters and industrialists imagined that immigrants might replace Blacks entirely. Thus, the immigrant laborers who came to Alabama found themselves poised uncomfortably between white employers and the Black working class, a liminal and often precarious position. White officials, citizens, and employers might embrace immigrants when they acted in ways that sustained Jim Crow. When they directly challenged the political and economic power structures of the New South order, however, even European immigrants might find themselves ostracized, jailed, or worse.

This racial fluidity applied to Southern and Eastern Europeans as well as, at times, to Anglo-Saxon, Nordic, and Germanic nationalities, and even, to some extent, to Chinese immigrants. Such "racial transiency" was especially apparent when considering working-class immigrants in urban areas and/or those caught up in often violent labor conflicts.[15] Both industrial employers and union officials lauded the hardworking and noble character of immigrants when it suited their purposes, and both denigrated and racialized them when immigrant laborers acted independently and for their own reasons.

The development of the coal and iron industries in the larger Birmingham District created an immigrant experience akin to that found in other parts of the country, wherever railroad building, coal mining, iron ore mining, or timbering predominated.[16] *Resident Strangers* thus illustrates the diversity of working-class life in the New South. The Birmingham District alone, for example, boasted multiple nationalities in the mines, camps, and towns, some of whom lived near African American residents and some of whom lived in their own separate enclaves. Italian, Greek, and Syrian peddlers in the Birmingham area, for example, maintained businesses in Black neighborhoods and catered to a Black clientele but typically lived on separate streets or in different neighborhoods. And while Italians and Slovaks often maintained extended families, other groups, such as the Chinese, Montenegrins, and Bulgarians, typically lived as single men crowded into camps or boardinghouses.

Chapter 1 examines the myriad efforts to recruit immigrants across the Reconstruction and New South eras to remake southern agriculture and to expand production in Birmingham's mines and blast furnaces. Recruiters construed immigration as a key element in a multifaceted strategy to transform Alabama's plantation economy and to maximize employer leverage over Black labor. As African Americans in the deep South migrated within Alabama and to other locales outside the region and country, public officials collaborated with private interests across the period to recruit immigrants in response. They cloaked such naked opportunism, however, in a language that marketed the state as a tropical Eden by offering glowing portraits of job opportunities and land availability, all the while struggling to hide the reality of poverty, harsh conditions, labor conflict, and the ensnarement of debt peonage. And while New South employers typically lauded Northern and Western Europeans as the ideal immigrants, they were more than willing to sidestep their racial scruples if it meant procuring obedient and cheap labor.

Chapter 2 examines Chinese immigrants in Alabama to establish much of the pattern of how immigrant laborers experienced the New South. Around two thousand Chinese men arrived in Alabama in 1870 to work on the construction of railroads. The Chinese proved unpredictable as dependable gang laborers, more expensive to procure than expected and prone to self-assertion on their own behalf when obtained. In the face of mistreatment, all the Chinese railroad workers soon fled the state. However, dozens of Chinese men made their way independently to Alabama's small towns and cities, beginning in the 1880s, to establish small hand-washing laundries. As a very small community of single men providing an essential service, they often benefited from white customers and patronage. However, with an appearance, language, and cultural practices conspicuously different from those Alabamians around them, their racial identity also shifted between the poles of Black and white. The tenuous position of Chinese immigrants in the New South left them vulnerable to depredations from both Black and white residents.

Chapter 3 examines the pattern of Italian and African American encounters in the state's urban and industrial communities. Italian immigrants and Black southerners often met as competitors or as customer versus proprietor in the fruit and dry goods peddling markets of urban street corners. And they often conflicted or collaborated as replacement miners, strikers, and union members in the district's mines and labor conflicts. When they collided with African Americans with more secure connections to local structures of power, or when they challenged the economic status quo, Italian laborers forfeited white racial inclusion. Performing acts of racial solidarity against African Americans, however, or serving as replacement laborers during strikes, earned Italian laborers white sympathy or support. The unpredictability of their racial status meant that immigrant laborers weighed every choice against the repercussions of stepping onto or being assigned to one side of the color line or the other.

Chapter 4 investigates the role of immigrants in key labor disputes in the Birmingham District, particularly the pivotal strike of 1908. Imported initially as strikebreakers, Italian, Slavic, and other European laborers also joined with U.S.-born Black and white miners in walkouts over wages and conditions and to secure the recognition of the United Mine Workers (UMW) union. Their presence complicated the efforts of operators and union leaders alike to shape strike outcomes. Ultimately, immigrant laborers discovered that challenging the New South economic order by joining the UMW and/or labor strikes against coal operators touched off a storm of racial and ethnic scapegoating that especially underscored their racial insecurity in the New South.

Chapters 5 and 6 examine immigrants ensnared by the state's capricious legal system, emphasizing those who ended up in the jails and the state prison, in the convict lease, and as defendants in a key trial to emerge from the failed miners' strike of 1908. Alabama's employers often lured immigrants under false pretenses and levied on them intimidation, violent abuse, or even arrest if they resisted or tried to flee. Such miscarriages of justice derived both from their exploitation as laborers and their uncertain and shifting place in the racial taxonomy of power that defined the New South legal system. Recruiters sold immigration to Alabama as a pathway to opportunity, and for some it surely was. For many others, such as the immigrant defendants who shouldered much of the blame for key incidents of strike violence in 1908, a sojourn to the South proved a decision much regretted. And that outcome helped to explain why more immigrants did not move south.

Whether they were Chinese railroad or laundry workers, Italian peddlers, or, like Dolphina's two husbands, Slovakian miners, thousands of immigrant newcomers from around the world committed their labor to the New South project. Yet historians once assumed that the new immigration credited with transforming the United States in the late nineteenth and early twentieth centuries largely bypassed the states of the former Confederacy. A couple of scholars paused long enough to consider the recruitment campaigns, but all concluded that few immigrants came to the South in response, or at least not enough to warrant much attention to their actual experience.[17] As a new stream of immigrant laborers, particularly from Mexico and Central America, began entering southern communities in the 1990s, however, scholars began to pay increasing attention to immigration to the South as a historical phenomenon worthy of attention.[18] As the historiographies of U.S. labor and immigration history intersected along the axis of "whiteness," the South emerged as a useful location to explore the process of immigrant racialization. Rendered "foreign" because of complexion, religion, language, nationality, and/or cultural practices, even European immigrants who seemed to be "white on arrival" actually existed as "in-between" peoples suspended between the rigid Jim Crow poles of Black and white.[19]

More recently, historians have challenged both the "white on arrival" and the "in-between" theses as the most useful way to explain the texture and tone of immigrant life in the New South. Such studies have countered the tendency to understand immigrant history in the South as primarily a story of striving toward "whiteness."[20] In New Orleans, for example, Bengali peddlers shifted among multiple racial identities, performing an expected role as the exotic "Hindoo" to market their "Oriental" goods to white, middle-class consumers, claiming whiteness in order to push for citizenship, but disappearing as "Black" among African American neighborhoods and families to evade immigration officials.[21]

Likewise, "multiple contingencies" shaped Mexican immigrants' economic, social, and political positions in New Orleans and the Delta farmlands of Mississippi, Texas, and Arkansas. Arriving in the 1910s, for example, Mexicans in New Orleans defined themselves as European "whites" and successfully integrated into southern white society, helped by their own middle-class background and the city's historic Spanish roots. When cast in the role of migrant agricultural laborers on Delta plantations, however, Mexicans struggled harder and longer, claiming "whiteness" to improve their social integration but rarely gaining economic security or advancement.[22]

Jessica Jackson identifies the racial fluidity among the New South's immigrant communities as "racial transiency," defined as the ability to move—or being moved by others—back and forth across the color line between Black and white. In examining the case of the Gulf South, particularly in Louisiana, Jackson concludes that Sicilians and other southern Italians exhibited a "racial flexibility" that cast them as white southerners in one context but as "people of color" in another. These Italians exercised some of the legal and political rights of white citizenship, such as voting, and might be construed by white southerners as "good citizens." However, their challenges to Jim Crow taboos and practices, such as by marrying Black residents or protesting disfranchisement, prompted their racialization as "degenerate" and "undesirable aliens." Thus, Sicilians in the New South, Jackson concludes, might be "both privileged as 'white' Italians and marginalized . . . as racially suspect 'dagoes.'" An established position as business proprietors in New Orleans, for example, did not prevent local whites from lynching Sicilians in 1891, nor did it impede their subsequent marginalization.[23]

Racial fluidity aptly applies to the case of immigrant laborers in New South Alabama. Whether they were digging the track lines for the Alabama and Chattanooga (AL-CH) Railroad, peddling fruit and dry goods in Alabama towns, washing the New South's dirty linens, sweating in Birmingham's mines, or languishing in the state's jails and prison, immigrant laborers in Alabama experienced "racial transiency," both by self-assertion and by imposition. Their racial identities fluctuated along with their usefulness to the New South project and the extent to which they accommodated or resisted the New South order.

Historians have long argued that the New South had much in common with the Old South.[24] *Resident Strangers* demonstrates just how much the New South had in common with the rest of the United States, as the forces of industrial capitalism, immigration, and empire transformed the nation and its reach in the world. In rejecting the suitability of free and independent Black labor, and in their frenzied search for the "perfect" replacement, Alabama employers had much in common with American and British imperialists who considered "indigenous labor" unsuitable for building the Panama Canal or for harvesting the sugarcane of the "tropics."[25] Fluctuations in European bond markets, especially in the 1870s, undermined the stability of financing for New South railroad projects and undercut public financing of immigration campaigns.[26] The long-established citrus trade between New Orleans and Sicily brought scores of Italians to Louisiana sugar plantations as well as to the mills and mines of Birmingham.[27] Labor agents from around the world circulated among deep South communities to lure African American farmhands for plantations to the West and abroad, even as white southerners sent recruiters to England, Germany, Scandinavia, and China in search of the "best" workers.

Thus, the New South was not a region isolated from the forces at work across the nation or in the rest of the world. Immigrant laborers brought home to Alabama the turbulent world of empire-building, as their presence and their agency complicated racial categorization, disrupted labor relations, and diversified southern communities. Focusing the lens on Alabama's immigrant laborers renders the New South as deeply embedded in national and global networks of finance, trade, and labor migration.

To get to Alabama in 1897, Dolphina boarded a Southern Railway train in New York and traveled south through Philadelphia, Baltimore, Washington, DC, Virginia, and the Carolinas before cutting through the heart of Atlanta and heading due west for around 110 miles to Birmingham.[28] At the Birmingham depot, Dolphina switched from the Southern Railway to a Georgia Pacific railcar that only departed from Birmingham once a day, arriving at the Brookside depot at 11:00 p.m. each night. Along the way, Dolphina passed "massive beehive ovens" that constantly "expelled foul gasses" to turn millions of tons of coal into coke. Like many visitors who arrived in the district by night, Dolphina saw a glowing red skyline that made Birmingham seem, as many recalled, a lot more "like hell from a railroad train" than "a heavenly place to live."[29] But the coal that gave north-central Alabama its industrial character actually dated to an earlier era.

At least six decades or more prior to Dolphina's arrival, white interlopers on Creek Indian lands knew of the coal and ore in north-central Alabama's Jones Valley. A veteran of Andrew Jackson's army during the War of 1812, David Hanby orchestrated the collection of coal from streams on his land near Pinson, Alabama, where he hired "large crews to pry lumps of coal from the bed of the Warrior River and floated eight to ten polar flatboats over rough shoals to market in Mobile, where he sold his coal for $4 to $7 a ton," accumulating as much as $6,000 per year. Publication of antebellum geological surveys of Jones Valley and Red Mountain spurred speculators, planters, and entrepreneurs in 1854 to hold a "barbecue" in order to gather the pledges of "money and slave labor to assist with railroad construction through Jones Valley."[30]

The coal lay in three mineral fields, from the great Warrior field, consisting of three thousand square miles of "high quality bituminous coal," to the smaller but still significant bituminous seams in the Cahaba and Coosa coalfields. In the middle of the district loomed Red Mountain, a giant deposit of "hematite red ore" with a 70 percent iron content. Along with the close proximity of flux agents such as limestone and dolomite, the district held all the ingredients "for the iron and steel-making process."[31]

The outbreak of the war initially disrupted developers' plans, but Confederate military demand stimulated new industrial development. Private investors collaborated with Confederate officials to construct blast furnaces and iron rolling mills, creating a nascent "industrial wartime economy which made Alabama the 'Arsenal of the Confederacy.'" In the furnaces of Tannehill, Oxmoor, and Ferndale, enslaved people provided much of that labor. Such industrial productivity, naturally, also made these sites military targets. Union troops burned Tannehill as well as "all iron-producing operations in Jefferson and Shelby counties," ultimately destroying sixteen of the seventeen known furnaces in operation. Rousseau's Union raiders also destroyed railroad tracks in central Alabama.[32]

After the war ended, in 1865, tapping the wealth of bituminous coal, hematite ore, limestone, and dolomite seams that spread across Jones Valley required labor, and plenty of it. Prior to emancipation, Alabama's mineral speculators typically leased enslaved people from Black Belt farms and plantations for off-season work digging out the coal and ore that lay just beneath the surface of slopes and creeks. An exception was planter and entrepreneur Robert Jemison Jr., who early on committed enslaved people to full-time mining of Jones Valley coal.[33]

Whether enslaved miners worked seasonally or year-round before the war, however, emancipation produced a new and chaotic labor environment. The urgent need for agricultural recovery *and* industrial development after the war put a premium on securing labor that could be worked hard, for long days, at low wages. In this context, Alabama's employers constantly worried about procuring the quantity and "quality" of labor needed to convert minerals in the ground to profits in the bank. Ordinances, codes, and laws to restrict the mobility of Black labor developed alongside schemes to recruit American and foreign-born laborers, both to discipline Black agricultural labor and to feed the booming mines and mills of the Birmingham industrial district.[34] Slovakians such as Dolphina Lesko ended up in Birmingham as part of this larger campaign to diversify Alabama's agricultural economy by converting the state's mineral district into a leading pig iron and steel producer.

By the time Dolphina appeared in Brookside, industrial capitalism had already transformed much of the rest of the United States, either directly through the development of mines, mills, and factories, or indirectly through timbering of the nation's old-growth forests, the rapid commercialization of farming, and the rise of agribusiness in the West. As in Alabama, railroad expansion spurred industrialization and vice versa. Once laborers drove the ceremonial last spike into the transcontinental railroad in 1869, track laying exploded. Workers built 125,000 miles of new railroad line by 1894, thereby creating the "most extensive transportation system in the world," a network that included the Alabama and Chattanooga Railroad and eventually the Southern and the Louisville and Nashville railroads. Together, these major railroads and their many feeder lines facilitated the development of the Birmingham District by providing a local market for coal and pig iron as well as transportation connecting the district's coal, coke, pig iron, and steel to regional, national, and foreign markets. Building railroads, of course, required timber, coal, iron, and steel, and train cars carried industrial and agricultural products to customers within the United States and to ports of departure for markets overseas.

Birmingham's industrial boom appears unusual only in comparison to the relatively scarce heavy industrial development across the rest of the deep South. Aside from the industrial corridor that extended north from Birmingham into the Chattanooga area of Tennessee, and the coal mining that transformed pockets of mountain communities in Kentucky, Tennessee, and the Virginias, textile mills remained the primary industry across much of the rest of the South wherever cotton, tobacco, or sugarcane plantations and farms did not predominate.[35]

America's industrial boom needed far more labor than the nation's struggling farms and rural towns could provide. As industrial capitalism destabilized economies and communities across the globe, displaced populations, along with adventurers, created a massive transfer of labor power across the Atlantic and Pacific Oceans, constituting one of the largest waves of immigration in world history. Between 1880 and 1920, more than 25 million immigrants left their farms, workshops, and mills across multiple continents for the United States. By the end of the nineteenth century and well into the early twentieth century, Southern and Eastern Europeans such as Dolphina and her two husbands increasingly outnumbered all other sending populations. Millions of Italians and Slavic peoples, more than a million Mexicans, "hundreds of thousands" of Chinese and "Hungarians, Greeks, Armenians, Syrians, Turks, Christian Arabs, Bulgarians, Latin Americans, Portuguese, and French Canadians," along with Russians, Ukrainians, Brits, Scots, Irish, and Welsh, fed into the industrial boom transforming the United States, including into the Birmingham District.[36] Along with U.S.-born white and Black workers, these newcomers were the real backbone of the Birmingham boom. Alabama's white elites may have envisioned it and gathered their investors, but it was these laborers who made it all work.

The Brookside community that Dolphina ultimately claimed as home emerged as one of many mining camps and towns that populated the Birmingham mineral district in the late nineteenth and early twentieth centuries. The Sloss Furnaces Brookside operation was one of its most productive coal mines, and a more mechanized one than elsewhere in the district. By the mid-1890s, around two thousand people, mostly U.S.-born Blacks and whites, lived in Brookside; however, Dolphina's Slovaks, along with workers from "Greece, Hungary, Italy, Poland, and Russia," had diversified the resident population by the late 1890s.[37]

Although coal and iron camps, villages, and towns differed in individual character and size, life in the southern Appalachian mineral fields was characterized by similarity. The coal, iron ore, and steel operators of the Birmingham District, much like those in Kentucky, Pennsylvania, Tennessee, Virginia, and West Virginia, employed ethnically and racially diverse workforces.[38] Some immigrants worked in the mines or mills while others pursued alternative occupations, often by providing goods and services to the district's thousands of industrial workers. Company towns and camps typically segregated communities of U.S.-born whites, U.S.-born Blacks, and foreign-born immigrants, and the latter groups preferred to live in close proximity to people who spoke the same language and practiced the same or similar religion—and who often hailed from the same villages, towns, or provinces in the old country.[39]

Some immigrants found living in the district too hard or bewildering, choosing to return to the old country or to relocate to other American locations, particularly in the wake of violent labor disputes, economic recessions, or international wars.[40] Many others, such as Dolphina and her husband, Joe Latenosky, chose to remain in Birmingham, or returned after

Joseph Sylvester Latenosky of Brookside, Alabama, a Slovakian miner and Dolphina Lesko's third husband. The patriarch of the Latenosky family, he continued to work in the Birmingham mines until his untimely death in a mining accident around the age of seventy-three. *Photo and details courtesy of Lesko descendant Ceara Comeau-Rosello.*

sojourns elsewhere, staying on for the rest of their lives. As the district developed, immigrant neighborhoods blossomed in Bessemer, Blocton, Blossburg, Brighton, Brookside, Cardiff, East Birmingham, East Lake, Ensley, Fairfield, North Birmingham, Pratt City, Thomas, Woodward, and Wylam, among other locations. Dolphina's Brookside alone boasted several different immigrant groups, with the largest ones being Slovakian or Italian but also including French, Greek, Polish, and Russian families, along with U.S.-born whites and Blacks.[41]

The thousands of immigrants who came to the New South paled in comparison to the millions who flooded into places such as the Garment District on the Lower East Side of New York City, the meatpacking district of Chicago, or the railroad and mining projects of the trans-Mississippi

West.[42] But even given these relatively small numbers, immigrants shaped communities across the region. The immigrants largely discounted by most scholars as an important factor in Birmingham's industrial labor history, for example, helped to account for the defeat of the United Mine Workers in 1908. And the varied outcomes of their encounters with African Americans exposed the provisional nature of immigrant laborers' racial status in the New South.

Immigrant laborers both accommodated themselves to the racial and economic hierarchies of the New South and challenged their harsh exploitation by their Alabama employers. Their experiences were not simply adjacent to the New South story but intrinsic to its history. The immigrant story of New South Alabama was a national one, but it was also an inherently southern one. The stories of immigrants such as Dolphina Lesko make a strong case for the importance of *presence* over *absence,* and of *quality* of anecdote over *quantity* of numbers.

CHAPTER 1

"THE BONE AND SINEW OF OTHER STATES AND COUNTRIES"

Planters, Industrialists, and Immigrant Recruitment in New South Alabama

Two decades before Dolphina Lesko arrived in Brookside, an excited crowd of white businessmen, planters, and boosters from around north-central Alabama gathered in Birmingham on a September evening in 1875 to hear a speech by Colonel H. S. Hyatt, an immigration agent from Saint Louis. This "large and respectable number of the representative farmers of the county and businessmen of the city," reported the *Birmingham Iron Age,* were "anxious to hear" Colonel Hyatt's impressions after several days spent touring the state's nascent industrial district. The attendees anticipated "an interesting address" from the man who credited himself with "inducing Western immigration from the Eastern and Middle States" by those who were "now prepared to exchange a frozen climate with grass hoppers and expensive lands" for a better climate, good soil, and cheaper living.

Hyatt did not disappoint, proceeding to outline the "comparative advantages of climate and season in favor of the South" and noting that while the long winter disrupted productivity on the plains of the Midwest, in the South "every day can be utilized in work." "The economy of living" proved more favorable in Alabama, as well, due to "cheaper fuel, less expensive clothing, and rentals." Hyatt also cited his success in relocating "respectable" immigrants to Mississippi and western Alabama, who were then able to purchase "their farms and workshops," thus assuring his audience that "his business was not with paupers and wharf-rats, but only with men of substance."

Hyatt's message particularly resonated with a group of men representing the Elyton Land Company, a joint stock outfit devoted to profiting from Alabama's mineral resources. "Many of the stockholders of the Elyton Land Company," reported the newspaper, promptly decided to "confer with Col. Hyatt, with a view to obtaining his services through his western agencies to bring capital and skilled labor to our city and county." Accompanied by Birmingham industrialist Colonel Sloss, Hyatt soon departed for Kentucky for a meeting with railway officials "in regard to transportation of immigrants over their line." Colonel Hyatt, gushed the editor, soon would return to the West "fully impressed" that "no region in the United States presented such attractions for manufacturing" nor offered such a "genial, equable, and healthful climate," all the while providing "every element which makes iron . . . close at hand." In fact, Alabama would reward "the farmer, and the horticulturist, the skilled laborer and common mechanic, the stock and fruit raiser and all trades, avocations, and employments of life" for "their labors by a liberal increase."[1] Indeed, as Colonel Hyatt's experience seemed to validate, the world was postwar Alabama's oyster.

Immigration fever swept up planters, industrialists and speculators across the region, spurring recruitment campaigns in nearly every southern community, animated as much by anxiety as by an optimistic faith in the future. Alabama's political and economic leaders ultimately hoped to recruit sufficient immigration either to relieve them of dependence on Black laborers or to compel those laborers' obedience. Like other Americans in the late nineteenth and early twentieth centuries, they believed race and nationality determined temperament and character. Thus, recruiters justified immigration campaigns with a rhetoric that both denigrated African Americans and heralded Northern and Western Europeans as the ideal replacements. Such rhetoric and intent placed Alabama's recruiters in the company of employers confronted with the new reality of emancipation across the plantation world and of imperialists confounded by the difficulties of coercing native-born laborers.[2]

Ultimately, availability, a reputation for docility, and a willingness to work for meager wages in rough conditions differentiated a good prospect from an unsuitable one. Much like British and American imperialists who rejected "indigenous" labor as too fractious and unreliable, Alabama's employers looked to foreign-born settlers and laborers as vulnerable populations they could more easily exploit. Their racialized inclination to define Northern and Western Europeans as the most capable of contributing to the New South project remained in constant tension with their basic hunger for any laborer who was available, obedient, and subject to being coerced.[3]

Colonel Hyatt's exuberant vision in 1875 of what New South Alabama could be stood in sharp relief to reality on the ground. The ruination of the southern economy, along with the physical devastation caused by the Civil War, still made recovery a daunting mountain to climb. Union General James Wilson described north Alabama in 1865 as "complete destitution," with the "entire Tennessee valley" devoid of supplies "in all directions, for a hundred and twenty miles."[4] Marching armies had burned depots and cotton bales and destroyed steamboats, industrial mills, and iron furnaces. Approximately forty thousand Alabamians perished in the war, with another thirty-five thousand veterans returning as partially or permanently disabled. Emancipation brought welcome freedom to the state's enslaved people, who numbered about half of the population, but it also cost the economy more than $200 million in "capital investment." And the plantation labor system that had long sustained southern agriculture was tilted upside down. Whether or not they had been worked by enslaved labor, all farms felt the disruption of lost population, abandoned fields, ruined crops, and stolen or slaughtered livestock.[5]

Emancipation especially amplified white fears about the future. Alabama's white landowners had only to glance across the Gulf to Santo Domingo and the British Caribbean to find out what this rocky transition to free labor might mean: a hurricane of labor disruption that upset every stabilizing feature of plantation society, most notably the presence of a regular and coercible supply of labor.[6] Moreover, severe flooding caused the failure of corn and cotton crops in Alabama during the first years after the war, and several smallpox, cholera, and yellow fever outbreaks created additional hardship.

Nor did Alabama have much of an industrial base in 1865 to mitigate the slack in the agricultural economy. In 1860, only eleven railroads and around 743 miles of track traversed the state, and Union cavalry raiders had ripped up miles of rails in central Alabama during the war.[7] State officials recognized the expansion of railroads as the critical step in boosting the state's economic recovery, particularly to facilitate the development of mineral resources in the northern tier of the state. Reconstruction Governor William Smith endorsed more than $4 million in bonds for the construction of the Alabama and Chattanooga Railroad, which eventually cut across the state to Mississippi to create a new avenue for Gulf Coast shipping. Other railroad building proposals soon followed.[8]

Issuing bonds to build railroads addressed one question.[9] But who would lay the track? The freed people across the South refused to assume the mantle of anything that even hinted at unfree labor, and they were quite anxious to obtain land of their own, if at all possible.[10] Such hopes drifted onto fallow soil, however, under first an ineffectual economic Reconstruction and then the conservative resurgence that overturned Republican rule.[11] As factories boomed in the northeast; cotton and sugar cultivation expanded in Mississippi, Arkansas, and Louisiana; sawmills and timber camps took root in the upcountry, piney woods, and wiregrass regions; and westward settlement accelerated, the freed people seemed to have choices where there had been none at all for so long.[12] That mobility played a central role in augmenting southern white employers' sense of labor crisis.

From the late 1860s onward, rumors of African Americans plotting to leave their communities for the promise of more hospitable locales, or at least better opportunities, flew across the plantations of the deep South. Nor were such rumors completely unfounded.[13] Alabama, specifically, had the added context of the Birmingham industrial boom that began in the 1880s, exerting even more pressure on the stability of the rural agricultural labor supply throughout the New South era.

Census data do not document the sort of steep population decline in Black communities before World War I that the litany of white complaints about labor shortages would suggest.[14] Natural increase also added to the southern Black population. However, the decennial snapshot that the census took could not easily track the actual flow of people moving in and out of rural and urban communities.[15] It was this mobility, both perceived and real, that kept many a southern planter pacing the floors at night, worried about having no crop harvested at all if they could not deflate African American pressure for better terms. Black laborers moved into towns such as Montgomery or Birmingham, or to expanding cotton or sugar lands and sawmill and turpentine camps in deep South states such as Alabama, Florida, Georgia, Louisiana, and Mississippi, or to other parts of the United States or even other countries.[16]

A sustained and widespread transfer of Black southerners out of the region required better nonagricultural employment opportunities elsewhere, which did not develop extensively until World War I opened the floodgates for the Great Migration to the Northeast, Midwest, and West Coast.[17] Even prior to World War I, however, plenty of schemes to recruit Black labor away from southern farms and plantations generated among southern white employers and their allies a persistent interest in using immigrant laborers to replace Black laborers or to discipline them at home.

Across the New South era, labor agents worked to deliver Black bodies to employers in competing southern communities, western territories and states, and in a number of foreign countries. A common interest in locating cheap labor that could be controlled united planters around the world, even as it simultaneously set them in competition with each other.[18] Labor agents intent on luring laborers to farms, plantations, and camps as close as the Mississippi Delta and as far away as Hawaii circulated among clusters of Black populations.[19] A New York City newspaper in 1887, for example, described labor agents operating throughout the deep South to recruit Black laborers to help develop new agricultural bottomlands now protected by levees in the Mississippi Delta. According to the paper, agents tried to lure recruits with tales of the Yazoo Delta "as a veritable paradise; where labor was scarcely needed to produce crops." Hundreds of hopeful African Americans reportedly came into Vicksburg each day from the Mississippi hill country, but also from Alabama. The writer estimated that around twenty-five thousand African Americans had arrived in the Delta by January of 1887. Upcountry planters now looked to "get white labor from the West" or to tap the supply in poorer Black regions of Alabama, Georgia, and the Carolinas, "from which there is also a marked emigration movement just at present." Indeed, "at every station along the Vicksburg and Meridian Railroad there are negroes awaiting transportation westward."[20]

If Mississippi, Louisiana, or Arkansas seemed too much of the same old thing, there was always the mythic West. William A. Ash, a "prominent and influential colored man of Montgomery, Ala.," reported one newspaper, had in 1880 recently returned from a trip to investigate "how the colored people were getting along who have been flocking to Kansas from the south for three years." Ash planned to report "the facts to the colored people of Montgomery and Madison County, Ala. who are now desirous of emigrating to Kansas in large numbers." African Americans felt utterly disfranchised in the state of Alabama, Ash explained, and so "they must seek a new home where their labor would do more [and] where their political rights would be guarded and respected." In Kansas, it seemed, "the prospects before the colored people . . . were good." Drought had been a problem for the crops in 1880, yet African Americans in Saline County had acquired modest homesteads, "paying for the land in installments, and . . . building neat and comfortable homes of their own." In "Tennessee Town," "the country is dotted with little cottages that have been erected by the colored people, within two or three years, who are now living independently in their own homes [and] the men find employment." Ash thus expected "to see a thousand colored people emigrating from Madison and Montgomery counties, Alabama, next spring."[21]

In 1889, Alabama whites appeared to be "tremendously stirred up just now," according to the *Indianapolis Journal,* "over the tremendous exodus of negroes from the Black Belt . . . [as] railroad agents 'have been ticketing hundreds of negroes to the West.'" A white Black Belt Alabama landowner lamented to the writer in early 1889 that "he had not been able to get negro laborers on his place, and feared he would have to turn the fields out to grass." Reportedly, forty Black families had fled one Wiregrass county in southeastern Alabama on the same day, destined for Texas and joining others heading there, or to Louisiana or Mississippi. Moreover, "an agent of the Alabama Midland Railroad is here to-day trying to get up some negro laborers to work on that road, which is now in the course of construction from Bainbridge, Georgia." The Midland agent stopped first in Bulloch County but found that "an emigrant agent had been ahead of him and shipped all the surplus negroes to Texas."[22]

Labor agents and land speculators attempting to lure southern Blacks to the Delta or the Midwest competed with others who hoped to tap southern Black disaffection to populate plantations abroad. A U.S. State Department official wrote to Alabama's Governor Patton as early as the fall of 1866, for example, about reported "schemes" to "induce freedmen to emigrate to foreign countries, and particularly Peru," and indicating that "all legal and moral means at your command should be used to prevent" their success. The official then noted the attachment of "dispatches" from the U.S. consul in Peru, apparently verifying such claims.[23]

A California newspaper pointed in 1882 to the ready population of "able bodied temperate and industrious colored men" in the southern United States who would reportedly be "glad of the opportunity of settling in the [Hawaiian] Islands and raising cotton and sugar cane . . . as free tillers and in many cases as owners of the soil which they cultivated."[24] A Hawaiian planter named Armstrong agreed, believing that in the deep South, perhaps as many as five thousand African American field hands could be obtained, particularly if agents targeted those "living in localities that were not prosperous."[25] But as Birmingham industries began drawing laborers out of the fields, Alabama planters naturally disavowed their schemes. One Hawaiian planter who "tried to organize a scheme for the colonization of the Southern negroes" found "the plan was so strongly opposed by the producers of the South, who say that, with the fresh impetus recently given to the industries of that section, and with the large developments of all branches of Southern manufacture promised, it will be but a short time before they will need all the negro labor that can be obtained, so that I was obliged to drop the matter."[26]

At least some African Americans took up the challenge to relocate to areas within the United States, or even to plantations abroad.[27] Whereas Mississippi planters in an earlier decade had lauded the transfer of Black labor from Alabama, Georgia, and the Carolinas to the Delta, for example, the *Grenada Sentinel* reported in the late winter of 1891 that "the rush of people desiring to secure homes in the Iowa and Sac and Fox lands ceded to the Government has commenced. . . . A large number of negroes are coming with the intention of farming in the new country."[28] That same month, reports from Denison, Texas, found that "a large number of immigrant negroes passed through this city on Friday en route to the Cherokee strip. If they cannot get in there they intend to squat on the land of the Sac and Fox, which is reported to them as being open for settlement. . . . The colony was recruited in Arkansas and eastern Texas." The lead wagon in the convoy reportedly sported a sign that read "Free land for free men; peaceful measures if possible, but forcible if necessary. The Indians must go."[29]

Along with the exodus to the Delta and to the western territories stood the well-known effort to continue populating the African American colony of Liberia. Oftentimes, the "back-to-Africa" movements were little more than thinly disguised campaigns by racist whites, particularly northerners, to prevent an exodus of southern Blacks into their own states. But that was not always the case. Amid the Populist turmoil roiling much of the South by the mid-1890s, one group of African Americans from Alabama petitioned U.S. Congressional Representative Joseph Wheeler in February of 1894: "We the Collered people of this, the 8th Congressional District of Alabama beg of you to assist us . . . if possible to go to Africa. As we beleive [*sic*] that it would be better for both the Collerd and White people of America."[30]

Such sentiments—that anywhere "not here" would be an improvement over what was definitely known in southern communities—brought some African Americans not only to the Delta, Oklahoma, or Liberia but also to the South Pacific. In October 1882, the *Pacific Commercial Advertiser* documented the evening traffic through local saloons and gambling enterprises in Honolulu, recording the various nationalities frequenting the establishments. In one billiard and bagatelle room, the reporter noted, "the following different nationalities were counted by the bar tender among his customers, viz.—Hawaiians, Chinese, South Sea Islanders, North American Indians, *Southern Negroes,* Lascars, Japanese, Americans, Englishmen, Irishmen, Germans, Portuguese, Spaniards, and Swedes" (my emphasis).[31]

Clearly, the permanent relocation of thousands of "negro laborers" to Kansas, Nebraska, or Oklahoma, or to the Hawaiian sugar plantations, failed to materialize.[32] However, that did not prevent Alabama's planters and employers from worrying that those orders *might* be filled. The assertiveness of Black laborers who remained in Alabama, the continued reports of labor agents operating in the deep South, and the reality that some Black families did in fact relocate generated persistent worries about the availability and quality of agricultural and industrial labor. Rumors about labor agents recruiting in Alabama for the Panama Canal project in 1906, for example, prompted A. H. Woodward, the vice president of Woodward Iron Company in Birmingham, along with D. H. Bacon, superintendent of the Tennessee Coal, Iron and Railroad Company, to telegram U.S. Congressional Representative Oscar Underwood in January: "Agents of the government are in this territory securing labor for the Panama Canal," the men wrote. "We request your vigorous protest against this, as the result will be disastrous to the manufacturing and farming interests of Alabama." Within days, Woodward received a response from Underwood that such rumors were baseless. The chairman of the U.S. Canal Committee had assured Underwood that "he has no agent in our district securing labor and will have none." Woodward noted that this "is certainly agreeable news to us," and then blamed the editors of a Birmingham newspaper for publishing the rumor as fact.[33]

Motivated by their fears of both Black assertiveness and the possibility that Black emigrationism undermined agricultural and industrial prosperity, southern white planters and their business-industrial allies deployed diverse tactics to control Black labor, from enacting punitive crop lien laws and implementing the convict lease system to regulating, fining, and arresting labor recruiting agents.[34] When riled up about their labor supply, planters and their allies could be quite devious.[35] An attorney representing the grand jury of Mobile County reported to Reconstruction Governor William Smith in 1870 that "very many laborers are passing through Montgomery and Mobile to Louisiana and Texas being under written contracts voluntarily entered into to go there because of the high price paid for such service in these states." However, at the Mobile harbor, "these laborers are met by an organized committee of persons on the boats and after being talked to and led to believe that they are to be taken to Brazil and then to be sold into Slavery." They are then informed that "under the Civil Rights bill they are not bound to adhere to their contracts." As a result, "in many instances they have thus been enduced [*sic*] to leave their employers" who then "have on several occasions appealed to the Mayor who appealed to the City Attorney and Judge of the City Court for relief." But these officials had "indicated they were powerless to oppose it."[36]

As they lamented their labor woes, planters and industrialists both highlighted immigration as a means to address them.[37] White booster J. J. Giers wrote to Alabama's Governor Patton in 1866 of his "firm convictions" about the need for immigration to resolve labor issues. "Just as long as our former slaves have the *monopoly* of labor," he argued, "they will make us pay dearly for it." As a result, he noted, "another race of people will have to show them *how* to labor, and how to make it most profitable."[38] The editor of the *Memphis Daily Appeal* justified the desire for Chinese laborers by noting that the absence of Blacks "from the fields is now sorely felt by the planters," and "the lack of steadiness, and the frequent interruptions of the labor of men, tells powerfully in the general result of the crop." To prosper, the state needed "capital and labor—capital for commercial and railroad enterprises, and labor for our fields, workshops, and households."[39]

Another disgruntled planter explained to Governor Patton, in 1867, that he had accrued debts "created upon the strength of the Negro," and now "they have been taken from us." Moreover, "the freedmen refuse to work for us." Indeed, "thousands and thousands" of citizens of Alabama "have laid the plow aside, [and] where corn and cotton decorated large farms, now you behold weeds." Thus, he called upon the governor for assistance, proclaiming that "the Sons of Alabama are in distress" and "are at a lost [*sic*] to know what step to take."[40]

The editors of the Black Belt's *Montgomery Advertiser* frequently commented on the labor situation in Alabama across the era, often denigrating the suitability of African Americans for either agricultural or industrial work. In 1877, for example, the editors applauded a New York writer for publishing a piece that lamented the reportedly deplorable state of "southern negroes" in the plantation belt. "The negroes on the large cotton plantations have actually retrograded toward barbarism," proclaimed the writer, adding that they lacked any "industry" or "habits of thrift and ambition." Though the "negro" had all the physical qualifications for agricultural labor, particularly an ability to "endure the heat and trials of southern summer fieldwork more successfully than whites," nonetheless, "what he lacks in the moral incentive to labor." Thus, the *Advertiser* declared, the South would find salvation when the flow of European immigrants into the North and West was diverted to Alabama.[41] Three years later, the editors approvingly cited a "paper" by one Major St. Paul who argued for the value of French and Italian laborers "as the best and the most available source from which the soil of the South may be supplied with industrious and intelligent tillers." The day was coming, he concluded, when "negro labor as a permanent 'institution' cannot be relied upon."[42]

Alabama employers were an economically diverse group that included planters, farmers, merchants, and large and small industrialists, and they were not always unified about how to stabilize the labor supply. Black Belt planters might vacillate about whether African Americans would ever be a reliable source of productive labor, even as industrial operators welcomed them into the mines to suppress or oust striking miners. A correspondent for the *Courier Journal*, for example, investigated the burgeoning Birmingham District in 1880, finding "a ceaseless whirr of business and a rush of humanity perfectly astonishing." In the various coal and ore mines, he found both Black and white miners, with the former typically outnumbering the latter. He also concluded that "the negro makes a superb miner, and can earn from $1.25 to $3.00 per day." Operators appeared to favor them because "the negro is less liable to engage in strikes than the white miner," because he enjoyed no inclusion into trade unions for protection. "The negro is not admitted into membership in any of the leagues, and if he should engage in strikes he would soon starve, because he cannot expect relief from co-operative miners, as the whites do."[43]

A decade later, during a strike at the DeBardeleben Coal and Iron Company, mine superintendent Captain L. W. Johns remarked that "the employment of negro labor as miners is the solution of the strike problem as reached by his company." Johns claimed to be working three hundred African Americans in his Blue Creek mines, who were proving to be so productive that the company was "now getting all the negro labor they want" and shortly would "have their mines running with full forces."[44]

Nonetheless, southern white employers, including those in agriculture, commonly expressed anxiety and concern about either relying on or being without Black labor. "Big mule" industrialists and "branchhead" planters found a convergence of interests, if temporarily, in recruiting immigrant labor to discipline or replace Black labor in the fields, timber camps, or mines, or to make underperforming agricultural lands newly productive.[45] These efforts in Alabama reflected similar campaigns in communities across the New South, wherever employers, merchants, and planters relied on Black labor.[46]

Promotional efforts that began right after the war led to the establishment of a separate Bureau of Immigration, which later continued as a subagency within the bureaus of Agricultural and Industrial Resources. Appointed by the governor, state immigration commissioners spent a great deal of their time pressuring the legislature for more funds while trying to develop and circulate promotional literature advertising Alabama's available lands, mineral resources, and employment opportunities.[47] Given persistently scarce resources and the lasting impact of Reconstruction politics, the legislature never fully invested state funds in the recruitment movement. This reluctance forced governors and commissioners to rely on a hybrid of public and private efforts among state officials and planters, industrialists, land speculators, and railroads.

In 1868, Republican governor William Smith and the state legislature established the Bureau of Industrial Relations and, among other duties, charged it with developing a program to "encourage immigration."[48] Governor Smith then appointed Alabama resident C. G. Baylor as immigration commissioner to the northeast United States and Europe.[49] In 1876, Alabama's Governor George S. Houston appointed three new commissioners of immigration, who were to earn individual commissions by recruiting prospective immigrants to buy or lease individual farms.[50] Commissioners also traveled to examine Midwestern recruitment programs and pushed for schemes to list all available Alabama lands on official forms provided by the bureau. State officials published lists of lands for sale in local, regional, and national newspapers, sent them to immigrant aid societies, and responded to any individual inquiries they received. After a visit to the Midwest around 1878, Commissioner C. F. Seviers planned to develop a new network of county recruitment agents who would operate from a central Montgomery office. They would gather completed land-for-sale forms, accepting a small commission fee in the process, and then disseminate that information "throughout the North and the West." Once funded by a $5,000 state appropriation, Seviers wanted to establish Alabama immigration-land offices in states throughout the West, the Midwest, and the Northwest.[51]

One of the more spectacular booster campaigns was developed under Commissioner of Agriculture and later Populist leader and gubernatorial candidate Reuben Kolb. With the support of the Louisville and Nashville (L&N) Railroad, Kolb created a special railcar outfitted with signs and displays, as well traveling quarters, to promote Alabama's land, agricultural, and industrial resources. His "Alabama on Wheels" then embarked on a whirlwind rail tour of the Midwest and West, twice in 1888, where he allegedly found a robust appetite for all things Alabama.[52] Through a mix of state aid and private donations, Kolb supposedly distributed 25 million pages of literature on the state and its resources.[53] And even as late as 1905, a publication by the Anniston Real Estate Exchange and Farm Agency noted the assistance of the railroads that "will sell on the first and third Tuesdays of each month a land explorers ticket at about one fare for the round trip."[54]

Alabama immigration boosters also made use of outside parties with a vested interest in the issue. In 1869, for example, fifty-nine leading Alabama men determined to establish a "State Immigration Company" and held a June convention to which many counties sent delegates. There they heard plans from a number of private individuals to promote the sale of Alabama's "surplus lands" to immigrants at "advantageous prices" and to send immigration agents to Europe and the American West and Midwest. The effort soon produced the Alabama Agricultural and Mineral Society for the Encouragement of Immigration.[55]

Speculators worked to connect prospective immigrant settlers to planters and others who were advertising lands for sale. In the fall of 1870, for example, the Stevens and Clark Real Estate and Emigrants Agency sent a detailed circular to Governor Smith, highlighting available lands in Chambers, Lee, Russell, and Tallapoosa Counties, addressed to "the Farmers and Mechanics."[56] And the Alabama Land and Immigration Company, headquartered in Alabama but planning to open an additional office in Chicago, announced to Alabama Commissioner of Agriculture R. R. Poole, in 1905, its availability and their preparation to "intelligently handle the better class of immigrants by showing farm, timber and mineral lands which we have listed and are daily listing all over the state."[57]

Much of the urgency for immigration derived from the immediate need to make idle land more productive.[58] Amid the persistent poverty and underdevelopment that plagued Alabama well into the twentieth century, planters who had once worked their plantations with enslaved labor still had to pay taxes on land that either was not producing or was underperforming. In this calculation of priorities, cotton needed planting, and right away. Thus, in the first years after the war, as planters struggled to control the labor of freed people, immigration schemes often centered on simply finding farm laborers. For example, a Mr. Mellen of Selma notified Governor Patton in February of 1867 that "I've held a meeting here today of planters and others to see if some steps can be taken towards inducing foreigners to emigrate here . . . with a view towards a class of laborers to settle the state which will develop its resources."[59] A Mr. Ganier wrote to Governor Patton in the summer of 1867 to introduce two friends "who are on their way to Europe to procure laborers for Pickens County and all other portions to the state who may interest them with business." The American Emigrant Company of New England was formed in 1867 with the express purpose of providing "laborers to southern planters and other employers on a commission basis."[60]

In April 1870, state immigration commissioner Paul Strobach solicited the support of the Mobile and Montgomery Railroad in a scheme to bring a "hundred laborers" to Alabama by having the railroad advance them the cost of passage, guarantee those who signed up at least two years of labor at twenty-five dollars per month, and provide each family with eighty acres of ostensibly railroad lands in the state, upon completion of their contract. Alternatively, families could pay their own way to Alabama, reside on the eighty acres for three consecutive years, and receive free title to that land.[61] A few months later, the *Memphis Appeal* reported that "some of the farmers of Alabama . . . have already sent an agent for four hundred Germans, and will have them comfortably provided for in ample time." Moreover, "a ship load of German emigrant laborers have arrived at New Orleans."[62]

Although the initial impulse aimed to secure immigrants as farm laborers, some recruiters and rural entrepreneurs hoped to restructure plantation agriculture entirely.[63] Immigrant settlers, not just farmhands or sharecroppers, might resolve the problems that plagued southern plantation agriculture in a post-emancipation world, providing a wedge to split large landholdings into smaller, commercially oriented, independent farms. "The interests of [plantations] owners will be greatly promoted," proclaimed J. T. Trezevant of Memphis, "by subdividing them into small farms, and selling or leasing alternate ones to industrious and thrifty immigrants who will soon seek homes among us." After all, "the improvement of one farm will add to the value of another."[64] In February 1867, one writer to Governor Patton called for immigration to "fill our vast and depopulated South," and mentioned the need for state agents to provide information regarding lands that Alabama planters and others wanted to sell.[65]

A few months later, J. T. Bernard, founder of the Southern Land and Immigration Company of Tallahassee, Florida, wrote to Governor Patton in response to the governor's recent editorial in a Mobile newspaper highlighting the need for immigration to the state. "I have concluded to send you one of our circulars," Bernard explained, "so that we may be of mutual service." More than anything, he noted "a revolution in our present system of labor" was essential "to introduce white labor in the South." Specifically, "suitable inducements must be held out to the immigrant by offering him lands at a low price," obtained by subdivision: "Our large plantations must be divided into small farms, . . . which could be sold or leased for a term of years."[66] Thus, immigrants would provide a ready market for arable lands, a market that Alabama's officials, planters, speculators, and others did not believe could, or should, be found among the state's freed people. All Alabama needed, concluded one recruiter, was the "hardy, industrious emigrant, whatever his nationality, or whatever section of the Union he may come."[67]

Beginning with the establishment of the German colony of Cullman in north Alabama in the 1870s and 1880s, several small European farming communities grew out along the trajectory of the L&N Railroad and the connecting lines across the state during the New South period. Typically, a particular national group relocated from the Northeast or Midwest anchored each colony, such as the Germans in Cullman, Scandinavians in Thorsby and Silverhill, and Italians in Daphne along the Gulf. Other nationalities soon filtered in to join the U.S.-born white and Black farmers there as well. Individual immigrant farm owners initially attempted to develop a mixed agricultural base, particularly focusing on cultivating fruit and vegetables for commercial markets. Italian growers in Baldwin County along the Gulf and in the rural areas of the Birmingham District proved most successful at developing truck gardening in the state. More common seems to have been the experience of Cullman, where cotton proved to be the most successful crop, thereby wedding the community thoroughly to regional agricultural tradition.[68]

Even as European and American imperialists increasingly construed tropical locales as vectors of disease and lassitude, immigration boosters advertised Alabama's climate, lands, and opportunities in nearly exotic terms, marketing Alabama as a "paradise," a place of arable lands and an ideal climate that promised bountiful rewards for anyone with capital or brawn and a lot of fortitude.[69] Yet robust and transformative immigrant colonies failed to materialize in the Alabama countryside on the scale recruiters and planters envisioned. The unpredictable weather, ghastly summer heat, constant threat of malaria, and a nearly despotic credit system undoubtedly proved a bitter pill to swallow. And those without the means to purchase land or to rent farms found conditions as farm laborers especially unbearable.

Soon after the Civil War ended, for example, a brief experiment by one

Alabama planter with Swedish immigrants ended ignobly within mere days when the planter housed the thirty men "in slave cabins and fed them the usual rations." Not surprisingly, "within a week the laborers had departed," having "informed him 'they were not slaves.'" A few years later, the British consul of New Orleans commented on the reluctance of immigrants to remain on southern plantations, noting that "a labourer is a labourer . . . whether he be French or German, Italian or Norwegian, British or Chinese, he is to be housed, fed, [and] treated as the Black race used to be."[70] Thus, while a sprinkling of immigrant farming colonies sprang up in Alabama, few lasted more than a few years. Neither immigrant settlers nor farm laborers would be sufficient to restructure the state's plantation model.

Planters and their merchant allies, however, were not the only ones interested in using immigrants to fill the gaps in the labor force or to deploy against African American independence. Unlike the rest of the region, Alabama developed a booming industrial center, beginning in the 1880s, which exerted additional pressure on the labor supply by attracting Black southerners intent on escaping the depressed conditions on the state's farms and plantations. As industrial laborers in the mining district, however, African Americans proved no more quiescent than they had been on the plantations. Whether serving as free or convict miners, as union members or strikers, Black laborers confounded the efforts of industrial operators to control them. Alabama's industrialists also turned to immigrant labor as a way to maintain or expand productivity without unduly antagonizing Black Belt planters.

W. Battaile of Mobile advertised in a newspaper his Foreign Immigration/Real Estate and Labor Agency: "I am prepared to furnish European laborers to Planters, Railroads, Salt Works, Iron and Coal Mines, Turpentine Works, Sawmills, Steamboats, Housekeepers, and Hotels, at short notice, in any number, on favorable terms, delivered here or in New Orleans."[71] Mellen wrote to Governor Patton that "Railroads and Emigrants for the state are most needed . . . I have lived several years in Ohio and watching the progress of Railroads in the West we have seen that every new Railroad has to develop the country enriching the value of its land." Another writer, in 1867, called on Patton to appoint a state geologist to promote the state's mineral resources, mentioning Patton's intent to invite "the labor and capital of the world to aid in the development of the wonderful resources of Alabama." Thomas Stephenson, thirty-six years old and English by birth, offered his services to Governor Patton that fall to recruit skilled labor from England's manufacturing and agricultural districts. That same month, a labor agent acting on behalf of a coal mine owner in Saint Clair County solicited the governor's support in a scheme to recruit Germans.[72]

With the completion of major railway arteries through the northern tier of the state by the late 1870s and early 1880s, the development of the state's coal and mineral fields finally accelerated.[73] The development of the Birmingham mineral district through its coal and iron ore mines and pig iron furnaces, however, also brought the labor strife that frequently disrupted industrial production.[74] In this context, industrialists joined planters to push for increased immigration. "WORKING MEN WANTED" trumpeted the *Pine Belt News* of rural Brewton County in September of 1897. "Birmingham District Reports a Scarcity of Laborers [for] The First Time in Seven Years." Reportedly due to the "unprecedented demand" for Alabama coal and pig iron, the district's mines and furnaces lacked "sufficient available labor" to "meet the demands," even though "there is not a strike or labor trouble of any kind in the state." However, labor strife "north of the Ohio river," along with "increased demands for Alabama iron in Europe," created increased pressure to find adequate labor. As a result, "coal mines and furnace operators are advertising for labor to meet the requirements of the situation and labor agents are being placed in the field."[75] Ernest Hive wrote from Huntsville to U.S. Representative Joseph Wheeler in 1898, for example, that "my cousin, Mr. Fred Sloss of Birmingham, will join me [here] under the fine name of Sloss and Mine, for the purpose of doing a Real Estate business and especially with the intent of inducing immigration."[76]

Ross Smith, commissioner of the Immigration and Industrial Association of Alabama, spelled out clearly for R. A. Mitchell of Alexander City the problem Alabama faced by the turn of the twentieth century: "The industrial sections have drawn very heavily upon the farmers, until now neither the farmers nor the industries have anything like adequate labor." Thus, Smith informed Governor Jelks that he had heard from several manufacturers who wanted to subscribe funds for the immigration campaign, including "a reasonable amount of money."[77] That same year (1905), the Immigration and Industrial Association produced an "application for labor" for prospective employers to complete. The first section stated "nationality preferred" but also provided an option to indicate one's second choice, or even to note that the applicant "would take any nationality." Both agricultural and industrial employers could make use of the application, though no record exists to indicate who actually did so.[78] In 1906, Governor Jelks took "a representative body of men from Birmingham and other places in Alabama" to Ellis Island in New York City "to study the immigration question." There, they witnessed "1,000 people unloaded from a ship from Hamburg," promptly concluding that "not one unloaded from this ship . . . would not have been acceptable to the people of Alabama."[79]

When Alabama's industrial employers joined planters to decry the "very serious labor situation" or the low productivity of too much of Alabama's agricultural lands, they saw in the stream of immigrants arriving in the United States the "right sort" of people, who could set the situation straight. But who did they mean, exactly? A massive wave of immigration from Southern and Eastern Europe, Mexico and the Americas, and Asia poured into the nation's factories and mills and spilled across the western United States after the Civil War, spurring anxiety among many U.S.-born Americans, as well as northern and western immigrants who had arrived much earlier, about the composition of a rapidly diversifying republic.

Under the influence of the scientific racism and ethnology of the age, Americans differentiated European nationalities by racialized character traits, segmenting the labor market by ethnicity and deeming some groups suitable for citizenship and others wholly undesirable. Thus, according to one scholar, white Americans distinguished between "superior" whites and "inferior" Blacks, Asians, and Latinx but also imposed varying degrees of civic suitability upon "Hebrews, Celts, Slavs, Finns, Italians, Teutons, Magyars, and Anglo-Saxons." Industrial employers, especially, applied this "racial typing," which rated the "particular 'racial' character" of various nationalities in reference to stereotyped expectations of job performance, applying such traits as "inherent tractability," "laziness," or "unruliness" to entire nationalities.[80] Alabama's recruiters and employers similarly imagined German, Scandinavian, Canadian, or British laborers or settlers to be capable of transitioning into landowning citizens without upsetting racial hierarchies. They did not regard the Chinese who moved into Alabama communities, or Italian, Greek, Slavic, or Syrian laborers, in the same way, but any of these groups were suitable as laborers if they were vulnerable enough to be recruited and exploited.

Thus, the New South's labor recruiters applied a highly racialized filter to the new immigration, which initially favored Northern and Western Europeans.[81] Such racial preconceptions reflected the deep-seated belief in the inferiority of Black labor, but also a conviction that certain European groups possessed positive racial-cultural traits that justified the expense and work of recruiting them.[82] As a result, most of Alabama's immigration recruiters emphasized people from the British Isles, Germania, or Scandinavia as the most welcome and, in their own imaginations at least, the most likely to succeed in the New South.

In 1866, immigration recruiter J. J. Giers pledged to Governor Patton that he would "go to New York and present the superior claims of our state for German immigration, to the leading . . . capitalists and shipowners."[83] In 1870, a few years later, the Allen Brothers of the Memphis Immigration Association proudly announced the arrival of "its first installment of WHITE IMMIGRANTS, consisting of able-bodied men of Teutonic and Scandinavian origin."[84] Mellen hoped to expand Alabama's railroad network, in part because railroads "will bring Emigration especially . . . of the class of laborers [of] Germans and Irish which have done so much to develop and improve the Northern states particularly the West." In applying to Governor Patton for an appointment as a recruitment agent, A. S. Tikes proclaimed his credentials: "I am thoroughly acquainted with the German language and have been a resident of this city for more than thirty years." Jonathan Gill Shorter of Eufaula endorsed another person to serve as an immigration agent, pointing out his ability to recruit from Scotland. However, William Byrd of Selma endorsed Robert Philpot for an appointment because he had lived in Germany for a year and spoke both German and French.[85] From Mobile in March of 1870, C. C. Pomeroy wrote Alabama's Governor Smith about becoming a state immigration commissioner, specifically for England and Scotland.[86] And W. T. Thompson notified immigration commissioner R. R. Poole, in 1905, that "there is some of us that will sell or lease our lands just any way to get our own country settled up with a good class of white people."[87]

Like U.S.-born citizens elsewhere, whites in Alabama typically drew these clear distinctions among European nationalities and classes along an ethnocentric spectrum from desirable to undesirable traits. But embattled planters and employers, particularly industrialists, also could be far less circumspect, prioritizing their desire for *obedient* labor as the paramount concern.[88] Ultimately, they were after warm bodies who were *not* Black laborers already engaged in sharecropping, domestic service, or as convict or free labor in the mines or lumber camps. What mattered the most was an immigrant's willingness to labor in an "industrious" and dutiful manner for low wages in harsh conditions. And the likelihood of that, in many cases, appeared to stem from the conditions in certain European countries that created impoverished and oppressed populations so anxious to escape that they would be willing to submit to less-than-ideal terms. Indeed, Alabama's employers appeared as besotted with an immigrant group's vulnerability as with its reputation.

Charles Hamacher wrote to Governor Patton from Saint Louis in 1867 to report on his immigrant recruitment efforts, noting that he had recently directed "some farmers" to Alabama booster J. J. Giers and pledging to "keep on sending over every farm hand which cannot get labor here." He especially hoped to target Germans, as "the services of the German farmer are valuable, for he is well-known as . . . a subservient and steady work man." In fact, he explained, without any apparent sense of irony, "Germany is so overpopulated and her laboring class is so poor, that a person brought up here in the United States has hardly any imagination of it." Moreover, "they are suppressed and kept down both by civil and military authorities and lead in short a most miserable life. No wonder they emigrate in such great numbers." After all, he continued, "they want to get a better home and a less despotic government—both is offered them here and therefore it is my opinion that a capable man has in Germany a right field to work upon." Indeed, "a man who is well known there, might induce a great many people to quit their pauper homes and seek a new and better one in Alabama."[89] F. S. Mount made a similar point when he also wrote to Governor Patton in August the same year to detail his own scheme to encourage immigration to Alabama. Writing from Paris, Mount noted:

> I feel confident that there is no real difficulty in obtaining every kind of labor necessary for the wants of our people. . . . From the German state, including Prussia, the emigration will be greater this fall than ever before known. The prospect of war, which sometimes seems imminent between France and Prussia, and the absorption of the entire male population into the army, has given an impetus to immigration which will continue for years.[90]

Mount then explained that "a home on their arrival, with *immediate* employment, and the sale or exchange of labor at very moderate prices of a homestead," would be an effective inducement to encourage German immigration to the state.

When planter Jacob Thompson delivered his speech to the planters' convention in Memphis, he referenced the revolutionary upheaval in France in 1868 and/or the Franco-Prussian War of 1870 to 1871 to explain that "the disturbed state of civilized Europe for the last twelve months presents the propitious opportunity for us."

> France has been stirred to its very foundations. Blood, destruction, and devastation have swept over her plains and cities. Thousands upon thousands of her best people have been reduced to poverty and want, and these thousands, seeing no other hope in their own country, will now seek new homes. Germany, too, has felt the wasting effects of war. Want, growing out of neglect and loss of private fortunes, will drive thousands of hardy Germans to seek their fortunes in new homes and under other governments.[91]

Thompson, however, did not see opportunity only in the turmoil and suffering of Central Europeans in the wake of German unification. He also referenced "restless Ireland" and the discontented of Spain and Italy. Ultimately, though, he explained, "It is from the enterprising people of the Northern States [that] I look for the largest influx of immigrants of the description we need." This was because "there the population is dense and the lands are held at a high price" while "here the population is sparse and the lands are low."

If political turmoil in Europe played to the advantage of Alabama's immigration schemes, the violence and chaos that accompanied settlement of the American West might accomplish similar ends. Some of Alabama's boosters smelled opportunity among immigrant homesteads disrupted by the Indian wars of the West that were in full swing by 1870. A Mobile gentleman wrote to Governor Smith in July of 1870 pressing for publications about "the Health, Advantages, inducements, offers, and Security in Alabama to persons in Europe who may desire to immigrate." Alabama, he reiterated, needed "immigrants, intelligent and skilled laborers . . . in very large numbers." And now, he emphasized, was the time "for us to turn the tide in our state—now while the Indians are making the Western States objectionable to Immigrants—we can now start them toward us and develop . . . the State."[92]

Land and labor agent Paul Stevens likewise sought to promote central Alabama to western residents, many of them first-generation immigrants. He drew a contrast between the alleged "morality, virtue, and refinement" of Alabama's townships and what he believed existed in the West: "Compare this picture of model home comforts in our Southern sunny lands with the bleak and savage inhospitality of a home in the far west, beyond the pale of civilization," he argued, where people were "deprived of all church, school, and postal privileges, and continually harassed with the fear of attacks from the Indian savages."[93]

Immigration commissioner C. F. Seviers explained to the Alabama legislature in 1876 that "if labor is capital, and who will doubt it, how much better can we restore the once prosperous State of Alabama and put her on the road to wealth than by inviting the bone and sinew of other states and countries to come and participate with us in the rich soil and climate which is ours?"[94] L. D. Saxton and Company advertised in Memphis in 1870 their readiness to provide "experienced farmers or laborers to work upon shares or for wages," along with "mechanics of various trades, and Emigrants and other Laborers *of all nationalities,* for Farm, Railroad work and business purposes" (my emphasis).[95] Editors of the *Manufacturer's Record* wrote to Governor Jelks that "we believe that the question of Southern immigration should be on an absolute business basis, with the advancement of the South and its whole welfare as the main objects." As soon as possible, they wanted to see "direct work in other parts of the country and abroad" to obtain "immigrants who in bettering themselves by moving to the South will be likely to benefit the South and likely not to become either a burden or an influence for ill." While they did not approve of campaigns undertaken for purely "altruistic" reasons, still they noted a definite campaign in the U.S. Northeast and in Italy to direct Italian immigrants to the South.[96]

Delegates of the Alabama Light and Traction Association resolved, around 1910, that "thousands of steady laborers without employment and often without bread" had "overrun" the Eastern Seaboard, while "a need for these same laborers is felt in other parts." Thus, they resolved, "whereas the Southern States are in need of laborers of all character and description. . . .

We, the delegates of the Alabama Light and Traction Association, assembled in Birmingham November 15th and 16th, do memorialize our senators and members of Congress to pass such laws as are needful in procuring free transportation, and other assistance in placing these said immigrants where they are needed and can find work."[97]

The chairman of the Tennessee Coal, Iron and Railroad Company likewise wrote to Congressmen Oscar Underwood, in 1906, to weigh in on the congressman's statements regarding the restriction of immigration. The writer objected in strong terms to Underwood's attempts to categorize nationalities by their "suitability," along with virtually every other statement he had made in a recent speech. First, the writer disagreed with Underwood's assumption that the Scandinavian immigrants who peopled the Northwest had come to the United States to flee despotic governments. Rather, he noted that TCI's experience with its diverse workforce in the Birmingham coal district showed that "a very large proportion of the Swedes, Norwegians, Danes, and Finlanders . . . all spoke kindly of their government, and of the laws to which they were amenable, saying that they came to this country because they could earn money, and that they often return to their native country after accumulating what will afford them a comfortable support there." In fact, he explained, "Really we don't care a rap how poor the immigrant is, but we do want him to have a reasonably muscular body, good breathing and digestive apparatus, and willingness to work, and moral qualities and ideals that are reasonably close to our own." He then both validated the currency of racial stereotyping of immigrants and handily dismissed it at the same time, pointing out that "the man from Southern Italy, Sicily, and Sardinia is in vindictiveness, and willingness to kill from ambush or in the dark, equalled by natives of Alabama, Georgia, North Carolina, Tennessee, and Kentucky, whose ancestors were English who came here from one hundred to two hundred years ago." He then went on to specify the multiple nationalities of the 985 men employed at the Chapin mine, with the single largest group being more than three hundred Italians.[98]

Frank Evans, an agent for the Immigration and Industrial Association of Alabama headquartered in Birmingham (and New York), wrote to Underwood in opposition to his comments about immigration by the "Southern Italian." Underwood supported restricting immigration by way of imposing a "head tax" on certain immigrant groups, a proposal Evans vociferously opposed. "In truth there should be no tax upon any good man, woman, or child entering this country." Certainly, he conceded, immigration officials should examine "all immigrants" on their "education, health, financial condition, and general moral standing," but he implored Underwood, "in behalf of the state which you represent, and especially your district that you put no tax upon these people." Rather than taxing immigrants, he pointed out, "Canada offers a premium for them, and is being rapidly populated." Yet "your committee proposes a tax upon them which will certainly retard the progress of our section." Moreover, Evans claimed, "since my arrival in New York and opening my office here I have sent several hundred worthy people to Alabama and I am anxious to continue the good work."[99]

The editors of both the *Birmingham News* and the *Montgomery Advertiser* also pointed to the benefits of Italian immigration, noting that "something must be done or many thousand acres of land in Alabama will have to go uncultivated next year." As a result, "everything tending to attract Italian laborers to Alabama should be done," while eschewing "an indiscriminate horde of ignorant, lawless immigrants." But, they took pains to note, "energetic and law-abiding" Italians were welcome.[100] Perle Smith of Birmingham chimed in, telling Congressman Underwood she found his recent speech on "The Protection of American Labor" an "interesting one," since "we are now making a systematic effort to secure the 'right' kind of immigrants as laborers here in Alabama." She noted, "I have a cousin who has a large plantation in Mississippi and I know what a blessing Italian labor has been to him at a time when the necessary farm hands were simply not to be had."[101]

Alabama's immigration boosters invested significant time, energy, and hope in the belief that, as Perle Smith articulated, immigrant settlers and laborers would "bless" their communities by relieving them of dependence upon African Americans. The persistent mobility that Black Alabamians used to structure their lives and to exert their freedoms both exasperated and distressed white landowners and employers. As in other post-emancipation societies, Alabama's white elites discounted Black landowning and independence as viable solutions for a prosperous future, denigrating Black labor and construing immigration as a means for disciplining or replacing it. And in keeping with planters and imperialists in the Americas and other sections of the world, they turned to Europeans and Asians as a pool from which to draw, perceiving in both populations a vulnerability and availability they aimed to exploit. They might have preferred Germans, Scots, and Scandinavians, but ultimately they would take Italians, Greeks, Russians, and initially even the Chinese, if they filled the bill.

Attracting immigrant laborers, as well as settlers, however, ultimately proved to be an unpredictable endeavor. After all, people migrating from one location in the world to another, however desperate their need or strong their sense of adventure, and however "suitable" their ethnic or national pedigree, arrived with their own ideas about what the terms of their labor should be. The expectations of recruiters and their planter and industrialist clients soon collided with the aspirations of the single largest importation of Asians to work in the New South: a group of almost two thousand Chinese men brought to Alabama to help build the state's first industrial railroad, the linchpin of the development of the Birmingham mineral district.

CHAPTER 2

"JOHN CHINAMAN" IN NEW SOUTH ALABAMA

On an early summer morning in August 1893, just around sunrise, Chinese laundryman Charley Sing encountered an unknown and decidedly hostile person in his downtown business. Asleep on an ironing board in the back, Sing awoke to a noise that prompted him to investigate. According to the police, he then surprised a "large negro" who struck him on the head with a wooden billet, "without a word." The man fled when Sing began yelling loudly to attract other merchants opening up their own shops nearby. When they rushed to his aid, reported the *Tuskaloosa Gazette,* they found "our laundryman" lying in a pool of blood "from a tremendous blow" to the head. A quick search nearby for the assailant proved fruitless, so the men returned to the shop in time to hear Sing relay the details of his assault to the police officers "in his broken way." Dr. J. L. Faut, one of Tuscaloosa's white physicians, treated Sing's wounds and ordered the distraught man to bed for the next few days to recover. "Robbery was doubtless the object of the attack," concluded the reporter. If it had occurred at a different hour, Sing "would have been robbed or murdered, or perhaps both, before help could have reached him."[1]

County Marshal King soon arrested an African American man named Jerry Haley, who worked as a "plasterer" on the local "government works," and brought Haley "before Charley who said it was the negro who struck him. Charley said he had changed clothes, but he knew him all the same." The county court found Haley "not guilty" of assault and battery, in September 1893.[2]

No doubt traumatized, Sing departed Tuscaloosa a few weeks later for San Francisco to catch a ship to Canton, China. He planned to visit his wife for the first time since he had left, thirteen years earlier. He eventually returned to Tuscaloosa, some months later.[3]

Sing's story might have concluded with his return to his homeland. However, he ended up in the local news again a few years later when he suddenly married Mary Matthews, a young Black woman he employed in his laundry. The marriage of Tuscaloosa's token "Celestial Washerman" to a local African American woman might be sufficient to attract brief mention in the local paper, but this event proved to be "a very unique wedding," though not because it crossed any perceived racial lines. Rather, it took place in the county jail. Local authorities had served a warrant on Charley Sing and Mary Matthews, incarcerating both on an unspecified but "serious charge." Sing reportedly earned his release by confessing before a judge and paying a fine. Matthews, however, remained in jail under a longer sentence.

Upon his release, Sing immediately contacted local Black minister Reverend Zacariah Taylor. The pastor then visited the county probate judge and procured a marriage license for Sing under the alias of "Joe Simon," but with Mary Matthews specified as the bride. Taylor then accompanied Sing, license in hand, to the jail, where he received permission "to step around to the jail and speak to Mary who soon appeared, poked her little hand through the bars," and, with Reverend Taylor's betrothal, became a "Celestial's bride." When the licensing probate judge discovered he had issued a marriage license to a "Chinaman," however, he pronounced himself as "considerably astonished." Nor did chief clerk Williams have any "intimation that Joe Simon and Charley Sing were one and the same." Nonetheless, the marriage successfully concluded this "rather sensational matter." Although initially sentenced "in durance vile," meaning for a long prison sentence, Matthew's release came with her marriage to her Chinese employer and subsequent payment of costs.[4]

In the late nineteenth and early twentieth centuries, Alabama's miscegenation statutes prohibited sexual relations between people defined as "white" and those defined as "Black," "Negro," or "mulatto." Such statutes aimed to erect a fortress against the dilution of white racial "purity" (power), a threat posed by long-term relationships that might produce mixed-race children. Thus, the state of Alabama prohibited not only marriage but also adultery or fornication between Black and white people. Adding miscegenation to a charge of adultery or fornication raised the offense from a misdemeanor to a felony, with both parties, as well as anyone officiating the union, risking a prison sentence and two to seven years of hard labor for the county. However, Alabama law did not specify how people who really were neither white nor Black fit into this legal proscription.[5]

The union of Charley Sing and Mary Matthews could mean that Sing held a racial identity closer to Black, thus explaining his ability to resolve the "serious charge" of adultery or fornication by marrying Matthews and paying their fines. However, the case might also suggest that someone perceived their relationship as an illicit one, construing Sing and Matthews as being of different races. Yet Charley Sing easily avoided worse punishment, not through a trial but by marrying Mary Matthews, which actually rendered them both bigamists, since Sing presumably still had a wife in Canton. The ambiguities that surrounded the Sing–Matthews union testify to the shape-shifting nature of racial categorizations in the New South, particularly as a diverse crop of immigrant laborers began residing in local communities.

The case of Charley Sing also exemplifies how Alabama's Chinese residents lived in a state of racial fluidity, a sort of bouncing back and forth between the poles of white and nonwhite racial identity. On the one hand, Sing endured a solo and precarious life in Tuscaloosa, working long hours in his laundry business and living very far from his homeland. He lived in his place of business, where he likely also kept the money he saved to pay his meager expenses and to send funds home to his family in China. Although this did not apply to all Chinese laborers and businessmen in the South, it applied to enough of them to generate the widespread impression that *all* Chinese kept potentially large amounts of cash in their businesses. Targeting a Chinese laundry, however, meant that thieves often encountered someone while robbing the business. Charley Sing's trauma, unfortunately, proved to be a common one for Chinese immigrants in New South Alabama, as well as in other southern states.

Sing's case also reflects the demographic contours of the Chinese in Alabama, namely, that their overall numbers remained sufficiently small to lessen the sense of threat that their presence might pose in communities structured by racial hierarchies amid economic transition.[6] Across the census years from 1870 to 1940, enumerators typically recorded only a few dozen Chinese individuals in Alabama at any one time.[7] Moreover, Chinese laundries served a function for white working- and middle-class communities, and particularly for single men, who were increasingly removed from family participation in their upkeep as they migrated off rural farms into towns and cities. Thus, to white Tuscaloosa, Sing was "our Chinese laundryman," and the newspaper accounts that mentioned him over the years clearly assumed readers knew who the writer meant.

The long relationship between southern missionary Protestantism and China, producing the popular yet contradictory perception of the Chinese as both "heathens" and converted "Christians," also influenced where Alabama's Chinese landed on the spectrum between Black and white. Chinese immigrants played on those notions to their advantage when possible. Although no record exists to document whether Charley Sing regarded himself as a Christian, for example, he clearly had nurtured a relationship with Reverend Taylor, who assumed the risk of obtaining a fraudulent marriage license. Perhaps Taylor's connection was to Mary Matthews and her family; still, he clearly aided Sing in securing Mary's release from jail through the marriage.

The tensions between Chinese and Black residents in New South towns and cities, evident in the frequent robberies, assaults, and other negative encounters that appeared in local and regional newspapers, also could align Chinese immigrants with the interests of white racial solidarity. Thus, white downtown merchants rushed to Sing's aid when he was assaulted in his place of business, a white physician treated his wounds, and police accepted at face value his identification of a Black man as his assailant.

Charley Sing appeared to benefit from a paternalistic white benevolence in Tuscaloosa, maintaining a base of white customers, the support of neighboring white merchants, and, after the assault, the attentions of a white physician and law enforcement, and a relatively sympathetic account in the local press.[8] He occasionally merited mention for his social activities as well, such as for a visit paid him by his Selma friend, the "prominent Celestial citizen" Sam Lee, just prior to his return trip to China in late 1893. Yet even relatively positive accounts described Sing in one-dimensional terms bordering on the derogatory, such as "our Chinese laundryman" or "the Celestial Washerman." And his identification of Jerry Haley as the Black man who assaulted him did not produce a conviction, whereas his relationship with his Black female employee landed both of them in jail.

As Sing's case demonstrates, the racial position of New South Alabama's Chinese immigrants ricocheted between racist white approbation as providers of useful drudgery labor and as Christian "converts," on one end, and as objects of resentment from African Americans as economic competitors or employers, on the other.[9] For Charley Sing and many other Chinese immigrants, experiencing New South Alabama thus meant maintaining an unpredictable footing in the shifting sands of racial and economic inclusion in the New South project.

Laboring in the infrastructure projects and service economy proved even rougher and more demeaning for Chinese workers in the American West, characterized by the intense exploitation, brutal conditions, and rampant anti-Chinese violence that accompanied the construction of the American "continental empire."[10] Still, the endurance and grit of Chinese railroad workers on the transcontinental railroad project astonished observers and employers alike. Moreover, Chinese railroad workers leveraged their importance as available and hardy laborers to demand more humane treatment by launching a failed strike in 1867.[11] That same resilience characterized the Chinese immigrant experience in New South Alabama, as railroad workers in the Birmingham District in 1870, and as Chinese laundrymen such as Charley Sing later carved out an economic niche in other New South communities. The transience of their racial identity in the New South allowed Alabama's Chinese residents a modicum more opportunity and agency than might be found in the West or Northeast. However, American xenophobia and southern Jim Crow still rendered their status insecure and vulnerable to victimization.[12]

Chinese nationals arrived in Alabama as early as the 1840s and 1850s, including visits to Tuscaloosa, through contacts with Protestant missionaries and as entertainers.[13] Elite white southerners also knew of the role played by Chinese laborers working in agricultural empires, particularly in the British colonies of the Caribbean.[14] The utilization of Chinese men as indentured laborers alongside enslaved Africans in Cuba drew the attention of southern white planters in the United States as the sectional crisis erupted into Civil War.[15] Under the leadership of the Republicans, Congress enacted the "Act to Prohibit the 'Coolie Trade' by American Citizens in American Vessels in 1862." The act forbade the transport of forced laborers by American vessels from China to Cuba, essentially barring American involvement in the transportation end of the "coolie trade." However, the act actually transformed the Chinese from the unfree "coolie" into the "voluntary immigrant," opening the door to their importation into the United States as laborers.[16]

The interest in Chinese laborers connected Alabama's planters and industrialists to a global community of coercion directed by agricultural imperialists to procure and secure laborers in response to emancipations.[17] Enforcement of the 1862 act, as well as of the later Foran Contract Labor Law, remained lax, allowing Chinese migrants to develop creative means to make it to the United States anyway, often by railway via Mexico or Canada. The recruitment of Chinese laborers to the deep South proceeded after the war, if under rather ambiguous terms.[18]

The Chinese men who came to the United States in the mid- to late nineteenth century typically originated in China's southeastern provinces, especially from the Pearl River Delta region of Guangdong, including the enclave of Canton (now known as Guangzhou), Charley Sing's hometown. Multiple factors pushed millions of Chinese such as Sing, mostly men but also some women, into the global diaspora in the nineteenth and early twentieth centuries. As the British suppressed the African slave trade in the early nineteenth century, a market for "coolie" labor developed by midcentury, especially for sugar plantations in the Caribbean.[19]

The Opium Wars and the subsequent capitulation of the Qing Dynasty to British demands further liberalized Chinese immigration.[20] Massive flooding in the 1850s also uprooted millions of peasants, who joined the Triad, Nian, Turban, and Taiping rebellions against the Qing rulers. The last of these insurgencies, among Muslim fundamentalists in Shaanxi and Gansu, only ended in 1872. The founding of the Taiping Heavenly Kingdom in 1851, however, proved to be the single most devastating event. The Taiping Rebellion produced a decade of civil war that caused the deaths of more than 50 million people from warfare, famine, and disease, possibly constituting the most destructive and bloodiest civil war in world history.[21]

Such turmoil propelled many Chinese men into the global diaspora in search of economic opportunity and security. Approximately 300,000 of these migrants came to the United States from 1852 to 1882.[22] With the discovery of gold in California in 1848 and the subsequent gold rush, the American West seemed especially attractive as a place to chase dreams of

"Gold Mountain," if not by prospecting then by servicing the needs of the laborers, settlers, and industrialists flocking to the region.[23]

To obtain Chinese laborers for southern employers, nevertheless, was no simple task. The Chinese Consolidated Benevolent Associations (*huiguans*) headquartered in San Francisco, more commonly known as the Chinese Six Companies, regulated the migration of labor between China and the United States, inserting an unfamiliar middle agent between southern planters and entrepreneurs and the workers they hoped to hire. Huiguans operated as mutual aid societies that provided jobs, shelter, and other basic amenities to Chinese immigrants. The leaders of the Six Companies profited from charging migrants for passage to the United States, including food, and then deducting that cost, plus interest, from their wages after arrival. Once they arrived in the United States, the workers then signed a contract with an American employer for a specific period.[24]

Although the Burlingame Treaty liberalized Chinese emigration to the United States in 1868, vague and often contradictory interpretations of the 1862 act and the subsequent Foran Contract Labor Law (1885) rendered the entire process difficult for either officials or civilians to predict or navigate.[25] This proved especially true for southerners arriving late to the game of tapping the global Chinese diaspora. Planters and entrepreneurs in the South relied on experienced labor contractors, such as W. A. Kissam and John Williams of Louisiana and Cornelius Koopmanschap in California, to work in collaboration with agents of the Six Companies.[26]

Louisiana's planters jump-started the process when they used agents to import a few Chinese men from Cuba in 1867 and over the next couple of years.[27] The southern news wire soon buzzed with glowing reports from Louisiana. On the Merrill Plantation near New Orleans, reported a Mississippi paper, "the first day's work of the Chinese in the cane fields of Louisiana was entirely successful. The hands showed themselves apt to learn and docile to obey," and, moreover, worked an entire day under "a broiling sun" with "no signs of fatigue." Railroad builders also took notice, anticipating "less trouble in the management of Chinese than American or European laborers." After all, the writer explained, "as a rule, the Chinese indulge in no intoxicating drinks; they work very steadily and are extremely tractable." And, perhaps best of all, "no desertions take place among them, as it is obvious that being in a strange country, they would not know in what direction to turn in search of employment."[28]

In other words, the vulnerability of the Chinese as laborers contracted to work in a foreign land in often isolated circumstances made them potentially even more easily exploited than the freed people. Frederick Douglass had recognized that intent, remarking that those "Southern gentlemen who led in the late rebellion . . . believed in slavery and they believe in it still" and wanted "laborers who will work for nothing; but as they cannot get the negroes on these terms, they want Chinamen who, they hope, will work for next to nothing."[29]

As work on the transcontinental railroad neared completion early in 1869, releasing thousands of Chinese railway workers, southern white interest in Chinese labor grew feverish.[30] Commercial conventions allowed for New South entrepreneurs to network with businessmen specializing in foreign labor recruitment.[31] A regional convention organized in Memphis in 1869 called on "all railroads in the South . . . to employ . . . as many as possible of the Chinamen recently discharged on the Pacific Railroad."[32] The organizers also invited Cornelius Koopmanschap to attend as "the principal importer of Chinese in California," and he quickly received top billing as a "main attraction" on the convention floor.[33]

Born in Amsterdam in 1828, Koopmanschap cut his teeth as a labor agent first in China and the Dutch East Indies, finally ending up in California for the gold rush by 1850. In San Francisco, he established a business importing Chinese goods as well as laborers, maintaining a business partnership with an agent in Hong Kong.[34] He cultivated a relationship with the Six Companies, delivering thousands of Chinese men from China to California to work on the transcontinental railroad project.[35] The conclusion of that contract in 1869 put Koopmanschap hot on the trail for new opportunities, and he followed the scent straight to the Memphis convention. There, the "House of Koopmanschap," along with Chinese labor agent Tye Kim Orr and former Confederate general Nathan Bedford Forrest, promised to bring up to thirty thousand Chinese laborers to help build the New South.[36]

Regional newspapers ran notices during the Memphis Chinese Labor Convention, calling for hundreds of railroad workers to assist in completing a line traversing the state of Alabama.[37] Bostonian entrepreneurs and brothers turned railroad builders, John C. and Daniel L. Stanton, soon took notice, collaborating with former Alabama governor Robert Patton to combine two defunct railways into the larger Alabama and Chattanooga Railroad. They hoped to build the first major rail line that would cut right through the heart of the state's budding mineral district.[38]

While the Stanton brothers held little personal capital of their own, they proved remarkably adept at securing support from financial backers in the Northeast and abroad, skills they soon deployed among Alabama's Reconstruction politicians. Although Daniel held the titular position as president of the railroad, John was the real mover and shaker, both on the ground as the actual contractor and in the legislative hallways and smoky backrooms of the state capitol. Described variously at the time as a "hard-working Scotchy fellow" and a "rustling rascal," the redheaded Stanton managed to obtain generous and possibly illegal subsidization via around $4 million in bond issues from the state legislature and Governor William Smith.[39] Daniel L. managed the financial end of the project while John C. headed up the construction of the road, simultaneously building southwest from Chattanooga and northeast from Meridian. Eventually, the two sections would meet at Eutaw, near Tuscaloosa, to complete the road.[40]

Stanton initially hired African American men to work in gangs under white overseers to grade the railroad beds and lay the track. Nimrod Bell, a former railroad conductor and white southerner, was hired on to manage Black laborers for Stanton, sometimes overseeing only a few dozen men but other times managing a gang amounting to more than one hundred.[41] Bell recalled that Stanton sent labor agents to recruit workers in East Tennessee and Virginia, and also brought a gang of around thirty Irish men down from New York City to work on the road. When the Irish men arrived on the project, according to Bell, they took one look at the work required, turned on their heels, and headed straight back North on the same day.[42] Not surprisingly, Stanton soon announced his frustrations with finding suitable labor for his project, although newspaper accounts focused primarily on his problems with "negro laborers." Stanton "has nearly lost patience," wrote one reporter, because "he finds it nearly impossible to keep them at work."[43]

Fueled by exaggerated press accounts and shady labor agents before and after the war, southern employers such as Stanton already construed Chinese laborers as a breed apart, as men who could be relied upon to dutifully labor at the hardest tasks of the New South without question—and to be grateful for the opportunity.[44] Unlike the freed people, many of whom were either leaving local communities they deemed inhospitable or asserting their rights as political and economic citizens, Chinese laborers were supposed to be docile, cooperative, and even self-sufficient, requiring only transport to the region, some basic supplies, and a contract to work under their own supervision.[45] Thus, as Stanton advertised for railroad labor in the late spring of 1869, he also contacted the Central Pacific Railroad with a view toward locating about one thousand or two thousand "Chinese coolies." A Tuscaloosa editor, with his eye on the Black Belt, interpreted this activity as "a warning to the negro . . . that his services can be dispensed with," and moreover, he noted, the "alternative" for Blacks would be "starving or immigrating."[46]

Stanton's song about his labor problems, naturally, played as sweet music indeed to the ears of Cornelius Koopmanschap, who was wrapping up his publicity tour of the southeast on the heels of the Memphis convention. He quickly promised Stanton up to two thousand Chinese workers at "$60 per head" to work for sixteen dollars a month plus board, along with eventual "free passage back" to California and China.[47]

Koopmanschap promised to begin "by employing his Chinese brokers in every province," and ultimately established a Chinese immigration agency in New Orleans, managed by labor agents John Williams and Sons.[48] The elder Williams was a "longtime sugar planter and commission merchant of New Orleans," of "great wealth," and the owner of several large plantations. His son reportedly lived in "interior China," where he worked to contract with the "best class of Chinese laborers," "forwarding them to the agents in New Orleans by sea," so "all who want laborers" could obtain them.[49] Williams, who had also attended the Memphis immigration convention, had already imported dozens of Chinese people for work on Louisiana sugar plantations.[50]

Koopmanschap then published in several newspapers the terms of the contracts for the Chinese labor he planned to import for the New South project. If planters or railroad builders could meet these terms, he noted, then he could procure the workers they needed. Specifically, the terms set out wages of eight to ten dollars in gold per month for "field hands" and fifteen dollars in gold per month "for railroad hands, plus board." Advances on their wages would pay for the cost of passage, along with other fees incurred along the way, such as blankets, clothing, and the like. Free provisions for the workers should include food, water, firewood, and "good quarters and weather proof sleeping places," and employers would pay all local taxes. Each laborer also would require a small plot for growing vegetables. The men would sign five-year contracts, and work in gangs under one Chinese interpreter/overseer for every fifty to one hundred men, who would "instruct and direct the men in their labors." They would work twenty-six days in each month, "that is to say to have Sundays for themselves," plus occasional holidays. A workday typically would begin at six a.m., with a one-hour break at noon, but the men could choose to have a two-hour break in the summertime if the workday commenced at five a.m. If a laborer became sick, his wages ceased; however, the employer must furnish all care and medicines, and pay for any provided. Finally, the notice stated, "It must be understood that these laborers are to meet with just treatment, and if errors are committed by them, a report must be made to the Chinese foreman, before any punishment shall be inflicted." In other words, the disciplinary authority ultimately lay with a Chinese overseer, not with the planter or railroad builder who hired them.[51]

Koopmanschap had failed to specify, however, the seriousness with which Chinese emigrants viewed the terms of the contracts they had signed. The American consular official in Hong Kong, D. H. Bailey, for example, described what amounted to "an organized business for trade" in Hong Kong and Canton by men "of large capital and firms of great wealth" that "bought and sold" Chinese men "for so much per head, precisely as a piece of merchandise was handled at its market value." These "rich traders," he alleged, contracted with Chinese laborers to work at low wages in a foreign country, then sold the contracts to a "dealer through his agents in the U.S." at "great profit." Although the U.S. laws did not recognize these contracts, Bailey noted that a Chinese laborer still "would comply strictly with all its terms," carrying a paper copy "written in Chinese characters on his person at all times."[52]

Thus, the first Chinese immigrant laborers in New South Alabama appeared a decade before men such as Charley Sing arrived to operate laundries in the state's cities and towns in the 1880s. In mid-July of 1870, hundreds of Chinese workers boarded trains in California bound for Alabama to start building the Stanton brothers' great railway. Conductor Bell reported that Stanton received as many as two thousand Chinese laborers or more.[53]

The men finally arrived in Alabama in early August 1870, bringing along their own "doctor, a storekeeper . . . a clerk, and treasurer." Crowds of curious onlookers greeted the men at railroad depots as they traveled across the country.[54] One account described them arriving in Tuscaloosa to march through town "in large force," impressing white onlookers as "an intelligent, orderly body of men" but generating "disgust, if not wrath" among local African Americans.[55] Stanton ended up splitting the group in two, sending about half to Meridian to begin work at the southern terminus and the rest to Chattanooga, the northern terminus.[56]

Cresting the Red Mountain Gap northeast of Birmingham late one midsummer day in 1870, a salesman named James Webb recorded his encounter with an "army of men" laying track for the AL-CH Railroad. Among these industrial "soldiers" were about four hundred Chinese men. "They are a queer looking race of creatures," Webb wrote to his wife. "They remind me, and would you also, of light colored Indian women." Citing their "peculiar dress," Webb noted that the men wore "loose trousers" and that "their hair is . . . straight and black, which they let grow long and plait . . . when at work they roll this round, like a lady does her braid, in a knot on the crown of the head." They wore very large straw hats, Webb noted, and "are very cleanly with their person." Moreover, the Chinese workers lived in separate encampments, "apart from the negroes and Germans." All in all, Webb concluded, "it was an interesting sight."[57]

As Webb's comments reflected, the Chinese working on the AL-CH were "the greatest objects of interest and curiosity," and though reportedly they were sometimes "stubborn and refractory," they were generally construed as "steady, industrious, and painstaking laborers."[58] One observer noted that initially they did not quite measure up to Black laborers, but once they had "hardened" to the work, they acquitted themselves well.[59] Likewise, Stanton told one reporter that "they were of little value for the first four months," but then "after they have become somewhat experienced, they are doing very well."[60]

Stanton's Chinese laborers appear to have diligently fulfilled the terms of their contracts. However, the same could not be said of the Stanton brothers running the show.[61] The first public sign of trouble emerged when John Stanton defaulted on a series of payments on the bonded debt that funded the construction. Political controversy ensued when Alabama governor

Robert Burns Lindsay refused to save the road from imminent failure. In June of 1871, U.S. District Court judge Richard Busteed put "Stanton's Road" into bankruptcy, prompting the editors of the leading Mobile newspaper to now describe the once favored J. C. Stanton as that "wily Yankee," and to call for his departure from the state because the "Railroad King" had now "become fatiguing."[62]

A "friend" of Stanton's attempted to explain what had happened, further demonstrating the international context that provided a backdrop to New South development. The AL-CH bonds ended up on the European market. When the "unexpected war in Europe" (the Franco-Prussian War) erupted, he claimed, the "stringency in money market" made it exceedingly difficult for all railroads in Alabama to continue "negotiating our bonds at the rates required by the internal improvement laws of Alabama." But even more importantly, he reported, "we have also been at considerable trouble and expense in procuring suitable labor."[63]

What his "friend" had failed to mention was Stanton's own failure to pay the wages due to the laborers he had already employed. Stanton argued that the choice had been either to pay the wages or to meet the interest payments due on the bonds.[64] But it appears that he managed to do neither. Nor was money the only issue upsetting Stanton's labor force. Even before Stanton defaulted, one observer reported a great deal of dissatisfaction among his Chinese workers: "They all wished to return to China," he found, "because they were not welcome here." The workers felt "there was a disposition to impose on them if they settled in the country," meaning the United States, generally. But in Alabama, specifically, the Chinese men discovered that "the negroes have no love for them, and they have not much for the negroes." In fact, he reported, "a difficulty occurred between the Chinese and the negroes on the road last week," in which "several Chinamen were very much injured." Stanton soon settled the trouble, and "all are now at work."[65]

The so-called difficulty mentioned, however, proved far more serious than the newspaper account suggested. As later recounted by Bell, the incident began when Stanton's Chinese workforce ran out of the rice provisions guaranteed in their labor contracts. Already forced to work barefoot, and most likely suspecting they might never see any wages either, losing access to a basic food staple proved to be the last straw. The men enacted a work stoppage: "After a while, the Chinese got out of rice and quit." Stanton, recalled Bell, "tried to get the Chinese to go to work," but the men refused to comply without first having their rice supply replenished. At this point, "Mr. Stanton commenced to strike some of them with the pick handle." But the men unexpectedly fought back: "I was afterwards told that the Chinese would have got the best of him had the negroes not taken his part and helped him out."[66] Apparently, Stanton beat several of the men so badly that they were unable to return to work. He sent some of the less injured men on to Chattanooga to work in the shops there. As for the others, "As soon as the ones that were crippled got well, they were sent back on the grade to work." Nonetheless, at least one of the men soon died from the beating, and possibly others did as well. "When one of them died he was buried in the ground on the side of the road," explained Bell, "as others that die are, with a head and foot board set up, both of which are covered with writing in the Chinese language."[67]

By the spring of 1871, about half of Stanton's Chinese workers had left the railroad because of these conditions. Reverend Brayfield Whilden, a Southern Baptist missionary who visited Stanton's Chinese camps in Alabama in March 1871, testified to a joint congressional committee investigating Chinese immigration in the United States that, initially, "there were some fifteen hundred Chinese in the South . . . most of them for the Alabama and Chattanooga Railroad Company." However, although "they completed this work, they received no money, and were fearfully abused."[68]

Moreover, when the bankruptcy decree stopped all work on the railroad, federal marshals tried to seize the railcars at the Meridian terminus. "Much excitement" then ensued, noted one observer, when "a mob of unpaid employees," including Black, white, and Chinese workers, stopped the trains in order to "secure their pay," holding the "locomotives and spare parts . . . hostage." The receiver appointed by Governor Lindsay to intervene described the men as "strikers" who protected the railway's physical property from damage but who also refused to yield control until someone met at least some of their claims against the Stanton brothers.[69] The disruption of rail traffic impeded the northward flow of supplies, leaving Stanton's workers "in a bad state." Around Tuscaloosa wandered "hundreds of laborers, composed of whites, Chinese, and negroes . . . among the swamps and in a starving condition," reported one observer. "Their condition is pitiable in the extreme." Bell recalled observing the Chinese laborers supplementing their diets with unripe persimmons, along with fish and frogs caught in a nearby swamp.[70]

Stanton never paid his workers' back wages, even with the railroad's completion in May.[71] The grading contractors he had hired obtained loans so they could pay some of the wages, but Stanton never reimbursed them. All of the contractors had to file for bankruptcy. Some lingering Chinese men wandered the "swamps" around Tuscaloosa, where they apparently subsisted on "roots, berries, and anything they could get," including "blackberries and crawfish."[72] Having heard that his former recruits were in "a bad way," but mostly interested in recouping his own losses, Koopmanschap visited Tuscaloosa to find the men "in an almost naked and starving condition." They demanded to be returned to California and were "willing to abandon their claims" to back wages in order to get there.[73] Such suffering did not motivate Koopmanschap to actually do anything for them, despite his initial promise that each Chinese worker would have free passage home to China. He departed without paying their wages, and he refused to fund any return passage to either California or China. He did, however, soon write to Alabama's Governor Lindsay to request reimbursement for his own expenses and losses.[74]

Once heralded as the beginning of an answer to the labor "problem" for the New South's entrepreneurs, the experiment with contracted Chinese labor floundered under the weight of global financial dilemmas, local labor challenges, and state Reconstruction politics.[75] Whether working on the Central Pacific in the West, the AL-CH in the deep South, or on plantations in the Delta or the Caribbean, Chinese workers did not prove to be the inexpensive or docile workforce upon which southern planters and entrepreneurs had banked.[76] Southern employers should have expected as much. Plenty of reports had circulated about how recalcitrant Chinese laborers could be.

In February of 1871, for example, reports from Jamaica declared that "the negroes and the Chinese are becoming very troublesome" as "they are burning sugar crops and houses, and much timber."[77] On one Louisiana plantation, the Chinese laborers' entrepreneurial independence confounded the plantation's overseer. Rather than labor all day in the fields, some of the Chinese workers reportedly stole tools and materials from the plantation, using them to craft "beadwork, toys, and trinkets" to sell at the nearby Napoleonville market, which earned them "more than their plantation wages."

Subsequently "docking their wages and withholding their rations" to discourage this behavior could be dangerous. Some of the Chinese allegedly fought back during one altercation with the overseer.[78]

The Chinese on the AL-CH Railroad project also proved surprisingly headstrong, working to control their own pace of work when they could and protesting jobs they did not want to do. For example, when Bell once directed about thirty Chinese men to hurry to rack an engine with a cord of wood, the barefoot men "would only carry one stick at a time," stretching the simple task to an hour.[79]

For his part, Koopmanschap blamed the Stantons' mismanagement for the failure of the Chinese labor experiment. "Stanton and Company have injured my whole business," whined Koopmanschap to Alabama governor Lindsay, and "on account of their non-payment (of wages) it is now impossible to make the Chinese go South."[80] Moreover, few "manufacturers" proved "willing to advance the $7,000 in gold necessary to bring a hundred of them hither."[81] By May 1872, the once grand "House of Koopmanschap" had declared bankruptcy.[82]

As the terms of Koopmanschap's contracts had indicated, Chinese workers, and often the agents who procured them, had specific expectations about the contracts they signed—at the very least, the expectation that they would not be beaten to death when they protested about working without appropriate food. The contract terms that insisted that a Chinese "overseer" serve not only as an interpreter but also as a bulwark against a southern employer's heavy-handed discipline injected an unfamiliar firewall that J. C. Stanton breached when he beat his recalcitrant Chinese laborers so badly he crippled several and killed at least one. Their response? Most of them fled at the first opportunity.[83]

Thus, the failure of the AL-CH Railroad project and similar efforts appeared to put an end to the experiment with Chinese labor. Nevertheless, Chinese nationals did not disappear from New South communities. In Mississippi and Louisiana, many plantation laborers shifted into other economic activities, particularly the dry goods and small groceries business, establishing a lasting economic foothold as the cotton and sugar economies expanded.[84] A nucleus of Chinese men made their way, often one by one, to the urban, small-town, and rural crossroads of the New South, seeking to establish an economic niche in the small service economies springing up along with the developing towns, factories, and mills. The men who came in this phase typically drew on kinship or village connections in a local community, utilizing a common chain migration process that brought them from other parts of the United States, such as San Francisco, Chicago, Saint Louis, New York City, and New Orleans, as well as from Canada, Mexico, and China. Charley Sing, for example, arrived in Tuscaloosa sometime between 1880 and 1893, well after the desperate men of the AL-CH project had left.

Although Chinese railroad workers had deployed their resistance and mobility against their exploitation whenever possible, their racial position in the New South as railroad workers had remained squarely on the nonwhite side of the color line. Thus, while J. C. Stanton could not easily control his Chinese workers, he could beat them to death without legal consequences. The individual Chinese men who arrived in Alabama starting in the 1880s likewise found their situations to be tenuous. But unlike the railroad laborers of 1870, these later Chinese arrivals, including Charley Sing, experienced more racial transiency through the services they provided and the connections they established to white Protestant Christianity. Nonetheless, their racial position in the New South remained unstable and their relationship with African American populations continued to be both contentious and often contradictory.

In 1882, Congress enacted the first federal immigration restriction bill, the Chinese Exclusion Act, inaugurating a protracted legal effort to restrict immigration into the United States by defining some immigrant groups as racially and/or economically preferable over others and coalescing a definition of "illegal alien" around the figure of the Chinese immigrant.[85] This act barred the entry of Chinese laborers into the United States for ten years and "set policies for admitting, tracking, and deporting Chinese immigrants unlawfully in the country," while also prohibiting "state and federal courts from granting Chinese residents U.S. citizenship."[86] The 1882 act exempted certain categories of Chinese people, most importantly those who could provide paper documentation proving that they were U.S citizens, merchants, students, or at least not manual laborers.[87]

The restriction acts established the beginning of an infrastructure of enforcement through the U.S. customhouse at ports of entry such as Angel Island in San Francisco; New Orleans, Louisiana; and Mobile, Alabama. But Chinese migrants continued to gain entry to the United States, including into Alabama. They regularly appealed deportation orders, evaded the law outright, and persistently optimized loopholes of enforcement at ports of entry or across the Mexican and Canadian borders.[88] Congress responded by imposing additional restrictions, seeking to pinpoint the definition of "merchant" and regulate the process used by customs officials to determine whether a Chinese applicant for entry was a ineligible laborer, an eligible merchant, a student, or other.[89] In 1892, the Geary Act "required all Chinese to register for certificates of residence or risk imprisonment or deportation." A further amendment narrowed the definition of "merchant" to "a person engaged in buying and selling merchandise" who did not "perform any manual labor," a status that also had to be validated by "two credible white witnesses in order to be readmitted into the country."[90] All people involved in the laundry business, whether as an owner or a hired hand, remained defined as laborers.[91]

Given this restrictive climate, it seems even more surprising that Chinese nationals ended up in Alabama after the AL-CH railroad debacle. Nevertheless, federal, state, and local records all indicate a persistent if small presence of Chinese immigrants in the state throughout the exclusion period. Many of the Chinese documented in the records of the Mobile customhouse appear to have been eventually deported from the United States through San Francisco under the terms of the acts.[92] As part of a wider Chinese diaspora, their journeys to Mobile and elsewhere in Alabama and the United States often originated in the Americas, with several traveling to Mobile from Bocas del Toro (near the Panama Canal), or Mérida, Mexico—and at least one from Havana, Cuba.[93] Chew Chan, for example, twenty-seven years old and documented as a "merchant," had last resided at Bocas del Toro when he arrived in Mobile aboard the vessel *Douglas* in July 1900, bound for Hong Kong. He left Mobile for California and then China. Ah Chin, a forty-year-old laborer bonded by the United Fruit Company, requested permission in December 1902 to enter Mobile. He also listed his last residence as Bocas del Toro.[94]

Along with such *transitory* Chinese who appeared in Mobile's customhouse records was a larger group that shared many of the same characteristics, such as age, gender, origination location, and occupation. These *permanent* Chinese requested permission, as required under the Exclusion Acts, to reenter the country and resume residency in Alabama. Their destination was not California, Hong Kong, or the like but homes and busi-

Ah Chin, a Chinese "merchant," who obtained permission in December of 1902 from a Customs House official to disembark from a ship in Mobile Bay in order to proceed on to California, most likely by rail. He was supposed to then depart from San Francisco to return to China. Ah Chin listed his last residence as Bocas del Toro, Panama, as did many of the Chinese men who passed through the Mobile Customs House in the very early twentieth century. *Photo and document found in 36.3.1, Federal Customs Service, RG 36, Collection District of Mobile, Alabama. National Archives and Records Administration, Atlanta, Georgia.*

nesses in Alabama. They intended to return to the United States after visiting other regions of the world, often to conduct business as merchants, according to their stated claims.[95] The true nature of their business abroad remains speculative; nonetheless, such requests revealed a small but thriving community of Chinese living in the state well after the AL-CH Railroad debacle.[96] Based on census records, however, as well as other documents, including newspaper accounts and naturalization records, most of these "permanent" Alabama Chinese worked in or operated laundries, relegating them to the category of "laborer" as defined in the Exclusion Acts.

Chinese immigrants lived in Alabama consistently from the 1880s through the formal end of the exclusion era in 1943. They resided not only in cities such as Birmingham, Mobile, and Montgomery but also in many towns and rural communities, including Demopolis, Evergreen, Florence, Greenville, Ozark, Sylacauga, Talladega, and Union Springs. Certainly, their numbers scarcely compared to the multitudes found in the cities of the East or West Coasts. Nonetheless, the global labor diaspora that brought the Chinese to Alabama in 1870 further diversified Alabama's New South population.[97]

Census records provide a glimpse of this population. In 1870, a census enumerator recorded only one Chinese immigrant living in Alabama, a man ignobly labeled "John China." He resided in Mobile with a Spaniard and his American wife, Jonathan and Johana Lazzo, along with a youth of sixteen named Thomas Ramsey, born in Virginia in 1854. The census taker defined the Lazzos as white, Thomas Ramsey as Black, and John China as Asian. Lazzo dealt in tobacco products, his wife kept house, and Ramsey worked as a "house servant." John China is listed as a "tobacco stripper."[98]

By 1890, at least forty-five Chinese men lived in Mobile, along with several others residing in Montgomery and Birmingham. Although a few listed occupations as dealers in tea and/or fancy goods, most worked in laundries, according to city directories.[99] A decade later, the federal census documented approximately thirty-seven Chinese in Alabama, virtually all still listing "laundry" as an occupation. By 1910, the Alabama Chinese population had grown to at least fifty-five, all of whom were born in either China or California and around half of whom listed occupations in the laundry business. Enumerators also recorded many as proprietors of laundries, not just as employees. The Chinese recorded in Alabama in 1910 had arrived in the United States from as early as 1870 to as late as 1909.[100] Ten years later, the overall numbers of Chinese in Alabama (approximately fifty-eight in 1920) had not changed greatly, according to the census, but occupational diversity had grown significantly, with thirty-seven identified as being in the laundry business. The rest listed other occupations, including cooks, restaurant managers and waiters, a bookkeeper, and an auditor.[101]

In theory, the Chinese in Alabama were neither white nor Black but Asian. Census enumerators in Alabama struggled to reconcile the Chinese presence with an essentially binary system of racial categorization.[102] Enumerators most often defined their Chinese subjects in Alabama as simply "Chinese." Sometimes, however, recorders defined them as white or Black. Chinese immigrants often lived in boardinghouses of one sort or another, sometimes with one another but often with other non-Chinese, who might be recorded as white or Black. In later census decades, many Chinese men were married, though often not with a wife living in the home, since they often left a wife and family back in China (or in other parts of the diaspora). But in Alabama, as in other deep South states, Chinese men such as Charley Sing also married American-born women, who might be recorded as either white or Black in the census.[103]

Immigrant laborers often moved around in the New South, a mobility that cannot be tracked easily through the decennial census. Moreover, the difficulty of identifying individuals who had names filtered through the racial proclivities of census enumerators, immigration agents, and local white and Black residents, combined with the need for dissembling to gain entry and avoid deportation, muddles understanding of just how many Chinese immigrants were in the New South, and who exactly they were. Nevertheless, by combining census records and other government documents with newspaper accounts, a pattern to Chinese immigrant laborers in New South Alabama after 1880 does emerge. Their overall numbers were small, from one or two in small towns or crossroads to several dozen in the Birmingham District and in other cities. They appeared in almost every Alabama community, especially in the Birmingham District and its surrounding hinterlands. The vast majority worked in the hand-washing laundry business.

Laundries had first evolved into the iconic Chinese occupation in western railroad and mining camps, due to racial discrimination barring more diverse occupational choices as well as the lack of Chinese women to assume the burden of domestic labor.[104] Alabama's Chinese immigrant launderers appeared to occupy a sort of transit point, networked to larger Chinese communities in Atlanta to the northeast and New Orleans to the southwest. These communities, in turn, all connected to the larger benevolent organizations established during the gold rush years in San Francisco, including the Six Companies. Alabama's Chinese population sustained kinship networks, as well as organizational connections, to Chinese people living across Alabama, in neighboring states, and in locations outside the South, including Chicago, New York City, Saint Louis, and San Francisco.

Such connections proved important because Chinese launderers such as Charley Sing often lived lonely lives as solitary men removed from families still in China.[105] Whereas in larger urban areas such as Atlanta, New York, or San Francisco such men benefited from inclusion in larger dynamic ethnic communities, the Chinese in Alabama lived in very small numbers in the state's urban, small-town, and rural locales. Few of the men had much more than a rudimentary command of English, and they worked extremely long hours at hard labor, working and living in small, dark, and dank environments, typically renting and living in a single storefront in a downtown commercial district.[106]

Although a start-up Chinese hand-washing laundry required only a little initial capital in the late nineteenth and early twentieth centuries, both poverty and frugality compelled Chinese laborers to form partnerships that shared the financial risk and labor.[107] Proprietors expanded operations initially by bringing to work in the business young men who typically were from the proprietor's village in China or to whom they were related (sometimes as "paper sons"), and who traveled from other American cities or directly from China or Canada.[108] A successful laundry might have multiple generations of proprietors who assumed the same name while living in the local community. For example, one local newspaper traced the advent of the Chinese laundry in town to the arrival, around 1878, of a man named "Charlie Loo," who then passed the business down to a number of other proprietors over the years, all of whom assumed the name of Charlie Loo, until the last man left in 1918 to service the U.S. Army in France.[109] Proprietors of prosperous laundries, particularly with the advent of electric-powered machinery in the early twentieth century, sometimes hired African American women as washer employees.[110]

Operating a laundry business in the New South without much facility in English could be a dangerous proposition. Chinese launderers often encountered troublesome customers who wanted to quarrel over rates or problems with their laundry, or who lacked a ticket to claim their clothes. Newspapers report incident after incident of such disputes, sometimes turning violent, with both white and Black customers. In October 1909, for instance, a dispute over laundry resulted in a Black customer levying an "embezzlement" charge that landed the Chinese proprietor in jail.[111] In Montgomery, three "white boys" beat a "Chinaman" named Ben Lee in a North Court Street laundry over a "misunderstanding" regarding a laundry ticket.[112]

Moreover, Alabama's Chinese immigrants confronted a deeply racist reception when they arrived to open their laundries in the state's communities. The press explored that arrival and their subsequent lives, as well as the presence of Asians in other areas of the country, in the highly racialized terms that prevailed across the United States. Local and state newspapers, for example, always identified a Chinese immigrant as a "Chinaman," and often as either a "Celestial" or an "Oriental." Anglicized names predominated as well, most commonly Joe, Charley/Charlie, or Sam, names that often appeared to be interchangeable among the men who worked in a given laundry. Individual depictions ranged from the overtly racist "almond-eyed Celestial" to the more paternalistic "hardworking, law-abiding Chinaman [with] his quiet unassuming manner."[113] These racist depictions defined how the American press and most citizens conceived of the Chinese throughout the United States and had a long history, dating back to at least the earlier nineteenth century.[114] However, a more positive (if still racist) portrayal could also be found in New South Alabama's press, which recognized the niche occupied by Chinese immigrants in providing this washing and ironing service to mostly white, but also Black, customers in southern communities. Moreover, their small numbers in each community prevented an obvious presence that provincial and xenophobic local residents might construe as more threatening.[115]

The Chinese connection to white Protestant missionary work, a popular pastime for southern white evangelicals, also provided a ready avenue toward the white side of the color line. Whereas the same dynamic did not work equally well for other immigrant groups, such as Austro-Hungarians, Greeks, Italians, Russians, or Syrian-Lebanese, Chinese immigrants could bolster their social position to some extent by regularly attending a Baptist Bible study, a Methodist church, or similar. The appearance (or in some cases the authentic reality) of Christian conversion nurtured relationships to a community's prominent white citizens, which could then be deployed when needed. Chinese immigrants in Alabama, for example, accessed white physicians, undertakers, and attorneys, and even the support, at times, of white law enforcement.[116]

However, these connections to local Christian communities, their smaller overall numbers, and their usefulness in providing a needed laundry service did not automatically translate into a secure membership in southern white citizenship, nor did it guarantee insulation from the racial tension characteristic of the Jim Crow South. As Charley Sing discovered,

Alabama's Chinese immigrants lived precariously poised between the unpredictability of both white largesse and Black resentment. Like other immigrants in the New South, the Chinese in Alabama experienced a racial fluidity that might provide opportunity but also often left them targeted and vulnerable.[117]

The case of Tip Chung, aka Joe Jung, exemplifies how particular circumstances sometimes allowed Chinese immigrants to establish a racial position closer to "whiteness."[118] Jung petitioned the U.S. District Court in Birmingham, Alabama, for naturalization as a U.S. citizen sometime around late 1944 or early 1945. In his application, he declared his birth date to be August 3, 1882, and his birthplace as Canton, China. The recorder documented him as sixty-one years old, five feet ten, 150 pounds, and "Chinese" in race and in nationality. As a young man, Jung had departed Canton for Hong Kong, where he boarded the SS *Iroquois,* landing first in Vancouver, Canada, and finally arriving in Seattle, Washington, in February 1910. At the time of his naturalization application, he worked as a "cook" and had made at least one return trip to China in 1927, departing from San Francisco aboard the *Pres. Lincoln* and returning to Alabama through the same port ten months later, this time aboard the *Pres. Madison.* He signed his application with both his own and his assigned name, with "Tip Chung" marked in blocky English print reminiscent of Chinese characters and the Anglicized "Joe Jung" written in cursive.[119]

If the record of his naturalization application documented the facts of Jung's travel from China to the United States and to Birmingham, Alabama, it did not quite capture the texture of that journey or of his life as a Chinese immigrant in the New South. A few years after he disembarked from the *Iroquois* at the Seattle harbor in the winter of 1910, Tip Chung, now Joe Jung, arrived in Alabama in 1914. Whereas many immigrant Chinese men remained single for years and even decades while in the United States, Jung did not. Only two years after his arrival in Alabama, in fact, Jung married the daughter of a white timber contractor, a young woman named Pearl Bradford, of Birmingham, prompting a brief article in *Franklin County Times.* Although describing Jung in racist terms typical of the American press, as "a full-blood Chinaman," the writer covered the remainder of the story with a more dispassionate tone. First obtaining a marriage license from the local judge, Jung reportedly then contacted Reverend J. W. Partridge, a prominent white Baptist minister, to officiate over a small betrothal ceremony in the Russellville home of a Mr. Orser, where "Mr. Orser's family and a few townsmen" served as witnesses to the union.[120]

By 1920, federal census enumerators had caught back up to Joe Jung and his wife, Pearl, listing them as residing in Birmingham with their toddler son named Howard Robert. They rented a home while Joe Jung operated his own laundry business. The enumerator decided to record Jung as "Chinese" and Pearl Jung and their son as "white." The Jungs even occasionally made the social pages of the local newspaper in Russellville, where they had married, such as in 1916 when "Mr. and Mrs. Joe Jung" arrived in Birmingham as "the guests of relatives," a sort of social validation frequently extended to local white residents but rarely, if ever, to African Americans in white-owned newspapers. Indeed, several aspects of Jung's life, as recorded in government documents and Alabama newspapers, suggest a racial identity closely, if not absolutely, aligned with the white side of the Jim Crow color line. Jung, though described in racist terms initially in the published marriage announcement, for example, successfully married a white woman with little additional commentary in the press. He easily obtained a marriage license as well as the services of a well-known white minister, and the couple married in the personal home of a local white family.[121]

During his life in the Birmingham District, Jung established a close relationship with other Chinese immigrants in the region. His connections to the prosperous white community in Birmingham, however, failed to shield Jung from a close acquaintance with the traumas and transience that also defined how Chinese immigrants experienced the New South.

Beginning in the late winter of 1916 and extending into the early spring of 1917, the Birmingham District experienced a string of disturbing and brutal murders of Chinese laundrymen. The murders occurred in very similar circumstances, typically involving a predawn attack by an unknown assailant, much like what had happened to Charley Sing in Tuscaloosa in 1893. However, although police officials consistently claimed robbery as the motive, in each case significant amounts of cash and or valuable goods remained untouched, and in at least two of the murders, the assailant or assailants thoroughly ransacked the business and living space. And while many aspects of each event appeared to testify to Chinese immigrants' more favorable spot in the Jim Crow racial hierarchy, the security of that position proved unstable at best, and not just because of the murders. These events nurtured local white suspicion of the Chinese as "Orientals" feuding in a "tong war" that, despite their relatively sparse numbers, nevertheless threatened to get out of control.

On February 20, 1916, an unknown assailant fatally shot "one of Birmingham's best-known Chinamen," Charley Fein Ben (Ben Chin Moon), in his laundry business. Ben lived long enough to relate the details of the assault, as well as his final wishes, to his friend, none other than Joe Jung. As he was preparing to open up in the early hours that Sunday morning, Ben answered a knock at the business's back door. When he answered, a white man (according to the police) immediately struck him with a wooden stick and a struggle between the two men ensued. Ben reportedly got the best of his assailant, overpowering him and running toward another room, possibly to fetch a gun. The assailant drew his own gun and shot Ben two times, then allegedly fled the scene across the Capitol Square park grounds.

Ben dragged himself to the front of his laundry and managed to break the front window to attract attention. A passerby or neighboring merchant found Ben and, interestingly, first called his friend and fellow Chinese laundryman Joe Jung, who called the police and then hurried to Ben's business. A "police patrol" rushed Ben to the hospital. He had lost an enormous amount of blood, prompting the need for a transfusion. Another of Ben's friends, this time a white man named S. Y. Hampton, who worked as a local messenger, volunteered his blood. Despite the transfusion, Ben died several hours later. He left not only his grieving friends in Birmingham but also a widow and a twelve-year-old son in Canton.[122]

Although the newspaper reports suggested some local suspicion that Ben's death originated from a feud among Chinese factions associated with Chinese lodge culture, that is, membership in Chinese fraternal and community organizations, police officials derided the notion, explaining that "there never was a tong that hired a white man to go after a person." Charley Ben had arrived in the United States in 1876 at only fifteen years of age, and he traveled to Birmingham in 1906 to open his second laundry business, the first having been in Prattville. Although he may or may not have belonged to a local, state, or regional *huiguan,* or "lodge," the *Birmingham News* reported that his friends believed Ben to be "very prosperous," and the police continued to point to robbery as a motive. The day after the murder, Joe Jung reportedly wired a contact with the Six Companies in California to notify them of Ben's murder, since they were known to offer reward money to facilitate the investigation and prosecution of such crimes. Jung also wired the Chinese ambassador in Washington, DC, for assistance. Local Chinese residents quickly raised $200 of reward money.[123]

Warner-Smith Undertakers of Birmingham, a business that typically serviced only white residents, took charge of Ben's body to prepare the corpse for eventual transit to Hong Kong for burial in China. Ben's "cousin," On Yick, soon arrived from New Orleans to begin making the travel arrangements. However, a dispute with the undertaker over the bill prompted Joe Jung, as the administrator of Ben's estate, to file a petition of attachment to force the release of the body. Ultimately, Ben's corpse remained, apparently embalmed, at the undertaker's for six weeks, until the probate judge ordered an extra $75 fee paid from the estate to Warner-Smith, in recognition of special preparations undertaken to prepare a "Chinese corpse" for a long trans-Pacific journey. The cousin from New Orleans finally accompanied Ben's "hermetically sealed remains" to China in mid-April 1916.[124]

As the war in Europe dragged on, the Chinese in Birmingham found no resolution to the murder of their kinsman Charley Fein Ben. The year ended with no assailant identified or arrested. Nor did the situation improve with the new year. In early March, an unknown assailant murdered another Chinese laundry proprietor, a man known as Sam Loo, who operated a laundry in east Ensley. This time, the victim appeared to have been taken completely by surprise. When he failed to open the doors early on a Saturday morning, antsy customers waiting to collect their laundry forced their way into the shop, where they found Loo facedown in a pool of blood, his toothbrush still in his mouth.

Given the gaping wound in the back of his head, police concluded that Loo had suffered a fatal shot from a large-caliber gun. This time, the assailant(s) ransacked the entire business, leaving no potential hiding place unexamined and smashing every piece of furniture. Nonetheless, police also found undisturbed $75 in cash and a $600 draft on a Hong Kong bank. Again, detectives preferred to believe that robbery explained the attack, much as they had in the case of Charley Fein Ben. Loo's "brother," Mock Loo, reportedly posted a $1,000 reward, but police continued to be "baffled" by the crime. A coroner's inquest met, to no avail. In late March, the coroner turned over Loo's personal effects, assets, and valuables to a man named Martin Cochran, an executor of his estate, which included more than $11,000 in cash spread across several local banks.[125]

As Loo's body followed Ben's across the Pacific Ocean to Hong Kong, having left Birmingham in late March or early April 1917, police remained stumped about who had murdered the laundrymen. And on April 13, 1917, shortly after Easter, disaster struck again. "Chinaman Found Murdered; Money Declared Missing," blared the headline when local residents awoke that morning. Much like the other two murder victims, Charlie Loo Soe died sometime around 4:50 a.m., right after patrol officers Whalen and Patterson had passed by and reportedly checked his front door. When they passed by again around one hour later, they claimed to have found the door open. Upon investigating, they discovered Soe behind the shop counter, dead from blunt force trauma to the head. The killer(s) again had ransacked the shop.

Officer Whalen appeared to have some acquaintance with Charlie Loo Soe, noting that the fifty-five-year-old man "was known to have money in his possession all the time" and reporting that valuable items possessed by Soe were missing, including a gold watch and chain, a pistol, and cash. Police officials again discounted suspicions of a "feud," noting that while Ben, Loo, and Soe were apparently "three members of the same family," still "all of the Chinese men killed had been known as moneyed men. . . . as men who have considerable cash in their places of business. The *Birmingham News* reported the three men to be "cousins," though at that time this could mean a variety of familial, kin, and village relationships among Chinese immigrants. A $1,500 reward specifically sought Loo's murderer. And while detectives allegedly collected multiple fingerprints from the crime scene at Soe's laundry, no suspect apparently emerged.[126]

The men who constituted the Chinese community in the district not only found the unsolved murders to be disturbing but also worried over the continuing suspicions expressed by the local newspapers that the murders represented some sort of gangland "tong war" come to Birmingham.[127] Such rumors threatened to override the advantage of constituting a small and quiet group of outsiders who had carved out an economic niche by providing laundry service to mainly white customers. The precariousness of their position—as a small cluster of "foreigners" with an ambiguous racial identity—was echoed in a statement developed and published by several

Chinese writers in an effort to quash the "tong war" rumors and to reassure their white patrons of their American loyalties. Most likely drafted on their behalf by their local white attorneys, a "Committee of Orientals" sent an open letter to the editor of the *Birmingham News* in late April, asking for their statement to be published.

The "Chinamen of the Birmingham District," reported the newspaper, stated that "there is no such thing as a tong war" in Birmingham, as the recent murders had occurred due to "other motives," which they left unspecified. They wanted readers to know that the tragic deaths of Ben, Loo, and Soe were in no way "the result of a tong war or some kind of feud existing among the Oriental citizens of this district," despite "frequent expressions [in the press] to that effect." In this letter, "the Chinese citizens of Birmingham District [are] declaring to their American friends that there is no tong war" nor any "feud of the slightest nature existing among the members of their race in and around Birmingham." They deplored the recent killings as tragic and certainly unwelcome but also lamented how "these killings have, to a certain extent, cast suspicion on their own race." Still, they trusted "their friends" to "withhold judgment in these matters until the guilty person or persons may be brought to justice." Moreover, they invited "the closest inquiry into their lives, habits, and conduct of living," inviting officers to visit their businesses at any time, where they would learn firsthand that the Chinese were, above all, "law abiding people, and lovers of peace and quiet." Finally, the committee asked the *News* to print their letter in full, and thereby "confer a great favor on the few members of the Oriental race who are living in this community and who are bearing their share of the burden of government, and who love and respect their adopted country." The letter concluded, "Respectfully, by Lee Looie, Charlie Looie, and Charlie Loo, Committee."[128]

In July of 1921, yet another brutal murder of a Chinese laundryman, in many respects reminiscent of the earlier ones in Birmingham, disrupted the tranquility of an Alabama town just to the south of the Birmingham District. Another "unknown murderer" delivered a fatal ax blow to the head of a "quiet and inoffensive Chinaman" named Tom Howell in his Gadsden laundry business. When local citizens stopped by to pick up their laundry on the morning of July 19, they found the front door open, yet they were unaware "that the proprietor was in the back of the building murdered." Howell's employees later discovered "his lifeless and stiff body." As in the earlier murders in Birmingham, the reporter claimed that Howell "was known to keep considerable money in his place of business" and thus concluded that robbery had to be the motive. Woodliff Undertaking, owned by the local coroner, collected Howell's body. A coroner's inquest before a jury assembled on the day after the murder. Labeling it "one of the worst crimes perpetrated in this city in many years," the *Gadsden Daily Times* lauded the victim as a "peaceable citizen" well "liked by all who knew him."[129]

Tom Howell had lived in the United States for approximately eight years, and in Gadsden for the last two. He apparently managed the laundry business for his brother, W. A. Howell, also known as Charlie Lee, who had departed Gadsden for San Francisco two years before and had left the laundry in his brother's charge. The transition from the generic "Charlie Lee," a name often assumed by Chinese laundrymen and assigned by U.S. residents to multiple generations of men working in the same laundry over time, to the Anglicized W. A. and Tom Howell likely came through conversion to Christianity. "Christian foully murdered," trumpeted the *Albany-Decatur Daily* about Howell's demise, also warning ominously that "police of other cities have been asked to watch for a strange Chinaman, who was seen in the Howell establishment." Whether Howell was a Baptist or a Methodist appears to be up for debate. One account proclaimed that he was "a member of the Baptist Church," but another noted that Howell "often attended the Bible class at the First Methodist church where he was always welcome."[130]

The Howell murder highlighted the relationships that connected Chinese communities from Alabama to Atlanta. As the coroner's jury continued to weigh evidence in the days immediately following the murder, including examining witnesses, "several Chinamen from Atlanta and Birmingham arrived in Gadsden . . . to attend the inquest and to take charge of the body of their deceased brother." The party included a "cousin and nephew" of Howell, as his brother had already embarked on a return trip to China at the time of the murder. Howell's kinsmen planned to ship his body to Atlanta for burial in Greenwood Cemetery. A few days after the murder, Howell's nephew, Lon Sing, reopened the laundry for business, promising to first turn out the clothes left there in the week prior to Howell's murder. The local newspaper reported that "there are several other Chinamen here who are assisting in getting the business of the late Tom Howell straightened out."[131]

A week after the murder, the coroner's inquest appeared no closer to identifying Howell's killer, prompting Alabama's Governor Kilby to post a $250 reward "for the capturer of Tom Howell, a Chinaman, who was murdered and robbed."[132] A rumor that "the secret order of the Chinese," likely a reference to the Chinese Freemasons lodge to which Howell belonged, would augment that reward seemed to attract the attention of the Montgomery police. "A long distance message from Montgomery yesterday afternoon brought to a local Chinaman," reported the newspaper, revealed that police in that city had arrested a man named Charlie Parr for Howell's murder. This report prompted a call from Gadsden Police Chief Littlefield to the Montgomery police department, but no definitive information: "It seems that the Montgomery officers want to know all about the reward before they tell all they know."[133]

Littlefield then sent a Patrolman Brown to Montgomery to "identify the man held there on suspicion of complicity in the murder of Tom Howell," though no information indicated why Brown would be able to do so. Meanwhile, the reward money increased to $1,250 when Howell's "relatives and friends" raised the funds and placed them in the Etowah Trust and Savings Bank "for the apprehension of the murderer." The local law firm of Disque and Disque also announced its representation of the interests of "the Chinamen in Gadsden" in the Howell case.[134]

A break in the case finally seemed to come in mid-October with the arrest of multiple individuals. This led to the arrest of a white man named George Whatley, the only suspect to appear before a preliminary hearing in early November. Attorneys for Disque and Disque assisted the prosecution on behalf of "the Chinamen of Gadsden."[135] According to newspaper reports, a "great deal of interest was manifested in the trial," with the courtroom filled to capacity at every session. The evidence against Whatley, who worked as a machinist, remained unclear, other than an association with other individuals apparently known to have robbed a local bank and who had schemed to rob his employer, Gulf State Steel Company, of its payroll. Whatley offered an alibi of traveling elsewhere in the state at the time of Howell's murder. Few local whites seemed to believe the evidence against Whatley to be sufficient, and on November 7, Judge Herzberg agreed, acquitting Whatley of Howell's murder, since "he had made it clear to the court that he was not in Gadsden at the time of the murder." Howell's murder never even made it to the grand jury stage.[136]

As indicated by the unsolved murders of Charley Fein Ben, Sam Loo, Charlie Loo Soe, and Tom Howell, cultivating a white customer base and maintaining other social connections to local whites did not guarantee protection from the often violent vagaries of working-class life in many New South communities. If Alabama's Chinese laundrymen held an uncertain position in relation to the white side of the color line, they also had an uneasy relationship with African American residents. Indeed, the insecurity of their racial identity rendered that relationship particularly fraught, as they encountered Alabama's Black citizens as economic competitors, occasional customers, and as exemplified by the case of Charley Sing and Mary Matthews, sometime employees.

As the most "foreign" outsiders among the newcomers who were expanding New South communities, and laboring in an occupation also held by African American workers, the Chinese often suffered from petty crime and harassment from local Black residents. In Florence, for example, a Chinese laundryman named Charley George resorted to firing his pistol in the air to stop a gaggle of "negro boys" from continuing to pelt his storefront and his person with rocks. In Birmingham in 1898, a Black man named Robert Jones allegedly assaulted a Chinese man named Ching Jung in a dispute over a laundry ticket. "Chinaman Charlie" of Prattville surprised a "negro man" at his main street laundry when he awakened to find him rummaging through his personal trunk. Chung Lee similarly interrupted a robbery in progress at his laundry in Selma, where police arrived from next door to nab the African American thief running out the back.[137]

Encounters between Alabama's Chinese laundrymen and local African American women proved especially complicated to navigate. Since handwashing constituted a foundational occupation for Black women in the New South, Chinese laundries posed an obvious risk to their livelihoods. In Jackson, Mississippi (1866), Galveston, Texas (1877), and Atlanta, Georgia (1881), for example, Black laundrywomen demonstrated a strong assertion of occupational entitlement, enacting work stoppages and strikes that they were more than willing to defend in violent terms, if necessary.[138] Control of their own wages and work conditions primarily motived these work stoppages, but the context also sometimes involved economic competition from Chinese laundries. Striking washerwomen in Galveston, for example, "told Sam Lee, Slam Sing, and Wu Loong and the rest that they must close up and leave this city within fifteen days or they would be driven away. . . . [The] Chinese got no business coming here taking our work from us." Indeed, they warned, "we mean what we say, cause your time is growing old. We are coming. . . . we will die for our company. Miss Brooks is ready to shoulder her rifle, Miss Sillese [her] sharpshooter."[139]

Shortly after the washerwoman strike in Atlanta concluded, a reporter for the *Atlanta Constitution,* in a thinly veiled effort to promote a new commercial laundry that had recently opened, undertook to "investigate," in December 1882, why Atlanta had only one Chinese laundry. The owner reportedly explained to the reporter, "They cannot compete with the negro washerwomen. Their rates are low and I suppose the Chinaman is starved out." Moreover, noted the reporter, "the colored people have a healthy hatred for laundries . . . They feel that to wash is the colored woman's birthright, and that any person who interferes is a usurper. The Chinaman comes in for a share of their dislike."[140] The Black washerwomen of Charleston apparently agreed, responding to a dispute in 1889 between city officials and Chinese laundry proprietors over business licensing fees by stating, "They have declared war against the heathen and will aid the municipal authorities in the fight."[141]

In New South Alabama, the low numbers of Chinese immigrants overall made it unlikely that Chinese laundry businesses posed a significant threat to African American livelihoods. More significant would have been other developments in the washing industry, such as the advent of steam and electrical machinery and the movement of larger capitalized interests into the laundry business in urban areas.[142] However, nearly all the Chinese men who came to Alabama after the Alabama and Chattanooga Railroad episode concluded in the 1870s operated or worked in laundry businesses, first as small hand-washing enterprises and eventually as steam laundries. Their appearance certainly created the impression that such a threat of real economic competition *might* exist. Moreover, as their businesses stabilized and grew, some Chinese proprietors employed African American women such as Mary Matthews in their laundries. Both situations provided opportunities for miscommunication, mistrust, and a general state of tension and conflict.

A writer for the *Evergreen Courant* in Conecuh County, Alabama, reminisced about the Chinese laundryman who once operated a downtown laundry in the early twentieth century. Known locally for handing out chestnuts to "the boys who had not abused him during the year by calling him names and running," the laundryman supplanted an African American freedwoman named Carolina Crosby, who had long taken in white washing.[143] In Florence in 1916, a racist advertisement called on local residents to eschew patronizing a Chinese laundry, asking "Who gets any return from patronizing these aliens?" and pointing out that "this kind of competition does no good and displaces honest, earnest, industrious women," who allegedly earned "good wages and under very excellent conditions." Residents should take their laundry to the "Florence women workers," who "are suffering for want of work."[144]

Two years later, Black women deployed the wartime atmosphere to their advantage against their Chinese employer in Ensley. Angered by his refusal to allow them to leave work to observe a Red Cross parade, the women publicly accused Gee Sen of a lack of patriotism. When one of the women allegedly announced her intent to attend the parade "because I am an American," the women accused their employer of declaring in response, "Damn America! I am running this place," and pulling down the front window shades to block the women's view. A Department of Justice official shortly appeared at the Ensley laundry, arresting Sen on a charge of "disloyalty," which also kicked off an investigation into how he had entered the United States at all.[145] Whether Sen had simply had a bad day or, more likely, the episode derived from long-simmering tensions, angering the Black women he employed brought Sen to the brink of deportation.

Starting in 1870, Chinese immigrant laborers diversified Alabama's urban, small-town, and rural communities, arriving first as gang laborers imported to help construct the Alabama and Chattanooga Railroad in 1870, and then, beginning in the 1880s, arriving as independent laborers to establish or work in laundries. Chinese immigrants experienced their Alabama sojourn as an often precarious balancing act between the extremes of white approbation as providers of needed labor or a useful service, and as Christian "converts," and objects of Black hostility as economic competitors. While the Chinese on the AL-CH Railroad labored alongside Black men who resented their presence, for example, such a feeling might well have been mutual. If the Stanton brothers did indeed hire Chinese workers fresh off the transcontinental railroad projects, they could have been some of the same men involved in strikes against the Union and Central Pacific railroads in 1867 and 1868, when railroad management imported Black strikebreakers from the deep South in order to more handily break the strike.[146]

What really prevented larger numbers of Chinese laborers from entering the deep South, however, was hard economic reality. New South industrialists and planters wanted, above all else, labor that could be worked like slaves. The freed people would not willingly resubmit to such conditions, but neither would the Chinese, and to add insult to injury, Chinese labor was more expensive to procure and sustain than had been anticipated. Southern planters and industrialists found they could not "bind" Chinese laborers in the way their Cuban counterparts were able to do.[147]

Chinese agent Choy Chew predicted as much in 1869, when a reporter asked him, during a visit to the United States, "What do you think of the scheme for bringing Chinese labor to the South?" At the time, Chew anticipated that most interest in the Chinese would come from southern planters in the deep South, but his point would have been useful for the railroad Stantons and others to hear: "I have no doubt that Mr. Koopmanschap will find little difficulty in procuring laborers for the Southern planters who want them," Chew remarked, "but I must wait to see the experiment tried before saying that millions of our people will rush to the States of the South." As he explained, "One peculiarity of the Chinese is that if the first reports which reach them of a new settlement whither some of their countrymen have gone are not of a flattering character they reject all subsequent invitations ... It will depend altogether upon the success of the first Chinese experiment at the South whether the millions will go there."[148]

Individual Chinese laborers controlled little except their mobility, and like the freed people, they exercised this one power whenever and however they could. When the Stantons failed to pay their railroad workers, they lost many of the Chinese men to others who could, particularly to Delta planters. The Chinese who ended up in Alabama after 1870 came on their own economic terms, as individuals, not as groups of contracted laborers. And they were not working in the fields or on the railroads.

Chinese immigrants succeeded in New South Alabama, where they could establish an economic niche providing drudge labor to white customers without growing into a sufficiently large community that it might pose a social threat to whites or a significant economic threat to Blacks. Ultimately, however, the conditions and treatment they endured in Alabama compelled many to leave. Even those who found economic success in the New South, such as Tom Howell of Gadsden, for example, or who nurtured relationships to prominent local whites, such as Joe Jung, remained vulnerable to the traumas exacted by the insecurity of life under Jim Crow. The racial fluidity that characterized Chinese life in New South Alabama also shaped the experience of other immigrants arriving in the state, many of whom landed, as did Dolphina Lesko and Charley Sing, in the communities within and surrounding the New South's industrial heartland, the Birmingham mineral district.

CHAPTER 3

"ITALIANS . . . IN THE COLORED QUARTERS"

Immigrant and African American Encounters in New South Alabama

When Italian laborers started to arrive in the Birmingham coal district in the 1880s to work in the mines, no one really knew exactly what to expect. By the fall of 1891, however, there seemed to be plenty of disenchantment to go around. Under the xenophobic headline "The Mafia at Greely,'" the *Bessemer Journal* reported the eruption of a "small riot" at the Greely mines one Saturday in early September. A dispute between a Black miner and an Italian miner took an ugly turn when the former sank his pickax into the head of the latter.

"The Mafia cry was raised at once," announced the article, as "every Italian miner in the different mines" came "running with his pick, shovel or any other kind of weapon he could get a hold of." Mine superintendent Major Miller raced to the scene and quickly concluded that "it was impossible to control them in their madness." To quell the angry Italians, he appointed thirty men to pursue the perpetrator into the woods and charged several others to carry the injured man back to camp. He then sent the rest back to work. As they dispersed, Miller prudently withdrew "all of his colored laborers" to work in a separate mine on the premises. A few days later, the *Journal* reported that "all difficulties originating from the riot between the Italians and negroes at Greely Mines last Saturday have been overcome, and everything is now running as smoothly and quietly as formerly."[1]

Although little record remains of this brief but dramatic event, the Greely mines incident demonstrated how the New South project often deployed immigrants and African American laborers in the South against each other. Yet the tension and violence that appeared to beset relations between the Italian and African American men in the Greely mines was not the only way that immigrants encountered Alabama's Black citizens. There were times when more cordial or even collaborative relations existed as well. For example, the Chinese men laboring for the Alabama and Chattanooga Railroad in 1870 joined with their Black coworkers to shut down the Meridian branch to protest J. C. Stanton's wage perfidy. Charley Sing wedded Mary Matthews. And an Italian woman recalled fondly the welcome she received shortly after her arrival in Birmingham, when an African American neighbor stopped by to offer an iconic platter of warm homemade biscuits.[2]

European laborers often shared with African Americans and the Chinese a precarious existence in New South Alabama, even if they never occupied an identical position in the region's racial hierarchy. In contrast to the Chinese, the Europeans' physical appearance of "whiteness" might afford some protection, even when accompanied by a "foreign" accent or no English at all, or by unfamiliar religious or cultural customs.[3] Both white and Black Americans, however, filtered their encounters with the immigrant peoples arriving in the United States at the time through stereotypes, prejudices, and racial typologies commonly held in the late nineteenth and early twentieth centuries.[4] And economic circumstances, as well as ideas about race and ethnicity, shaped where someone from Greece, Hungary, Ireland, Italy, Scotland, or elsewhere landed along the boundary between safety and vulnerability in the New South. To labor in harsh and unsafe conditions for low wages was to have far less power than employers.

The racial hierarchies that structured power in the New South complicated how African Americans and immigrants met each other in Alabama, creating opportunities for collaboration against white employers but also generating tensions, conflict, and sometimes violence. Immigrant racial identity thus proved to be both mutable and contingent, marching European immigrants in lockstep with southern white supremacy, in one context, but subjecting them to the discomfort and trauma of being racialized victims, in another.[5]

Alabama communities witnessed a diverse influx of immigrants from around the world, which included people from virtually every continent. Europeans constituted the largest group in the wave of immigration of the late nineteenth and early twentieth centuries, both to the United States and among the immigrant laborers who arrived in the New South. Exact numbers across the decades from the post-Reconstruction era to the World War I period are hard to pin down, given the mobility of immigrant laborers within the state and region. However, for each decennial census, immigrants enumerated as born in Italy often were the single largest group of European laborers in the state and in Jefferson County, the heart of the Birmingham District. Thus, while accounts of other European laborers occasionally surfaced, Italian immigrants appeared most often in newspaper accounts describing European encounters with African Americans. Additionally, oral interviews conducted with Italian American descendants still living in the Birmingham area in the 1980s provide further details on how this group of immigrant laborers experienced New South Alabama.

Jefferson County, Alabama, Immigrants' Country of Origin, 1880–1920

Country	*1880*	*1900*	*1910*	*1920*
Austria	2	102	371	260
Canada	19	218	312	509
China	0	12	12	18
England	101	1,119	1,194	1,045
Germany	64	788	897	614
Greece	0	104	313	481
Hungary	1	194	136	89
Ireland	148	481	402	298
Italy and Sicily	1	517	1,877	2,196
Norway	1	26	46	31
Russia	5	240	781	820
Scotland	46	806	688	658
Syria	0	8	48	267

Source: Federal Census, Population, 1880, 1900, 1910, 1920, Ancestry.com.

Alabama's Italian laborers belonged to a much larger diaspora of approximately 16 million citizens who left Italy during the "long nineteenth century," from 1789 to 1914. Of these, about one-third came to North America, with approximately 50 percent ending up as "birds of passage," or sojourners who eventually returned home. Italy's emergence as a new nation-state in the 1870s had failed to ameliorate economic problems rooted in a rapidly growing population within a depressed agricultural economy. Officially sanctioned discrimination against southern Italians exacerbated difficult economic conditions in the late nineteenth century, even creating "rampant starvation."[6]

"The conditions in . . . Sicily, were very sad," explained Charlie LaRocca, whose parents immigrated to Birmingham in 1908. "There was no work and people had a hard time there. People had to go anywhere to find jobs."[7] Approximately 90 percent of the Italians who went to the New South originated in southern Italy, especially Sicily.[8] Those who ventured into the deep South of the United States often worked seasonally as sugarcane laborers in Louisiana or on cotton plantations in the Delta, sometimes finding off-season work in Gulf Coast railroad construction. Many of these Italians also made their way into the coal mines of Appalachia, often having worked in sulfur mines in the old country. Their presence in the lowest-paid occupations, doing unskilled, hard labor, earned the Italian diaspora, according to one scholar, the moniker of the "Chinese of Europe."[9] Unlike the Chinese, however, Italian immigrants could bring over family members to the United States if they could accrue the funds to do so, and they could apply for naturalized citizenship.

The Italians who ended up in the Birmingham District often had been farmers in the Sicilian villages of Campofranco, Bisacquino, or Agrigento, where labor-intensive agriculture had long struggled amid persistent economic depression. Lured to the United States and then to Alabama by their connections to family and extended kin already there, or persuaded by labor agents of better opportunities in the mines and mills of the district, Italians usually landed first in New Orleans, where they worked briefly on the outlying sugar plantations. They eventually made their way to Birmingham, having heard from relatives about job opportunities in the mines, rolling mills, and furnaces of the district.[10]

Second-generation Italian American Rose Maenza recalled that her father, Louis, arrived in New Orleans as a teenager in 1887 but ended up working as a "waterboy" in Birmingham for the Tennessee Coal, Iron and

Immigrant "Pioneers of Ensley," Birmingham District, Alabama, August 20, 1905. *Left to right* (first row), Louis Maenza, John Cuilla, Joseph Maenza, Joe Rizzo; (second row), Charles Rouss, Tony Artale, [unidentified], Jacob Pumilia; (third row), Joseph Pumilia, Tony Cuilla, Joe Tortorigi, [unidentified]. *Birmingfind Collection, 829.3.8, Birmingham, Ala. Public Library Archives.*

Railroad Company, making less than one dollar a day. He soon left that job and returned to New Orleans to open a small grocery with his brother. A levee break, however, flooded the store, ruining the business and souring her father on New Orleans. In 1904, he returned to Birmingham, specifically to the large Italian enclave at Ensley, where he and his brother again tried their hand at the grocery business, renting a small market. By 1907, they had expanded into the wholesale grocery business selling bulk goods in the largely African American neighborhood of Tuxedo Junction.[11]

In the Italian American Lorina family of Birmingham, however, it was Paul Lorina's mother who devised an alternative when his father could not earn enough as a young man in the TCI yard. "We can't make a living at this," she told her husband, but "get me a little grocery store and I'll help you." As Paul remembered, "My daddy bought a little corner grocery store. I don't know how in the world he paid for it but he bought the property and all." He

Rouss and Maenza Wholesale Company, an Italian business in Ensley, Birmingham District, Alabama, 1912. Foreground, *left to right,* Louis Maenza, [unidentified], Dennis Echols, "Mr. Dupuy." Included in the group to the rear are Phillip Rouss and Joe Rouss. *Birmingfind Collection, 829.2.51, Birmingham, Ala. Public Library Archives.*

kept his job at TCI "during the day and at night he'd come home and cut the meat and put it in the icebox for my mother. Other Italian stores were all around us but there was enough for everybody. It was fair competition. We wasn't jealous of one another."[12]

Charlie LaRocca's father worked in the coal mines when he first came to Birmingham, but he found the work too dangerous. His parents then tried the grocery business, but his father ultimately found it was easier to peddle to workers around the district than to manage a store. In LaRocca's memory, many Italians worked in the mines, particularly for the Republic Company, and flooded into the Ensley and East Thomas neighborhoods. But he also recalled that many Italians left industrial work to set up "papa and mama stores" or to peddle goods, often purchasing from Italian truck farmers around East Lake.[13]

The father of Italian descendants Francis and Nellie Saia, for example, tried the dry goods business in Birmingham but soon abandoned it because "he was a gardener first." He managed to rent land for thirty years, hiring "all kinds of immigrants" to help him grow "his first class fruits and vegeta-

Italian fruit and vegetable store in Wylam, Birmingham District, Alabama, undated. *Birmingfind Collection, 829.11.6.68, Birmingham, Ala. Public Library Archives.*

bles," including "lettuce, tomatoes, [and] okra," which he sold to hotels and hospitals.[14] Much like the Italian laborers of Louisiana, Alabama's Italian immigrants shifted among occupations, often choosing fruit peddling, groceries, or truck gardening as safer and sometimes more lucrative alternatives to mining.

Also in keeping with their experience in Louisiana and elsewhere, Alabama's Italians encountered discrimination as a daily part of life in the New South. On the sugar plantations north of New Orleans, Italian immigrants served as field hands, working in the same low-skill hard labor as African Americans. They also experienced a racialization that derived, in part, from that association with Black labor. To improve their social and economic status, according to one scholar, Italian field hands had to disassociate themselves from African Americans and embrace "whiteness" in order to move into alternative occupations, such as truck farming and retail grocery service.[15]

In the Birmingham District, in contrast, Italian immigrants moved into a variety of occupations right from the start, and when they did enter the coal mines, they worked alongside both U.S.-born Black and white southerners as well as other immigrants.[16] Nevertheless, Italian residents suffered verbal insults, particularly the "dago" slur, and often found that white residents refused to trade with them.[17] "The reason so many Italians put their stores in the colored quarters," explained Italian descendant Mrs. Argentina Morganti, "was that the white people wouldn't trade with them."[18] African American residents would, however, and the dearth of stores in the outlying towns and camps of the district created opportunity for enterprising immigrants. Paul Lorina's parents, along with many other immigrants, "set up stores in Black neighborhoods because there weren't stores there and it made it convenient for them to set up business."[19] These ventures provided a needed service, generating primary or supplementary income for the Italian families and offering closer and cheaper foodstuffs and products for laborers.

An Italian "floating gang" crew of miners that "moved from one task to another, at the Woodward Iron Works in Brighton." Vincent Costa, pictured in the center of the front row, directed the crew. *Birmingfind Collection, 829.3.28, Birmingham, Ala. Public Library Archives.*

White merchants of brick-and-mortar establishments, however, did not welcome competition from itinerant immigrant peddlers and grocers. In many southern communities, "blue laws" kept licensed businesses closed on Sundays, which created an opportunity for peddlers, who could find a steady market when other businesses were closed. That niche also led to conflict with city and town merchants, who used local governments to periodically push for new licensing fees and other regulatory mechanisms aimed expressly at shutting down immigrant peddlers and competitors. The proliferation of fruit stands and vendors emerged as a persistent source of tension as the working-class neighborhoods and downtown district of Birmingham developed.[20]

Labeling these immigrant proprietors the "fruit stand nuisance," the *Birmingham News* called for their removal in 1889. The Birmingham Board of Aldermen heard an ordinance, "To Prohibit Stands on Streets and Sidewalks," in November 1889, which aimed to stop "any person, firm or corporation" from placing any "fruit stand, booth, auction stand or stands" that obstructed any portion of city streets or sidewalks. Moreover, at the same meeting the board considered another ordinance to forbid the "running of post-cart fruit vendors after January 1st, when the present license expires." Passage of the ordinance, announced the *News* editors, "ends the career of the dago." Ten years later, the district's Retail Grocers Association again went after the small proprietors of fruit and cigar stands, many of them immigrants, convincing city police to arrest multiple vendors for violating Sunday blue laws.[21]

African Americans not only traded with immigrant peddlers and grocers but also often resided alongside the streets, alleyways, and company quarters where immigrants lived. Alabama Italian Francis Oddo's father and uncle opened "a little bitty store [in] a small room" and traded with many Black families nearby. But the communities also maintained residential segregation. "We had to live there; we didn't know any better," remembered Frances Oddo, but "we didn't mix with the colored families in the company houses." As Charlie LaRocca reminisced in the 1980s, "In those days, Blacks and whites didn't mix."[22] Immigrant quarters might be clustered according to nationality, but they usually lived in separate camps, along separate if sometimes adjacent streets, with immigrant families on one side of the quarters and Black families on the other. The liminal racial status of immigrants in the New South, especially of Italians, thus generated both proximity and familiarity with their African Americans customers and neighbors but also nurtured a competitive difference that could be contentious.

Given that Alabama's immigration boosters commonly trumpeted their campaigns as a means of disciplining or replacing Black labor, African Americans often perceived European and other immigrants as unwelcome guests whose presence promised to further erode their own tenuous position. The dust of the Civil War had scarcely settled, for example, before the *Memphis Daily Appeal* called on the Freedmen's Bureau to ignore the request of "respectable white and colored laborers around Mobile" and prevent the importation of German laborers by planters anxious to set them to work "for lower wages than a negro can subsist upon."[23] Several years later, in 1886, Reverend A. N. McEwen, pastor of a large African American Baptist church in Mobile, delivered a fiery sermon to a Knights of Labor assembly gathered at the Dexter Avenue Baptist Church in Montgomery. To answer his own query, "What means the establishment of bureaus of foreign emigration?," Reverend McEwen answered, "It means the bringing in of foreign labor as competition with home labor in the interest of monopoly and against labor organizations of this country." In his view, "the importation of European paupers and bandits for the purpose of oppressing the laboring classes of this country and lowering wages cannot result in any good." And while Reverend McEwen declared, "I am not a member of the K. of L.," he endorsed the Knights' "Declaration of Principles," including section XVI: "That the importation of foreign labor under contract be prohibited."[24]

When a national bill to appropriate $600,000 for a "Colored World Exposition" arose in October 1886, the editor of Alabama's *Marion Herald* questioned the inclusion of "Indians, Chinese and Maylays" along with "Africans" by the bill's sponsors: "Does the gentleman think that the Chinese, Maylays etc., have as great a claim upon the National Treasury as the Negroes?" After all, he explained, "the Negro is a citizen, pays taxes and does all he can to promote the general welfare," unlike the others. "The Indian, as a class, is not a citizen, pays no taxes and does all he can to obstruct the navigation of this ship of state. Now the Chinaman, what does he contribute to the Commonwealth? Nothing, he comes here, works like a beaver, subsist[s] upon what we consider unclean, and dispatches his earnings, in toto, back to the Flowery Kingdom." He then asserted that "the Negro has an inalienably [*sic*] claim upon the national treasury."[25]

Several years later, the officers of the Colored Farmers Progressive Union in Alabama followed suit, addressing Congressman Oscar Underwood in support of a plan for the U.S. government to designate all of New Mexico "for the purpose of setting it apart as a reservation for the Negro race, under the same terms and Conditions under which the Indian Territory was set apart for the Indians." After all, T. G. Fowler reminded Underwood, "We believe that the Negro has greater claims on our Government than the Indians or any other alien race—for provision and legislative protection."[26]

With his dependence upon white elite benefactors and their frequent support of schemes to recruit immigrant labor and farmers to the state, Booker T. Washington trod lightly on the question of immigration. On the one hand, Tuskegee Institute profited from the enrollment of foreign-born students of color, most of whom hailed from Caribbean countries and territories such as Cuba, Haiti, and Puerto Rico. On the other hand, schemes to use immigrants to replace Black labor undermined Washington's program to nurture Black prosperity through self-reliance and white support. Thus, Washington opposed efforts to bar the immigration of people of color but also undertook a European tour to investigate the conditions compelling outmigration to the United States. He tried to make the case that impoverished southern Blacks and European peasants actually had a lot in common. Yet he also planted stories highlighting moments when immigrant recruitment schemes had floundered, in order to draw attention to the superiority of Black labor.

In 1910, for example, he wrote to Oswald Garrison Villard of Huntington, New York, about the alleged failure of the Italian labor experiment on the Percy plantations in Sunnyside, Arkansas, and he shared an article "which shows that Mr. John Gracie, the man who employed the Italians ... has gotten rid of the Italians, and replaced them with Negro labor." In 1915, Washington wrote to the editor of the *New York World*, siding against a bill prohibiting the immigration of people of African descent as an obstacle to the school's expansion of the college's foreign-born student population. Washington also pointed out that "the bill puts an unnecessary slight on colored people by classing them with alien criminals." Most African immigrants, Washington noted, were of "West Indian descent," were "law-abiding," and "have never become anarchists or as a class given trouble to the Government," a clear slap at European immigrants.[27]

While Black elites such as Washington may have approached the issue of immigration with some ambivalence, or at least caution, the same was not true necessarily of Black workers, who often construed immigrants as a direct threat to their own livelihoods. As seen in the case of the Chinese launderers and Black washerwomen, the most intense conflicts between European immigrants and African Americans emerged in the state's more urban areas. Local newspapers often reported incidents of crime involving Black residents and European immigrants, from petty theft to murder. To what extent African Americans actually were responsible for these crimes is hard to determine, given the highly racialized operation of law enforcement and the sensationalized nature of the era's print journalism. Nevertheless, such stories testify to significant tension between European immigrants and African American laborers, tensions that sometimes prompted conflict and even violence. The incidents also highlighted the proximity of immigrant and African American laborers in New South communities.

Many encounters echoed what Chinese immigrants experienced in Alabama's towns and cities. In the spring of 1897, for example, Greek fruit stand and restaurant operator Vecillios Leckas died during a robbery of his store, which was located next door to a local saloon in Birmingham. Police arrested four African American men for the crime, the only evidence of their guilt apparently being their habit of frequenting the saloon.[28] When a white teenager ended up stabbed for stealing peanuts off the stand of another Greek proprietor in the city, in 1901, the *Birmingham News* was far more sympathetic to the thief, described by the writer as "the little fellow," than to the "strange boy [who] had been left there by the Greek who runs the stand."[29] The sympathy tables turned, however, when the ethnicity and race of the victim and perpetrator reversed. In 1906, the *News* reported "Fruit Merchant Foully Murdered . . . Negro Shoots Anastasius Argiro Through the Heart and then Escapes." Having only resided in the United States for a few months, Argiro was "murdered in cold blood by an unknown negro." After buying a dime's worth of eggs, the assailant allegedly helped himself to some nuts. At that point, "a small boy, the son of the dead man, told him to put the nuts back, and when the negro refused the little fellow called his father." When Argiro told the man to replace the nuts, the assailant allegedly took *more* nuts instead, and when Argiro moved toward him, he "pulled out a pistol and fired on him, the bullet entering the heart" and then "ran away." Argiro and his fifteen-year-old son had only been in the United States "a short time and neither could talk English very plainly. The son is now alone in America." Police were determined, the newspaper reported, to "capture the negro and avenge the foul murder."[30]

In 1902, authorities in Blocton, a mining town within the Birmingham District, arrested Ed Walker, an African American male, for the murder of Mrs. Costello, an Italian woman married to a miner who also ran a store. According to the report, nearby friends, who allegedly witnessed a Black man enter and leave the store, found Mrs. Costello soon after, dead from an ax blow to the head. Police allegedly gave "pursuit of the murderer" and settled on Walker, who was unfortunate to be found in the vicinity with seventy-three dollars on hand. "If he is the right man," reported the *Union-Banner* of Clanton, Alabama, "it is supposed . . . he hid the remainder of the money" that he allegedly stole from Mrs. Costello.[31] When victimized by a white petty thief, an immigrant proprietor might appear "foreign" and "strange." But when targeted by Black crime, their racial identity landed more solidly on the white side of the line.

Such incidents also underscore how Black Alabamians and immigrant laborers contended for vending space and markets on the streets of the state's urban areas, in Birmingham, Mobile, and Montgomery. Italians, Greeks, Syrians, and Eastern Europeans found an economic niche hustling fruit and other small goods in the urban commercial districts, where both blue- and white-collar workers provided a ready market. But they likely were not the first ones there.

African Americans had long used informal commerce to earn income, a tradition stretching back to the era of slavery and the rural practice of "deadfall" markets. Essentially, these roadside markets allowed enslaved people to sell to each other the food and small goods they had either produced or purloined. With emancipation, such deadfalls also became a potential means toward economic independence for both the seller and the buyer. As "sources of cloth, molasses, sugar, cheap jewelry, and cottonseed," however, rural roadside vendors increasingly angered Black Belt merchants, because they offered spaces free of white control for Black farmers and wage workers, along with the possibility of avoiding the inevitable debt that came with doing business with white merchants and planters. By the end of the 1870s, Alabama's political leaders had defined deadfalling as a serious crime, and multitudes of Alabama's Black men and women found themselves imprisoned for traditional practices that now constituted larceny. In 1875, for example, selling a product in Alabama before sunrise or after sundown could earn a person twelve months of hard labor, at least if the seller was Black. In fact, both Blacks and whites engaged in "nighttime trading," but white officials typically arrested only Black vendors, further contributing to the rapid growth of the Black convict population.[32]

As the Birmingham District boom began in the 1880s, the population of African Americans grew accordingly, and most of those who relocated there came from rural Alabama, particularly the Black Belt. They likely brought with them the practice of supplementing their incomes through this tradition of informal commerce. Although African Americans were both the primary sellers and main customers in rural Alabama, however, they now encountered competition from the immigrants of Greece, Syria, Eastern Europe, and especially Italy and Sicily, who sought to do the same. Thus, Alabama's immigrant peddlers and small grocery proprietors faced not only resentful and competitive white merchants but sometimes hostile African Americans as well. As a result, a stream of tense and occasionally violent encounters played out on the state's urban street corners. Incidents that appeared, at first glance, to be merely individual disagreements often morphed into something else. As in the Greely mines incident, or the conflict over purloined peanuts, a misunderstanding or argument could quickly escalate into a deeper and more dangerous confrontation. The xenophobic prejudices common to all Americans at the time, combined with little personal connection to any prominent local whites, left immigrant peddlers in a potentially dangerous position when confronted with hostile African American competitors. The way in which newspapers reported such incidents reflected the unsettled racial position of immigrant laborers in communities stratified by race and class but also in a nearly constant state of transition and change.[33]

In the fall of 1910, the *Montgomery Advertiser* gleefully employed nearly every racist and xenophobic trope possible to report on a confrontation between fruit vendors in downtown Montgomery, in an article headlined "No Right Sella Da App . . . Italian Fruit Vendor and Negro Mammy Fight

... Arrival of Police and Large Crowd of Negro Servants." According to the writer, immigrant peddler G. Snider had obtained a city license to peddle his fruits along Court Street. On the day in question, he encountered a competitor, Mary Walker, "an old negro woman" who had an established peddling business of her own in the same area. Described as a "huckster" in the article, Snider took exception when Walker set up to sell her fruit as usual. He physically accosted her, striking her in the face and then running to find a police officer. When he returned with two policemen, Snider demanded that they arrest Walker. By this point, however, a crowd of displeased Black locals had begun to gather. The writer deployed an arsenal of racist language to describe what happened next: "By this time every old 'mammy' in the neighborhood was gathered around the two huckster wagons making unladylike remarks about 'Dagoes.' A large number of small boys also were present and added interest to the affair by making faces, throwing pebbles, and teasing the Italian. After questioning everyone near the trouble, the police officers decided the Italian was the guilty party."

The police proceeded to arrest Snider, not Walker, for disorderly conduct. And "several people who had watched the trouble added to the Italian's discomfort by purchasing apples from the old negro woman right under the Italian's very nose." In the aftermath, reported the newspaper, "Mary Williams is still selling apples on Court Street, and white people who know her say that the Italian will make few sales in the neighborhood where the difficulty took place."[34] Snider had assumed that he could publicly assault a Black woman and then rely on the police to defend his claim. That did not prove to be the case, however, as the police instead sided with Walker, who appeared to enjoy more connections to local downtown whites.

A particularly tragic incident erupted from yet another chance encounter between Birmingham's Black and Italian immigrant residents. In this case, the local Italian community deployed Jim Crow practices to exact revenge on a Black man accused of murdering one of their own.[35] Whereas Snider's attempt to claim white membership backfired, the Italians in this case successfully asserted white entitlement by lynching John Chandler; they landed squarely on the white side of the color line.

On a Friday evening in the late winter of 1912, in Bessemer, an industrial town a dozen miles southwest of Birmingham proper, a local Black man named John Chandler walked into a grocery owned by Italian immigrant, Joseph Gagliano. Little evidence remains about what transpired next. Newspapers reported that Chandler allegedly refused to pay for about a "dime's worth" of fruit. When proprietor Gagliano insisted on payment, Chandler reportedly shot and killed him.[36] Within a few hours, a coroner's inquest identified Chandler, along with two other African American men, Forney Smith and Charles Page, as either the perpetrators of the crime or at least privy to information about Gagliano's murder. Deputies placed all three men under arrest in Bessemer, then prepared to transport them by streetcar to the Jefferson County jail on Sunday morning.

In the wake of Joseph Gagliano's murder, devastated family and friends quickly made funeral arrangements, which included a traditional procession carrying his body through the streets of Bessemer. Led by prominent Italian residents and the members of the Italian Society, the procession began on Sunday morning. According to one report, "a strong undercurrent of excitement" had been evident on Bessemer's streets the day before, and while no organized plan had developed to attempt to seize Chandler and the other men, many of the Italian participants nonetheless brought pistols to the funeral march.[37]

About the time that several hundred of Gagliano's family and friends, along with many members of the broader Italian community, traversed the industrial district in funereal lockstep, county deputies departed the Bessemer courthouse with Chandler, Fortney, and Smith in shackles, heading for the county jail. As they waited on the curb for a streetcar, the Gagliano procession of several hundred grieving and no doubt angry Italians began passing by. When the streetcar stopped on the far side of the street, the deputies, incredibly, cut through the crowd of marchers with the shackled prisoners in tow.

At this moment, Louis Gagliano, Joseph's bereaved brother, stepped up and shot Chandler in the back four times, killing him instantly. As Chandler's body slumped, Deputy Parker grabbed Louis around the waist and began to shout for assistance. Amid the chaos prompted by the assault on the prisoners, a large crowd of Italians stopped marching to surround the deputies, and half a dozen struggled with the officer to free Louis Gagliano. When the deputies stood their ground, the Italian men gave up on freeing their friend and instead turned to fire multiple shots into Chandler's prostrate body. Only the appearance of further multitudes of Black onlookers, reported one newspaper, convinced the "Italian mob" to desist and continue with the funeral procession. Authorities transported Chandler's bloody remains to a local undertaker, and the deputies, minus one who had received a flesh wound in the leg, continued with Forney and Smith to the Birmingham city jail.[38]

In the immediate aftermath of this assault, "an immense crowd [and] a steady stream of people," namely, African American residents, visited "the undertaker's parlor to see the body of the negro, which had been hauled away in the dead wagon still with handcuffs on his wrists." Sheriff McAdory sent Louis Gagliano to the county jail. Meanwhile, on Monday morning "crowds" loitered on the corner where the events had transpired, "viewing the place" where Gagliano and his comrades had exacted vengeance for his brother's murder by butchering an unarmed Black man.[39] Despite the plethora of witnesses to the crime, including officers at the scene, a coroner's inquest quickly concluded that Chandler "came to his death at the hands of a number of Italians, to the jury unknown." While dozens, perhaps hundreds, of people obviously had witnessed Louis Gagliano's shooting of Chandler, and even though a deputy had grabbed him while he stood over Chandler's body and still held his freshly fired pistol, Gagliano denied any involvement.[40]

When it became clear that Chandler would never receive any semblance of justice, African Americans in Bessemer organized. Several hundred people met in early February at an African Methodist Episcopal church on the outskirts of the city and resolved to implement "a boycott of Italian merchants." Black citizens who continued to trade with the Italian merchants would be fined $2.50.[41] "The recent killing of a negro in that town by Italians," explained one newspaper account, "is given as the reason for the resolution."[42] Within a month, reported the *Montgomery Times,* the "Negro boycott" had proven "very effective." Describing the effort as "one of the most complete boycotts ever reported," the previous two months had seen "no trading at all . . . by the negroes with the men they formerly patronized largely." Soon, "at many of the stores not a negro has entered for weeks and the Italian merchants have not only lost a large portion of their trade, but they are unable to dispose of the stock they have on hand." Many of the targeted merchants had already decided to sell their business and property "to go into business elsewhere." As a result, "negroes in some instances have opened stores themselves, while many of the grocery stores in Bessemer now carry heavy stocks of fruits, a thing not done in the past." According to the *Advertiser,* many of the Italian merchants and grocers were relocating to Birmingham and nearby Ensley.[43]

The most frequently cited example of Italian encounters with racial violence in the New South has been the notorious lynching of eleven Italian nationals by a white mob in New Orleans in 1891.[44] However, the Gagliano case demonstrates the other, but still contradictory, side of immigrant racial flexibility. Joseph Gagliano met a fate not uncommon for immigrant laborers and proprietors in the New South, much like the spate of unsolved killings of Chinese laundrymen. But Gagliano's family and friends seized a quasi-white identity to seek their own, completely southern form of extralegal justice to defend the Gaglianos and their community's honor. They achieved this through the murder of an unarmed Black man, and they did so with no lasting legal consequences.

A relationship steeped in both dependence and competition brought Alabama's immigrant and African American residents into testy proximity in the state's urban and small-town neighborhoods, highlighting the unpredictability of navigating the region's racial hierarchies. The contradictory nature of Italian immigrant–African American relations similarly emerged in the contentious labor environment that brought so many newcomers to New South Alabama's coal district. In the earlier years of the Birmingham industrial boom, as mining provided employment to scores of Black and white southerners, immigrant miners arrived as replacement laborers, to stave off organizing and undermine strikes. From their first appearance at the Warrior Coal and Coke Company mines in 1884, African American miners greeted the arrival of these newcomers with deep suspicion and great alarm.

The railroad companies feeding into and out of the Birmingham District colluded in 1884 to cut the purchase price per ton of coal.[45] Five hundred miners in the Warrior fields struck in May over the accompanying wage reduction.[46] Newspapers reported ominously that "the coal companies announce their intention to get miners from the North," while the strikers "threaten that they will prevent any new comers from working, by violence if necessary." By May 20, mine operations in the Warrior fields had been suspended "for several weeks," while miners in the "upper" part of the district "held out against the reduction" but then "were forced to yield after" miners in the "lower" district allegedly "conceded." Yet, according to the editor of the *Montgomery Advertiser,* the strike was far from over. "One concern is offered 150 . . . Hungarian miners, or the same number of Italians from New York City." Work had resumed in some of the mines, but not in others. By mid-August, the newspaper reported that "the striking coal miners at Warrior today induced a force of newly arrived Italians not to work."[47]

More specifically, the striking miners had encountered a small group of ten Italian men, who arrived in the district under contract with the Warrior Coal and Coke Company.[48] The strikers, many of whom may have been members of the Knights of Labor, "persuaded" the men not to work, and most of the mines at Warrior remained idle.[49] The situation, however, remained tense, and "trouble is anticipated."[50] Indeed, a letter to the *Montgomery Advertiser* communicated "grave fears of an outbreak on the part of the striking miners at the Warrior mines," and in a not so subtle warning to the strikers, stated, "It is even hinted that troops may be called for." Because the Italian miners "have been recently brought to the mines to fill the places of miners" on strike against the wage cut, "serious trouble may result at any time."[51]

Trouble appeared certain when the Warrior coal operators continued to import Italian strikebreakers from outside the state. In early September, an additional group of around twenty men arrived at Warrior; however, operators deployed them into the mines before the strikers knew what had happened. The train hauling the men to Alabama stopped a couple of miles north of the Warrior depot to let off the men at the junction of Warrior's trunk line with the Louisville and Nashville Railroad. The Italians commenced their first day of work in the mines before the strikers could intervene. Nonetheless, reported the *Advertiser,* "the idle crowd at Warrior have . . . already found means of communicating with the newly arrived Italians and, it seems, will persuade them not to work if possible." Whereas the company initially had trouble communicating with the first two loads of Italian workers, lacking an interpreter and relying instead on "French and German, aided by signs," this time they had brought along a "first rate interpreter." The Italians "who came first," reported the newspaper, were "working steadily" while "the ten men who were won over by the old miners, are still at Warrior."[52] A day later, however, the paper discounted a rumor that ten of the Italian imports at Warrior "were killed by resident miners," noting that "there was no truth in this." Rather, "the residents induced the Italians to leave the mines . . . but there was no breach of the peace." Meanwhile, work in many of the area mines was to resume at "the old price of 80 cents," whereas the Warrior Coal and Coke Company planned to hold out "at 65 cents."[53]

Alone among the operators affected by the strike, Warrior continued to sell coal to the L&N Railroad at the reduced rate. A mass meeting of the striking miners resolved to withhold their labor from any operator who sold coal to the L&N at a rate less than $150 per ton, and to pressure any miners who had resumed work at the eighty-cents-per-ton labor rate to stop working. Most importantly, the resident miners reportedly raised sufficient funds to pay the fare for the Italian miners at Warrior to leave. Fifty-nine Italian miners left for Decatur to board another train for new jobs at Muscle Shoals.[54] Meanwhile, the conflict between the strikers and the Warrior operators escalated through anonymous property violence. A standing locomotive was mysteriously released one night, plunging down a steep grade to derail into a gondola; another night saw Warrior's thirty-five-foot-high railroad trestle erupt into flames.[55]

By October 10, the dispute in the Warrior fields appeared to have resolved.[56] The strikers had reportedly induced the Italians to leave Warrior with the promise of jobs in north Alabama.[57] The Warrior operators initially had conceded to the demand for eighty cents per ton for wage labor, but then almost immediately reduced the amount to seventy cents, closing the mines for one day to enforce the change. However, the company agreed to at least implement a semimonthly pay schedule, rather than a monthly one, while in return the defeated miners agreed to the reduction to seventy cents.[58]

By the summer of 1885, however, a second strike erupted against the importation of yet more Italian laborers. Among the group of Italian men who had arrived to help break the strike in 1884 and who were "induced" to depart back to the North were about five men who had persuaded the resident miners to allow them to remain longer in Warrior. No evidence remains to indicate what these men did in the Warrior district for the remainder of the strike of 1884, or if they went to work in the mines when the resident strikers conceded to the operators in the fall of 1884. However, at least one of the men returned to New York, where he persuaded another group of Italians to travel back to Warrior to work in the mines. He returned with almost two dozen "compatriots," in August, a mere ten days after work had resumed in the mines, and "the other miners have struck against these."[59]

This new squad of Italian imports this time came armed with loaded pistols. When the men hopped off the train at the Warrior mines, they fired into the air several times, allegedly to celebrate the "completion of their journey." However, the *Huntsville Gazette,* an African American newspaper, claimed that the men "shot off their pistols like desperadoes," continuing "at various times until Saturday morning." Angry strikers threw rocks at the wagon driver hauling the Italians' baggage as they traveled from the Warrior depot to the mines. Salvatori Filina, the young man who had remained behind in Warrior during the 1884 strike but then returned to New York to gather a new squad of Italian laborers, fired his pistol into the air to scatter the rock throwers. "Indignant" miners subsequently assembled in a mass meeting to demand a response from the company, but they did not get the reaction they wanted with regard to removing the Italian laborers. "We intend to work them," was the reply.[60]

With "nearly every miner in the Warrior fields being represented in the mass meeting," the miners obtained the support of the sheriff and deputies, who likely had kin among the miners.[61] "Accompanied by a procession of 400 miners," law enforcement officials "went to the mines of the Coke and Coal Co." and arrested twenty-one Italian workers for carrying concealed weapons. Warrior bonded out all the other men, who then waited in the Birmingham jail pending trial.[62] Company officials, meanwhile, "declare that they will defend to the Italians to the last." Nonetheless, "the home miners have laid down their tools," and having "sworn not to work with them," they had all, "save one," now "stopped work."[63]

Beyond rock throwing, however, and even with the apparent support of at least some local deputies and the sheriff, the resident miners could do little to remedy the situation. By September 1885, the coal market for the Warrior product had slowed, leaving "light orders" at all the mines in the district. In this environment, local coal operators united with Warrior to import additional Italian laborers. "The Warrior Coal and Coke Company's Italians were put to work this morning with little interference on the part of the old miners," reported the *Montgomery Advertiser,* and the other operators were likely to "follow the lead of the Warrior people, and get new men as fast as possible."[64] Within the week, miners agreed to a compromise that ended their strike at Warrior "against the introduction of Italian laborers," settling for far less than what they initially had hoped. "The strikers agreed to the reservation" of a separate entrance "for Italians and will resume work at once."[65]

Black miners at Warrior, understandably, resented the immigrant workers imported to undercut their strike, and when they lost that battle, they opted, ironically, for the segregation of the Italian miners from their own work entrances. That seemed like a victory to Birmingham's coal operators, who duly proceeded to expand the immigrant labor base wherever and however possible across the next few years.[66] They gambled that ethnic-racial resentments would be nurtured and not diminished in the mines, further undermining union organization. A similar calculation had informed the decision by J. C. Stanton and Nathan Bedford Forrest to import Chinese railroad laborers in 1870, and other coal operators and timbering entrepreneurs likewise turned to immigrant laborers in other parts of the South.[67]

However, the big coal operators, such as Sloss-Sheffield and TCI, as well as the smaller commercial mine owners, had miscalculated. As the Birmingham mineral district exploded in growth in the next decade, union membership grew as well. And when labor disputes inevitably erupted over the terms of union work contracts, the open shop, and other issues, the inclinations and loyalties of those immigrants imported as competitors to American-born miners proved to be unpredictable, to say the least. Indeed, Black *and* white, American-born *and* foreign-born workers participated on all sides of the labor conflicts that roiled the mineral district from the 1890s to at least the 1920s. This pattern characterized the Birmingham strikes as well as labor disputes in industrial communities throughout the United States.

A matrix of factors, such as the state of the local or regional economy, the historical or social position of Black labor within a particular industry or locality, or even just individual resentments or character, influenced how immigrant and Black laborers encountered each other in the New South. The urban and commercial spaces of Alabama's industrial districts and towns made such contingencies especially apparent. Relations between Blacks and immigrants could be pleasant, as when a resident Black woman brought homemade biscuits to welcome a newly arrived Italian neighbor. Nonetheless, the insecurity that defined life for both African Americans and immigrant laborers in the New South often shaped Black/immigrant relations into something much different. Sometimes that simply meant keeping a distance in the crowded company towns and camps. But the Greeley Mines incident, the Gagliano affair, the walkout by Black miners over the employment of Italian laborers in Walker County, and other labor conflicts in Birmingham all testified to how unpredictable these encounters could be.

This would be even more evident as Birmingham's industries continued to grow and a diversity of laborers continued to arrive, including immigrants from around the world. Warrior's U.S.-born miners had failed to win the concessions they wanted on wages, hours, and the use of immigrant miners, but no one would forget what had happened. Coal operators understood that immigrant laborers offered them useful leverage against organizing miners; U.S.-born miners recognized the threat to their solidarity that such laborers posed. And the immigrant miners themselves learned just how fraught with danger a sojourn to the Birmingham District could be, and how uncertain was their position in the state's racial and economic hierarchies.

CHAPTER 4

"A FEW DEPRAVED WHITE MEN AND THE WORST ELEMENT OF NEGROES"

Immigrants, African Americans, and the Birmingham Strikes

Jean-Francis Rion disembarked from the *Chateau Lafitte* in New York harbor on a clear, chilly day just before Christmas of 1888. After surviving a stint in the French army, at thirty-eight years of age he had finally departed Bordeaux for the United States.[1] At some point, Jean-Francis left New York, ending up in Alabama by 1894, working in the Tennessee Coal, Iron and Railroad Company's Jefferson County coal mines and living among the other French residents of Pratt City.[2] Jean-Francis might have remained entirely forgotten in the historical record but for two factors. First, miners in the United Mine Workers Union of Alabama (UMWA) walked out on strike at TCI mines in the spring of 1894 to protest wage cuts, inaugurating a bitter and violent conflict that revolved around the importation of Black replacement miners.[3] Second, Rion joined the strike and soon after became its most infamous participant.

After the Warrior Coal and Coke Company strike, coal operators worked hard to encourage immigration schemes and build up a ready pool of replacement labor.[4] During the 1894 strike, however, they also relied on African American replacements and convicts. Their first effort to use them, at the Blue Creek mines, stalled because the men refused to enter the shafts when confronted by angry Black strikers.[5] Powerlessness against the continued deployment of strikebreakers dramatically escalated the violence of the strike.[6] Nighttime shootings into nonstrikers' homes, dynamiting of mine properties, the murder of a nonunion Black miner, firefights between assailants and special deputies guarding the mines, and various incidents of arson that burned railroad bridges and trestles characterized the strike.[7]

In Alabama, Jean-Francis Rion transitioned to "Rion Regis" and joined a closely knit community of French mining families who lived in Pratt City. He joined the desperate coal miners enacting the 1894 work stoppage against TCI over further reductions to the "starvation wages" they already earned.[8] The culmination of these bitter feelings came in July. A group of strikers, possibly as many as a hundred, departed a mass union meeting on the evening of July 16 to sneak to TCI slope 3, where African American "blackleg" miners had recently started work. As the men emerged from the shaft at the end of their shift, the strikers opened fire with their Winchester rifles. The terrorized men scattered into the surrounding woods, deputies and guards fired back, and some of the strikers pursued the fleeing men.[9]

The aggressive actions of Regis, however, captured the most press attention. As he fired on the Black miners, Regis took a guard's bullet in the arm or leg, which knocked him to the ground. As multiple accounts related it, Regis then sat back up and continued to empty his gun into the ranks of the miners, guards, and deputies, thereby demonstrating "the bitterness of the strikers" as he "continued firing at the negroes and deputies refusing to surrender." A deputy managed to flank him and bring him down with a shot through his side. Newspaper accounts thereafter grew confused about his fate, sometimes relating that he had been killed and other times reporting that he had been "seriously wounded." A reporter for the *Montgomery Advertiser* remarked on "the air of mystery" about Regis, noting that "no one has been able positively to ascertain what became of his body," and speculated that "it is supposed to have been secretly buried by strikers."[10]

In fact, Regis did not die at the site or soon thereafter. Captured by the deputies, he ended up in the Jefferson County jail under the attention of the county physician.[11] Along with a fractured arm and leg, Regis also had been shot through the left lung, leaving him "dangerously wounded." Visited by a curious reporter, Regis remained largely taciturn, relating only that he was forty-five years old, not married, unable to speak English, and had not attended the strikers' meeting that preceded the assault. The reporter described Regis as a "raw-boned but strong-looking fellow," pointing out that he had "proved to be the most daring one in the mob."[12]

But Regis was not the only immigrant incarcerated as a result of the attack. Another reporter described what he heard when he visited the jail: "A perfect jabber of French and Welsh and Scotch and British was kept up between the prisoners and their wives." In fact, one could "stand by for half an hour without hearing any good, old-fashioned Alabama accent. One might have closed his eyes and imagined himself very far from the south, so far as the tongues of the prisoners and their wives would indicate." These "foreigners and assassins," the writer concluded, were "the same class of people that threw the Haymarket bomb in Chicago."[13]

Governor Thomas Goode Jones worried about these signs of radicalism emerging rather dramatically among the immigrant laborers that TCI had imported into the Birmingham District. In the wake of the assault and reports about Regis's highly publicized role in it, Governor Jones requested that Mobile's Catholic diocese immediately dispatch a French-speaking priest to the district. Although offering a largely self-serving assessment meant to dispel any white disquietude about who, exactly, Alabama's big mule industrialists had been inviting into the state, Father Beaudequin's report did reveal important elements about what brought about that fateful assault.

"Led Into It. This Is What the French Miners Claim," blasted the headline in the July 28, 1894, *Daily News* of Birmingham, which reprinted the priest's report. Beaudequin arrived at Pratt City in late July, expecting to find "a nest of French socialists and anarchists," but he found himself "agreeably disappointed" when he received a warm and cordial welcome from about two dozen French families. Living in "comfortable homes" with "well-cultivated garden patches," and often keeping poultry and a cow, the families all agreed that they had been duped into participating in the assault.

> They were led into it without knowing what it was all about. They were informed by the leaders that by attending the meeting and acting with them, they would get fresh meat two times a week. As they could see no objection to that, they all voted affirmatively by raising their right hand, and all rushed out together until they got into the fray and fought with their English-speaking companions.

After hearing this rather implausible account, Beaudequin next visited the Jefferson County jail to meet the offenders in person. In the jail, he found "thirteen Frenchmen, including Regis, the one who is probably fatally shot." These men then "corroborated the stories of the others at the mines, that they were led on . . . until it was too late to retreat." He then took pains to note that the notorious Regis was "a fine type of an inhabitant of the French Alps, and is a man of peaceable disposition." In fact, he noticed "no hint of anarchism about him."[14] Such observations sought to interpret the French laborers coal operators had employed in Alabama as more akin to the "superior" northwestern Europeans than to the Mediterranean nationals that most Americans at the time regarded as culturally suspect and racially inferior, and tainted by association with radical ideologies, particularly anarchism.[15]

Father Beaudequin next met with Governor Jones, who seems to have provided some specific marching orders regarding what message the priest should relay to the miners he planned to assemble for Sunday morning mass in Pratt City. To a "packed" church of French and Irish attendees, the priest laid out a typically conservative message: "I spoke to them for over an hour, showed them how wrong they had been in violating their contract, and that they should have abided by it up to the hour of its expiration. I impressed upon them the necessity of obedience to the laws and authorities, and to do away with so much clannishness."[16]

Along with reporting this typically antiunion, antistrike message, however, Beaudequin also documented at least some of the immigrants' grievances, particularly their dependence on the TCI company stores, where the "exorbitant prices for provisions . . . reduces them to poverty." Indeed, the Irish miners became "so worked up" on this issue that Beaudequin "had to speak to them as a priest and condemn the language they used. They were then profuse in their apologies and quieted down." Beaudequin also interpreted the cause of the assault at TCI slope 3 in much more racialized terms in order to dismiss it as a significant protest against the company's use of strikebreakers. Although the UMWA strike ranks included both Black and white miners, the priest claimed that "another grievance, and a very great one, is to see the negroes mounting guard with Winchesters on their shoulders. The Irish, especially," he explained, "complained of this, and it arouses their ire a great deal." Indeed, he concluded, "I fear . . . that the miners will never brook the sight of negro guards."[17] He did not, however, provide any evidence that such a concern explained Regis's actions or those of the other Frenchmen involved in the assault.

Officials arrested more than a hundred men for what newspaper reports termed the "Pratt City massacre," though all but a dozen or so ended up released without charges.[18] Of the remaining men, three received capital murder indictments for the death of Deputy T. W. Pierce: W. J. Kelso, Bill Brock, and Rion Regis.[19] As the men awaited trial, Regis's physical condition fluctuated. A month after the attack, he underwent a painful operation in the jail hospital to remove parts of two ribs and relieve pressure on his wounded lung. Still describing him as "the Frenchman who distinguished himself by shooting at the guards and deputies even after he himself had been shot down," reporters expressed a sort of grudging respect for Regis: "It is common talk at the jail . . . that Regis can stand anything."[20] A month later, he seemed to be on the mend, as he "has recovered from his frightful wounds and is now in the county jail gaining in flesh every day."[21]

The men's case finally appeared in criminal court in early 1895, where "friends and relatives, witnesses," and the morbidly curious packed the courtroom. However, mistakes by officials in pooling the jurors and the illness of the assigned judge led to delays that pushed the case well into the fall. When Regis reemerged, his case had been severed from the others and he appeared on the docket list as a "non-capital felony." By early 1896, however, it was too late; "Rion Regis is dead," reported the *Birmingham News*. Regis had finally succumbed to the lingering effects of his injuries during the night of February 14. He had "not been well since he was shot," noted the account, but had not been expected to die, since he seemed "no worse than usual." Still, over the previous few days, he "had frequently pointed to his breast over the left lung, and said in broken English, 'No good feel there.'"[22]

In his personal effects, Regis had only three dollars and some memorandum books in which he recorded his life events, including his original name, his birthplace of Saint-Martial, France, his drafting into the French army in 1871, his close relationship with a sister still at home in Saint-Martial, and notations "showing where he had paid his dues to labor organizations in the old country." Recalling Regis's role in the 1894 strike, the writer remarked that "he fought in that conflict with remarkable fierceness, still firing after being shot in the lung and with a ball in his right hand." In fact, when arrested, the "peaceable" Frenchman, who allegedly held no radical intentions but who had, like his fellow immigrants, been "duped" into the fight, still had his rifle in his hand and "fifty bullets strung around his waist."[23]

Amid economic depression, and as the Pullman Railway strike violently roiled out of the Midwest to spread across twenty-six states, both the UMWA and the coal operators in Birmingham recognized the important lesson of the 1894 strike.[24] Whether companies were bringing it in or keeping it out, replacement labor continued to be a critical element in future strikes. TCI, Sloss, Republic, and Alabama Consolidated, the key large operators, along with the smaller commercial ones, usually relied on the supply of African Americans residing in mostly rural areas across the region to fill this need. However, as the number of immigrants coming into American ports to the north and west, and to Galveston, Mobile, New Orleans, and Savannah, swelled, they joined Alabama's planters and town boosters in seeing their utility.[25] And they typically conflated "European" with "white."

TCI superintendent Don Bacon used European laborers specifically to rout the UMW's strike of 1904 to 1906, importing "Huns, Slavs, Greeks, Servians [*sic*], Italians, and Finns to replace" the Black laborers deemed too "unreliable." Sloss Furnace's president, John Maben, followed suit, declaring that "whenever I can put a white man in the place of a negro, I do," and noting in 1907 that "the only final solution is white labor, and I expect that we shall be driven to bring in Italians and Hungarians from the north." The editor of the *Birmingham Herald* agreed on the value of immigrant labor for the district, noting, for example, that "Negro labor is as good as far as it goes, but there are not enough negroes 'to go around.'" As a result, "foreign labor is increasing in demand. Within the last three or four years, thousands of foreigners, mostly Italians and Slavs, have settled in Jefferson County."[26]

Although exact numbers are difficult to determine across the decades, immigrant numbers in specific mining towns, camps, or operations appear to have gradually increased from the 1890s through the early 1900s.[27] In 1886, geologist Henry McCalley reported from the Jefferson County coalfields that along with U.S.-born Blacks and whites, he also found in the mines "Germans, Irish, Welsh, English, Swedes, French, Scotch, Austrians [and] Bavarians.[28] A visitor to the Pratt mines in 1881 commented on the "hundreds of laborers of nearly all races and colors" and specifically cited the British, Irish, and Welsh immigrants laboring alongside U.S.-born Blacks and whites. A little over a decade later, another traveler commented on "an even broader diversity," with Alabama convicts working alongside the "diminutive Hungarian Slav, or Slavisch . . . the industrious German or Frenchman . . . the honest Scotchman with his twang," with the majority being African Americans, and "all are here in one and the same mine." By 1910, African Americans numbered more than half of the district's coal mining population, while white miners "represented a broad, continually shifting mix of ethnic backgrounds."[29] As the number of U.S.-born Black and white miners grew, the overall percentage of immigrants in the mines remained more stable. The nationalities shifted from primarily those from Western Europe and the British Isles in the 1880s to a greater diversity of Italians, Greeks, Syrians, Eastern Europeans, and others in the early 1900s.[30]

How an increased supply of immigrant laborers would complicate things for the UMW in District 20 soon became evident.[31] The big operators signed an agreement with the UMW's District 20 in August 1903 that established a wage scale contract, in force until June of 1904.[32] Contract renewal negotiations stalled, however, in early June, and the union imposed a work stoppage until negotiators could resolve the dispute. Smaller commercial coal operators, who mostly sold coal in the local market, quickly signed temporary contracts with the UMW as everyone waited the outcome of negotiations between District 20 leaders and representatives of the large coal and furnace operators.[33]

Again, Tennessee Coal, Iron and Railroad Company officials escalated the conflict by announcing in mid-July their intention to shift convicts from one mine slope to another, previously worked with free miners, and to bring in additional convicts. TCI began building a new stockade at the Pratt City mines, removed free miners' tools from slope 3, and posted eviction notices for idle miners living in company-owned housing. Officials then brought in several hundred replacement convict miners, most of whom were African American, derailing contract negotiations between the UMW's District 20 leadership and the big coal operators and pushing the union, on July 25, to declare a district-wide strike against operators who had not signed a temporary contract.[34]

As with the conflict in 1894, the 1904 strike soon revolved around the question of replacement labor. As census schedules indicate, immigrants already worked in several of the mineral district's mines by then, including those operated by TCI or Sloss-Sheffield.[35] This time, UMW leaders knew to prepare for an infusion of immigrant strikebreakers.[36] In early August, the national UMW had "Slav," Polish, and Italian interpreters hard at work in Birmingham to convince "foreigners" to not accept jobs in the striking mines.[37] The UMW also added Black organizers to perform the same job among potential African American strikebreakers, but it was the "foreign" element on either side that attracted the most media attention.

UMW president Ed Flynn noted that while "there was some apprehension in union circles that the Slavs at mines in the western portion of the county were likely to desert the union organization," the "national organizer" from Pennsylvania, "who is a Slav," had addressed a large union meeting at Brookside and felt confident, as "he received pledges from the men to remain loyal to the union."[38] In an interview many decades later, Birmingham Slovak resident Steve Slovensky recalled a Slovak man sent by the UMW leadership to the district from Pennsylvania or Ohio to organize in his community of miners, very likely during the 1908 strike: "I do remember when he was here. I remember the old folks talking in a group. The men were talking about the fellow organizing and wanting to go ahead and start a union. Of course, they'd go ahead and listen to him because they felt he had more sense than they did. They went ahead and joined the union."[39]

The UMW's struggle to stop the stream of replacement laborers emboldened Sloss president John Maben to publicly restate the coal and furnace operator's vow to never concede to the union.[40] In these circumstances, as in other disputes in the mineral district, including in 1894, violence soon erupted, with a typical spate of dynamiting and sporadic gunfire. This served to provide the county sheriff with motivation to deputize more men and assign them to guard mine property, the governor to send in more militia troops to protect replacement workers, and operators to successfully seek court-ordered injunctions against the strikers.

As coal production increased in the late summer despite the strike, the UMW pitched a last-ditch effort by redeploying a "Slav" organizer named Petok to the district, as "there are quite a number of Slavs working in this field."[41] In October, TCI announced the placement of more than one hundred additional workers in its Blocton mines in Bibb County; the UMW countered that many of these men quit when they realized they had been enlisted under false pretenses as strikebreakers.[42] However, later that same month, the UMW dispatched Joseph Poiggani, an Italian organizer assigned to the

Birmingham District, to New Orleans "to inform his countrymen of conditions" in the Birmingham District. While there, he witnessed the landing of a ship carrying a hundred Italians who were rumored to be headed to north Alabama.[43] In late November, the UMW circulated to districts a flyer alleging that the strike was still in force, but it actually appeared to be over. In December, all miners in the district, union and nonunion, received a temporary wage increase.[44]

That the district's coal and furnace operators interpreted the 1904 outcome as validation for the use of immigrant replacement labor (at least in principle, if not at the actual scale achieved) soon became evident in the following months.[45] In the spring of 1905, the Birmingham Commercial Club held a conference on the efficacy of immigration for Alabama's farms, plantations, and manufacturing establishments, upon the heels of a tour of the mineral district by Italian ambassador Baron des Planches. The ambassador found Alabama's industrialists already importing "a large amount of foreign labor to the District to work in ore and coal mines, around furnaces, factories, and mills" and, reported the *Monroe Journal,* "Poles, Hungarians and others have already been brought to this section in numbers."[46] Around fifty German immigrants arrived in June 1905 to work at the Western Steel Car and Foundry Company in nearby Anniston. And according to Frank V. Evans, stationed at Ellis Island on behalf of Alabama's immigration bureau in December of the same year, a "large number" of immigrants had arrived on the island and would be headed to "Alabama at the earliest possible moment."[47] The *Jones Valley Times* duly reported in July 1906 that iron, steel, and coal operators in Birmingham were "importing [from Ellis Island via Savannah, Georgia] quite a number of Germans, Italians, Poles, and Slavs to work in the different industries here," as "this class of labor, especially the Italians and Poles, have proven to be good laborers."[48]

Farther to the south, the Southern Steel Company in Gadsden obtained "two carloads of Italian laborers," men and women, via the Southern Railway, straight from New York City.[49] In the summer of 1907, another report circulated that a hundred German immigrants recruited directly from Europe by an Alabama state immigration agent had arrived in New York, with their destination set as Birmingham.[50] One mine operator reported to the *Birmingham News* that four-fifths "of the men who dig the coal that makes Birmingham famous are not native-born Americans. They come from Germany, France, Belgium, England, and Italy," having found in Alabama a ripe field "for skilled labor." In his own operation, he pointed out, there labored "eight distinct and separate nationalities" from "Norway to Italy." Of these, "Austrians led the list of men who had turned most coal into coin, and Hungarians came next."[51]

In August 1907, Saint Paul Catholic Church in Birmingham celebrated the Feast of the Assumption of the Blessed Virgin Mary with four different masses to accommodate almost two thousand attendees. Similar services occurred at smaller parishes in the district, including at Saint Thomas's Church of San Marco, where people gathered to hear an "eloquent" address in Italian. In all, the "Italians and Slavs of the Birmingham District attended mass in great numbers that day."[52] From New Orleans came the news, just before Christmas of 1907, of the arrival of a steamer with thirteen Greeks and many "Slavs," prompting the reporter to explain that "often, these arrivals come through New Orleans on the way to Birmingham."[53]

Industrial employers commonly relied on strikebreakers to replace striking union miners in the rest of the United States. However, industrial operators in the rest of the country commonly preferred African Americans in this role, because they often confronted large immigrant communities, particularly Southern and Eastern Europeans, as strikers and unionists.[54] African Americans from rural areas sometimes played a similar role in the Birmingham District, but a longer history of Black labor in Alabama's coal mines, along with the organizing of the UMW, increasingly pulled Black miners into the union orbit. With the experience of the 1894 strike in mind (though apparently forgetting their actual role in the Pratt City massacre), Birmingham's coal operators gambled that diversifying the workforce with various groups of foreign nationals would erect a firewall against expanding union organization. This conviction would soon be tested.

On July 6, 1908, after contract renewal negotiations broke down once again, the Alabama UMW called a district-wide strike, citing a series of unacceptable wage decreases and the need to reorganize and finally establish permanent union recognition.[55] UMW leaders again dispatched immigrant organizers to District 20 (Birmingham), including two men named Pascue and Pugenni. At a mass meeting in Wylam in mid-July, Pugenni addressed a large audience of miners "in his native tongue of Italian."[56]

Foreign-born laborers held an ambiguous position in the Birmingham strikes, with the UMW courting some as members, even as operators imported ever more immigrants as strikebreakers. By 1908, however, the immigrant mining population now resident in the district had worked alongside U.S.-born Black and white miners for several years. When operators set out to once again deliver replacement workers into the striking mines, they confronted a population of immigrants that included men who were more seasoned by their work in the Birmingham District than they had been years earlier.[57] Within two weeks of the initial walkout, according to news reports, tensions again permeated the mineral district. Striking miners stood against the operators, replacement workers, and scores of "special deputies" appointed to guard mine properties, and the state's militia soldiers stood delicately poised between them.[58]

Striking miners besieged union headquarters "all day long," reported the *Birmingham News*, some to report on the progress of the strike in their mines and camps. Others had grievances to share, and still others needed provisions for their families. "Many of them," reported one writer, "were Italians and several interpreters made plain the wants of the foreigners to officials at the headquarters."[59] The situation alarmed union officials and operators, but especially local law enforcement.[60] In corresponding with Alabama Adjutant General Bibb Graves during the 1908 strike, Chief Deputy Sheriff Lucien Brown of Jefferson County registered his alarm at the coal operators' behavior in importing immigrant laborers and arming their guards. "The strike situation here is at high tension," reported Deputy Brown. "There are more men out than ever at one time before and as result of the two previous strikes . . . most of them now are of a foreign nationality, and hard to work on except with force." But the operators, he noted, "are determined to run 'Open Shop' and are importing men." In fact, he noted with some dismay, "a car load came in last night. When it becomes general at all mines [I] am afraid we will have some serious clashes." The situation at Blossburg, where many Slavic immigrants worked, had become especially threatening, after TCI officials "mounted a 'Colts Rapid Fire Gun" on a mine car." When Deputy Brown "refused to request a Gatling gun from you for them," TCI officials "paid about $600.00 for their own gun." That was not at all a good sign: "Am afraid this place will have a difficulty. They are importing men."[61] The *United Miner Workers Journal* further pointed out that "Bulgarians" and "Hungarians" at Blocton in Bibb County were some of the eight thousand miners who had joined the strike by July 30.[62]

Given these circumstances, some of the district's miners opted to leave the area: "It was learned today that a number of men who formerly worked in the Alabama mines are making preparations to leave here," reported the *Montgomery Advertiser*. "A party of five Frenchmen, miners, left Wylam this morning for Illinois mining fields."[63] Not everyone left, however. According to one account, about sixty-five other "imported miners" walked along the railroad tracks from the mines to the town of Wylam, where they approached strikers staffing the union commissary. Much like Regis and his fellow French strikers in 1894, they claimed to have been transported from Tennessee to Birmingham under false pretenses, having had no knowledge of the ongoing union strike. They announced they had summarily quit their jobs upon learning of the strike, which prompted cheers from the union men. Local UMW officials reportedly signed all of the men into the union on the spot.[64]

Amid sporadic but increasing violence in the district, strikers and operators continued to grapple over the "Negroes, Dagoes, and Slavs" who were still working.[65] Newspapers reported that deputies kept the men under armed guard in the mines, which they were afraid to leave unless to join the strike.[66] At Republic, one of the big coal operators, a union meeting erupted in chaos when a deputy "squad" reportedly showed up along with a wagonload of "strikebreakers."[67] The ensuing gunfire wounded four men, possibly fatally.[68] Deputies arrested at least twenty-four others, including Sam Parafuione, Mitno Baratka, Casimer Dorso, Joe Tamborallo, Mike Stooko, and Paul Lazarino.[69] Around the same time, deputies reportedly arrested fifteen Italians and around thirty African American strikers at the Bessie Mines for "intimidating" replacement workers.[70] In still another incident, a union organizer claimed that company guards had forced a group of Greek miners at Searles back into the mines at gunpoint when they managed to escape and tried to catch a train to Birmingham.[71] Meanwhile, reported a union miner, "At Johns last week, guards came into some of the Bulgarians' houses and ran them out and gave them five minutes to get off the company's property."[72]

Replacement workers continued to flow into the district over the Southern and the Louisville and Nashville railways.[73] In July, Governor Comer dispatched a cavalry battalion without its mounts and an artillery battalion without its guns to assist the operators in evicting strikers from company housing.[74] Sporadic violence continued at the Republic, Sayreton, and Bessemer mines, among other locations in Jefferson, Bibb, and Walker Counties.[75] Strikers reportedly tried to peacefully persuade a car full of strikebreakers at Chattanooga and Attalla to "not to take up work against the union." Despite these efforts, reported the *Montgomery Advertiser,* "no less than 1,000 strikebreakers were put to work in the mines today, and the statement is made by officials that there has been an appreciable increase in the output of coal." In these circumstances, workers on all sides registered the stress, including immigrants.

> Bulgarians in the furnace quarters of the Tennessee, Coal, Iron and Railway Company had a personal difficulty today, and one of them wielded an axe, inflicting a fatal injury on the head of one of his fellow-countrymen. The man with the axe made good his escape. There was a rumor that this trouble was connected with the strike, but investigation showed that the men involved were not even employed about the mines.[76]

Several weeks into the conflict, a military escort convoyed two more carloads of replacement workers into the Wylam mines. And District 20 UMW leader W. R. Fairley reported, "At Croker, I am told . . . the deputies and guards are intimidating and threatening the colored miners on strike at that place. They are trying to force the men back into the mines."[77] Amid the violence and the pressure exerted by the continuing influx of replacement labor, the UMW called a mass meeting of strikers at West Blocton, in Bibb County, late in July.[78] A new UMW local had reorganized in mid-July at Blocton with around five hundred members, including numerous immigrants who hailed from the Austro-Hungarian Empire. A UMW official visiting the mining town in July found "the men there in good spirits," with coal production cut from 2,500 to 500 tons. He also found that "all the men they have at work are Hungarians" and hoped that "they will quit just as soon as the union get(s) houses for them to live in."[79]

Fairley provided an update on the strike and called on union miners to "stand firm." As the prolabor *Blocton Enterprise* reported, "The foreign element was largely represented in the gathering, and they were addressed in the mother tongue by . . . a national organizer, and others."[80] J. T. Wood, a Black miner and preacher, also made a short speech, announcing that "the best element of his race were with the white miners in their demands for better wages and conditions." On the morning of July 29, about four hundred striking miners marched en masse along the highway to West Blocton, adding to their ranks as they proceeded, and arriving six hundred strong, a group the sympathetic *Enterprise* described as "representative of the intelligent workers in the coal fields of Alabama who are now seeking to obtain by peaceful methods redress of grievances of long standing."[81]

As more "blackleg" labor continued to arrive, strike violence increased even more by the end of July, with miners' homes dynamited near Wylam and personal altercations mounting between strikers and working miners and between deputies and strikers.[82] UMW leader Fairley, however, claimed that "many of the imported men were joining the union." Indeed, reported the *Montgomery Advertiser,* officials of the Frisco Railroad reported that "many foreigners are being brought in from the West . . . [and] quite an experience is reported, twenty-five of the foreigners coming in one day the past week and buying tickets right back to the place from whence they came the next day." Meanwhile, county and state officials reportedly continued to stockpile ammunition.[83]

In early August, events took a particularly tragic turn. The dynamiting of the home of Black miner Finlay Fuller at Brighton resulted in the arrest of Black union miner William Millen. Although Millen reportedly had an alibi, assailants removed him from a jail cell in Brighton, murdered him, and then hung his body from a tree. Officials held the coroner's inquest before a crowd of almost a thousand onlookers—under the same tree, while Millen's body continued to hang. Millen's lynching broadcast a strong message to other strikers, particularly Black miners, about their participation in any action against replacement workers.[84]

The incident also provided the pretext for the state and local courts to crack down further on the strike, preventing picketing, public marches, or loitering of any sort near the mines. Officials justified such measures as necessary to stop provocative daily marches by strikers through mining camps, and as essential to those men who were still working or who wanted to return to work. Nonetheless, Polish miner John Hughico had his house dynamited, which destroyed his porch and killed all of his chickens. Deputies allegedly fired on six men who ran away from the scene, following them into the Italian neighborhood of Ensley, where they arrested six Italians, one of whom reportedly had a pistol ball lodged in his scalp.[85] According to one report, Hughico boarded Italian miners but had refused to join the strike. His boarders left his house as a result, and Hughico had received threatening letters just prior to the explosion.[86]

Even as the violence escalated, operators accelerated the arrival of immigrant replacement workers. J. L. Knoepfler, of Louisiana's state board of agriculture and immigration, reported in early August that Birmingham's coal operators had arranged for "two hundred and fifty men, consisting to a large extent of foreigners, but with a few negroes among them," to be "rushed out of New Orleans" in order to "assist in ending the mining strike in Alabama." Although this caused a near "labor famine" in the Crescent City, "the workmen have been sent off in batches of twenty to fifty. The bulk of the foreigners were Austrians, with a scattering of Italians."[87]

The event that most highlighted the complicated encounters, and sometimes collaboration, between immigrant and African American miners in Birmingham occurred near Blocton in early August. The Blocton train ambush proved to be a key incident of the 1908 strike, propelling the UMW along the road to defeat, an outcome in which both immigrants and African Americans played pivotal roles. Although U.S.-born Black and white strikers also suffered arrests, beatings, and in the case of Millen, a lynching, it was the Slavic immigrant laborers who were scapegoated for the worst incident of violence in the 1908 strike.

The late night broke hot and humid on Saturday, August 8, 1908, when a train engine pulling three railcars departed Birmingham proper around 11:30 p.m., heading for the Blocton coal mines in Bibb County. Having packed the cars to capacity with strikebreakers, special deputies, mine officials, and a few militia soldiers, TCI aimed to sneak the men into Blocton without alerting striking miners, who often clustered along the tracks to keep watch for exactly that reason.[88] An informant, however, clearly had already alerted the strikers to expect the train.

About one mile from the Blocton depot, as the train entered a cut between two hills, it encountered railroad ties piled onto the tracks ahead. As the engineer slowed the cars, a signal shot was fired, followed by a deadly fusillade from the left into the railcars. The cut between the hills dropped the height of the track substantially, allowing the assailants to fire directly into the windows. A few deputies and soldiers on the train returned fire (most carried still unloaded weapons), while the engineer used the train's cowcatcher to push the timbers out of the way and then sped to the Blocton depot. But it was too late. The conductor, a deputy sheriff, and an "imported strike breaker" were dead, and at least eleven others, including three TCI officials, were wounded, some seriously.

The train returned to Birmingham at daybreak, carrying the dead and wounded as well as all but a few replacement workers, who had refused to leave the cars in Blocton. Bandaged and bloody men departed the train before a large, shocked crowd in Birmingham. TCI officials and deputies transported the dead to funeral homes and the wounded to Saint Vincent's hospital.

The Blocton incident was the second ambush of a train carrying strikebreakers during the 1908 conflict; the first occurred at Blossburg on July 17. Both involved fatalities, but the Blocton ambush involved multiple deaths and injuries of operators, law enforcement officials, and strikebreakers. The Blocton ambush also resulted in mass arrests of both Black and white strikers, U.S. and foreign-born. It was the only known ambush to involve immigrant perpetrators, and the only known incident of the 1908 strike to result in highly public trials.[89]

According to newspaper reports, law enforcement officials soon arrived at the ambush site, where they deployed bloodhounds brought in from Birmingham. "Dogs were hurried to the scene," reported the Huntsville *Morning Mercury,* "and took trails through the woods directly to the union quarters. Eight negroes were arrested this afternoon and others are expected."[90] The prolabor *Blocton Enterprise,* however, disputed this account, reporting a couple of days later that militia soldiers arrived at the site a few hours after the attack, where they met up with local Deputy Sheriff Oakley: "Four bloodhounds had been brought along from Birmingham and were placed on the scent, but according to our information were a failure."[91]

Another account, in contrast, reported that "the hounds were turned loose and while the trail was nearly ten hours old it was taken at once." The hounds tracked "for some distance, breaking several times, but always being picked up again," when the trail stopped in a "small settlement" of Blocton.[92] Deputies and militia soldiers searched several houses, allegedly locating numerous rifles and shotguns, along with ammunition, and arrested several African Americans. According to one report, "at one time, things took on a squally look," with several people reportedly "suggesting that they be lynched."[93]

All told, officials detained eight Black men and one Black woman, though officers also arrested around fifty other suspects as well. Of these, the vast majority were "foreigners," specifically, "Slavs" imported by TCI during the 1904–1906 strike.[94] "More than half of the men arrested are Slavs and Bulgarians," reported the *Birmingham News*, men "who were brought into this district four years ago as strike-breakers."[95] Deputies traced a bloody sock left at the scene of the ambuscade back to another individual, a man named Wasilije Wainovich, when he was found in the nearby Blocton settlement with one sockless foot and a badly mashed toe.[96]

Of the "Slavs" arrested, reported local and state newspapers, five "are said to have confessed to having taken part in the shooting."[97] More specifically, in an account largely validated by other newspapers that quoted Deputy Sheriff Oakley's statements at the later trial, the *Blocton Enterprise* reported that, "some of the arrests were said to have been made on the strength of an alleged confession of a frightened Hungarian who had been put through the 'third degree.'" Trial testimony revealed the "frightened Hungarian" to be Bose Durkovich, who had been in the United States only twenty days when the ambush transpired. Acquainted with Wainovich from the "old country," Durkovich claimed to have not participated in the ambush but to have seen Wainovich and others going to and returning from the incident.[98]

Governor Comer, who had resided in the district for much of the 1908 strike, said little in public about the train ambush. Privately, he admitted to his secretary on the following day that "I do not see any chance of my leaving here" as the "affair at Blocton yesterday was very bad and much deplored."[99]

For District 20's UMW leadership, the train ambush appears to have prompted some soul searching. The blatant and deadly attack on strikebreakers, deputies, and soldiers, not to mention TCI officials, put the UMW on the defensive. It was hard to understand how anyone *other* than the union strikers would have perpetrated this deed. One of the first people arrested for the attack was Robert Hayes, the white president of the Blocton UMW local. The *Blocton Enterprise* described Hayes as "a young man well known and respected in this community" and declared that "no one here believes for a moment that he was in any way connected with the affair." In fact, the

Gadsden Daily Times erroneously claimed, Hayes was "the only American arrested yet."[100]

Acting president of the Blocton local, W. M. Lewis, tried to deflect union responsibility by pinning the attack on the "special" deputies assigned to police the strikers and to protect mine properties and strikebreakers, and by dismissing the confessions as obtained by "cruelly whipping ignorant foreigners."[101] UMW strike leader W. R. Fairley went even further to discount union involvement while accounting for the role of the alleged immigrant participants: "Nearly all of those who are charged with any participation in this Blocton affair, as shown by the correspondence in the daily papers," announced Fairley, "are Slavs and other foreigners, who were imported to that place by the Tennessee Company as strikebreakers during the strike three years ago." Nonetheless, he took pains to point out that the UMW had "at all times and do now, beg and implore all union miners to desist and refrain from any violence and unlawful conduct." Fairley went on to note that, aside from the Blocton incident, local courts had already dismissed sixty-two of the sixty-three cases brought against union miners. Fairley took pains to add that "I, together with every officer of the United Mine Workers, unqualifiedly condemn the atrocious and inhuman conduct of those who fired into the train near Blocton, murdering and maiming some of the men on it."[102] By denying any culpability for strike violence while simultaneously validating the guilt of the "foreigners" arrested for the ambush, UMW officials avoided alienating the Black miners, who were the real backbone of the union's strike efforts.

A couple of days after the ambush and arrests, the *Blocton Enterprise* reported receiving an update from a "prominent" Blocton attorney: "The foreigners charged with shooting in the train Sunday morning are being taken one at a time to the office of Mr. Lavendar," where they also met with another attorney, named Ellison, and an interpreter. Attorneys Lavendar and Ellison "are taking statements behind closed doors from the defendants." Moreover, a phone call "from a respectable citizen says that the solicitor's door is guarded by three or four men with guns." The editor decried, "Ethics, shades of ethics! Where is honor? Where is justice? Where is common decency?"[103]

Moreover, the sheriff and his deputies, along with a militia company led by Lieutenant Leon Schwartz of Mobile, searched homes in "Dagotown" and in a hall "occupied by negroes" the day after the strike, seizing weapons and ammunition and locating the apparent owner of the "bloody sock" found at the scene of the ambush. Schwartz reportedly stated, "It may not have been lawful, but it was the thing to do, and it ought to be done in every mining camp in the district." Blocton, reported the *Montgomery Advertiser,* was a coal town very sympathetic to the UMW and the striking miners: "Nearly all the citizens of Blocton sympathize with the mines," since many businessmen and professionals there had started out digging coal, and most people depended upon the mines in one way or another. Thus, the newspaper reported, "there is much indignation in Blocton over the searching of houses. Peculiarly enough the resentment among the white people," the reporter noted, "is directed chiefly at the searching of the hall used by negro secret societies."[104]

In accounting for the quick arrests of the large number of immigrants after the ambush, and to dispel the rumors that a confession emerged because deputies tortured the owner of the bloody sock, Deputy Sheriff Oakley provided his account to the *Advertiser.* He claimed, "When we had secured good evidence implicating the union miners, we went out and arrested fourteen of them. Most of them were foreigners who do not speak English." The sheriff then carried the men to Blocton's TCI offices and located "an intelligent young Hungarian miner" (a man named John Hollek or Rollek), who explained the seriousness of the situation to the men and obtained confessions from seven of them. Hollek then reportedly gave the sheriff the story he gleaned from the arrested men:

> Saturday afternoon Robert Hayes, President of Blocton Local of the United Mine Workers, went to Dagotown, where the foreigners who are on strike are staying, and told them that the Tennessee Company would bring a number of men down that night from Birmingham to take their places, and that they must not permit those men to come to Blocton. Without much excitement the foreigners and negroes planned the attack. After dark about forty of them marched out from Dagotown and around the mountain. They went north to a point about two miles from Blocton. Here they rolled cross ties on the track and waited. When the train came along they began to shoot. Then they left the place hurriedly and went back to Dagotown.

The sheriff indicated his trust in Hollek's accounting of the confessions and also specified that the only time any of the men were hurt occurred when one of the immigrants (likely Wainovich, with the injured toe) attempted, upon arrest, to seize a deputy's firearm, receiving a beating in return. "Not one of them has been whipped," the sheriff promised, "and no harsh language has been used to them," a statement that testimony from both sides in the later trials proved to be a bald-faced lie. In the jail at Centreville languished thirty-one men, including UMW Blocton president Robert Hayes, five African American miners, and twenty-five "foreigners," including "Italians, Slavs, Huns and Frenchmen." The Bibb County grand jury arraigned the men in Centreville on August 14.[105]

In the wake of the ambush, a mass meeting of around five thousand Birmingham businessmen assembled to register their alarm and indignation at the state of affairs in the district due to the strike. The angry crowd cheered speeches by prominent Birmingham businessmen, such as real estate developer Robert Jemison, who pledged to end the lawlessness of the strike and to support Governor Comer's effort to reestablish law and order in the district. Birmingham banker John E. Morris also addressed the crowd, noting that there were "1,000,000 men in Alabama ready to shoulder arms," reported one journalist, "and drive bad men out of the state." Moreover, he continued, "if we allow *a few depraved white men and the worst element of Negroes* to continue to commit such acts . . . we may expect bloody anarchy for an indefinite period" (my emphasis). The only other mention of African Americans in reference to the mass meeting, which had to be adjourned early to avoid its devolution into possible mob action, was the Millen lynching.[106]

In Luverne, southwest of the state capitol of Montgomery, the editor of the *Crenshaw County News* commented on the "acts of lawlessness" roiling the Birmingham District during the strike, noting that the "leaders of the Miners' Union claim [this] was done by foreigners, who were imported to the district as strikebreakers three years ago." The editor hoped for a peaceful resolution of the strike, since "coal has become as necessary to the business and comfort of a large part of the people of the state as is bread and clothing," and with many of the mines closed, people were suffering. Indeed, "the *News* agrees . . . that the operators of the mines are doing themselves, and the state an injustice by importing foreigners as strikebreakers." After all, he explained, "many of them are only half-civilized and are in no doubt responsible for many of the acts of violence that have been suffered in the mining district."[107] The editor of the Bibb County *Centreville Press* noted that "a part of the responsibility of the recent outrage should and is being charged up to the [TCI] Company who would import such a class of men into any community."[108]

While newspaper editors and journalists certainly exaggerated details or slanted their accounts to match their own political inclinations, still both sides agreed that Slavic immigrants perpetrated the train ambush, along with a scattering of African Americans, who largely escaped mention and apparently avoided culpability. Both sides also agreed that the immigrants involved likely arrived in the district as replacement labor during either the 1894 or 1904 strikes.[109] By pointing the finger at the Slavic participants as the negative "foreign" influence, operators and union officials avoided antagonizing the larger group of African American miners who served both as replacement workers and as key union members and strikers.

From the beginning of the 1908 strike, mining officials, unsympathetic newspaper editors, other Birmingham business interests, and local law enforcement complained about Governor Comer's apparent reluctance to fully enlist the military arm of the state to suppress the strike.[110] Republic Steel officials, especially, wanted a forceful response, telegramming Adjutant General Bibb Graves an urgent message to "wire at once advice regarding guns requested in our telegram of yesterday," which Graves dutifully forwarded to Governor Comer.[111] In mid-July, Walker County's Sheriff J. O. Long urgently pressed the governor to designate militia companies to stand ready to deploy as "I am expecting trouble in this county at any time, and should it come I will call on the state for help." Although he found that "things are quiet here at this time," he had nonetheless "been informed that there is apt to be trouble within the near future." And he stated, "Please advise me at once."[112] Deputy Sheriff Lucien Brown had explained to Graves in July that "I am up against it," with "over 200 deputies out on strike duty." Brown had been "up all night last night and it's 9 am Sunday night and still no sleep in sight." While he hoped "we can handle [the strike] without the troops," truthfully, he felt "it looks bad now."[113]

The governor did deploy militia companies from the outset, and he spent a good deal of time meeting with company and union officials while he personally traversed the mineral district as the strike progressed. Yet he initially opted for a more restrained response than had been the case in earlier strikes. Indeed, union officials hoped for the state militia assigned to the mines and camps to provide a buffer between the strikers and the "special" deputies, who regarded each other with deep antipathy. The continued influx of replacement workers guarded by both deputies and soldiers, however, clearly aligned the state with the mine and furnace owners as the strike dragged on. Prior to the train ambush, Governor Comer resisted calls to declare martial law to end the strike. But with three dead and several wounded in a mass assault against the companies' use of replacement workers, pressure intensified on the governor to act. "Many are calling for the governor to declare martial law," announced the *Gadsden Daily Times*, "and to jail, disarm, or deport all strikers."[114]

A few days after the ambush, Comer did just that in a proclamation that made clear that the "right to work" was at the heart of his decision. First noting the "disorder, lawlessness, murder and other crimes committed by certain lawless parties in their efforts to prevent peaceable citizens from working in the mines of the district," the governor's proclamation stated that "it is the intention of the state government of Alabama to protect every citizen in the borders of the state in lawful employment." Therefore, he explained, "as governor of the state of Alabama," he would enlist "the whole power of the state" to protect "everybody who desires to work, even if it should be necessary to use all the military forces of the state for that purpose, and to summon every citizen of the state to act as a member of the posse comitatus."[115]

Soon after the governor's proclamation of martial law, journalist Bruce Kennedy deftly racialized the strike's context, reporting for the *Montgomery Advertiser*, "There is a mixing of the white and Black races at the mining camps that portends an evil day for Alabama." The UMW "puts the white man and the Black man on an equal plane in the organization," Kennedy trumpeted, and many of the Birmingham area locals even had Black officers. Moreover, Black miners stood as the "recognized leaders" in many of the district's mining camps. Nor was this merely a case of Black and white Alabamians belonging to the same union locals: "When it is considered that perhaps 50 per cent of the union members are foreigners, many of whom do not speak English, the domination of the negro leaders over the white man is apparent."

While Kennedy conceded that he could not "state it as a fact," still he understood from "reputable" sources that at the camps' schools and churches, "the negroes and the white people mingle and mix as equals." Indeed, at one picnic, a "negro preacher" made a speech to "black and white miners and their wives and children," who reportedly applauded his references to "social equality." When a "young white man" made another speech later in the day, Kennedy alleged, a "big black negro advanced to the platform and putting his arms around the shoulders of the white speaker, whispered in his ear as though advising him what to say." Most disturbingly, "as repugnant as the scene was to some white men," Kennedy noted, "it appeared to meet with the favor of the white men, women, and children in the audience." Kennedy made it clear who he assumed those supportive whites were: "It might be safe to say that 25 per cent of the coal diggers in the mineral district are native white men of Alabama. No one doubts that these white men are opposed to mixing the races on social lines." Kennedy's readers could easily infer that immigrant whites were another matter. There was no racial taboo, apparently, that they were not willing to violate.[116]

Governor Comer used this highly racialized context as a pretext to order the destruction of the strikers' camps that hosted the evicted miners, terminally eroding the UMW's ability to sustain the walkout. As a result, the UMW called off the strike on August 31.[117] Miners specifically blamed Comer's actions prohibiting the "erection of camps" for evicted miners, and the race-baiting slander about "social equality" in the union camps, as key factors in the strike's defeat. The Birmingham District would be open shop now, averred union leaders: "Miners have been forced to swallow a bitter dose of defeat." The District 20 UMW leadership alleged that the governor brought the strike to a climax when he broke up the camps and prohibited public meetings, essentially undercutting the foundation for strikers to continue to hold out.

One editor made it clear whom he blamed for it all: only a fraction of Black miners took part in strike violence, such as the train ambush; the real offenders were "some lawless men who were imported here and who stay awhile and move on." Exonerating the Black strikers and blaming the "foreigners," the editor claimed "the miners did not bring them here. They are not citizens, not immigrants, just imports." Indeed, "the really guilty were men brought into the district by the mine operators and not miners, and were foreigners who are not even citizens of this county, and for whose conduct the miners themselves should not, and could not, by law, be held responsible."[118]

The press treatment of immigrant participation in the strike of 1908 demonstrated the complex and often fluctuating racial position of immigrant laborers in New South Alabama. On the heels of the train ambush, newspaper editors and company officials defined the immigrant participants in the strike as "white" in order to attack the UMW for violating racial taboos in the mixed union meetings and tent camps. At other times, commentators, including some within the UMW, described the immigrant participants as uncivilized "scum," relegating them to the status of nonwhites when their actions proved difficult to control.

Strikes were rough affairs in the New South, because everyone, especially in the Birmingham District, had a lot riding on how each event turned out—miners, operators, local businesses, and residents alike. In this highly charged context, as Regis had discovered earlier, the "Slavs" arrested for the train ambush in 1908 found little security on either side of the labor conflict or within the racial hierarchy. African Americans and foreign-born laborers, even so-called white ones, shared a precarious existence in the New South, even if not an identical one. Their vulnerability set them in competition with one another while also creating opportunities to establish solidarities, as demonstrated in the Pratt City massacre and in the Blocton train ambush. Immigrants such as Regis also shared with Black southerners a determination to resist their exploitation, an agency that landed many in Alabama's county jails, state prison, and the convict lease system. There, they quickly discovered just how isolated and vulnerable an immigrant could be when trouble reared its head in New South Alabama.

CHAPTER 5

"THE LAND OF SNAKES, CROCODILES, NEGROES, YELLOW FEVER, AND DEATH"

The Immigrant Experience in New South Alabama

On an early June morning in 1903, James Parrish and Antonio Turk surprised local residents in downtown Selma when they stumbled off a train, covered in mud, sweat, and grass burrs. Brothers James and Henry Parrish owned and operated the Parrish Brothers and Company lumber mill, which produced barrel staves in a timber camp hard by the Tombigbee River, about three miles north of the small railroad town of Myrtlewood, in Marengo County. Described as a "Slavic" foreman, Antonio Turk hired Parrish's laborers and settled the terms for wages and conditions. Parrish had recently contracted with Turk to hire more than sixty Slavonian "stavegetters," who lived at the camp and worked turning out hardwood staves.[1]

While Parrish and Turk spent an hour cleaning up at the local barbershop, rumors flew around town that the men had barely escaped the camp with their lives. Although the obviously embarrassed Parrish proclaimed such stories to be " greatly exaggerated," one reporter concluded that the men had arrived in Selma so filthy from a hasty trek through the swamp that "this went to indicate that there was something in the story about Mr. Parrish and his foreman being held up by the excited Slavs."[2] In fact, Parrish and Turk had been threatened by their Slavonian laborers during a wage dispute.

Immigrant laborers often worked on contracts arranged through labor agents or foremen, who in turn set the terms of wages and living conditions with the employer.[3] Turk apparently had settled on a wage for staves produced by the Slavonians, who expected to be paid in full each month. Parrish had arrived in camp the previous day carrying about $3,500 "to pay off the Slavonians who [were] engaged in getting out the staves." That payment, however, amounted to only half of what the Slavonian laborers had expected. The angry and agitated men, some of whom held shotguns, surrounded Turk, demanding that he intervene with Parrish to have new checks written on the spot in the proper amounts. Turk wisely convinced Parrish to issue new checks. The laborers then locked both men in a building while at least one headed to Myrtlewood to attempt to cash one of the checks. Once they had received their due wages in full, surmised one reporter, the Slavonian workers had planned to release the men unharmed.

Feeling an urgent need to not lose several thousand dollars more than he wanted to pay, however, Parrish signaled to one of his "trusted negro" employees, who snuck away to Myrtlewood to alert merchants. During the night, Parrish and Turk managed to escape, kicking off a desperate race to arrive at area banks and merchants before the Slavonians could cash any of the checks. Parrish and Turk thus spent "a very disagreeable night" in "an exciting trip through a swamp" to arrive at Linden, where they caught the train to Selma.

Within hours, the deputy sheriff in Myrtlewood had arrested and jailed eight Slavonian "ringleaders." Fifteen others who had participated in the holdup had already escaped by walking across the county to Cuba Station, where they caught a train to "parts unknown." About forty other Slavonian men remained in the timber camp, now "thoroughly cowed and subdued" and "perfectly willing to go to work and do what Foreman Turk wanted them to do." Telegrams quickly sent to all the neighboring communities prevented the men from successfully cashing any of the new checks. "The men who have been arrested will be vigorously prosecuted," noted one newspaper, "and there is a great deal of excitement in the neighborhood of the camp."[4]

Like many of the immigrant laborers who arrived in Alabama, the Slavonians at Myrtlewood resisted their employer's effort to fully exploit their labor. They had been hired to provide hand labor producing timber staves, and much like the Chinese on the Alabama and Chattanooga Railroad, the Slavonian stavegetters expected the terms of their contract to be enforced. At least some of the men felt no compunction in asserting that right in a very forceful manner, strong-arming their foreman and threatening their white employer. That assertiveness suggests that they either felt a certain measure of racial security as "white" Europeans challenging a labor boss or they were simply desperate enough to act, regardless of the consequences. However, since they lacked any local relationships with the white establishment in southern Alabama and had no labor organization to protect them or advocate for their interests, their brief rebellion quickly failed. At the same time, they at least survived their protest with their lives intact, though they likely were incarcerated as a result. Like other immigrant laborers, the Myrtlewood Slavonians experienced a dynamic and fluid racial identity in New South Alabama, one that made the outcome of every act of self-assertion unpredictable and risky.

The case of the Myrtlewood Slavonians also illuminates how immigrant laborers often experienced New South Alabama not only as a disappointing place but often as a downright dangerous one. Their experiences posed an uncomfortable answer to the question that most vexed Alabama's immigration boosters across the era: Why didn't more European immigrants come South, when employment opportunities appeared to be plentiful and arable land bountiful? Alabama's boosters and labor agents may have marketed relocation to Alabama as a solid investment for the industrious laborer, but they also found making that case to be an uphill battle against hyperbolic stereotypes of a pathological South that ruthlessly exploited its laborers, immigrants included.

In fact, European laborers such as the Slavonians did encounter significant discrimination, xenophobia, and legal injustices in the New South. As nominal "whites," European immigrants, even Southern and Eastern Europeans, did not experience a situation *identical* to what African Americans suffered. It is hard to imagine, for example, that Black laborers holding up their white boss at gunpoint would escape severe punishment, including extralegal lynching or legal execution. Nonetheless, the immigrant laborers who arrived in Alabama discovered that neither a white appearance, in the case of Europeans, nor reputations for docility and industriousness, in the case of the Chinese, guaranteed protection against the cruelties, injustices, or poor conditions that typically defined working-class life in Alabama. As it turned out, the New South economy churned up foreign-born workers almost as much as it did African Americans.

Soon after the war ended, Alabama's boosters recognized the dilemma posed by competing with other labor agents to recruit immigrants to a region beset by the complications of recovery. The chaos and violence of Reconstruction provided ready fodder for state agents engaged in a heated battle in the United States and abroad to procure labor for plantations, mills, and mines.[5] The still recovering South made an easy target. For example, booster F. S. Mount forwarded to Alabama governor Robert Patton an article he had found in a Mobile newspaper, about negative propaganda against the South that had been published in a New York German-language newspaper, describing it as "injuriously affecting the entire South." Mount found that the article "was produced in Germany, never very favorable to the South," and generated "considerable feeling." He also enclosed a newspaper clipping from the *New Orleans Bee* that reported on a sensational story, widely circulated in Germany and allegedly based on private letters and on newspaper reports, about the mistreatment of German immigrants in the deep South. The story detailed immigrants who were forced to live in old slave quarters, subjected to a subpar diet with little medical care, and faced dire consequences if they tried to escape. In short, according to the article, southern employers treated European laborers like "Dutch n——s." Mount blamed such bad publicity on "unscrupulous labor agents."[6]

Lurid accounts of the South apparently made it to England as well. A Mr. J. Watson wrote to Alabama's Governor William Smith in 1867 about the "fallacies and falsehoods" complicating recruitment efforts there.[7] A few years later, in 1870, a convention speech by Alabama planter Jacob Thompson condemned those who derided the South: "They may raise their howls over the Ku Klux bills, they may parade the slanderous stories of the disorders and dangers of our society, they may attempt to frighten away for selfish ends the emigrant by telling him that there he will be regarded as no better than a negro." Nevertheless, Thompson hoped his more positive portrayal of Alabama would be heard by "the class of men that we need."[8]

Paul Stevens, proprietor of the Stevens and Clark Real Estate and Emigrants Agency, wrote to Governor Smith:

> We would do injustice to truth, our own feelings and our people generally if we did not brand with falsehood the many malicious slanders of our people with which the press is every day teeming. . . . These newspaper accounts

> of cruel murders, brutal inhumanity to the freedmen and universal proscription, mobbing, and maltreatment of Northern men, particularly, are all, without a single exception, manufactured by base, designing men, along for political purposes. . . . We boldly assert these outrages exist only in name and the filthy subjects in which they are published. These lying reports have seriously injured our people politically, besides retarding our progress in wealth and recuperation from the desolating ruin of the war, by delaying and diverting from our more fertile lands, mild climate, and more pleasant homes, that sturdy class of emigrants so much needed to rebuild our waste places and render our beautiful South land once more a blooming garden of beauty.[9]

The development of the Birmingham mineral district and its accompanying labor conflicts drove immigration boosters to exert even more pressure on state officials to deliver the goods. However, propaganda concerning the maltreatment of immigrants and the less-than-stellar conditions in Alabama and the South continued to circulate well into the early twentieth century. In 1905, Ross Smith, commissioner of the Immigration and Industrial Association of Alabama, referenced "the maps being circulated in Europe" that allegedly "had marked across the face in black letters: 'The Southland, the land of Snakes, Crocodiles, Negroes, Yellow Fever, and Death; avoid it.'" Smith first encountered this story in a Tallahassee newspaper, "which so incensed me that I began an investigation. I found several different wordings of the map, as seen by different Southerners in different parts of Europe." He ultimately located a Mr. Payne,

> who, while traveling in Europe, and in some steamship or other office, saw a Western railroad map hung on the wall, with the South marked off with crayon and indicated, as far as Mr. Payne could remember, the words about as suggested above, possibly stronger, in warning emigrants against going to the South. From parties traveling in Europe about that time, they saw several Northwestern Railway maps had been marked in similar manner."[10]

That same year, C. B. Carter, secretary treasurer of the National Association of Hosiery Manufacturers, sent to members an article "which appeared recently in the Chicago Chronicle in regard to the South being boycotted by

European immigrants." In response, Carter explained, "prominent southerners have gone abroad" during the past summer months to investigate "the conditions that affect the destination of the immigrants who land in this country." They learned that American railroad agents across Europe played an important role in fixing immigrants' destination to their own advantage, "so that when they leave their homes abroad they are sure to locate on certain lands of the west and northwest, and in that way help in settling up vast areas belonging to certain railroads, and at the same time building up the traffic of those roads." However, they also discovered to their dismay that "the south is absolutely boycotted by the immigrants because the maps distributed among them have the portion of the United States south of Mason and Dixon's line painted black:

> "It is all black and unfit for the settlement of white immigrants," it is said the prospective immigrants are told. They are impressed with the idea that the south is laboring under such social conditions that any white man settling there will be obliged to associate with colored people and that he can never hope for the opportunities that are easily attained in the great northwest. Because of these representations, it is said, it is impossible to secure a single European settler for the southern states.[11]

Prospective settlers and laborers from the Midwest, New York, or abroad, as well as foreign consuls and immigrant associations, grew increasingly savvy about the prospect of relocation below the Mason–Dixon line. Eliot Norton of the Society for Italian Immigrants in New York City, for example, wrote to Governor Jelks in 1905 that Italians wanted to know what to expect before they came South, particularly the terms of their labor or settlement, and the conditions they could expect to find. Given the clear need for "laborers, mill workers, and settlers," Norton noted, "people wonder why more immigrants arriving in [the] U.S. don't divert to the South." In fact, Italians had to be "familiarized" with both conditions in and the advantages of the South: "Only when the conditions under which they come are studied and understood, and the requirements for their southern settlement met with," would they venture to the state and region in significant numbers.

Indeed, he averred, it was "absurd to suppose they will travel farther if they know nothing about the country they are going to. Some immigrants can be informed of the advantages of the southern settlement *after* they land here but to be really effective such instruction must be given to them before they sail." Thus, his society would endeavor to "make sure any manufacturing plant, mine, or plantation, the owners of which desire workmen or settlers, [would] be examined by a competent person, who will report full thereon . . . These reports will cover all the conditions that concern the prospective settler, such as climate, house rent, cost of living, rate of wages, hours of work, etc., etc."[12]

An application for labor supplied by the Immigration and Industrial Association of Alabama in 1905 tried to do just what Norton wanted, pinning down the expectations held by both sides regarding immigrant laborers. On the blank form, a prospective employer specified the type of work offered, the term of employment, proximity to a rail line, expected hours of labor per day, and the level of wages to be paid per day or per month. Additional details included the terms for "farming on shares," the "class of houses furnished," and whether an employer provided "quarters separate from blacks." Employers also indicated whether the food would be to immigrants' liking and clean water would be provided, and offered details on the state of the general "health of the community" and the provisions for medical care. Employers also had to detail whether schools were free for children over the age of seven, and for how many months; to certify that "there is no strike on at these works"; and to note whether it was an "open or a union shop." Finally, the application indicated that an employer would forward to the immigrant the cost of transportation, including rations for the trip to Alabama, and deduct this cost from an employee's paycheck each month. If an immigrant stayed on the job or the farm for at least six months, then the employer would refund the money.[13]

The following year, even as immigration commissioner Ross Smith reported to the Birmingham Commercial Club the settlement of more than eight hundred people along Alabama's rail lines since December 1905, he also worried that more immigrants would not come because "a prejudice exists among the consuls and foreign benevolent associations in New York against the South, and these are not friendly to our movement in any sense. This prejudice is brought about by the alleged ill treatment of Southern foremen against white laborers." Moreover, the reputed low southern wages, combined with "lynchings, inadequate school facilities and inferior houses for the accommodation of foreigners," though "grossly exaggerated by designing agents," still "have militated greatly against the South in securing her share of the best class of people."[14] Booster Frank Evans agreed with Smith's assessment, explaining to Governor Jelks in September 1906, "You are correct in your suggestion that the tenants' houses in our state will repel immigration. That is, the cheap negro houses."[15]

While Alabama's recruitment leaders wanted to believe that unfair propaganda mostly explained immigrants' reluctance to go to the South, they constantly had to contend with incidents that testified otherwise.[16] As outsiders, immigrant laborers such as the Myrtlewood Slavonians often lacked acquaintances or connections who might protect them if something went awry. Two cases demonstrated how vulnerable such immigrants could be in the New South. The cases of H. C. Bailey and Robert Wiederkehr both involved Europeans who arrived in the state from countries preferred by Alabama's immigration boosters but, much to their surprise, ended up imprisoned within a short time of their arrival.

THE CASE OF H.C. BAILEY

In the summer of 1870, as immigration boosters closely watched the Stanton brothers' experiment with Chinese railroad labor unfold, Alabama governor William Smith received a curious inquiry. "Mr. Gridland, Her Britannic Majesty's Consul at Mobile presents his compliments to His Excellency Governor Smith," wrote Mr. Gridland, "and will be glad to receive an answer to his communication . . . in the case of H. C. Bailey, a British subject imprisoned at Livingston, Alabama." Smith's personal secretary had scribbled a handwritten notation: "See letter to Mr. Gridland, June 18, 1870."

In early June, Gridland had forwarded to the governor a letter received from Bailey, who was "now confined in Jail at Livingston in this state." Gridland had no way to determine the veracity of Bailey's claims. Yet he pointedly noted, "If true it would seem that the said Bailey has not been dealt with according to the laws of Alabama, which doubtless Your Excellency is at all times willing to have enforced." Thus, Consul Gridland asked Governor Smith to investigate Bailey's case.[17]

Born in England around 1847, Henry Bailey resided in Sumter, Alabama, in 1870, where a census enumerator recorded him as a white, male citizen over twenty-one years of age and his occupation as "in prison."[18] Bailey's own account of his troubles highlights the unexpected dangers attendant to many an immigrant's sojourn to the deep South, even if he were an English-speaking white man.[19] Essentially, authorities in Demopolis arrested Bailey for a burglary he swore he did not commit. "I am a Butcher by trade and left England about ten months ago for America where I have been ever since," Bailey explained.

Early in January, having heard "a good account of this Country up North," Bailey arrived in Alabama. However, "this has proven a failure," as he almost immediately became too ill to work for a period of time. He soon departed to Demopolis in March, where "I engaged myself to Mr. John Ground as a butcher there." Much to his consternation, however, he found himself very shortly under arrest "with a partner of Ground's in the butchering business." Demopolis authorities apparently accused Bailey of burglary on the strength of a Black witness who Bailey believed "had been bribed by some one to come up and swear false against me[,] being a stranger." The perpetrators, he alleged, left their tools behind when they were apparently surprised in the act by the same witness "who said he thought it was a man like me that he saw there."

Bailey could provide an alibi: "I have got good witnesses to prove when I went to bed and when I got up the next morning and they have not got anything to shew it was me." He also pointed out that the man who owned the forgotten tools arrived to claim them soon after the incident. Nevertheless, "he being a citizen there was no questions put to him only he said that he had not missed his tools till he heard they was in the courthouse." Bailey ended up accused, arrested, and incarcerated.

A hung jury failed to end the case. The presiding judge sent Bailey back to prison to await a new trial, where he now languished. "I think they will try and put it on me anyhow," he told Gridland, "being a stranger and no one to see into it for me." He pleaded for the consulate's assistance, declaring that "I am quite innocent of it as you are yourself" and pointing out that "I served my apprenticeship in England and have got my indentures with me to show what I am and what sort of character I have always maintained." Bailey noted that when in good health, he could earn "200 dollars a month so I did not need to commit a Burglary or disgrace myself in that way." Finally, he asked the question certain to make every southern immigration booster squirm: "Sir, I would like to know your opinion . . . if this is the way they treat people in this Country because they have no friends to protect them?"[20]

The record does not indicate what ultimately happened to H. C. Bailey. Another case a few years later, however, proved the truth of the warning that coming to the deep South might well be an adventure much regretted.

THE CASE OF ROBERT WIEDERKEHR

Early in 1877, Robert Wiederkehr, barely eighteen years of age, left his home in Switzerland to board a ship, either at the port of Bremen, Germany, or somewhere in France.[21] Swiss "nationals" such as Wiederkehr had immigrated to the United States as early as the eighteenth century, but the largest single immigration took place amid the centralization of the Swiss state and its subsequent industrialization after 1848. Technology in the form of expanded railways and refrigerated ships opened Switzerland to a flood of agricultural goods from North America and Eastern Europe in the 1870s, plunging small farms into economic depression and prompting a flood of farmers off the land to far-flung places such as Australia, New Zealand, and North America. In the United States, most of these immigrants ended up on farms in the Midwest.[22] Robert Wiederkehr, unfortunately, trod a different path.

Shortly after his arrival in New Orleans in March, Wiederkehr allegedly fell under the sway of an Irishman of questionable character named Daly. This man reportedly brought him to Mobile, where he hired out to an elderly German immigrant named John "Fritz" Dahm. Dahm maintained a farm along Polecat Bay, across from Mobile proper, accessible only by boat. He lived there with his children of various ages.[23]

In June 1879, something terrible happened at Polecat Bay. Early one Friday morning, Wiederkehr appeared outside his employer's house, where he announced to Dahm's children, at work in the garden, that "the Devil was in the house." Their father then staggered outside, unable to speak and covered in blood from grievous wounds to his head. "Being frightened by the appearance of his father and the statement of young Wiederkehr," according to the *Daily Register,* Dahm's son appears to have "fled to a boat and rowed to a neighboring garden, where, securing assistance, he rowed back home."[24]

Wiederkehr had not moved, but the wounded Dahm made his way back into the house, where he lay dying in his bedroom. According to a later newspaper account, someone, likely police officers, found a bloody shirt and an ax hidden away on the site. Officers delivered Dahm to the city hospital, where he died the next morning, and placed Wiederkehr in a cell at the Mobile jail. After allegedly "freely" confessing to having murdered his employer, with the assistance of Daly, in order to steal money to fund a departure for California, Wiederkehr was held without bail. According to one account, "lynching was threatened by the friends of Fritz Dahm, the murdered gardener, and one time, even before the boy had been put on trial, the rope had been placed around his neck and the voice of passion and indignance [*sic*], cried 'Hang him!,' but finally the law prevailed and the boy was allowed a fair trial."[25]

That "fair" trial ensued when, a month later, the Mobile city court arraigned and indicted Wiederkehr. After a two-day trial, a jury of "good and lawful men," comprising white, U.S.-born citizens of Mobile County, convicted the Swiss teenager of Dahm's murder. He received a life sentence. Although Wiederkehr had pleaded "not guilty" and appeared not to understand English, the presiding judge denied a defense motion for a new trial. The court then directed "the Sheriff of Mobile County . . . to convey the said Robert Weiderker [*sic*] to the penitentiary of the state of Alabama . . . and that he be confined at hard labor therein for the term of his natural life."[26]

Most of Wiederkehr's story comes from the local paper or from the letters his family and benefactors wrote to Governor Rufous Cobb, asking for a pardon. All of those sources agree that Wiederkehr could not understand much English. While awaiting the grand jury decision, and just one day after the murder occurred, a reporter for the *Daily Register* visited Wiederkehr in his cell. He reported his impressions of this young Swiss immigrant with prejudicial flair. Wiederkehr seemed incapable of understanding the significance of his situation. As he allegedly explained, "He got plenty money; me hit him on the head," but it is hard to know what he actually said. "'Tis hard to believe that this blue-eyed, happy-faced boy is a self-confessed murderer," clucked the reporter, and "the contemplation [of it] is sickening."[27]

That Wiederkehr's story was more complicated than it might first appear becomes ever clearer over the course of an exchange of letters from a benefactor, and from family members petitioning the governor for his pardon. Eccentric Swiss jeweler A. C. Huguenin claimed to be an informal ambassador to the Mobile city government, where he had lived since before the Civil War. Huguenin petitioned for pardon on the grounds that "gross exaggeration and the pressure of many to deception and errors" misled "the judge and city court." Indeed, Huguenin and sixty-four "good" white men and citizens of Mobile, many of whom appeared to be immigrants themselves, agreed that Wiederkehr "was unable to speak or to understand English." After visiting Wiederkehr several times in the Mobile jail, Huguenin was "thoroughly convinced that he was not capable of realizing the nature, extent, or consequences of the crime with which he is charged."[28] Huguenin continued to push for clemency, at one point asking, in June of 1880, that the Mobile County sheriff deliver the youth to him so that he would not "fall into bad hands again." The county solicitor, however, refused to intervene in the case because a jury had, after all, convicted Wiederkehr of murder.[29]

Soon, Wiederkehr's letters were postmarked from Helena, bordering the Birmingham coal and iron district, more than two hundred miles from the Gulf Coast.[30] While dreams of a better life, and perhaps of adventure, had brought him to Mobile in 1877, this young Swiss immigrant soon found himself leased as a convict to work out his life sentence in some of the state's most abusive convict mines.[31]

In a letter most likely dictated to someone on his behalf, given his limited facility with English, Wiederkehr wrote to Huguenin in 1880, "I am well and getting along finely" and thanking him for all his kindnesses. While continuing to hope for "my happy Deliverance from prison," Wiederkehr asked Huguenin for "a box of nice things to eat" because "in prison I get nothing but coarce [*sic*] diet and my appetite longs for somethings of luxury." In another letter, dated the same day and also postmarked from Helena, Wiederkehr repeated the news of his good health and remarked on the beautiful spring flowers. He added, however, that "I am still at the same place—but I am controlled by a Different Company: Messrs. Comer and McCurdy," who, Wiederkehr took curious pains to note, are "very nice and feeling Gentlemen" who "treat me very kindly for all of which I am truly very Thankful."[32]

Curiously, two days later, Huguenin wrote urgently to Comer and McCurdy at Helena, pleading, "Gentlemen, for God Sake, please let me know . . . , why my boy, Robert Wiederkehr, do not answer my letter to your care and kindness." A couple of weeks later, J. W. Comer reassured Huguenin that while Wiederkehr "has written to you and I fear the letter had miscarried," nonetheless, "his health is better than for a long time." Indeed, Comer gladly reports, Wiederkehr is doing "quite well."[33]

Wiederkehr proved luckier than many convicts, Black or white, who succumbed to the hardships of life in a New South prison or convict lease mine. He survived his ordeal. He eventually received a pardon from Alabama's Governor Edward O'Neal in the spring of 1886, possibly because the "crafty fellow who put the crime on Wiederkehr," that is, the mysterious Irishman named Daly, "was afterwards convicted and sent to the penitentiary for another crime." Despite Robert's earlier confession, the *Montgomery Advertiser* reported in 1886 that "it is pretty certain now that Wiederkehr did not commit the crime." Indeed, Wiederkehr reportedly had demonstrated "excellent conduct" during his nine years of imprisonment, "and it was partly in consideration of that fact that the pardon was granted."[34]

Family members and a "sweetheart" forwarded money to Robert for his immediate return to his homeland, according to newspaper accounts. However, he remained in the United States, applying for a passport in 1921 at sixty-two years of age, declaring a "permanent residence" in New Orleans, and an occupation as a "painter." He lived "uninterrupted" in the United States for forty-eight years, from 1877 to 1921. In February 1906, Wiederkehr became a naturalized U.S. citizen, applying for a passport in Jefferson County, Alabama, so he could "travel and visit relatives" in Switzerland, England, France, Italy, Belgium, and Holland, and return to the United States within a year.[35]

H. C. Bailey in 1870 and Robert Wiederkehr seven years later were not the only hapless newcomers who arrived in New South Alabama thinking one thing about the future but who then ended up experiencing a very different fate. Under the Redeemers and the Bourbon Democrats, southern states, including Alabama, had enacted labor statutes premised on the draconian enforcement of written and verbal work contracts.[36] If a laborer or sharecropper agreed to work for a defined time and received any wages, but then left prior to a contract's conclusion, he or she could be arrested, convicted, and sentenced under so-called false pretenses laws.[37]

The codification of the false pretenses law in Alabama, in 1885, made abandoning a work contract despite having received a wage advance the same as stealing money from an employer. However, these cases remained in civil court rather than criminal court, unless the accuser could prove the laborer had intended to defraud his/her employer by fleeing rather than completing the contracted work. The burden of proof rested with the employer or the county/state rather than with the accused, and according to one scholar, even African American laborers often won these cases prior to 1900.

Along with the strengthening of segregation and disfranchisement in the 1890s, however, the state legislature amended the false pretenses law in 1903 to dramatically favor the employer over the laborer. Now the mere act of failing to complete the contracted work, or failing to reimburse an employer for any advances, constituted adequate proof of a laborer's intent to defraud, raising what had been a misdemeanor to the level of a felony. The U.S. Supreme Court did not overturn such laws as unconstitutional until the *Bailey v. State* case of 1911. However, federal enforcement proved relatively lax, and imprisonment for false pretenses violations, as well as peonage, persisted well into the mid-twentieth century.[38]

Under such discriminatory laws and ordinances, a Black "underclass" proliferated, feeding the New South's agricultural and industrial engines through increasing levels of incarceration. As immigrant laborers entered Alabama's mines, turpentine and lumber camps, and urban and town peddling markets, they also showed up as convicts in the state prison records. The state government leased these immigrants to private economic interests to serve out their sentences at hard labor, just as the state did with the much larger population of African American convicts.[39]

The convict lease system played a critical role in the growth of the New South economy, particularly in the Alabama coal and iron ore industry.[40] Officials leased convicts, who were overwhelmingly African American, from county jails and the state prison to the proprietors of coal mines, plantations and farms, lumberyards, and turpentine camps. Leasing convicts made the Alabama coal industry especially productive and state and county incarceration profitable.[41] By 1878, more than five hundred state convicts worked in Alabama's "lumber mills, plantations, and coal mines, with the majority working in agriculture."[42] By 1888, TCI and Sloss Furnaces together absorbed nearly all "able male prisoners" for the Birmingham District, paying up to $18.50 per prisoner. By the early twentieth century, Alabama's convict lease system had grown into a large and profitable operation that helped keep the per capita tax burden low but likely depressed wages for free workers.

From 1910 to 1914, for example, the state netted "over $2 million from convict labor, more revenue than ever before."[43]

Planters and lumber and turpentine operators, among others, made quick use of this system, but no outfits exploited prison labor more thoroughly and efficiently than the Pratt mines, Sloss Furnaces, and ultimately, TCI.[44] In Shelby County, for example, industrialist Daniel Pratt owned the Eureka mines, managed by his son-in-law, Henry DeBardeleben. Organized into two operations, one mine ran with free labor and the other with convicts. Pratt hired former slave owner J. W. Comer, brother of later governor B. B. Comer and cofounder of the labor "agency" Comer and McCurdy, to run these prison mines. Comer initially leased around fifty state convicts and an "unknown" number of county prisoners for his mines. He and his partner, William McCurdy, also a former slave owner, leased convicts to work their plantations in Barbour and Lowndes Counties.[45] Comer and McCurdy apparently leased Robert Wiederkehr from the Mobile county jail after his conviction in 1877, because he appears to have ended up in the Eureka mines.

The convict lease system rang up its profits through exceptionally brutal methods. In Alabama, the convict death rate "far outstripped every other comparable state" throughout the late nineteenth and early twentieth centuries.[46] Before the Civil War, men such as Comer and McCurdy invested significant resources in enslaved people as a form of liquid capital. Emancipation, however, seemed to evaporate whatever weak scruples such economic interests had once sustained. To the scores of employers who worked them throughout the region, prisoners were worth no more than the wealth their labor could extract from the mines or the land.[47]

After emancipation, Comer and McCurdy started a labor contracting business to "fiercely compete" for this entrapped pool of "surplus" labor. They held convicts for years, often past the terms of their prison sentences, to labor in the coal and ore mines or on their plantations. These convicts not only confronted rough working and living conditions and the constant threat of injury and disease but also the depraved cruelty of the men who supervised them. Alabama prison inspector Reginald Dawson found "extremely high death rates" and "miserable accommodations" in the Pratt mines runs by Comer and on the plantations owned by both men.[48] Convict laborers lived chained to bed racks in filthy, crowded shacks, and they ran back and forth to the mines in snow and rain, chained and often shoeless.

They labored for sixteen-hour days, working in dangerous and desperate conditions, sometimes in standing water up to their necks. Accidents were common, the most well known being the Banner mine explosion in 1911 that killed 123 prisoners.[49] Convicts who could not keep up, who talked back or resisted, or who failed to win favor with the guards routinely suffered beatings and even torture. Between 1878 and 1880, twenty-five of the eighty-six convicts Comer worked died on his watch, a mortality rate of more than 30 percent. "Every day some of us were carried to our last resting, the grave," recorded prisoner Ezekiel Archey about the Eureka mines. "Day after day we looked Death in the face," and it was a time of "pure suffering."[50] The state of Alabama had condemned Swiss immigrant Robert Wiederkehr to work out his life sentence in these same mines.

In 1924, four years before the state of Alabama removed the last privately leased state convicts from the coal mines, historian Frank Tannenbaum described the southern prison system as one of the "Darker Phases of the South," specifically citing reformer H. H. Hart:

> It is next to impossible for the average citizen . . . to grasp or comprehend the horrors attending such a system. It is hard to describe the cruelty, woe, and misery. [The convict's] physical, moral, and religious welfare are as completely abandoned as if he were a brute . . . when maimed or injured he has no remedy, however great may be the negligence, or however willful may be the act causing his injury.[51]

Tannenbaum also noted that "the color line exists in the prison. The colored population of the South is predominant. The management is white." Yet Tannenbaum also remarked that "the white prisoners do not escape the mood and the temper the treatment of the colored generates—and so they suffer with their darker fellows."[52] In typical fashion for a white Progressive era reformer, Tannenbaum's horror at this system stemmed as much from the lack of distinction between Black and white prisoners than from the sheer brutality overall. But his recognition that whites *were* incarcerated in this highly racialized system of forced labor is instructive.

Prior to the Civil War, whites, often immigrants, "made up a disproportionate share of the [southern] prison populations." Punishment of enslaved people typically occurred on the plantations or farms where they lived, exacted by the owner. Convicted whites went to a county jail, or to the state penitentiary at Wetumpka, after it officially opened in 1842.[53] But emancipation ultimately overturned this system, and the number of imprisoned whites shrank dramatically. First the Black codes and then subsequent Jim Crow laws ensured that the number of imprisoned Blacks exploded.

In Alabama, prison officials had experimented with leasing white convicts even before the Civil War, both within the walls at Wetumpka State Prison and to outside quarry contractors. S. D. Morgan sent his approval for the convict lease scheme to Alabama's Governor Patton in 1866, since this notion "has long been a favorite theory of mine as far back as the year 1834."[54] In his capacity as president of the commission that built the state capital in Montgomery, Morgan claimed that he "had obtained as labourers in the quarries, and as stone cutters from 100 to 200 convicts a year—a large portion of them I kept engaged on quarries outside of the prison, and I assure you I never had under me so valuable a gang of labourers in all my various operations."[55] It was a logical step, after the war, to recognize the utility of expanding misdemeanor and felony crimes to create a readily available supply of coercible labor, particularly once the Birmingham industrial boom exerted additional pressure on agricultural labor.

The white men and women incarcerated in Alabama's postwar jails and prison often ended up there for similar "crimes" as African Americans. The sheer volume of Black prisoners, however, overwhelmed the numbers of white prisoners, obscuring the immigrant convicts in the historical literature. Despite what Tannenbaum concluded, white convicts likely experienced less brutal treatment than Blacks, but because virtually all studies of the convict lease focus nearly exclusively on Black lessees, the actual treatment of other convicts is essentially unknown.[56] In 1908, however, officials of the United Mine Workers condemned the use of whipping and other abuses at the Pratt mines, noting that "there are some whites among the Blacks and they get theirs too."[57]

Immigrant prisoners, who were overwhelmingly male, often appear in the federal census for Alabama and in the state's convict records. Census enumerators as well as state prison officials usually defined their nativity as being from Europe or the British Isles, and often listed them as newly arrived. State and county officials leased them to the same private contractors that swallowed up the legions of Black convicts.

Ascertaining a precise understanding of *how* many immigrants ended up in Alabama's postwar prison and lease complex is exceedingly difficult. Their names, along with identifying information such as "nativity," appear in the state convict records from the 1880s through the 1910s, and in federal census records from 1870 through 1920. Prisoners who show up in the census are not easily cross-referenced to those who appear among the state convict records or vice versa. The records do yield at least two significant points. First, immigrants such as H. C. Bailey, Robert Wiederkehr, and the Myrtlewood Slavonians, often newly arrived in the United States, *were* incarcerated in the postbellum South. And second, state and county officials leased many of these men to private operators such as TCI. And, as the pardon, parole, and clemency records indicated, a young Swiss man convicted of murder named Robert Wiederkehr was one of them. But he was not the only one.[58]

The lease system compelled Alabama's prison officials to document the identities of prisoners in custody in order to keep track of them as lessees, especially if they escaped. Standard information recorded included a prisoner's name, birth date, nativity (birthplace), and a detailed physical description, including birthmarks, scars, or tattoos. Prison recorders also noted an inmate's perceived race and individual "habits" as well as the location of close family members. The records included the charge, the county, and the details of sentencing, and often indicated whether a prisoner received "short time" (early release) and/or assignment as a lessee to a contractor such as TCI. Escapes, recaptures, and deaths also appeared in each record, if relevant. The inconsistency of racial descriptions constitutes one of the more striking features of Alabama's convict records. Prison staff struggled to align their own understanding of who was "white" or "Black" with the diversity of the men who appeared before them.

In 1870, for example, a young man named Fredrick Coly, who was born in Russia, ended up as a "convict in (the) state prison." In 1888, Dick Gillespie, a forty-year-old man born in Scotland, ended up convicted of grand larceny in Montgomery city court. Described as only five feet three inches tall, white, with a "fair complexion," bad teeth, and tattoos, Gillespie received a ten-year sentence. The Montgomery city court also convicted Fred Rohen, born in 1865 in the West Indies, of grand larceny in 1892. He is described as white but with a "dark complexion," including black hair and eyes, and he had been working on the railroad. Sporting several scars, including from "gunshot wounds in both thighs," Rohen received a two-year sentence. Octo Vogel, a twenty-six-year-old male born in Germany around 1866, worked as a cook and lived in Birmingham before he ran afoul of the law as an accused "horse thief." Described as having a "good German" education, and with a son still living in the old country, Vogel was also convicted of grand larceny and received thirteen months.[59] In 1892, embezzlement charges caught up with a man named Asite Bailey, identified as twenty-two years old with a "very dark" complexion and black hair and eyes, who ended up sentenced by a Marengo County court to two years in prison. His official record lists his occupation as "pedler," his birthplace as "Turkey," and his race as "Turk." The state of Alabama leased all of these men to TCI.[60]

Albert Wyman, born in Switzerland and identified by local prison officials as "white" with a "sallow" complexion, ended up in the Jefferson County criminal court in 1907, convicted of "false pretenses" and sentenced to one year and one day. And a few years earlier, John E. Schmidt, born in Holland, thirty-two years old and working as a cook in Birmingham while his wife and children resided in Macon, Georgia, received the same sentence for the same crime: false pretenses.[61]

As Asite Bailey's example demonstrates, people recorded as "white" by prison officials were not the only immigrants ensnared in the state's convict lease system. For example, the 1910 census records an Alabama prisoner named Frank Shaw as born in Africa around 1876. Shaw's father was born in Kentucky, his mother somewhere in Africa, and Shaw, who was identified on his prison record as "black," either lived in or was imprisoned in Montgomery.

Sexto Rodrigues was born in Cuba and is identified in the Alabama convict records as a Black male with "good teeth" but a "bad habit" that resulted in a conviction for "felonious adultery" in 1909. He earned early parole by being leased to the Henderson Lumber Company, where he died on February 16, 1910, crushed to death by a "log train." George Sasker, born in the West Indies around 1848, ran afoul of the law in Russell County and ended up convicted of burglary and grand larceny in 1891. Identified as "Negro" or "carrib" with black hair, good teeth, and no education, Sasker spoke mostly Spanish, worked as a laborer in Montgomery, and lived with his wife. Shortly after his conviction, officials leased Sasker to TCI to work off his four-year sentence. A few years later, Lazarous Welcome of Honduras, twenty-two years old, appeared in the federal population census of 1900 as a prisoner in prison number 1 at the TCI complex. Identified as a single Black male who arrived in the United States in 1892, he worked as a sailor, so he likely ran into trouble either while living along the coast or while in port at Mobile.

This makes three Latin Americans among this sample defined as "Black," while the case of one Joseph Zamora—like that of the Turkish national Asite Bailey—illustrates how fluid such categories could be. Born in Peru in 1866, Zamora's convict record defines him as a "Spaniard" and "white." But he is also described as having a "dark" complexion, black hair, dark brown or black eyes, and "bad teeth." He could read and write and allegedly maintained "good habits," but he nonetheless received multiple convictions for property crimes, including grand larceny and burglary. Like the others detailed here, and despite being ostensibly "white," Zamora also ended up leased to TCI in 1888.[62]

The point is not that immigrant convicts identified in these records shared precisely the same fate as U.S.-born African Americans, who were by far the larger group incarcerated and leased. Information about many more individual cases, particularly including details about the circumstances that landed immigrants in jail, is needed to develop a deeper understanding of how the experiences of immigrant laborers compared to the discrimination and injustice African Americans lived on a daily basis. However, the anecdotal evidence, combined with the information that census and convict records do yield, clearly establishes how immigrants of various nationalities with fluid racial identities often encountered the Jim Crow system of injustice.

Immigrant prisoners may very well have committed the crimes that landed them in Alabama's jails and prisons. Nevertheless, many of the cases traceable by combining the convict and census records with newspaper accounts highlight similar features, especially that immigrant laborers often lacked meaningful ties to local white structures of power. This made them especially vulnerable to the arbitrary nature of the southern system of justice. Thus, H. C Bailey and Robert Wiederkehr both lacked local white defenders to intervene for them at the time of their arrest, when they had the misfortune of being in the wrong place at the wrong time. Another immigrant, this time from Africa, discovered firsthand what could happen if one was accused of tampering with the Black labor supply.

THE CASE OF RICHARD STRICKLAND

Richard Strickland appears in the federal census of 1900 as a prisoner housed at TCI's prison mine number 1 in Jefferson County. The enumerator described Richard as a fifty-year-old Black male who had been born around 1849 in the Congo Free State in Africa, as were both of his parents. He had been married to Annie Strickland for thirty years, with no indication that their union produced any children. He arrived as an immigrant in the United States in 1893, eventually making his way to Alabama with a citizenship status listed as "alien" and the occupation of "house painter." This was akin to being a day laborer, though Richard could read and write and also spoke English.[63]

The Congo Free State emerged from the Berlin Conference of 1885 as a personal colony for King Leopold II of Belgium, who rapidly established a brutal regime intent on exploiting central Africa's rich mineral and rubber resources. The Congolese people included many different ethnic and language groups and had a migratory history that dated back thousands of years. By the year 600, "over 200 different ethnic groups" resided in the territory, and these had "consolidated into a number of kingdoms and empires" by the sixteenth century. European contact came with the Portuguese in the fifteenth century and increased over time, through "exploration, missionary work, and the expansion of the slave trade."

Scholars estimate that Europeans took as many as 1.5 million Congolese for the international slave trade. That tragic history only grew worse under King Leopold II, who gained notoriety in the late nineteenth and early twentieth centuries for the brutalities perpetrated against the Congo's men, women, and children in the name of colonial rubber profits. Thus, the "abuse and exploitation of the local population" not only enriched Leopold and Belgium but also resulted in "the death and maiming of millions." Belgium sent Catholic missionaries to the Congo early on, whereas Protestant missionaries active in the Congo Free State originated from the United States or Great Britain.[64]

At the heart of Richard's story, as in the case of Robert Wiederkehr's, appears what initially seems to be a question of "criminal character," or at least poor judgment. But the evidence strongly suggests that this Congolese immigrant landed in Alabama's convict lease system because he dared to recruit African Americans to leave Alabama for employment elsewhere.[65]

Procuring and controlling the labor supply obsessed Alabama's employers, from the plantations and farms to the mines, camps, and mills, across the New South period. Agents hired to lure workers from one plantation or industrial operation to another, often to other states, territories, or even countries, inspired persistent opprobrium and retaliation. In 1875, the finance committee of the state legislature, for example, heard a bill that proffered to levy a tax of $1,000 on "labor agents" in order to "prevent the depopulation of Alabama." Local officials arrested several labor agents in the cotton village of Uniontown, Perry County, in 1880, "for procuring hands for other states without having the tax."[66]

Planters objecting to the "incessant persuasion" of such agents in Courtland, located in northwest Alabama, informed chief "labor herder" W. H. Doll, in 1892, that "his presence here is unnecessary," prompting his quick departure. Agents such as Doll had obtained "several hundred negro families" from the area for the "promised land" of Texas and other western locations. Planters were especially angry because "many of those who have joined the exodus have violated contracts, turned their backs on obligations, and have left debts behind them."[67]

In 1903, railroad contractors involved in expanding lines in the mineral district complained about the "foreign labor agents" spread throughout north Alabama, who tried to entice Black laborers "with a long ride and a little better wage" to head west for "Arkansas and the Indian Territory." Local officials arrested Black agent Gilbert Shipe for conducting such business without a license. Shipe had succeeded in spurring "a movement to the Western country [of] twenty-five good, strong negro laborers."[68]

Such concerns caught up to Richard Strickland in the spring of 1898. The *Montgomery Advertiser* reported on the case of a "negro preacher" named R. H. Strickland, arrested by Deputy Sheriff Robert Warnock on the Jefferson–Shelby county line and then returned to the Jefferson County jail. Warnock arrested Strickland for "swindling," specifically, for "going around the many public works in the Birmingham District and approaching the many negroes employed there," and offering to pay fifty cents per person for anyone who wished to leave Alabama for work in the Congo Free State. Strickland allegedly promised to pay to transport enlistees to Washington,

DC, "at which point the negroes would be presented with a tag which would carry them to the Congo, Free State, Africa." Reportedly, about 2,500 African Americans took Strickland up on his offer, which came to light when large groups gathered at railroad depots in Birmingham proper, as well as in Irondale and Gate City, "ready to make the trip." Strickland, the newspaper reported, "who fled after working his scheme[,] was once in Africa, and is therefore able to tell fancy stories concerning that country."[69]

White authorities and observers were convinced that these people had been duped, unable to fathom why any of Alabama's Black citizens would decide to sell all their property and embark to an Africa with which none of them were at all familiar. "The rascal finds a fertile field for his activity in persuading the ignorant negroes of the South that plenty of rest and nothing to do is awaiting them in Africa." Indeed, "it is stated that many negroes who gave up their money sold all of their personal property . . . so as to make the trip unencumbered, and a number are now reported in needy circumstances."[70]

The fraud case, however, might not entirely explain the reasons for Strickland's arrest. This becomes apparent upon review of his actual record of incarceration. Strickland's convict record lists "assault to murder" as the charge, not fraud. The charge could well have been the result of an attempt to resist arrest on Strickland's part, or it could reflect local white efforts to manufacture a more serious crime against someone who was effectively recruiting Black laborers away from the Birmingham District. In either case, Strickland received a harsh punishment: a ten-year sentence. The prison record describes his nativity, curiously, as "African prince," noting that he had a Black complexion and "good" teeth and that he received a pardon on September 27, 1900.[71]

In an article under the headline "Native of Congo Free State Released by Governor Johnston and Will Return to Africa," the *Weekly Advertiser* reported Strickland's case as the "most interesting" of the many recent pardons awarded by the governor. Strickland allegedly pleaded guilty to assault to murder in July 1898. Whereas, two years before, a reporter had believed Strickland had merely once *been* in Africa, now the reporter recognized Strickland's Congolese nativity: "Strickland is a genuine African and a native of Congo Free State. He was brought to the United States by missionaries as a specimen of the converted heathen." Strickland received a pardon because, according to the prison physician, he suffered from an "incurable disease." He gained parole on the "condition that he leave the U.S. within thirty days," and he had "money to pay his railroad fare to New York and a steamer pass to return to Africa."[72]

That both Richard *and* his parents were born in the Congo Free State suggests that, against significant odds, at least some of his ancestors and family had avoided the Atlantic slave trade. And with his arrival in the United States in 1893, Richard had miraculously escaped the brutal imperial regime imposed by Belgium's King Leopold II. But less than a decade after his arrival, having avoided one forced labor regime, Richard ended up essentially enslaved by TCI in Alabama, the victim of another.[73]

From James Weir and H. C. Bailey to Robert Wiederkehr and Richard Strickland, immigrants who accepted offers to come to New South Alabama often found more trouble than they had bargained for. The ambiguity of their racial identity, together with their appearance as "foreign" outsiders lacking ties to white structures of power, created an insecure position in New South Alabama's racial and economic hierarchies, even for many European immigrants. Their ensnarement in the legal injustices characteristic of the New South exposed the vulnerability many immigrant laborers experienced in Alabama. That maltreatment, in turn, attracted the attention of foreign consuls, and even prompted a federal investigation of peonage among lumber and turpentine camp operators in the deep South.[74] None of the aforementioned men won clemency, pardon, or release through the intervention of consular officials.[75] Each case that hit the headlines, however, made recruiting immigrants all the more difficult.

Not everyone, of course, could be deterred by sensationalized and macabre accounts of life in the South, or even authentic stories of hardship that arrived by word of mouth or in the mail sent to friends and relatives waiting in the North or in the old country. As Slovakian Birmingham resident Steve Slovensky remembered, "One would come down, and he'd write to his friends or relatives up there. Then they would start coming down."[76] However, the flip side of the coin mattered, too. Labor agent George Gift, for example, found his high hopes of bringing thousands of Chinese laborers to the deep South dashed once he arrived in China in the 1870s: "The local Chinese . . . had no desire to go to the South, a destination they dreaded even worse than Cuba or Peru."[77]

Immigrant recruiters and the planters and industrialists who supported their campaigns preferred to believe that competing agents unfairly maligned the South and that accounts of mistreatment of immigrants were either gross exaggerations or propaganda. Many of the laborers who answered their call to come to Alabama, such as the Slavonians, Wiederkehr, and Strickland, found out otherwise. As it turned out, the hardships that one knew, whether in a New York tenement or on a bleak Midwestern farm, still were preferable to the unanticipated challenges one might very well encounter in the land of "snakes, crocodiles . . . yellow fever, and death."[78] It was the aftermath of the UMW strike of 1908 in Birmingham, however, specifically the fallout from the Blocton train ambush, that provided the most dramatic case that relocation to the sunny South might not be the best choice, even for the Europeans recruited to come.

CHAPTER 6

"THE SCUM OF THE FOREIGN ELEMENT"

The Trials of the Blocton Four

The Blocton train ambush in the summer of 1908 effectively brought the United Mine Workers strike in the mineral district to a standstill. The arrest of dozens of immigrant Slavic laborers, along with a few African American strikers, for the bloody assault provided Governor Comer with the pretext to move even more aggressively to end the strike. Demolition of the tent encampments, derided by the governor and his press allies as hotbeds of radical unionism and interracial mixing, destroyed the communal network erected by local UMW officials to help the miners through the dislocation of evictions. UMW president W. M. Lewis declared the strike over by the end of August, conceding the ground to the coal operators.

With the strike itself concluding, press attention shifted quickly to the fates of the Slavic men arrested for the train ambuscade. The subsequent trials of the Blocton Four highlighted the racial fluidity of the Slavic miners as they gained firsthand experience with the New South's system of legalized injustice. Industrialists wanted immigrants to lend their labor to the New South project; they did not recruit them only to have these laborers join U.S.-born miners in resisting their exploitation. This challenge to the Tennessee Coal, Iron and Railroad Company, Sloss-Sheffield, and the other coal operators exposed just how tenuous was the position of immigrant laborers in the New South order.

As the statements of union officials and media reports reflected in 1908, the role of immigrants in the Blocton train ambush initially attracted far more interest than their apparent collaboration with African American strikers in perpetrating the attack.[1] Indeed, the dozen or so African American miners arrested for the ambush remained anonymous in both the pro- and antiunion Alabama press, and none went to trial.[2]

The grand jury empaneled to consider the evidence in the murder of train conductor Joe Collins ultimately returned fifty-eight indictments.[3] However, the jury declined to indict the local Blocton UMW president, Robert Hayes, Italian merchant Frank Narcissus, or any of the African Americans arrested.[4] Thus, the trials revolved around the remaining immigrant miners charged with the murder, typically identified as "Slavs," Bulgarians, or Hungarians.[5] The editor of the *Gadsden Times* found that what was most significant about the trials was "that most of the Slavs and Bulgarians arrested for the crime were brought into the district four years ago as strikebreakers by the Tennessee company."[6]

Hayes denied knowledge of or involvement in the ambush, claiming to have spent the night at home with his father. As a locally known white man born and raised in Alabama, Hayes benefited from both his racial and his nativist privilege when the Bibb County Court accepted at face value his alibi as exoneration from participation in the ambush. Italian Frank Narcissus (sometimes called Nuse) also escaped indictment. He likely had a longer history in the community as an established merchant with ties to local whites of influence, including possibly law enforcement. Officials also released the African American miners who had been arrested, and none faced indictment over the ambush. Of all the people arrested in the affair, the dozens of Slavic immigrants, many of whom had only recently arrived in Alabama, had the fewest connections to local whites that could have offered a similar escape hatch.

Upon the strength of the evidence gathered at the scene of the Blocton train ambush, particularly the "bloody sock" and the "alleged confessions" of several of the immigrants arrested, the Bibb County grand jury ultimately indicted at least six "foreigners." Four men, Boriseo Dabetich, Mihaila Lazarovich, Mileto Popovich, and Wasilije Wainovich, actually went to trial.[7] Severance of the cases allowed each man to be tried separately. The trials began with the cases of first Wainovich and then Lazarovich, followed by Dabetich and Popovich. Juries convicted the first three of the men on essentially the same evidence and arguments and sentenced them to life imprisonment. A plea agreement between defense attorneys and the prosecution led to a manslaughter conviction and a three-year sentence for Mileto Popovich. Presiding Judge Miller eventually dismissed the other outstanding cases.[8]

The prosecution's case against the four immigrant miners revolved essentially around the bloody sock located by a deputy sheriff at the scene of the ambush and the alleged confessions of some of the "Slavs" arrested for the incident. When deputies and members of the state militia descended on the nearby homes of Black and immigrant miners residing in Blocton, shortly after the ambush, they allegedly found Wasilije Wainovich sitting on the stoop of his boardinghouse, nursing a badly smashed toe. On the bandaged foot he wore a sock, while the other foot was bare. When officials perfectly matched Wainovich's sock to the soiled one taken from the ambush scene, they arrested him. In searching Wainovich's boardinghouse, as well as the other nearby homes in which either Black or immigrant miners lived, deputies and soldiers allegedly located multiple shotguns, rifles, and pistols, along with a large amount of ammunition.[9]

Chief Deputy Oakley, with the assistance of the state militia, transported the men to the county jail in Centreville. Interrogations proceeded through the use of an interpreter, most likely provided by either TCI or Sloss-Sheffield officials. Both the prosecution and the defense agreed that physical intimidation induced either one or more of the confessions entered as evidence. Oakley earlier had proclaimed in the media that he and his men had treated the immigrants with great solicitude, except for one individual, who received a beating when he reportedly attempted to seize a deputy's pistol. Nonetheless, prosecution witness Boze Durkovich, upon cross-examination, testified at the trial that he was struck in the head by a Deputy Cole at least once and that "guns were laid on the witness's head and he was commanded to 'tell all you know'" and to disclose whether he was at the "shooting up of the train."[10]

Prosecution witnesses included the TCI physician who had treated Wainovich's smashed toe, special deputies, militia soldiers, TCI officials who had been wounded during the ambush, and several of the immigrants presumed to have knowledge about the events preceding and following the ambush.[11] The prosecution's case rested heavily on the immigrants' statements about what happened in the mining camp the day of the attack and in the hours after it occurred. The prosecution witnesses generally testified to seeing Wainovich and/or Lazarovich in the company of a group of "Italians, Slavs, and people of many nationalities" in the late afternoon of the ambush, and then, the next day, seeing Wainovich with a bandaged foot, though he had not sported an injury the day before.

Boze Durkovich, for example, "a Slav employed as a cook," had lived in Blocton only twenty days when the ambush occurred. Although he had been asleep at home during the incident, he recalled seeing Wainovich the prior afternoon among a large crowd at the union commissary, along with local UMW official Robert Hayes. Hayes allegedly received a message during the meeting and then discussed its contents with the crowd. Although Durkovich had been too far away to hear what he actually said, he noted that everyone left the store soon thereafter and proceeded to "Big John's house." When Durkovich saw Wainovich the next morning, he noticed his injured foot. Wainovich allegedly told Durkovich "that he hurt his foot when a heavy piece of timber had been dropped upon it." Durkovich also noted that "he had seen guns in the house that he had not known before." Durkovich testified that Wainovich confessed to having participated in shooting into the train, and that "forty men, altogether, twelve of them negroes," constituted the ambush party.

Another witness who lived in the boardinghouse with Wainovich offered the same tale: he saw Wainovich leave the house, uninjured, around five p.m. the day of the ambush, along with five or six other men. The next day, Wainovich told him how he had injured his toe and that he had shot into the train. Mileto Popovich, described by one reporter as "a Slav and by far the most intelligent witness placed upon the stand whose speech was necessary to translate," testified that Wainovich told him "that the negroes who were placing the log across the tracks had dropped it on his foot" and that "after the shooting he [Wainovich] had run away from the scene with the crowd." Popovich testified that he had seen Wainovich the afternoon before the shooting with a "crowd of Italians, Slavs, and Hungarians." Livco Vanilorich, another "Slav" who lived near the railroad tracks, also recalled seeing Wainovich with "a large number of people" the evening prior to the ambush. He saw him "going along the railroad track past the Italian store" and noticed that "he carried a gun." Wainovich told him about injuring his foot, and that he had left his sock at the scene. The prosecution used these statements, along with the bloody sock, to tie Wainovich and Lazarovich to the cascade of events that culminated in the train ambuscade.

Led by Birmingham lawyer Frank S. White Jr., counsel for UMW District 20, defense attorneys first entered a not guilty plea for Wainovich. They then set their sights on undermining witness statements about how Wainovich injured his toe and protesting their inability to independently depose prosecution witnesses before the trial. They also tried to make the case to the jurors that "the most important of the state's witnesses were employed by the Tennessee Coal and Iron Company and that in reality the Tennessee Company was prosecuting the case against the prisoner(s)." The defense also used cross-examination to attempt to undermine Bose Durkovich's testimony by questioning the voluntary nature of his confession, given the beating and intimidation he endured at the hands of the arresting deputies: "The cross examination here took a peculiar turn in that witness was asked how many times Deputy Sheriff Cole hit him in making the arrest . . . The witness replied that Mr. Cole struck him once and showed the scar to the jury and judge. No one else hit him, but several revolvers were placed at his head." Judge Miller ultimately refused to disallow his testimony as based on a coerced confession.

Various witnesses for the defense offered alibis for Wainovich or Lazarovich on the night of the shooting, claiming to have seen the men asleep in their beds in the boardinghouse that night. Moreover, reported one observer, "The counsel for the defense are endeavoring to prove that the defendant was not hurt by the falling timber at the scene of the shooting." Rather, defense attorneys enlisted the witnesses to argue that "the injury to Wainovich's toe was caused by the axe with which he was chopping wood . . . to make a fire for the Sunday morning breakfast."

Mardelo Wainovich, brother to Wasilije and boardinghouse roommate to Lazarovich, testified for the defense that he typically shared a bed with both men and had seen both in the bed, asleep, on the night of the shooting. He slept in the middle of the bed, with his brother to one side of him and Lazarovich on the other. And "he explained his brother's hurt foot, saying that it was Wasilije's turn to do the cooking, and that Wasilije had gone downstairs early in the morning to cut the wood for the fire. In a little while, he came back with his foot smashed." Milo Dabetich, who shared the house with the

Wainovich brothers, similarly testified to seeing Wasilije "in his bed by his brother's side during the whole of the night." Dabetich claimed that he "had waked him up on Sunday morning that he might go out to cut wood for the breakfast fire. He stated that Wasilije had hurt his foot in cutting the wood." Mileto Popovich, who also shared the house, testified to the same story.

An Italian woman named Catrina Maria took the stand. Her father or husband apparently owned the store that served as the union commissary. Described by a reporter as "the most important witness for the defense," Maria testified to seeing Wasilije chopping wood "in the front yard with a big axe" on Sunday morning, and then "seeing him suddenly reach for his foot and go into the house. The next time she saw him, his foot was bandaged."[12]

Finally, Lazarovich took the stand in the afternoon session and testified to the same course of events as the other defense witnesses: Wainovich slept at home all night, then hurt his foot chopping wood the next morning. Moreover, Dabetich, who had offered damning testimony for the prosecution on the first day of the trial, now "was recalled to the stand for the defense," where he essentially recanted: "He swore he did not hear the defendant say in his presence anything about shooting into the train, or anything about leaving a sock near the railroad tracks."[13]

Blocton UMW president Robert Hayes denied on the stand any prior knowledge that a train bearing strikebreakers was headed into Blocton late that Saturday night. He also denied knowing how the "foreigners" had obtained guns and ammunition, and specifically denied that the union had provided the weapons. Hayes claimed that he only learned about the ambush when reading the Sunday morning newspaper. Finally, Hayes testified that "he had not advised the prisoners to keep their mouths shut nor had the negro trusty in the jail acted as his agent."[14]

On September 12, after all-night deliberations, the jury in the Wainovich trial returned its verdict: guilty of murder in the first degree. The jury also imposed a sentence of life imprisonment. According to newspaper reports, ten of the twelve jurors had favored the death penalty; they compromised with a life sentence in order to end deliberations. Defense attorney White made a show of demanding that the jury be publicly polled on the verdict and sentence, which Judge Miller allowed. The result was the same: "Without exception every member of the jury clearly and unhesitatingly stated that the verdict as read was his verdict." Nonetheless, noted one reporter, "both attorneys for the defense and the State regarded the verdict as a victory for their cause." The state, he explained, "was happy, in that the verdict was a fitting punishment for a tool in a great conspiracy, while the defense expressed themselves as well satisfied that the client was not given the extreme penalty."[15] Judge Miller directed the defense to "acquaint the prisoner, Wasilije Wainovich, of the finding of the jury." With no hint of irony, the reporter stated, "This the interpreter did, the defendant replying that he was not guilty. He accepted the verdict, however, in the same stoical manner which he has worn since the opening of the case."[16] Wainovich's conviction, stated one Alabama reporter, constituted "one of the first convictions ever brought about for rioting in the mine territory."[17]

Three more cases involving the "Slavs" implicated in the train ambush proceeded after the Wainovich verdict, beginning with Mihaila Lazarovich. The first trial had proved sensational enough, however, that the court encountered difficulty in seating a new jury. Although Chief Deputy Charles Oakley called on "nearly every man" in the county seat, still "the citizens of Centreville were soon run through, as all of them had a fixed opinion or were challenged by the defense." Judge Miller directed the deputy to pool a new jury, and "deputies then mounted horses and went to the country for jurymen." The court adjourned until the afternoon, when "the freeholders of Bibb County could be summoned from their farms at varying distances from the county seat."[18]

Lazarovich's trial then proceeded, with the UMW counsel again taking the defense lead, along with A. S. Vandergraff, while Bibb County solicitor W. W. Lavender led for the state.[19] Given the detailed coverage of Wainovich's trial, the press provided fewer details on this one, largely because the prosecution offered essentially the same evidence, witnesses, and argument.

As before, "the foreign witnesses were sworn in through the medium of interpreters."[20] Several "Slav" witnesses testified that Lazarovich told them, on the afternoon prior to the ambush, that "a train load of men were coming to Blocton that night and that a crowd was going to wait on them and that the defendant and others went in the direction of where the shooting was done." The jury found Lazarovich guilty of first-degree murder in the death of train conductor Joseph Collins, and again imposed a life sentence.[21]

Five months later, the court took up the next case in the Blocton train ambush saga, with the trials of Boriseo Dabetich and Mileto Popovich. Of the two, Dabetich's trial attracted the most attention in the media and from the community, likely because the defendant was a youth of sixteen. Again, attorney A. S. Vandergraff mounted the defense. In a striking departure from the prior two cases, however, this time the defendant took the stand on his own behalf, speaking through an interpreter. Dabetich swore to being sixteen years of age and "stated that he had been in America six months when Conductor Collins was killed." He denied "all knowledge of the crime." Although one reporter noted that "some predict there will be a mistrial," indicating some doubt about the strength of evidence and testimony, he offered no further explanation. In the end, his doubts did not matter. Nor did the interest of local "ladies," who apparently attended to see the young man state his case, or of "Mr. Wheeler," the Russian consul from Mobile, who visited Centreville "on business conducted with the trial of the defendant." The jury found young Dabetich, like Wainovich and Lazarovich, guilty of murder in the first degree, and also imposed a life sentence.[22]

In the wake of the life sentences in all of the first three cases, defense attorneys found it prudent to seek a plea bargain in the next case on the docket. Attorneys for Mileto Popovich accepted a conviction of manslaughter in the first degree and a sentence of three years in the state penitentiary.[23] Although several cases against the "other Slavs" in the train ambush had yet to be tried, County Solicitor Thompson dismissed the remaining cases, which cleared the docket. Thus ended the legal saga of the Blocton train ambush.[24]

The testimony in the Blocton trials demonstrated the difficult conditions in which many of the miners labored in Alabama. The witness testimony combined with census records, for example, portrays a rough existence in the mining camps, though not one that was unusual for workers who toiled in the Birmingham District or in many other industrial locales across the United States. The Wainovich brothers and their comrades shared close quarters in boardinghouses in Blocton, as did many miners, immigrant or otherwise. All of the "Slavs" who testified in the trial mentioned sharing beds with each other. "They bring 4 or 5 [of] every nationality, Italians, Greeks . . . Hungarians, Bulgarians," recalled African American TCI laborer Will Battle, "and put em in one house. They'd wash and iron and cook for they self. They didn't bring no woman with them."[25] Based on the manuscript census records, immigrant laborers in the mining camps often lived in such rooming houses. For example, the state's key witness in the first trial in 1908, Durkovich, arrived in the United States in 1907 and traveled immediately or within a few weeks or months to the Birmingham District. There, he found lodging among a dozen or so fellow Montenegrins, the oldest being thirty and the youngest nineteen, in a boardinghouse.[26]

More telling than their living quarters, however, was the fact that the harsh conditions both inside and outside of the mines created a path for immigrant laborers to identify with their fellow miners, including those born and raised in Alabama or elsewhere in the United States.[27] Though they were hated and reviled as strikebreakers when they arrived in the district during earlier conflicts, many imported laborers reportedly had transitioned, by the summer of 1908, into full-fledged strikers and likely union members. Neither the Alabama press nor union officials knew exactly when these men had arrived in the Birmingham District, but they agreed that they initially came as strikebreakers and then transitioned along the way. The *United Mine Workers Journal,* at different times, reported the men as having been imported in 1894 or 1904, during union strikes against the operators.[28]

One such miner penned a letter to the editor of the sympathetic *Blocton Enterprise* shortly before the train ambush. Objecting to the falsehoods that allegedly besmirched the strikers, while portraying the "open shop" miners as "peaceful and satisfied with the 'open shop' prices and conditions," this "Friend of the Union" wanted to set the record straight: "I write a few cases I have seen in some 'open shop' mines in my journey in Alabama." First, in Walker County:

> I saw myself two months ago a lot of barefoot miners carrying timber on the shoulder from woods to the mine. I asked them how much the company pay them for the each timber. I received the answer that the company not pay nothing for the timbers; only they pay for a car of coal 40 cents. If a miner needs some timbers he must make them and bring them in the mine without to have right to ask any pay for it . . . I know a lot of miners which have paid to the mine bosses and to the driver bosses money to give him some cars. Can a miner be satisfied under these conditions?[29]

He went on to note that the "open shop" the operators professed to want was "a mistake; is not an 'open shop' mine in Alabama. Is either 'union mine' or 'scab mine' because if will be an open shop mine will have the same right to work the union and non-union men together," the writer argued. "But here in Alabama in an 'open shop' mine, can't be a union man therein, because if they found a miner only talking about union he will be discharged for that." Thus, he asked, "Is not it shameful to call those mines 'open shop'?" Such mines, he explained, would be better described as "open trap" because "are like the trap; also the miners like the mouse."

> The open shop corporation treat the open shop miners kindly and promise them all from heaven until caught them in the open shop or open trap; then they know well that they can't get out without help. Now the U.M.W. of A. have seen the mouse in the trap, also have heard their cry from all the open shops, and they are willing to help them to come out from the trap. So today of 20,000 coal miners who are living in Alabama 15,000 of them are union members, and every day increase the number, so I am sure in a short time all will be union members.

But this immigrant striker articulated more than a straight-up UMW justification for the strike. He also cannily appealed to the sentiments of *U.S.-born* Alabamians in making his case for the union's cause: "Of course the coal operators will import some scabs from the other states," he pointed out, "to take the place from the good Alabama citizens who are honorable and like to change the open shop system."

> I don't know if is that right or not to put to work such subjects which haven't paid any tax for the state, or such subjects which are coming from Bulgaria or other states with the intention to steal the bread from the Alabama citizens to make some money and then go elsewhere, such subjects which are coming with the intention to rob this beautiful land and to put the Alabama citizens in a deplorable and bad position.

Pointing out that the "coal corporations" and "also the farmers and all the classes of labor" already were organized, he added that "this land is a land of liberty and freedom, and the right of every one is guaranteed by the Constitution." After all, he pointed out, "we ask only honest pay for our work, and eight hours is enough for a miner in the bad air and the smoke in which we work inside. Also we ask to be treated as men, not as beasts. That is all we want." And he had a warning or two to add as well: "I advise all the union men not to believe if some company spy tell them to go to work under any kind of promise, because they lie, betray and sell you for a few silver dimes."

> Like the Judas has sold the Jeus Cristos for thirty silver coin. Brothers, I know a lot of miners who came from different points here on the last strike under the promise that the company would pay them $3.50 a day, and here they have received only $1.25 for a day of labor . . . Remember the New Testament, that our Lord Jeus Cristos did start our religion with twelve apostles only, and they had a very hard time, and they had all the world; but we are only the State of Alabama, not all the world, and we are as many apostles to build the union for all the Alabama miners.[30]

After years laboring in the mines, the immigrant "Friend of the Union" who penned this letter clearly identified his interests with his fellow strikers and union members in Alabama more than with the replacement imports, such as the "Bulgarians," who continued to pour into the district and, like young Dabetich, became ensnared in the sudden and unfortunate turn of events after they arrived. In the wake of the train ambush, however, even "Friend of the Union" would have had to admit to the fragility of protection afforded by union membership. As the coverage of the trial proceedings indicated, the four men tried and convicted for the ambush murder of L&N conductor Joe Collins barely understood what was happening to them. They may have appeared to be white men, but like Robert Wiederkehr, H. C. Bailey, and the Slavonians, among countless others, they were white men of a "lesser sort." They ended up entangled in the indiscriminate vagaries of the highly racialized southern legal system, unable to mount an effective defense on their own behalf.

Whether the men directly participated in the ambush, as seems likely in the case of Wasilije Wainovich, with his badly smashed toe, or they were simply unfortunate enough to be seen in proximity to those who perpetrated it, as is probable in the case of Boriseo Dabetich and Mileto Popovich, these men did not find in Alabama the opportunity lauded by the state immigration boosters and labor recruiting agents. They did find at least a modicum of community with their fellow strikers, both Black and white, but in the end the "Slavs" shouldered the entire blame for the train ambush, assigned that role by the press, the prosecution, and UMW leaders.

Deputies arrested upward of fifty people in the incident, with about a dozen of them identified as "negroes" and the rest as "foreigners" and/or "Slavs." But it was only Wainovich, Lazarovich, Dabetich, and Popovich who ended up convicted and sentenced. In discussing those arrested for participation in or knowledge of the ambuscade, neither the press nor the prosecution identified a single Black individual by name. In other incidents of the strike, Black miners did end up identified, as either victims or perpetrators of strike violence, but not in the train ambush, the most sensational event of the strike and arguably the pivotal event for the UMW's defeat.[31]

One newspaper account in the *Birmingham News* suggests why African American miners escaped blame for the train ambush. To explain how officials ended up targeting the immigrant community at Blocton for the ambush, most reports pointed to the bloodhounds that allegedly brought deputies and members of the state militia straight to Wainovich's smashed toe. One report, however, posited a different account: deputies had already arrested the African Americans *before* the militia arrived at the scene. And when they did arrive, "close questioning," that is, the use of threats and possible violence, led these initial prisoners to disclose the "first clue" to the identity of the "real assassins." Indeed, concluded the reporter, "the negroes proved to the satisfaction of the authorities that they were innocent but they imparted information that proved valuable before the man hunt was over."[32]

Eyeing the racial landscape at hand, the Black strikers under arrest wisely chose to meet white officials' demand for information rather than to maintain solidarity with immigrant strikers. In return, they escaped culpability for any participation in the ambush. As replacement workers, immigrants such as Wainovich and the others earned praise and protection from employers. But when they challenged the New South order by striking or engaging in strike-related violence, they suddenly had fewer options than even African American miners.[33]

Indeed, the men appear to have been unclear about why they were being tried for murder in the first place. Popovich, for example, who indicated during his testimony that he did not know the name of the company for which he labored in the district, also indicated, upon cross-examination by the prosecutor, that he did not "know what the charge against him was." Prosecuting solicitor W. W. Lavender queried whether the interpreter had explained on the morning of his arrest "what the charge was," to which Popovich replied, "Don [*sic*] remember the interpreter." Through the court interpreter, the prosecutor then asked Popovich, "Isn't it a fact that Deputy Oakley and the interpreter told you of the charge when you were jail?" Popovich answered, "Yes, but didn't understand the interpreter."

Clearly trying to make the case that Popovich was dissembling on this point, the prosecutor then instructed the state's interpreter to discuss with the witness the internal layout of the house where the men boarded in Blocton. Whereas Popovich claimed to not understand the interpreter when arrested, now he engaged in a "rapid" discussion with an interpreter before the jurors, Judge Miller, and trial observers, "showing the jury," according to the reporter, "that the witness readily understood."[34] But it remains unclear whether the trial interpreter for the state was the same person who interpreted for law enforcement when the deputies arrested the men. Moreover, if the account of the trials in the *Montgomery Advertiser* can be believed, these men were not Hungarians or Bulgarians but were from Montenegro, in the southern Slavic region of the Balkans.[35]

Montenegro, or "Black Mountain," lay just below Croatia in the southern portion of the Austro-Hungarian Empire. Incorporated into the Serbian Empire around the fourteenth century, Montenegro had a geography that yielded little in the way of viable occupations. Described as "rough" or "rugged" mountainous terrain, it had little arable land for market agriculture, other than sheep or goat herding. It was bordered on the north by Serbia and Kosovo and on the south by the Adriatic Sea, and steep mountains climbed up from the coast. Much of the rest of the land was either covered with dense forest or consisted of a largely "barren" limestone plain.

"The land was too poor to support its population," and hunger stalked Montenegro throughout the twentieth century. The "extreme poverty of the land" propelled outmigration, typically to other lands within the Austro-Hungarian Empire, to Russia, or to the United States. Almost "continual turmoil and warfare" in the western Balkans, with Montenegrins often at the apex of struggles between the Habsburg, Ottoman, Russian, and Serbian empires, also played a role in propelling emigration.[36]

Few Americans in the early twentieth century understood the ethnic, political, or social complexities that defined the Balkans of south-central Europe. Newspaper editors and reporters, government and union officials, and employers alike commonly misidentified immigrants from the Balkans as Austrian, Bulgarian, Greek, Hungarian, Italian, Polish, Russian, "Slavic," or even German. What language would an interpreter for the Bibb County sheriff, the state militia, TCI officials, the presiding judge, or UMW officials have used? As Montenegrins, the Blocton Four would most likely have spoken Serbo-Croatian.[37] Like Popovich, however, Lazarovich indicated during his trial that he "did not know why he was being held at the Centreville jail at the present time."[38] Upon their conviction, the interpreter even had to explain the verdicts to the defendants.

Moreover, in the charge to the jury on the first day of Wainovich's trial, Judge Samuel L. Weaver made it clear where his sympathies lay, and it was not with the defendants. "I do not believe, and I think your investigations will reveal the fact," proclaimed Weaver, "that [these] violations have not been committed by native Alabamians." And while he averred that "I shall say nothing against foreign immigration," still he called on jurors "to execute the law that these foreigners who come within our borders be awakened to a lively sense of their duty as citizens by receiving punishment they deserve for the violation of the law."[39]

As Jessica Jackson has found in examining Italian immigrants on trial in the Gulf South states, jurors commonly viewed immigrant defendants through a racialized lens that combined preexisting xenophobia, nativism, and racism with a "commonsense" understanding of who they thought the defendants were, one that derived from community proximity, personal experience, and assigned reputations. In practice, juries placed immigrant defendants and witnesses along a spectrum between "whiteness" and "Blackness."[40] In this context, the Blocton Four hardly experienced a fair trial before a jury of their peers. At the conclusion of the first trial, the *Birmingham News* published the names of the twelve jurors (all white men). Among the ten identified through 1910 census records, all were farmers, nearly all owned their own home, free of mortgage debt, nine were married with children, and all were born in Alabama, as were nearly all of their parents. None was even a second-generation immigrant.[41]

And such bias extended beyond the courtroom. *Montgomery Advertiser* reporter Frank Glass, who offered a detailed account of the train ambush trials, gleefully trumpeted dehumanizing stereotypes of the immigrant laborers on trial. Initially, Glass romanticized Wainovich as a "newcomer [with] a striking general appearance," though one "common to the mining district." Wainovich "is well set up physically with clear, grayish, blue eyes, eyes which become hard and flinty. His hair is a shock of auburn with a tendency to curl." Indeed, despite his rough miner's apparel, Glass reported, Wainovich "presents an almost distinguished appearance. With high cheek bones, a good nose, and square chin, this view of his face is excellent."

There the flattery ended. Glass quickly degenerated into racist tropes that demonstrated the ambiguous position of these "semi-white" men caught up in the New South judicial system. "The full profile" of Wainovich, Glass wrote, actually presented as "bad, repulsive to the word . . . the face is broad in the extreme, and taken with the general physique brings out to the fullest the brute in the man." Moreover, he sniffed, "the mustache, Kaiser Wilhelm, adds to the brutish appearance of the man." Glass also commented on the men's language, describing their names as "musical" but also quoting Prosecutor Thompson's derogatory comments made in his closing remarks. First, Thompson had derided the defense charge that "the defendant did not speak the English language and could not know what was being said against him" as "pure rot." Next, Thompson arrogantly proclaimed that "if he had his way at Ellis Island any person 'who spelled his name by slinging a handful of type,' would be excluded from the country just because of that fact." Finally, Thompson slurred Wainovich as "the type of man . . . who assassinated Kings and Presidents," deftly linking the defendants to popular memory of European and anarchist involvement in the earlier Haymarket Square bombing in Chicago in 1886 and the more recent assassination of President William McKinley in 1901.[42]

Americans often racialized immigrants, particularly Italian and Slavic people, in the wake of violent labor conflicts in other parts of the United States.[43] In the racial ordering of European immigrants common among Americans in the early twentieth century, the national identity of the Blocton Four as Montenegrins set them very low on the European ethnic "ladder," ranked as the lowest of the "black Austrians," along with Bulgarians and Serbians.[44] Glass's derogatory descriptions fit this broader national pattern. He derided the men on trial as "Monte-Negron," remarking that the "language of Bulgaria, even that of the lowest class of Bulgarians, that of the

Monte-Negro, when spoken by the interpreter, and by the most intelligent of the witnesses, flows along without a sound that is harsh to the ear." Moreover, appealing to the provincial and xenophobic proclivities of his readers, Glass noted that the Slavic men used "graceful and smooth" gestures while testifying: "Not one of them had the quick gesture of the Frenchman, or the uplifted eyebrow and shoulder of the more commonly known descendants of the Latin."[45]

During the Birmingham strikes, both sides of the labor conflict denigrated or lauded the immigrant laborers, including the Montenegrin strikers, when it suited their purposes to do so. Their racial position varied by context, much like what the Chinese, Italians, and other immigrants had experienced in Alabama. Once the Slavs appeared to be deeply embedded in the strike, and once they were charged with perpetrating the worst of its violence, they became useful scapegoats, or undesirables, for both sides. Their treatment by local officials, journalists and editors, and even UMW officials demonstrated the fluidity of the immigrant laborer's place in the New South lexicon of race and class.

To union officials, for example, these men were a sort of noble victim when their story involved mistreatment by the coal operators in a way that validated the strike's cause. But when their story appeared to put union officials or editors sympathetic to the strikers on the defensive, as in the train ambush, these men became something far less "noble" and certainly less "white." The *Centreville Press,* relatively sympathetic to the strikers, for example, blamed TCI officials for the ambush, specifically for having imported "hundreds of foreigners" and "such a class of men" into the mineral district. In fact, noted the editor, TCI had "no moral right to force upon a community, *the scum of the foreign element*" (my emphasis).[46]

Indeed, it seems this perspective was shared by UMW officials, who vacillated between condemning the train ambushers as "bad immigrants" and posing them as "immigrant victims" of the perfidy of the operators and their flunkies in local law enforcement. One UMW member, "Piper," admitted in the sympathetic *Blocton Enterprise* that "some of those criminals could have been members of our organization," but he also explained, "I am sure they are not all members, nor even sympathizers of the union but bitter enemies."[47] UMW officials wanted to portray the men as strikebreakers, deciding that "out of [those] in connection with this shooting, all except one or two were brought in to break the strike four years ago and given arms by the Tennessee Coal and Iron Company at that time," ignoring the fact that the same applied to the many African Americans, who produced an explosion of membership in the UMW during the 1908 strike.[48]

The UMW also preferred to draw attention away from the train ambush, understandably, by highlighting the many incidents of violence against the strikers perpetrated by special deputies, soldiers, or TCI thugs. District 20 UMW official and strike leader W. R. Fairley, for example, told a mass meeting held by the Birmingham Trades Council about TCI's alleged stockading of a group of "Bulgarians" who had just arrived in the District: "At the present moment . . . 65 Bulgarians who left their native country after listening to the siren song to come to the land of the free and the brave, are penned up at Wylam," accused Fairley, "and they have met in Alabama their second unspeakable Turk, and the atrocities of Bulgaria are being repeated . . . That was done by the powerful Tennessee Company." The company allegedly had brought the men to the district under false pretenses, assuring them that no strike existed in Birmingham, but then "they had been forced into the stockades at the point of bayonets of 'Gov. Comer's tin-horn soldiers.' They said at Wylam 65 Bulgarians were confined in stockades, and that they had been driven in."[49]

A later statement in the *United Mine Workers Journal*, published during the trials of Wainovich and Popovich, again drew attention to the incarceration of immigrant laborers, this time confusing the "Bulgarians" with "Greeks," in order to condemn Governor Comer for citing a lack of hygiene and unsafe conditions as justification for shutting down the strikers' encampments. "The men who will drive into one of these dens a bunch of 50 or 100 Greeks, or men of any nationality," condemned the union miner, "and horde [*sic*] them together like cattle, where the black snake whip is the symbol of authority, care not for sanitary conditions."[50]

Despite the miscarriage of justice that landed the Blocton Four in prison, none of the men served a full sentence. Just prior to leaving office, Governor Comer amended the terms of Wainovich, Lazarovich, and Dabetich from life to five years. According to the *Montgomery Advertiser*, Comer's change of heart derived from "the request of both the trial judge and the solicitor that five years would be ample punishment for the men."[51] Although the UMW shied away from admitting publicly that the men were either union members or legitimate participants in the strike on the union's side, union officials did not entirely forget the men once they were convicted. District 20 president John R. Kennemer reported at the annual district convention in June 1911, "I am working on a parole and the prospects are good and I hope to have all released before the expiration of their terms." Governor Emmett O'Neal, a bit more sympathetic to organized labor, granted three of the four men early parole. Mileto Popovich received neither pardon nor parole but was released on "short time," completing twenty-six months of his three-year sentence "on account of good conduct."[52]

The years in prison or as convicts in the mines, however, took their toll. Three of the four men served out their years in the dismal Flat Top prison mine in the district, while one went to the state penitentiary at Wetumpka, or "the Walls."[53] Of the other three, as Kennemer reported in 1911, "there is only one of them that is really able to work." This man, likely Dabetich, "is working in the mines at Flat Top, while the other one is doing little chores around the prison." Wainovich may have been able to handle light duty around the Walls, but Lazarovich was not even that fortunate. By the spring of 1911, he was "in the last stage of consumption," prompting Kennemer to work with the deputy Russian consul, a Mr. Fuller, to apply for an immediate pardon.[54] A few days later, the *Centreville Press* reported that Lazarovich, "having participated in the general riot which occurred at Blocton," had been paroled by Governor O'Neal, "upon the condition that his family take care of the convict." Regrettably, "it is said the man has only a short time to live."[55] The UMW subsequently paid $12.40 to Lazarovich to aid in "transportation," presumably when he left the prison, and ten dollars to the destitute Popovich, for "relief," when his time at the Walls ended in May of 1911.[56] From that point onward, the historical record appears to be silent on the subsequent fate of the Blocton Four or of any of the other participants in the train ambush.

When immigrant laborers such as the Montenegrin defendants came to the Birmingham District, they confronted strike violence, ill treatment, and legal jeopardy. "Thousands were inveigled to Alabama by the operators' promise of 'steady work, no strike, and good wages,'" explained UMW officials. "But when they arrived there they found there was very much of a strike, and those of them who were not driven into the stockade made haste to the strikers' headquarters and joined the strikers." This response "was not because they were intimidated but because they had been deceived."[57] Yet as Dabetich, Lazarovich, Popovich, and Wainovich also found out, joining the strike community offered little protection from Alabama's racialized and arbitrary system of justice.

Although UMW's President Lewis never publicly acknowledged that the immigrant participants in the train ambush were not only strikers but likely also union members, he did accurately diagnose the problem that vexed the state's immigration boosters. In doing so, he exposed the UMW's own racial myopia: "They have a problem in the South of handling labor that would not be tolerated in other parts of the country," Lewis explained. "And this is probably the chief reason why the operators there have so much trouble securing a desirable class of miners." The operators, he pointed out, "complain that negro miners are not reliable and that immigrants cannot be persuaded to settle in the South in large numbers."

> The trouble seems to be that the coal company officials, in common with other employers, as well as the civil authorities, have become so used to dealing with negro labor that they are not very successful in handling any other class. Treatment that the colored class submits to as a matter of course, having always been used to it[,] will not work at all even when applied to the poorest class of foreigners.[58]

In an article reprinted from the *Coal Trade Journal,* published in the *United Mine Workers Journal,* another writer echoed Lewis's analysis, commenting, in the wake of the ambush trials, that actions targeting strikers "may have the effect of causing a return to work, but it is not good advertising for employers of labor anxious to get a better class of workmen. The men accorded such drastic treatment, unless they are natives who have always been used that way, will leave for other parts at the earliest opportunity and warn their friends to keep away."[59] And it was that warning, from those who *had* risked it all to come South, who had taken boosters or labor agents at their word and yet ended up pretty much on the wrong side of everything, that convinced many immigrants making their way to the United States in the decades following the Civil War to avoid the South.

CONCLUSION

Neither immigrants nor Catholics were overrunning Alabama in the 1850s, but that did not stop Reverend John Hinchey Willoughby from hating both groups anyway. Born in North Carolina in 1816 and residing in Alabama since at least the 1830s, Willoughby served during the Civil War as the chaplain for the Eighteenth Alabama Infantry, until he was captured at Mission Ridge.[1] He was apparently an avid consumer of national politics well before then, and he appeared to be caught up in the nativist political movement of the mid-nineteenth century that morphed into the Know Nothing Party, amid the nation's developing sectional crisis.[2]

Willoughby wrote to a newspaper editor in July 1855 to condemn the Catholic peoples of England, France, Portugal, Russia, and Spain as "dupes" of the pope. He then noted, "I am in favor of a repeal or amendment of the naturalization laws so as to prevent the landing of paupers and criminals upon our shore." In fact, he declared, "I would not vote for a Roman Catholic if nominated by Uncle Sam himself." More specifically, Willoughby opposed the foreign-born people he erroneously believed braved the Atlantic crossing simply to cast a vote in American elections: "If they come here on purpose to vote they should not be allowed to do so."[3]

Around the time that Willoughby scribbled his indignant xenophobic screed, Alabama's state population recorded around 7,500 "foreigners" and Catholics as resident in the state, most of whom lived in Mobile. The single largest group in 1850 was the Irish (3,817), followed by German (1,252), English (1,025), Scottish (597), and French (497) nationals.[4] Given Alabama's overall population of more than 700,000 in 1850, the "paupers," "criminals," and "dupes" about whom Reverend Willoughby decried amounted to less than 1 percent of the state's total population, scarcely constituting a threat to the state's U.S.-born residents.[5]

One hundred and fifty-six years after Willoughby's letter to the editor, in 2011, the Republican-dominated Alabama state legislature sparked a firestorm of controversy and a tsunami of negative publicity by enacting the Beason-Hammon Alabama Taxpayers and Citizens Protection Act (HB-56).[6] Republican governor Robert Bentley, an ordained Baptist minister, lost no time in signing the nation's harshest anti-immigrant bill into law. HB-56 rendered the act of being an undocumented noncitizen in the state a felony crime, along with virtually all efforts to lend assistance to that population, including through employment, education, housing, medical care, law enforcement services, and help with food or utilities.[7]

At the time, the state's population of undocumented people amounted to less than 4 percent of the population, a bigger proportion than in 1855 but still a far cry from threatening the state's resources, employment opportunities, law and order, or cultural identities.[8] Nonetheless, the Republican majority in the statehouse enacted the nation's most punitive anti-immigrant law anyway. Republican Mo Brooks, U.S. representative for Alabama's Fifth Congressional District, channeled the hateful spirit of Reverend Willoughby to declare that, to rid the state of this conjured menace, "I will do anything short of shooting them, because illegal aliens need to quit taking jobs from American citizens."[9]

From the xenophobia of Reverend Willoughby in 1855 to the nasty political grandstanding of Representative Brooks in 2011, Alabama residents have recorded a long history of opposition to immigration and immigrants. The politicians, officials, and boosters who wanted to attract immigrant laborers and settlers to the state often complained about the resistance to this program they sometimes encountered. The earliest opponents directed their most strident complaints at the question of Chinese labor, reflecting both the prominence of the issue nationally, after the completion of the transcontinental railway in 1869, and the fallout of efforts to use Chinese laborers on railroad construction in the early 1870s. Republican Governor William Smith, for example, opposed the importation of Chinese labor during Reconstruction because it threatened to create "a super abundance of cheap labor [that] would be detrimental to the state." Ostensibly, Smith sought to protect the freedmen, as Republican constituents, from a race to the bottom on wages that increasing the availability of surplus labor would likely produce.[10]

Others, however, opposed bringing Chinese laborers to Alabama for reasons more aligned with Reconstruction controversies, such as the accusation that railroad magnate J. C. Stanton sought to use Chinese labor not just to build the Alabama and Chattanooga Railroad but also to create new citizens who would vote for Republican candidates and policies, particularly on future bond issues to fund railroad construction.[11] In 1878, immigration commissioner C. F. Seviers noted to the governor that "it is well known that statements prejudicial to the introduction of immigrants into Alabama are prevalent, and it is equally well known that Alabama has never taken any measures to remove this unfounded prejudice."[12]

The "unfounded prejudice" Seviers identified in Alabama echoed the nativism found across the United States as an expanding and increasingly diverse wave of immigrants from around the world arrived in the late nineteenth and early twentieth centuries. Like many other Americans of the era, Alabamians at times responded to the arrival of these new immigrants in xenophobic, ethnocentric, and nativist terms, drawing on a deep pool of ignorance and racism when it came to peoples and cultures beyond their own experiences. Thus, anti-immigration sentiment in New South Alabama did not sound any more virulent than what existed in many other sections of the United States, including in the Northeast, the Midwest, or the West.[13]

In the New South, popular reaction to immigrants also depended on the position held by local residents in the region's political, economic, and racial hierarchies. Coal operators and planters often perceived immigration as a potential boon to their own economic prospects. African American washerwomen, striking miners, or petty merchants, on the other hand, often perceived immigrants as a real economic threat.

Certainly, there were plenty of U.S.-born residents who viewed Alabama's New South immigration campaigns with skepticism and even suspicion.[14] But African Americans, especially, had good reason to react with hostility and resentment. Southern white employers publicly stated their intentions, backed up by their actions, to hire immigrants in order to bring recalcitrant Blacks to heel. "I am preparing to get independent of the freedman," announced Alabama planter and later immigration booster and Birmingham real estate developer Robert Jemison Jr., in 1870, because "until he is taught that we are or can make ourselves independent of him . . . he will be a poor and unreliable laborer."[15] Several decades later, the *Birmingham News* reported on the labor difficulties experienced by the owners of the Black Warrior Lumber Company in central Alabama: "They have been having such a hard time with their laborers," reported the writer, "that the company has decided to put in a force of Slavs instead of Negroes." Moreover, "the first installment has arrived [and] it is expected that about one hundred more" would soon follow. Most importantly, "they are said to be excellent workers and the company is well pleased with this change."[16] The message, and there were plenty of them across the era, was clear: African Americans who stood up for their economic and political rights would confront, at the very least, campaigns to bring in immigrants to replace them.

This book could easily have simply logged instance after instance in which Alabama's U.S.-born residents, like Americans elsewhere at the time, voiced opposition to the wave of new immigration entering the country and the state during the New South era.[17] Such an approach also would offer some obvious similarity to the later anti-immigrant climate that produced HB-56 in 2011. The larger task for this project, however, was to address a more fundamental historical amnesia, one that allowed many citizens in a state actually built by a diversity of peoples to pretend that their experiences and sacrifices on behalf of the New South project never even happened.

Alabama's entrepreneurial and political leadership recruited with great fervor and fanfare, marketing the state to the industrious and thrifty immigrant willing to make a few sacrifices in the short-term for gains in the long run. In the booster imagination, such people were almost always Northern and Western Europeans, and most often German, Scandinavian, or from the British Isles. However, because disciplining or replacing Black labor always remained the fundamental aim, and because Alabama's boosters and labor agents ultimately depended upon whatever immigrant "material" was available, they also embraced at various times, if ambivalently, Chinese, Italians, Greeks, Russians, Hungarians, and other such "new" groups who increasingly arrived at American ports of entry after the Civil War.

For many immigrants, the South, and Alabama in particular, had a fearsome reputation in the wake of a destructive war to preserve slavery and the counterrevolutionary violence that accompanied Reconstruction and the adjustment to emancipation. Negative perceptions of the South, the possibility of higher wages and better job opportunities in the North, or land availability in the Midwest, along with preexisting connections to kin and immigrant communities located elsewhere, meant that many immigrants either avoided the South entirely or left soon after they arrived. "The fact has just been developed," announced a Birmingham reporter in the fall of 1907, "that 280 Poles and Slavs have left this place [Ensley] for Mexico within the last few months." Furthermore, some Italians in Ensley had remarked that "they like the climate and are satisfied with the wages, but they say they are not satisfied with their treatment." More specifically, "Owing to a number of persons being placed over these foreigners who are not in sympathy with them, a great deal of dissatisfaction exists."[18]

But whereas immigration boosters at the time recognized some of these obstacles, very few dwelled for long on the actual implications of what immigrant laborers experienced when they did come to the New South. In the accounts of people such as Chinese laundryman Charley Sing, French gunman Rion Regis, Swiss "murderer" Robert Wiederkehr, Congolese labor agent Richard Strickland, and the Slavonian stavegetters, or in the tribulations of Wasilije Wainovich and his Montenegrin comrades, lies another reason why more immigrants did not heed the call to come to Alabama and the South. Stories of mistreatment circulated as widely as recruiters' tales of opportunity, creating an incentive for immigrant laborers to leave if they ventured South and convincing others to not risk coming at all.

Nevertheless, like Dolphina Lesko and the other Slovakians of Birmingham, thousands of immigrants did choose to labor and eventually reside in New South Alabama and other southern states. Their stories establish immigrants as an integral part of the New South project. Alabama's New South story, then, is about more than the *absence* of immigrants in comparison to the rest of the industrializing nation. If we consider immigrant communities to be noteworthy only if they numbered in the hundreds of thousands or more, then we miss their *actual* presence in the villages, towns, and cities that populated the region, including the outlying rural crossroads and camps. And if we accept a small presence as virtually no presence at all, then we accept a truncated version of what the New South, and Alabama, really were.

The largest demographic groups in communities throughout the state always remained Blacks and whites born in the United States. Nevertheless, people from around the world found their way into many of the state's rural crossroads, small towns, and urban communities. The nationalities laboring in Jefferson County in 1910, for example, originated from every inhabited continent. British, German, Italian, and Russian nationals worked in the district's mines, and Greek, Italian, Russian, and Syrian-Lebanese peddlers traveled throughout the district. But there were others as well, and not only the Slavic men who ultimately took the blame for the Blocton train ambush. Scandinavians, Poles, twelve Chinese men, around thirty Tunisians, and between twenty and thirty Mexican nationals resided in the county in 1910. Many of the Mexicans worked in the coal mines.[19]

Immigrant agricultural settlements along the Southern and the Louisville and Nashville railroads that crossed the state included the German colony of Cullman in north Alabama, the Scandinavian colonies of Fruitdale, Silverhill, and Thorsby in Central Alabama, and the Italian colony of Daphne along the Gulf Coast.[20] By 1910, the population in each of these settlements had been diversified further, not only via U.S.-born Alabamians but also through the arrival of several other nationalities, including more than thirty Hungarians in Cullman.[21]

Farther to the east, on the edge of the mineral district, Talladega County registered forty-four Russians, ten Austrians, eight Greeks, two Chinese, and almost three hundred Italians in 1910. The presence of the latter began with an Italian national who had narrowly escaped lynching by white men "of the most pernicious character" for having the brass to teach the freed people in the vicinity in the spring of 1869.[22] Farther south, in Tallapoosa and Bulloch Counties, resided six Russians, in addition to sixty-five more in Dallas County, home of Selma, and seven Russians in each of the Black Belt counties of Marengo and Barbour. Twenty-five Russians resided in Covington County, home of the Jackson Lumber Company, which was the target of federal investigations, prosecutions, and convictions for peonage involving immigrant laborers in 1906. The timber industry also brought multiple nationalities to rural Wilcox County by 1910, including twenty-six Hungarians, eleven Austrians, and four Puerto Ricans. Meanwhile, a French clothing store in Eufaula, county seat of Barbour County, employed eleven Croatian laborers. And the Bryce Mental Hospital in Tuscaloosa, along with Wetumpka State Prison in Elmore County, registered multiple nationalities among their respective patients and prisoners in 1910.[23]

Although approximating "whiteness" sometimes defined how immigrants accommodated to the New South, a fluctuating racial position offers a more accurate characterization of what many immigrant laborers experienced in Alabama. Immigrants of the Austro-Hungarian Empire collaborated with African Americans against coal operators in the Birmingham District, for example, but also confounded union officials who struggled to understand or control them. Immigrant fruit peddlers and Chinese launderers clashed with the African Americans on whom they relied, even as they competed against them, in urban areas. But they also found that they could not necessarily count on Alabama's white officers to defend them when they clashed with African American citizens with more established histories in a local community.

Such diversity in a region that conflated race with nationality and citizenship with color complicated the development, implementation, and regulation of Jim Crow. Thus, New South Alabama's immigration story is both similar to the rest of the nation and distinctly southern. Laborers from around the globe worked alongside U.S.-born Blacks and whites to build the region's railroads, mine its coal and iron ore, timber its piney woods, and wash its dirty laundry, contributing their blood, sweat, and sometimes their very lives to the New South project. Their experiences make a strong claim for the active participation of immigrant laborers in building the foundations of the New South. These stories—of the Dolphina Leskos, the Charley Sings, the Wasilije Wainovichs—should be integral, not marginal, to how we understand the history of the New South and its place in the world.

NOTES

INTRODUCTION

1. The brief historical accounts of Dolphina Lesko's journey to Brookside, Alabama, all describe her dilemma upon arrival at Ellis Island as involving a missing passport, ostensibly issued by the Austro-Hungarian state when she applied to legally depart for North America. Tara Zahra similarly describes the emigration documents issued by that government from as early as the 1850s as "passports." Zahra, *The Great Departure: Mass Migration from Eastern Europe and the Making of the Free World* (New York: W. W. Norton, 2016), 11, 38, 45. For a review of the broader history of the passport, particularly as it developed in the U.S. context, see Craig Robertson, *The Passport in America: A History of a Document* (Oxford: Oxford University Press, 2012).

2. Annie Latenosky Patchen interview, file 809.3.1.2.32; and Brookside staff research notes, file 809.3.1.2.24, both in Birmingfind Papers, Birmingham Public Library, Department of Archives and Manuscripts (collection is hereinafter cited as Birmingfind). There are conflicting accounts for some of the details of Dolphina's life story, including whether her delay in arriving at Brookside occurred at the point of embarkation in Germany or after she arrived at Ellis Island aboard the *Victoria.* The account relied on here derives from the oral history interview conducted with her daughter as part of the Birmingfind immigrant histories project.

3. "Adophina 'Anna' Lesko," posted by descendant Ceara Cameau, Ancestry.com.

4. Dr. Cathleen Giustino, historian of Central and Eastern Europe, Auburn University, email to author, May 4, 2020.

5. Tara Zahra, "Travel Agents on Trial: Policing Mobility in East Central Europe, 1889–1989," *Past and Present* 223 (May 2014): 168–170.

6. Annie Latenosky Patchen interview, file 809.3.1.2.32; and Brookside staff research notes, file 809.3.1.2.24, both in Birmingfind.

7. On the Birmingham-to-Brookside route, remembered her daughter, "everybody knew everybody . . . If you was lost, they were talking about you. If somebody got hurt, you knew about it." Annie Latenosky Patchen interview, file 809.3.1.2.32.

8. Annie Latenosky Patchen interview, file 809.3.1.2.32, Birmingfind. Immigration historian Tara Zahra notes that "on both sides of the Atlantic, single [female] migrants were generally

either suspected of prostitution or seen as real or potential victims of sex trafficking." Zahra, "Travel Agents on Trial," 180. Such suspicions and fear possibly accounted for the unease Dolphina manifested toward the policeman offering her assistance at the Brookside depot.

9. Annie Latenosky Patchen interview, file 809.3.1.2.32; and Brookside staff research notes, file 809.3.1.2.24, both in Birmingfind.

10. "Adophina 'Anna' Lesko," posted by descendant Ceara Cameau, Ancestry.com.

11. Although she was never fluent in English, Dolphina picked up enough words over the years to pick out the news from family letters and to communicate with local merchants and doctors. Annie Latenosky Patchen interview, file 809.3.1.2.32; "Dolphina Letanosky [Dolphina Lesko]," *Alabama, Deaths and Burials Index, 1881–1974* [online database] (Provo, UT: Ancestry .com Operations, 2011).

12. The understanding that "race" exists not as an authentic biological condition but as a political and social construction deriving from specific historical contexts represents one of the most singular historiographical developments of the past couple of decades. An essential corollary is that constructing racial categorizations as a foundation for white economic, political, legal, and social power renders those categories unstable. If notions of "white" or "Black," for example, derive from historical circumstances, then those notions are not immutable but subject to redefinition and evolution as communities, states, regions, and nations undergo periods of significant change. Individual and group notions of "whiteness" and "Blackness" in the South and in the United States, across time, have coalesced, both in opposition and in relation to conceptions and perceptions of each other. Essentially, the terms of "whiteness" and "Blackness," of white, Black, and African American, have a history in the United States, including in New South Alabama, that is both distinct and interdependent. This work examines a period, 1865–1920, when a particular locale, New South Alabama, experienced sufficient economic and social change to further destabilize—and illuminate the cracks in—the racial foundations that defined southern life from emancipation through World War I. The lens bringing those cracks into focus, at least in this work, is the recruitment and arrival of immigrant laborers as participants in building the New South order.

A complicated matrix entangled racial categories, understandings, and experiences in the New South; articulating that complexity requires one, sooner or later, to make choices about how to deploy language. Thus, a particular terminology guides the descriptions of foreign-born people, but also U.S.-born residents, who appear in this work. Unless otherwise indicated, the term "white" means a person born in the United States, with an ancestry commonly rooted in Northern and/or Western Europe. Such people benefited from political, legal, and social recognition as American citizens and most likely identified strongly as "southerners," that is, as people who had lived in Alabama for several decades, typically dating to at least the antebellum period and often earlier. Southern whites might hold significant wealth, wield political influence, and enjoy social prestige in their communities. But they also could be much poorer or lack sanctioned social standing, and they may or may not have had access to political participation or influence. Nonetheless, to be "white" in the New South meant to have the expectation of a least a modicum of the legal protections of full citizenship, and the social validation among other whites of being not Black.

Similarly, the terms "Black" or "African American" utilized in this study describe a person whose ancestry derived originally from the African continent but whose ancestors arrived in North America as either indentured servants or enslaved laborers. The term "freedmen" or "freedpeople" refers to the formerly enslaved African Americans who survived slavery, the Civil War, and the turbulent transition of emancipation. As this study focuses on laborers, most African Americans described in these pages worked in various low-wage agricultural, commercial, or industrial occupations. Most importantly, to be Black or African American in the New South, regardless of class, typically meant to be without most of the legal protections afforded by full citizenship and to be subjected to the whims and power of southern whites of all classes. Thus, to be "Black" in the New South meant also to be "not white."

Inserting immigrants of diverse nationalities and ethnicities into a history commonly understood and described in, literally, Black-and-white terms presents a unique challenge. Thus, when I use the qualifier of "white" to describe immigrant laborers, as in the term "white immigrant," I typically am referring to European immigrants, although immigrants of various nationalities moved back and forth between the poles of Black and white identity in the New South. In chapter 5, readers meet African immigrants, that is, immigrant laborers identified in census, convict, or other records as "Black" individuals born in Caribbean, South American, or African nations. Most importantly, readers should not construe the racial terminology used here as an argument for the static nature of any racial categorizations in the New South. Indeed, the inherent mutability of racial identities, categorizations, and experiences conveyed through the lens of immigrant laborers constitutes a fundamental premise of this work.

The literature addressing these themes of racial construction and categorizations and the like is voluminous. Some key works are David R. Roediger, *The Wages of Whiteness: Race and the Making of the American Working Class* (New York: Verso, 1991); Gail Bedermann, *Manliness and Civilization: A Cultural History of Gender and Race in the United States, 1880–1917* (Chicago: University of Chicago Press, 1995); Matthew Frye Jacobson, *Whiteness of a Different Color: European Immigrants and the Alchemy of Race* (Cambridge, MA: Harvard University Press, 1998); Grace Elizabeth Hale, *Making Whiteness: The Culture of Segregation in the South, 1890–1940* (New York: Vintage Books, 1999); Eric Arnesen, "Whiteness and the Historians' Imagination," *International Labor and Working-Class History* 60 (Fall 2001): 3–32; Barbara J. Fields, "Whiteness, Racism, and Identity," *International Labor and Working-Class History* 60 (Fall 2001): 48–56; Matthew Guterl, *The Color of Race in America, 1900–1940* (New Brunswick, NJ: Rutgers University Press, 2001); Stephen Hahn, *A Nation under Our Feet: Black Political Struggles in the Rural South from Slavery to the Great Migration* (Cambridge, MA: Belknap Press of Harvard University Press, 2003); Mae M. Ngai, *Impossible Subjects: Illegal Aliens and the Making of Modern America* (Princeton, NJ: Princeton University Press, 2004); David R. Roediger, *Working toward Whiteness: How America's Immigrants Became White* (New York: Basic Books, 2005). For a discussion of the "disorderly" approach to this issue of immigrant racial identities, see James R. Barrett and David Roediger, "Inbetween Peoples: Race, Nationality, and the 'New Immigrant Working Class,'" *Journal of American Ethnic History* 16, no. 3 (Spring 1997): 3–44. Also see John J. Bukowczyk, "The Racial Turn," *Journal of American Ethnic History* 36, no. 2 (Winter 2017): 5–10.

13. This is not to suggest that these are the only immigrant stories that mattered in Alabama or in the rest of the New South. A European Jewish population, for example, established roots in many southern towns, including Mobile and Montgomery, even before the Civil War. Birmingham had a small resident population of Greeks and Syrian-Palestinians, and several small agricultural colonies of European settlers emerged along the railroad lines and on the Gulf Coast. But these all represent somewhat different stories than the one told here, which emphasizes immigrant industrial or retail laborers, particularly those who resided in the Birmingham District, while also occasionally referencing examples in other areas of the state.

14. Hahn, *A Nation under Our Feet*, 4.

15. I am adopting the term "racial transiency" from the excellent work of Jessica Jackson, *Dixie's Italians: Sicilians, Race, and Citizenship in the Jim Crow Gulf South* (Baton Rouge: Louisiana State University Press, 2020), 8. Jackson coined the term as an apt description of the fluidity of racialization and racial identity experienced by southern Italians in the Gulf South during this era. I find this definition also accurately captures the experience of many of the immigrant groups in New South Alabama, including not only Italians but also the Chinese, the French, the various nationals of the Austro-Hungarian Empire, and others.

16. The historiography of mining labor and communities in the United States is rich and voluminous. Some excellent examples are Ronald L. Lewis, *Coal, Iron, and Slaves: Industrial Slavery in Maryland and Virginia, 1715–1865* (Santa Barbara, CA: Greenwood Press, 1979); Joe William Trotter Jr., *Coal, Class, and Color: Blacks in Southwest Virginia, 1915–1923* (Urbana: University of Illinois Press, 1990); Crandall A. Shifflett, *Coal Towns: Life, Work, and Culture in the Company Towns of Southern Appalachia, 1880–1960* (Knoxville: University of Tennessee Press, 1991); Scott Martelle, *Blood Passion: The Ludlow Massacre and Class War in the American West* (New Brunswick, NJ: Rutgers University Press, 2007); Ronald L. Lewis, *Welsh Americans: A History of Assimilation in the Coalfields* (Chapel Hill: University of North Carolina Press, 2008); James Green, *The Devil Is Here in These Hills: West Virginia's Coal Miners and Their Battle for Freedom* (New York: Atlantic Monthly Press, 2015); and David LaVigne, "The 'Black Fellows' of the Mesabi Iron Range: European Immigrants and Racial Differentiation during the Early Twentieth Century," *Journal of American Ethnic History* 36, no. 2 (Winter 2017): 11–39.

17. As early as 1945, sociologist Rupert B. Vance concluded that, statistically, "the Southeast received but little of [European] immigration after the 1820s," and any population increase resulted from "the forces of natural increase and internal migration." Vance, *All These People: The Nation's Resources in the South* (Chapel Hill: University of North Carolina Press, 1945), 15. Thus, decided historian Rowland Berthoff in 1951, "the appeal to foreign laborers and settlers was but a minor and futile phase of the New South." Berthoff, "Southern Attitudes toward Immigration, 1865–1914," *Journal of Southern History* 17, no. 3 (August 1951): 328–329. Eminent southern historian C. Vann Woodward followed suit, by and large, when he concluded that "the flood tide of European immigration, in 1899–1910, swept past the South, leaving it almost untouched and further isolating it in its peculiarities from the rest of the country." Woodward, *Origins of the New South, 1877–1913* (Baton Rouge: Louisiana State University Press, 1951, 1971), 299. Gavin Wright agreed, designating postwar immigration to the South as an "evanescent pass-through." Wright, *Old South, New South: Revolutions in the Southern Economy since the Civil War* (New York: Basic

Books, 1986), 76. An irreconcilable conflict between those white southerners who wanted immigration to help break up large plantations in the deep South as a crucial step toward diversifying the economy and those planters who wanted immigrants as a subservient labor force to sustain the plantation system ultimately doomed recruiting efforts, according to Eric Foner. Moreover, he concluded, "European immigrants did not relish the idea of taking the place of Blacks as plantation laborers," and "nearly all the immigrants who entered the country remained in the North and West." Foner, *Reconstruction: America's Unfinished Revolution, 1863–1877* (New York: Harper and Row, 1988). In his synthesis of New South history, Edward L. Ayers completely ignored the intense interest in immigration that feverishly absorbed boosters in nearly every southern community well into the early twentieth century. Ayers also fails to acknowledge the immigrant laborers who did come, even as he offers an exhaustive account of urban, small-town, and rural life in the New South. Ayers, *The Promise of the New South: Life after Reconstruction* (Oxford: Oxford University Press, 1992). Brian Kelly similarly argues that the efforts of Birmingham's industrial barons to recruit large numbers of Europeans to labor in the Tennessee Valley industrial-mineral district produced only "meager results." The harshness of daily life under the Jim Crow system, low wages, debates over immigration and the "proper" type of immigrant to recruit, among other issues, created too many challenges. And "with other options available to them, foreign-born laborers were unlikely to settle in the district voluntarily." The Tennessee Coal, Iron and Railroad Company did bring in some "Huns, Slavs, Greeks, Servians [*sic*], Italians, and Finns" as strikebreakers in 1906 and 1906, but ultimately "the immigration campaign never delivered the relief its sponsors had hoped for." Kelly, *Race, Class, and Power in the Alabama Coalfields, 1908–1921* (Urbana: University of Illinois Press, 2001), 39–40, 42–45, 47. A recent textbook notes in passing this immigration of Eastern Europeans to the Birmingham area after the Civil War but neglects to explore it. The author does describe in more depth immigration to the South before the Civil War. See William A. Link, *Southern Crucible: The Making of an American Region* (New York: Oxford University Press, 2015), 236–237, 412–413.

18. See, for example, Raymond Mohl, "The *Nuevo* New South: Hispanic Migration to Alabama," *Migration World* 30, no. 9 (2002): 14–18; Leon Fink, *The Maya of Morganton: Work and Community in the Nuevo New South* (Chapel Hill: University of North Carolina Press, 2003); and essays in Arthur D. Murphy, Colleen Blanchard, and Jennifer H. Hill, eds., *Latino Workers in the Contemporary South* (Athens: University of Georgia Press, 2001); and in Linda Allegro and Andrew Grant Wood, eds., *Latin American Migrations to the U.S. Heartland* (Urbana: University of Illinois Press, 2013).

19. Examples of this historiographical intersection include David Roediger, *The Wages of Whiteness: Race and the Making of the American Working Class* (New York: Verso, 1991); Mathew Frye Jacobsen, *Whiteness of a Different Color: European Immigrants and the Alchemy of Race* (Cambridge, MA: Harvard University Press, 1998); George Sanchez, "Race, Nation, and Culture in Recent Immigration Studies," *Journal of American Ethnic History* 18, no. 4 (Summer 1999): 66–84; Matthew Frye Jacobson, *Barbarian Virtues: The United States Encounters Foreign Peoples at Home and Abroad, 1876–1917* (New York: Hill and Wang, 2000), 85–89; Mae M. Ngai, *Impossible Subjects: Illegal Aliens and the Making of Modern America* (Princeton, NJ: Princeton University Press, 2004); Moon-Ho Jung, *Coolies and Cane: Race, Labor, and Sugar in the Age of*

Emancipation (Baltimore, MD: Johns Hopkins University Press, 2006); Sarah M. A. Gualtieri, *Between Arab and White: Race and Ethnicity in the Early Syrian American Diaspora* (Berkeley: University of California Press, 2009); Bukowczyk, "Racial Turn," 5–10. For a contrary view on the "whiteness" historiography, see Eric Arnesen, "Whiteness and the Historians' Imagination," *International Labor and Working-Class History* 60 (Fall 2001): 3–32. The "in-between" thesis is specifically addressed in Barrett and Roediger, "Inbetween Peoples, 101–140. The "white on arrival" thesis is outlined by Thomas Guglielmo, *White on Arrival: Italians, Race, Color, and Power in Chicago, 1890–1945* (New York: Oxford University Press, 2003). For an excellent historiographical discussion of these terms, see Jackson, *Dixie's Italians,* 7–9, 160 notes 31–32.

20. For an excellent example of the current approach of immigration historians to the "whiteness" theme, see the essays in the special volume on "The Racial Turn" in *Journal of American Ethnic History* 36, no. 2 (Winter 2017), but particularly the discussion of editor John Bukowczyk, "The Racial Turn," 5–9.

21. Vivek Bald, *Bengali Harlem and the Lost Histories of South Asian America* (Boston: Harvard University Press, 2013), 6, 8, 48, and generally.

22. Julie Weise, *Corazon de Dixie: Mexicanos in the U.S. South since 1910* (Chapel Hill: University of North Carolina Press, 2015), 3, 6, 8, 14–15, and generally.

23. Jackson, *Dixie's Italians,* 8–10.

24. For a historiographical discussion of this traditional theme in New South historical study, see James C. Cobb, "Beyond Planters and Industrialists: A New Perspective on the New South," *Journal of Southern History* 54, no. 1 (February 1988): 45–68.

25. Julie Greene, *The Canal Builders: Making America's Empire at the Panama Canal* (New York: Penguin Books, 2009); Jung, *Coolies and Cane,* 66–67.

26. Historians have long acknowledged the part that foreign capital played in building the physical, industrial, and financial infrastructures of the postwar South. On the role of foreign capital, see Woodward, *Origins of the New South,* 120–121; Daniel Letwin, *The Challenge of Interracial Unionism: Alabama Coal Miners, 1878–1921* (Chapel Hill: University of North Carolina Press, 1998), 15, 17–18; and Scott Nelson, *A Nation of Deadbeats: An Uncommon History of America's Financial Disasters* (New York: Alfred A. Knopf, 2012), 165–168. On the financial structures of post–Civil War railroad building in the United States, see Richard White, *Railroaded: The Transcontinentals and the Making of Modern America* (New York: W. W. Norton, 2011), 380–382. Also see Scott Nelson, *Iron Confederacies: Southern Railways, Klan Violence, and Reconstruction* (Chapel Hill: University of North Carolina, 1999); Michael Fitzgerald, *Reconstruction in Alabama: From Civil War to Redemption in the Cotton South* (Baton Rouge: Louisiana State University Press, 2017), 205–228. For an earlier, yet still useful, examination of Reconstruction-era railroad building, see A. B. Moore, "Railroad Building in Alabama during the Reconstruction Period," *Journal of Southern History* 1, no. 4 (November 1935), 424.

27. On Italian labor on southern cotton and sugarcane plantations, see Jean Ann Scarpaci, *Italian Immigrants in Louisiana's Sugar Parishes: Recruitment, Labor Conditions, and Community Relations, 1880–1910* (New York: Arno Press, 1980); Jeannie Whayne, *Shadows over Sunnyside: Evolution of a Plantation in Arkansas, 1830–1945* (Fayetteville: University of Arkansas Press, 1993); Stefano Luconi, "The Lynching of Southern Europeans in the Southern United

States: The Plight of Italian Immigrants in Dixie," in *The U.S. South and Europe: Transatlantic Relations in the Nineteenth and Twentieth Centuries,* ed. Cornelis A. van Minnen and Manfred Berg (Lexington: University Press of Kentucky, 2013); Justin Nystrom, *Creole Italian: Sicilian Immigrants and the Shaping of New Orleans Food Culture* (Athens: University of Georgia Press, 2018), 61; and J. Vincenza Scarpaci, "Labor for Louisiana's Sugar Cane Fields: An Experiment in Immigrant Recruitment," *Journal of American Ethnic History* 36, no. 2 (Winter 2017): 19–41.

28. The Southern Railway (through consolidated lines) ran from Meridian, Mississippi, on Alabama's western border and proceeded roughly northeast through the mineral district before cutting northward up the Atlantic Seaboard. The Louisville and Nashville (L&N) Railroad took a more central route from Birmingham, shooting almost due north to southeastern Kentucky, then southwestern Virginia, West Virginia, and finally to Cincinnati, Ohio, and beyond.

29. Marjorie Longnecker White, *The Birmingham District: An Industrial History and Guide* (Birmingham Historical Society, 1981), 237.

30. White, *Birmingham District,* 40–42, and scattered generally.

31. White, *Birmingham District,* 33–34.

32. White, *Birmingham District,* 40–41; William Warren Rogers et al., *Alabama: History of a Deep South State* (Tuscaloosa: University of Alabama Press, 2018), 216–217, 228.

33. Joshua Shiver, "Robert Jemison Jr.," *Encyclopedia of Alabama,* http://www.encyclopediaofalabama.org/article/h-4138; and Dr. Keith Hebert, historian of the Reconstruction and New South eras, Auburn University, email to author, May 7, 2020.

34. William Cohen, *At Freedom's Edge: Black Mobility and the Southern White Quest for Racial Control, 1861–1915* (Baton Rouge: Louisiana State University Press, 1991); Alex Lichtenstein, *Twice the Work of Free Labor: The Political Economy of Convict Labor in the New South* (New York: Verso, 1996); Mary Ellen Curtin, *Black Prisoners and Their World, Alabama, 1865–1900* (Charlottesville: University Press of Virginia, 2000); Scott Nelson, *Steel Drivin' Man: John Henry, The Untold Story of an American Legend* (Oxford: Oxford University Press, 2006); Douglas Blackmon, *Slavery by Another Name: The Re-Enslavement of Black Americans from the Civil War to World War II* (New York: Anchor Books, 2008); Hahn, *A Nation under Our Feet,* 154–155, 441; Talitha Leflouria, *Chained in Silence: Black Women and Convict Labor in the New South* (Chapel Hill: University of North Carolina Press, 2015).

35. Christopher Clark et al., *Who Built America?: Working People and the Nation's History,* 3rd ed. (New York: Bedford/St. Martin's, 2008), 28–35.

36. Leonard Dinnerstein, Roger L. Nichols, and David M. Reimers, *Natives and Strangers: A History of Ethnic Americans,* 6th ed. (New York: Oxford University Press, 2015), 101–107.

37. W. David Lewis, *Sloss Furnaces and the Rise of the Birmingham Industrial District: An Industrial Epic* (Tuscaloosa: University of Alabama Press, 1994), 168, 173, 188, 210.

38. David Montgomery notes that "there were many Slavic and Italian miners in Alabama and northern West Virginia" but that southern Appalachian mines "were worked primarily by migrants from the region's own farms—in stark contrast to the rest of the country, where few local farmers joined the immigrants in the mines." Among the multiple groups working in the mines across the United States in the late nineteenth and early twentieth centuries were the Chinese and "Chicanos . . . [and] Slavic, Greek, Italian, British, and Mexican immigrants," as

well as U.S.-born whites and Blacks. Montgomery, *The Fall of the House of Labor: The Workplace, the State, and American Labor Activism, 1865–1925* (Cambridge: Cambridge University Press, 1989), 334–345. Also see James Sanders Day, *Diamonds in the Rough: A History of Alabama's Cahaba Coal Field* (Tuscaloosa: University of Alabama Press, 2013).

39. On immigrant communities in southern Appalachian coalfields, see Shifflett, *Coal Towns;* Day, *Diamonds in the Rough,* 89–90, 124, 142, 144, 154; Letwin, *Challenge of Interracial Unionism,* 23–26, 73–75, 114–115, 143–145; and Brian Kelly, *Race, Class, and Power in the Alabama Coalfields, 1908–1921* (Urbana: University of Illinois Press, 2001), 38–40, 42–45, 47–48, 81, 135.

40. For example, the *Birmingham News* reported in the winter of 1908 that "one hundred and ten foreigners will leave Ensley tonight to return to their fatherland." Of those who planned to leave that night, "eighty-nine are Italians and twenty-one Greeks," and "various reasons are given for their departure." That summer, during the peak of the 1908 United Mine Workers (UMW) strike, the newspaper reported the flight of "a number of foreigners recently brought to the district from New Orleans" for work "in the mines of the Alabama Consolidated Coal Company." Although the men reportedly "worked contentedly for a few days," they soon "began dropping away very rapidly," with little explanation. But the writer sought to provide a reason: a "mysterious letter," written in Greek and allegedly dropped by one of the departing men, turned out to be a warning that the UMW did not have their best interests at heart. In fact, the letter claimed that while the union could deliver "good wages" if it won the strike, the UMW might also opt "to kill you." Whether the letter represented an authentic warning is hard to know; it clearly represented an antiunion message that effectively targeted some of the Greek miners at work in the district's mines. See *Birmingham News,* February 4, August 15, 1908. Slovak Steve Slovensky remembered that some of his parents' generation returned to the old country at one point but usually then found life too different and would return to Birmingham and head back into the mines. Some Slovaks did return to stay but, as he recalled, "it was rare to go back." Steven Slovensky interview, file 809.3.1.2.34, Birmingfind.

41. Annie Cameau and John Bensko interviews, file 809.3.1.2.31; Alice Slovensky Harmon interview, file 809.3.1.2.33; and Steve Slovensky interview, file 809.3.1.2.34, all in Birmingfind. Zahra, "Travel Agents on Trial," 168, finds that around 400,000 Austro-Hungarian citizens returned to their homelands from the United States, once they acquired sufficient funds to purchase land or pay off debts. Italian immigrants, in particular, had a high rate of return from emigration abroad, as so-called birds of passage, with approximately 50 percent of those who initially left returning. See Jessica Barbata Jackson, "Reconsidering the Experience of Italians and Sicilians in Louisiana, 1870s–1890s," *Journal of Louisiana Historical Association* 58, no. 3 (Summer 2017): 300–338; Donna Gabaccia, "*Gil italiani nel mondo:* Italy's Workers Around the World," *OAH Magazine of History* 14, no. 1 (Fall 1999), 12–16; and Gabaccia, *Italy's Many Diasporas* (Seattle: University of Washington Press, 2000). Also see Max Paul Friedman, "'Voting with Their Feet': Toward a Conceptual History of 'America' in European Migrant Sending Communities, 1860s–1914," *Journal of Social History* 40, no. 3 (Spring 2007): 557–575.

42. There exists a voluminous literature on immigration and immigrants in the United States in the late nineteenth and early twentieth centuries. In addition to works cited in earlier endnotes, some examples include John Higham, *Strangers in the Land: Patterns of American*

Nativism, 1860–1925 (New Brunswick, NJ: Rutgers University Press, 1955); John Bodnar, *The Transplanted: A History of Immigrants in Urban America* (Bloomington: Indiana University Press, 1985); Roger Daniels, *Asian America: Chinese and Japanese in the United States since 1850* (Seattle: University of Washington Press, 1988); Daniels, *Coming to America: A History of Immigration and Ethnicity in American Life* (New York: Perennial, 2002); Donna Gabaccia, *Militants and Migrants: Rural Sicilians Become American Workers* (New Brunswick, NJ: Rutgers University Press, 1988); Gabaccia, *Italy's Many Diasporas;* Gunther Peck, *Reinventing Free Labor: Padrones and Immigrant Workers in the North American West, 1880–1930* (Cambridge: Cambridge University Press, 2000); Ryan Dearinger, *The Filth of Progress: Immigrants, Americans, and the Building of Canals and Railroads in the West* (Oakland: University of California Press, 2016); Manu Karuka, *Empire's Tracks: Indigenous Nations, Chinese Workers, and the Transcontinental Railroad* (Oakland: University of California Press, 2019).

1. "THE BONE AND SINEW OF OTHER STATES AND COUNTRIES": PLANTERS, INDUSTRIALISTS, AND IMMIGRANT RECRUITMENT IN NEW SOUTH ALABAMA

1. *Birmingham Iron Age,* September 23, 1875.

2. See, for example, Elizabeth Clune, "Black Workers, White Immigrants, and the Postemancipation Problem of Labor," in *Global Perspectives on Industrial Transformation in the American South,* ed. Susanna Delfino and Michael Gillespie (Columbia: University of Missouri Press, 2005): 200–201; David R. Roediger and Elizabeth D. Esch, *The Production of Difference: Race and the Management of Labor in U.S. History* (Oxford: Oxford University Press, 2012), 15; Sven Beckert, *Empire of Cotton: A Global History* (New York: Vintage Books, 2014), 290–291, 304–306.

3. For another example of how southern employers reconciled their racialized understanding of Southern and Eastern Europeans with their need for cheap labor, see J. Vincent Lowery, "'Another Species of Racial Discord': Race, Desirability, and the North Carolina Immigration Movement of the Early Twentieth Century," *Journal of American Ethnic History* 36, no. 2 (Winter 2017): 32–59.

4. Quoted in Rogers et al., *Alabama,* 228. My description of the Civil War's impact on the state of Alabama borrows heavily from the account in this work.

5. Rogers et al., *Alabama,* 228–229, 235–236.

6. See, for example, Thomas C. Holt, "The Essences of the Contract: The Articulation of Race, Gender, and Political Economy in British Emancipation Policy, 1838–1866"; and Rebecca J. Scott, "Fault Lines, Color Lines, and Party Lines: Race, Labor, and Collective Action in Louisiana and Cuba, 1862–1912," both in *Beyond Slavery: Explorations of Race, Labor, and Citizenship in Postemancipation Societies,* ed. Frederick Cooper, Thomas C. Holt, and Rebecca J. Scott (Chapel Hill: University of North Carolina Press, 2000); David Brion Davis, *The Problem of Slavery in the Age of Emancipation* (New York: Vintage Books, 2016), 259–260, 286; and Eric Foner, *Nothing but Freedom: Emancipation and Its Legacy* (Baton Rouge: Louisiana State University Press, 1983).

7. Wright, *Old South, New South,* 22, table 2.2.

8. Smith's decision fired the first shot in a long round of railroad building and fraud that would bring the state to the brink of bankruptcy by 1875. Railroad companies, according to

historian Edward Ayers, "worked feverishly in the New South," and the region "built railroads faster than the nation as a whole" as states rushed to recover from the devastation wrought by the Civil War. By 1890, Ayers concluded, nine of ten southerners "lived in a railroad county." Ayers, *Promise of the New South,* 9–10. Both the Louisville and Nashville and the Alabama and Chattanooga railroads received "extravagant state government aid" amounting to around $17 million of a total of $25 million in state debt, which ultimately "bankrupted the state." Woodward, *Origins of the New South,* 8–9. For more on railroad building in the Reconstruction and New South eras, see Rogers et al., *Alabama,* 253–254; Wright, *Old South, New South,* 38; Alex Lichtenstein, *Twice the Work of Free Labor: The Political Economy of Convict Labor in the New South* (New York: Verso, 1996), 44–48; Scott Reynolds Nelson, *Iron Confederacies: Southern Railways, Klan Violence, and Reconstruction* (Chapel Hill: University of North Carolina Press, 1999); and Mark Summers, *Railroads, Reconstruction, and the Gospel of Prosperity Aid under the Radical Republicans, 1865–1877* (Princeton, NJ: Princeton University Press, 2014). For an examination of railroad building during the Civil War, see Kenneth Noe, *Southwest Virginia's Railroad: Modernization, and the Sectional Crisis in the Civil War Era* (Chicago: University of Illinois Press, 1994). For an assessment of the financial corruption endemic to railroad building during the era, see Richard White, "Information, Markets, and Corruption: Transcontinental Railroads in the Gilded Age," *Journal of American History* 90, no. 1 (June 2003): 19–43. On railroads in Reconstruction-era Alabama, see Moore, "Railroad Building in Alabama." On the various railroad building proposals, also see Moore, as well as Michael Fitzgerald, *Reconstruction in Alabama: From Civil War to Redemption in the Cotton South* (Baton Rouge: Louisiana State University Press, 2017), 205–228.

9. From 1865 to 1875, Alabama led the former Confederate states in the mileage of new railroad track constructed, according to Lichtenstein, *Twice the Work of Free Labor,* 44.

10. In an 1867 letter to Alabama Governor Robert Patton, Lewis Wyeth of Guntersville noted that many poor southerners, Black *and* white, hoped to obtain lands under the Homestead Act. See Lewis Wyeth to Gov. Patton, October 16, 1867, reel 2, Governor Robert Miller Patton Papers, Administrative Files, ADAH (hereinafter cited as Patton Papers). For the most recent discussion of how Alabama's freed people made the transition from slavery and Civil War to emancipation and Reconstruction, see Fitzgerald, *Reconstruction in Alabama,* particularly chapters 5 and 7. Also see Hahn, *A Nation under Our Feet,* 129.

11. The best overall discussion of Reconstruction in Alabama is Fitzgerald, *Reconstruction in Alabama.*

12. Kelly, *Race, Class, and Power,* 30; Foner, *Reconstruction,* 139–140, 210, 402.

13. Black migration, historian Steven Hahn notes, "took hold almost immediately after emancipation and then erupted into a mass movement in the cotton belt of the Deep South during the late 1870s." Hahn identifies this "grassroots emigrationism" as a constituent element of Black political mobilization during the Reconstruction and New South eras. When they did move, African Americans typically exchanged one community for another within their home state or among southern states. But they sometimes made their way west to Kansas, Nebraska, or Oklahoma, or even to lands outside the United States, including Liberia, Hawaii, Mexico, and the Philippines. During the Redeemers' period, the strongest support for emigrationism

came from "cotton-growing areas with large and numerically dominant Black populations," with a recent history of "political mobilization," and where freed people in plantation areas "had made major efforts . . . to organize themselves and create stable communities, but then suffered or were threatened by serious reversals." Such "reversals" took various forms, from "paramilitary violence" against Black economic or political independence to disenfranchising state constitutions. Although the economic crisis of the 1870s had eased somewhat by 1886, still another "'colored exodus' west took hundreds of black workers from the cotton fields" of the deep South, including Alabama, leaving white landowners again "indignant at the 'demoralization which always accompanies a movement of this kind.'" See Hahn, *A Nation under Our Feet*, 9, 331, 361. For an emphasis on Reconstruction violence as a counterrevolutionary reaction by Confederate whites, see Douglas Egerton, *Wars of Reconstruction: The Brief, Violent History of America's Most Progressive Era* (New York: Bloomsbury, 2014).

14. In examining the Reconstruction South, Eric Foner concludes that southern white fears of labor shortages after the Civil War were "no mirage" as "the supply of Black labor dropped about one third" after Appomattox. Foner, *Reconstruction*, 139–140, 210. But Alex Lichtenstein questions the veracity of planters' claims that a labor "shortage" existed in the postwar South. "How do we reconcile the presence of a low-wage labor market" in the New South, he rightly asks, "with fears of chronic labor scarcity?" In fact, he finds, no true labor "shortage" existed; rather, it was an "ideological fiction" enlisted by disgruntled planters and frustrated industrialists to describe Black labor that was too mobile to control easily. "African Americans insisted on their status as free laborers." Lichtenstein, *Twice the Work of Free Labor*, 12–13. All of these points have merit and plenty of evidence. However, perceptions of labor scarcity also derived from conditions that were inherently local, differing from place to place. Moreover, the development of the Birmingham District, beginning in the 1880s, created an additional "pull" factor for rural labor in Alabama and surrounding states that likely exacerbated Black Belt planters' anxieties.

15. Hahn, *A Nation under Our Feet*, 330–331, 335, 337–338, 345, 355–359, 360–361.

16. Ayers, *Promise of the New South* notes that "once Black workers began to leave, whites found it almost impossible to stop them for long" (157). The most well-known examples of this "grassroots emigrationism" was the migration to Kansas and Nebraska that began around the time that the conservative Bourbons defeated Reconstruction. The standard work on these "Exodusters" is Nell Irvin Painter, *Exodusters: Black Migration to Kansas after Reconstruction* (New York: Knopf, 1977). Also see Robert G. Althern, *In Search of Canaan: Black Migration to Kansas, 1879–80* (Lawrence: Regents Press of Kansas, 1978); Hahn, *A Nation under Our Feet*, 332, 360–361. The Exodusters fled the familiar South for the unknown for various reasons, but especially due to the "threats, coercion, vulnerabilities, insecurities, and limited prospects for themselves, their families, and their children." As emigrationist leader Henry Adams explained about "Kansas fever" and the Liberian colonization scheme, "It is the idea . . . that pervades our breast 'that at last we will be free,' free from oppression, free from tyranny, free from bulldozing, murderous southern whites." Quoted in Hahn, *A Nation under Our Feet*, 336–337. Two decades later, the "Negro Emigration Club" of Marshall, Texas, called on all "negro emigrationists" to convene on August 27, 1891, to "take counsel and advice for the best plan for emigration, and

such other matters as we may think best for the negro people of Harrison, Panola, Marion, Smith, Upshur, Gregg, Rusk, and Shelby counties." And for "the discouraged," noted the club officers, "we have but one remark to make: join with us; and try, by one united effort, to better our condition, financially, morally, politically, and socially, and aid each other to get lands and homes, where we may not have to give all we make to stay on a plantation, and at the end of the year have nothing but a distressed wife, half fed, poorly clothed children, with a poor and sorrowing father." "To the Negro Emigrationists," *Forth Worth Gazette,* August 17, 1891. The great majority of those southern Black families who packed up what little they had to head for new horizons were "landless farming folk" organized into families connected by kinship, work, and "land tenure" networks. Hahn, *A Nation under Our Feet,* 338. Such people appeared ripe for the picking to labor agents operating throughout the South, many from the Delta, the western territories, and even from overseas. Ayers notes the proliferation of labor agents in the New South, who often worked for "large planters, railroads, and labor agencies." Ayers, *Promise of the New South,* 150–151. See also Cohen, *At Freedom's Edge,* 45, 126, and elsewhere.

17. The best overview of the Great Migration, as well as the most eloquent storytelling, is Isabel Wilkerson, *The Warmth of Other Suns: The Epic Story of America's Great Migration* (Random House, 2010). Also see William J. Collins, "When the Tide Turned: Immigration and the Delay of the Great Black Migration," *Journal of Economic History* 57, no. 3 (September 1997): 607–632.

18. "The nation was at a crossroads in 1869," notes Moon-Ho Jung. On the one hand, African American leaders and Radical Republicans "forged ahead to recast the United States into a multiracial democracy," but "southern planters, on the other hand, plunged into the global competition for plantation labor, fueled by revamped dreams of white supremacy and enslaved labor." Jung, *Coolies and Cane,* 108–109, 114. Jung interprets this global context in the age of emancipation as critical to generating the campaigns for immigrant labor and to their ultimate failure in Louisiana.

19. The Republican *Dalles Times-Mountaineer* (Oregon) reported on October 26, 1889, that allegedly ten thousand Black citizens were planning to migrate to Mexico from Texas: "Some of the evils they complain of are real . . . others are imaginary. There will be no prejudice because of color in the Mexican Republic, and a black man will be accorded the same privileges as one of lighter color. Society and business will be open to them." For more on the southern African American colony in Mexico, see J. Fred Rippy, "A Negro Colonization Project in Mexico, 1895," *Journal of Negro History* 6, no. 1 (January 1921): 66–73; and Cohen, *At Freedom's Edge,* 260–264.

20. "An Africa in America," *The Sun,* January 3, 1887.

21. *The Advance,* September 11, 1880. The editors validated Ash's view by discounting other newspaper reports that African Americans were suffering in Kansas: "From the above, we should judge that it is all false. Everything is perfectly serene and the colored are wonderfully prosperous out in Kansas."

Adolph Munter, born in Prussia in 1852, arrived in the United States around 1869 and resided in Alabama by 1870. By 1887, however, he had relocated to Spokane in Washington Territory. The *Montgomery Advertiser* reprinted a letter from Munter in the summer of 1887 describing life in Spokane, where "everybody is given a fair chance—the laboring people and the mechanics occupy a social position here which the southern white people would not believe unless they could see it." Specifically, he cited racially mixed church congregations and public accommodations open to both Blacks and whites. Though the climate was chilly, still he had found "no malaria, no chills and fever." And farmers were able to raise "wheat, oats, barley . . . watermelon, cantelopes, linseed, and hops" along with "grapes and apricots." Railroad and construction laborers earned two dollars a day while farm labor earned one dollar per day, but also "food and lodging." Importantly, "there is demand for all kinds of labor," and carpenters, masons, and mechanics enjoyed even higher wages. Fertile farmlands could be obtained at reasonable prices. Munter concluded that "I believe our Alabama colored people would get along very well here." *Montgomery Herald,* July 23, 1887. See also "Adolph Munter," *1870, 1910, United States Federal Census* [online database]. Provo, UT: Ancestry.com Operations, 2009 (hereinafter all census records cited as U.S. Federal Census, Ancestry.com).

22. *Indianapolis Journal,* reprinted in *St. Louis Globe-Democrat,* January 2, 1889. The *Daily Gazette* of Fort Worth, Texas, reported the same year on a stream of southern Blacks headed to Oklahoma, and the *Crawford Avalanche* of Michigan similarly claimed that thousands of African Americans were planning an exodus from Alabama, Georgia, Louisiana, Tennessee, and the Carolinas to Kansas. *Daily Gazette,* July 8, 1889; *Crawford Avalanche,* October 10, 1889.

23. William H. Leonard to Governor Patton, October 17, 1866, reel 23, Patton Papers. Also mentioned briefly in Jung, *Coolies and Cane,* 130.

24. *Pacific Commercial Advertiser,* August 5, 1882.

25. Like their cotton-growing counterparts in the United States, sugar planters in the islands spent a good deal of time experimenting with, and then judging, the qualities of field and sugar mill labor of different nationalities, especially the Chinese, the Portuguese, and South Pacific Islanders, along with indigenous Hawaiians. Supposedly, for example, Fijians made "excellent laborers" when young and "were easily satisfied as to their food so long as it was clean." They were "not difficult to train," responded well to directions if civilly delivered, and "in disposition and willingness to work they were superior to both the Chinese and to natives." The Portuguese, however, were expensive to obtain, and as far as fieldwork, "at stripping and weeding they did not do much more work than a Chinaman, and certainly not as much as a native." The Chinese, moreover, were viewed as "more docile and less expensive" but also were hampered, in the planters' eyes at least, by their apparent cruelty toward livestock. *Pacific Commercial Advertiser,* March 25, 1882.

26. *Pacific Commercial Advertiser,* January 6, 1883. The *San Diego Union* reported in 1900 that in Hawaii "a number of leading planters have decided to experiment with negro labor on their sugar plantations, as there are not enough Japs coming into their country to supply the increased demand." English emigre John Hind, one of Hawaii's "pioneer sugar, coffee, and pineapple men" and manager of the family-owned Hawi Mill and Plantation Company in the Kohala district, traveled for several months through the United States in search of labor. Indeed, "another gentlemen thoroughly familiar with the South has preceded Mr. Hind to Louisiana. It is their present intention to employ thirty-five families at least to return with them to Hawaii." The wages offered for field labor would be "from $16 to $20 per month." *Honolulu Republican,* August 14, 1900; *Honolulu Star-Bulletin,* obituary, August 15, 1933.

27. When the flooding Mississippi River breached the levees in April 1890, the situation in the Delta grew "more and more alarming," according to the reports from New Orleans and Vicksburg. Railroads recently built into the Delta now stood "at a standstill," rising waters threatened to inundate "the greater portion of this vast area of cotton land," as well as the "40,000 people, most of them negro immigrants from the Carolinas, Georgia, and Alabama," who had recently settled there. A few months later, reported merchant John A. Servent, "from all the surrounding states thousands of well-to-do colored people, with their families" had rushed into Guthrie, Oklahoma, and "taken up land and settled." *Asheville Daily Citizen,* June 3, 1890.

28. *Grenada Sentinel* (Mississippi), February 21, 1891.

29. Nervous whites intent on preventing such an exodus of African Americans from the South to the West took pains to point out the hardships Black emigrationists encountered, though it is hard to differentiate between what actually happened and what whites fabricated as scare tactics. "They are now opening their eyes to the fact that the land is all taken by white men. They are on the verge of starvation." *Mitchell Capital* (Dakota Territory), March 6, 1891. On tensions between American Indian communities and migrant African Americans in Oklahoma, see Sarah Deutsch, "Being American in Boley, Oklahoma," in *Beyond Black and White: Race, Ethnicity, and Gender in the U.S. South and Southwest,* ed. Stephanie Cole and Alison Parker (College Station: Texas A&M University Press, 2004), 97–122.

30. Thomas Gamble to Hon. Joseph Wheeler, Limrock, AL, February 10, 1894, folder 2, box 76, Joseph Wheeler family papers, LPR 50, ADAH.

31. *Pacific Commercial Advertiser,* October 7, 1882. Charles R. Buckland, the "government agent" for the Boston Exhibition, issued a report in the summer of 1883 on his travels throughout the Hawaiian Islands to "His Excellency, the Minister for Foreign Affairs." At Pahala, Buckland found "a curious mixture of labor comprising, as it does, natives of European countries, China, Manila, Chile, India, the Azores, and the *American negro*" (my emphasis). Buckland investigated the conditions and operations of multiple sugar plantations and production facilities across several islands, as well as rice plantations and cattle ranches. He toured the Hawaiian Agricultural Company's Pahala Plantation, which covered 2,600 acres and contained the islands' largest sugar mill. The company directly cultivated 1,600 acres, while "Chinamen on shares" planted the remaining thousand acres. *Pacific Commercial Advertiser,* July 7, 1883. Colonel W. O. Bean of Nashville, Tennessee, brought to the islands in January of 1901 more than twenty Black laborers, including mostly young men and women, and promised to bring ten thousand more. The group came from Nashville and immediately set off for Sprecklesville upon arrival in the islands. "These negroes are the first lot," announced the newspaper, "and their reports to their fellows in Tennessee and other southern states will, if the conditions are found to be favorable, mean that the supply of negro labor for the islands will be practically unlimited." In fact, "the men said that there were at the present time ten thousand negroes who would be willing to come here to work if they were sure [of] everything as represented." The men and women from Nashville represented "a fair sample of the negroes of the south, male and female," as "nearly all can read and write" and demonstrated a "keen interest" in the "customs of the country and prices." Importantly, they also asked "many questions as to the form of government . . . and if there was a board of supervisors and the numbers of white voters." One of the party

was a J. T. Mason, of the Knights and Daughters of America, "a powerful negro organization." He arrived in Hawaii with the express "purpose of looking into the prospects and on his report depends in a good measure the further importation of negro laborers to this country." Mason stated that "we have heard great things of this place," but "now I am here to see for myself." He continued, "If I find that things are favorable there is no doubt in my mind that the planters can have all the negro labor that they will pay for. There are thousands of young people in the southern states who will be willing to come and make their homes here. The people with me are most all young folks and their impressions of things as they find them here will be the means of the coming or staying away of many thousands of our race." The newspaper identified the group as consisting of "voters and staunch Republicans." Upon arrival, "he went to Wailuku with the laborers last evening," about twenty-five miles into the country, to stay overnight at a Mr. Bishop's place. The laborers' baggage was light, mostly "hand luggage," with one person carrying belongings tied up into a gunnysack and "slung over his shoulder." And "several of the women of the party had big tin pails which they were specially careful to look out for." *Honolulu Republican,* January 3, 1902. Charles E. Royce, a "planter with large farms on the island of Maui . . . prepares to go to Philly to order new refinery equipment to be built near Sprecklesville. He reports that sugar crop very good this year, and prices good. Only problem is need more labor." Thus, "every effort is being made at the present time to get a sufficient number of negroes from the United States, and while many have been taken, there is still a shortage that must be filled." Royce told the reporter that "what we want now in the islands is more negro labor." He said reports in American papers that "American negroes were a failure in the islands" were false. Those people "know nothing about the labor conditions here. The American negro has been a success and what we want now is more of them. It is the Porto Rican that has been a failure." *Honolulu Republican,* July 31, 1901.

32. The majority of African Americans remained concentrated within the Black Belt, coastal plains, and Piedmont regions across the New South era, from the late 1860s through 1920. See data in Walter F. Willcox, "The Negro Population," United States Census Bureau, https://www2.census.gov/prod2/decennial/documents/03322287no8ch1.pdf.

33. A. H. Woodward to Hon. Oscar Underwood, January 10, 1906; R. H. Banister, Secretary, Woodward Iron Co., to Hon. Oscar Underwood, January 9 and 13, 1906, all in folder 4, box 8, Oscar Wilder Underwood Papers, LPR 29, ADAH.

34. Woodward, *Origins of the New South,* 180–184; Cohen, *At Freedom's Edge,* 275; Ayers, *Promise of the New South,* 13, 44.

35. Planters were not averse to losing itinerant Black laborers during economic downturns or periods of crop failures, but they typically used imprisonment, debt peonage, violence, and local and state laws to attempt to prevent Black migration when economic times were better. See Ayers, *Promise of the New South,* 150–151, and Cohen, *At Freedom's Edge.*

36. M. S. Poole, Foreman, Grand Jury of Mobile County, to Gov. William Smith, February 14, 1870, folder: February 1870, reel 8, General Correspondence, Administrative Files, SG006058, Governor William Smith Papers, ADAH (hereinafter cited as Governor Smith Papers). For more on the reenactment and expansion of Black codes and other measures to restrict Black labor mobility, see Cohen, *At Freedom's Edge;* Hahn, *A Nation under Our Feet,* 426–428, 440–443.

37. Hahn, *A Nation under Our Feet,* 436–441. "The most common complaint of planters and industrialists alike was the difficulty of recruiting and retaining adequate labor," argues Lichtenstein, *Twice the Work of Free Labor,* 12–13. Also see Matthew Pratt Guterl, "After Slavery: Asian Labor, the American South, and the Age of Emancipation," *Journal of World History* 14, no. 2 (June 2003): 226–227; and Clune, "Black Workers, White Immigrants," 199–201.

38. J. J. Giers to Governor Patton, Nashville, November 11, 1866, reel 23, Patton Papers, ADAH. Alabamian F. S. Mount warned Governor Patton a few months later that "with the Negro labor of the South becoming more and more reduced and unreliable even when obtained... unless [labor] can be supplied from some other means... at once... the condition of our people in a few years will be deplorable." F. S. Mount (or Blount) to Governor Patton, August 10, 1867, reel 25, Patton Papers, ADAH. Booster Gideon Pillow reported from Memphis in 1869 that at least a third of Black laborers have "left the corn and cotton fields" and "taken to other vocations," including steamboat work, where they "have supplanted the Irish, Dutch, and Germans." *Memphis Daily Appeal,* July 15, 1869.

39. *Memphis Daily Appeal,* July 14, 1870. British citizen Robert Somers, traveling the South after the war, described an encounter with a white planter near Montgomery, "a Scotchman who had spent the early part of his life in a tropical clime" and recently had purchased a plantation near Montgomery. He noted, "Mr. Ross... complains of the difficulty of cultivating his land by negro labour (and) the danger of falling into lawsuits with overseers and labour-contractors." See Robert Somers, *The Southern States since the War, 1870–71* (Tuscaloosa: University of Alabama, 1965), 179.

40. Unsigned to Gov. Patton, Eutaw, AL, January 1867, reel 23, Patton Papers, ADAH.

41. *Montgomery Advertiser,* July 14, 1877.

42. *Montgomery Advertiser,* February 5, December 29, 1880. The editors ran an article promoting the lands of central Alabama around Troy for immigrant farmers, noting the spread of cotton cultivation to the area and the continued abundance of wildlife for foraging. They also declared that "the idea that cotton cannot be produced in the South by white labor" to be a "most pernicious fallacy," and pointed to the "fact" that "cotton raised by white (skilled) men is worth more in the markets than that raised by negroes, because the white man is a nicer farmer, gathers his crop clean, handles it carefully, excluding dirt and trash, and bales it well and attractively." Indeed, "it would amply pay the laboring whites of the North to come South and raise cotton, because lands are cheap, and because most of them are trained and skilled farmers, economical and cleanly, and their cotton would bring the highest prices as compared with that made by careless, indolent negroes."

43. *Montgomery Advertiser,* December 11, 1880.

44. *Montgomery Advertiser,* December 24, 1880.

45. The terms "big mule" and "branchhead" reference the descriptive title of Carl Grafton and Ann Permaloff, *Big Mules and Brancheads: James E. Folsom and Political Power in Alabama* (Athens: University of Georgia Press, 1985). The two factions together dominated Alabama politics throughout much of the New South era. The branchheads were Black Belt planters; timber, lumber mill, and turpentining operators; farm industry proprietors; and large rural merchants, while the "big mules" were the "economic elites of industrial Alabama," including

coal and ore mining operators and railroad and utility companies. See Anna Permaloff, "Black Belt–Big Mule Coalition," *Encyclopedia of Alabama,* encyclopediaofalabama.org/article/h-1434.

46. See Clune, "Black Workers, White Immigrants."

47. See, for example, Rogers, *One-Gallused Rebellion,* 80–97.

48. Carolyn Laverne Watson, "Immigration to Alabama, 1865–1890" (master's thesis, Auburn University, 1963), 16.

49. Salaried at $300 a month, C. G. Baylor began a turbulent and ultimately disappointing tenure as a state commissioner, developing plans with the American Missionary Association in New England to encourage immigrants to relocate to Alabama but ultimately failing to implement any concrete program. Declaring his suspicion that "Mr. Baylor is making a sinecure of his position," Governor Smith soon terminated his appointment. See Watson, "Immigration to Alabama," 16–17; and C. G. Baylor to Gov. Smith, February 18, March 24, 1869; Gov. Smith to Secretary Dalton, April 11, 1869, both in Governor Smith Papers.

50. Watson, "Immigration to Alabama," 23.

51. None of this came to fruition, however, as the state legislature neglected to provide the funds. See Watson, "Immigration to Alabama," 23–25.

52. Katharine M. Pruett and John D. Fair, "Promoting a New South: Immigration, Racism, and 'Alabama on Wheels,'" *Agricultural History* 66, no. 1 (January 1992): 19–41.

53. Rogers, *One-Gallused Rebellion,* 117–118, 170; and Watson, "Immigration to Alabama," 25–28, 48.

54. J. H. Mountain to R. R. Poole, February 20, 1905, Alabama Commissioner of Agriculture and Industry records, 1888–1914, folder: Correspondence, 1905 (Immigration), ADAH (hereinafter cited as Agriculture and Industry records). Alabama officials also participated, along with other southern states, in various commercial conventions and world exhibits meant to profile what they believed were the state's many advantages. Alabama sent agents, along with information on land and mineral resources, to the 1867 International Exhibition in Paris, to Vienna in 1873, to Atlanta in 1881, to New Orleans in 1885, and to other locales. The degree to which such ventures were worth the time and expenditure is hard to calculate. Alabama did win recognition at the Paris exhibition, though not for its suitability for immigrants or for its mineral resources but for its display of short-staple cotton—not exactly a testament to changing times. Certificate of Award (1868), State of Alabama, Paris Exhibition, reel 26, Governor Patton Papers, ADAH. Also see Watson, "Immigration to Alabama," 31–32.

55. Watson, "Immigration to Alabama," 31, 33–35.

56. Paul Stevens to Gov. Smith, October 17, 1870, reel 10, Governor Smith Papers, ADAH.

57. R. D. Alexander to R. R. Poole, February 18, 1905, folder: Correspondence, 1905 (Immigration), Agriculture and Industry records, ADAH. Planters, mill owners, and mine proprietors also took matters into their own hands. In 1905, E. F. Ellsberry of Geneva, Alabama, proprietor of the South East Alabama Colonization Company, contacted Commissioner of Agriculture R. R. Poole about his own efforts to attract immigrant farmers: "I noticed in the Advertiser a day or two ago that you are seeking to get immigrants for Ala.," he wrote, noting that "I am doing what I can to the same end, and have some 8 or 20 thousand acres of both farm and timber lands and any hands for sale." Offering his list to Poole, Ellsberry closed by stating his efforts: "Am

doing as much correspondence as I can without interfering too much with my profession to get Northern and Western farmers to come to the Wiregrass." As his letterhead stated, "You Will Probably Be Dead Thousands of Years So Why Not Live in 'God's Country' When You Can?" See E. F. Ellsberg to R. R. Poole, February 20, 1905, folder: Correspondence, 1905 (Immigration), Agriculture and Industry records, ADAH.

58. On Alabama's continuing agrarian crisis, see Rogers, *One-Gallused Rebellion,* and Hahn, *A Nation under Our Feet.*

59. Governor Patton soon appointed Mellen as an immigration agent for the state of Alabama to attend the Paris exhibition of 1867. See Mellen to Governor Patton, February 8, 19, 1867, both letters in reel 23, Governor Patton Papers, ADAH.

60. Ganier to Governor Patton, August 22, 1867, reel 25, Governor Patton Papers, ADAH; Watson, "Immigration to Alabama," 31.

61. Watson, "Immigration to Alabama," 18–19. Governor Smith had appointed Paul Strobach specifically as an immigration agent to Europe, where he would recruit especially from the British Isles. He soon became ensnared, however, in a conflict over Smith's dual appointment of his protégé, John Flanagan, as an agent to Ireland, remarking, "I feel myself very much injured by the appointment of another person for the Different States in Europe." After all, he noted, "another one may be appointed for Denmark and one for Sweden and for Germany . . . and where [will] the Commissioner of Europe . . . be then?!" See James Flanagan to Secretary Dalton, April 27, 1870, and Paul Strobach to Gov. Smith, May 5, 1870, reel 9, Governor Smith Papers, ADAH.

62. *Memphis Daily Appeal,* November 2, 1867.

63. Rogers, *One-Gallused Rebellion,* vii–viii, 91, 95, 121.

64. Trezevant, Jones, and Company, *Memphis Daily Appeal,* December 13, 1865.

65. [Illegible] to Gov. Patton, February 1, 1867, reel 23, Governor Patton Papers, ADAH.

66. J. T. Bernard, Tallahassee, FL, to Gov. Patton, April 1, 1867, Governor Patton Papers, reel 24, ADAH.

67. Paul Stevens to Gov. Smith, October 17, 1870, Governor Smith Papers, ADAH.

68. The best account of these agricultural colonies in Alabama remains Robert S. Davis, "The Old World in the New South: Entrepreneurial Ventures and the Agricultural History of Cullman County, Alabama," *Agricultural History* 79, no. 4 (Autumn 2005): 439–461. Also see Erwin Ledyard, "An American Italy," from *The Southern States: A Illustrated Monthly Magazine Devoted to the South* (March 1894), available at http://alabamayesterdays.blogspot.com/2016/11/an-american-italy-in-baldwin-county.html. Further details about the communities of Cullman, Daphne, Fruitdale, Silverhill, and Thorsby may also be found under each place name via the online *Encyclopedia of Alabama,* www.encyclopediaofalabama.org. I have found less evidence of European immigrants employed in significant numbers as plantation laborers in Alabama than in the states of Mississippi, Louisiana, and Arkansas. For examples in other states, see Whayne, *Shadows over Sunnyside;* and James C. Cobb, *The Most Southern Place on Earth: The Mississippi Delta and the Roots of Regional Identity* (New York: Oxford University Press, 1992), 110–112.

69. On connecting the southern region and climate to broader imperial notions of "tropicality," see Natalie Ring, "Inventing the Tropical South: Race, Region, and the Colonial Model," *Mississippi Quarterly* 56, no. 4 (Fall 2003): 619–631; and Ring, *The Problem South: Region, Empire, and the New Liberal State, 1880–1930* (Athens: University of Georgia Press, 2012).

70. Foner, *Reconstruction,* 213; Watson, "Immigration to Alabama," 81, citing Berthoff, 330–331.

71. Advertisement, *Memphis Daily Appeal,* December 13, 1865.

72. Mellen to Gov. Patton, January 24, 1867, reel 23; [Illegible] to Gov. Patton, Greensboro, AL, July 1867, reel 25; Thomas Stephenson to Gov. Patton, September 2, 1867, reel 25; [Illegible] to Gov. Patton, September 6, 1867, reel 25. Also see Thomas Stephenson to Gov. Patton, September 30, 1867, reel 25. All in Governor Patton Papers.

73. Lewis, *Sloss Furnaces,* 58.

74. From the Knights of Labor to the United Mine Workers, Birmingham's industrial workers organized to defend their rights, and they frequently employed work stoppages and strikes to advance their interests. Amid the economic depression of the 1890s and insurgent agrarian politics, the strike of 1894 proved particularly difficult to resolve. And despite contracts signed by operators with District 20 of the United Mine Workers, additional damaging strikes erupted in 1904, 1906, and especially in 1908. Robert D. Ward and William Warren Rogers, *The Great Strike of 1894* (Tuscaloosa: University of Alabama Press, 1965), 20–21, mentions immigrants during the strike but dismisses their importance to the labor movement or to strike events in the district. Letwin, *Challenge of Interracial Unionism,* 99–114, discusses in detail the 1894 strike but offers little about the immigrants who arrived during it.

75. *Pine Belt News* (Brewton, Alabama), September 9, 1897. Newspaper editors in the plantation belt who relied on planter subscriptions had a vested interest in pushing for out-migration of Black labor during times of economic depression and agricultural–political strife. All of these came together in the decade of the 1890s with growing agricultural unrest, the depression of 1893 to 1897, and the emergence of the biracial Populist challenge.

76. Ernest Hive to Wheeler, December 8, 1898, box 104, folder 3, Wheeler family papers.

77. Ross Smith to R. A. Mitchell, August 2, 1905; and Smith to Gov. Jelks, November 16, 1905, both reel 24, Governor Jelks Papers.

78. Application for Labor, 1905, reel 24, Governor Jelks Papers.

79. Ross Smith, "Alabama and Immigration," report to the Birmingham Commercial Club, June 11, 1906, Agriculture and Industry records.

80. Jacobson, *Barbarian Virtues,* 4–9, 13–14, 17, 57, 60, 70, 72, 217–218, and generally. Also see Jacobson, *Whiteness of a Different Color.*

81. See, for example, Roediger, *Wages of Whiteness,* generally; Jacobsen, *Whiteness of a Different Color,* generally, Jacobsen, *Barbarian Virtues,* 85–89; Sanchez, "Race, Nation, and Culture," generally; Ngai, *Impossible Subjects,* generally; Jung, *Coolies and Cane,* generally; Gualtieri, *Between Arab and White,* generally; and Bukowczyk, "Racial Turn," 5–10.

82. Jacobsen, *Barbarian Virtues,* 14, 37, 61, 65–67, 69–72, 85–86.

83. J. J. Giers to Gov. Patton, November 16, 1866, reel 23, Governor Patton Papers.

84. *Memphis Daily Appeal,* February 17, 1870.

85. Mellen to Gov. Patton, January 24, 1867, reel 23; A. S. Tikes to Gov. Patton, February 7, 1867, reel 23; Jonathan Gill Shorter to Gov. Patton, March 22, 1867, reel 24; William Byrd to Gov. Patton, March 25, 1867, reel 24; Robert Philpot to Gov. Patton, April 12, 1867, reel 24, all in Governor Patton Papers. Thomas Stephenson also offered to be an immigration agent, this time to England, where he would recruit agricultural and skilled labor to the state. See Thomas Stephenson to Gov. Patton, September 2, 1867, reel 25, Governor Patton Papers.

86. C. C. Pomeroy to Gov. Smith, March 30, 1870, reel 8, Governor Smith Papers.

87. W. T. Thompson to Commissioner R. R. Poole, Alpine, Alabama, February 20, 1905; and Poole to Thompson, Montgomery, February 25, 1905, Agriculture and Industry records.

88. In North Carolina, for example, white employers, politicians, and voters debated the racial pedigrees of various immigrant groups, attempting to pin down either the "desirability" or the "racial inferiority" of Southern and Eastern Europeans. Although the debate itself indicated a certain amount of fluctuation in definitions of "whiteness" in the New South, concerns about the racial undesirability of Southern and Eastern Europeans also fluctuated by the availability of farm and industrial labor. See Lowery, "Another Species of Racial Discord," 32–59.

89. Charles Hamacher to Gov. Patton, 1867, reel 25, Governor Patton Papers. Andrew Zimmerman, *Alabama in Africa: Booker T. Washington, the German Empire, and the Globalization of the New South* (Princeton, NJ: Oxford University Press, 2010), 70–87, discusses the rocky transition to "freedom" in Prussian serfdom that, as in the American South, left German peasants without independent landholdings and often merely reemployed as day laborers. They remained under the control and coercion of landlords, who saw their own landholdings increase, along with their economic and political power. Such conditions spurred a "mass exodus" of German agricultural laborers, labeled by Zimmerman the "German freedpeople," in the late nineteenth and early twentieth centuries, particularly to the United States.

90. F. S. Mount to Gov. Patton, August 10, 1867, Reel 25, Governor Patton Papers.

91. Jacob Thompson, *Memphis Appeal,* June 3, 1871.

92. [Illegible] to Gov. Smith, July 2, 1870, reel 9, Governor Smith Papers.

93. Paul Stevens to Gov. Smith, October 17, 1870, reel 10, Governor Smith Papers. Commissioner Seviers agreed, in 1878, that the western states still afforded "a fine field for our own operations," but not because of the cumulative effects of the Indian Wars. Rather, "those who have settled there," though able to "accumulate considerable means and estates," nonetheless desired to leave, as they "have become dissatisfied on account of the severe climate, and other disasters detrimental to their general health and interests." C. F. Seviers, "Report of the Commissioner of Immigration . . . , November 1878, Agriculture and Industry, Annual Reports. By the early twentieth century, with the Indian Wars long over, a new tactic emerged. Along with again emphasizing the state's warm climate in contrast to the upper-Midwestern and Western winters, immigration boosters also highlighted the persistent difference in land values as a motivation to come South. "I see no reason why people should pay from $100 to $150, for lands in Iowa," remarked Commissioner Ross Smith in 1905. "Lands equally good can be bought in Alabama for from $10 to $20." Ross Smith to R. A. Mitchell, Alexander City, Alabama, August 2, 1905, reel 24, Governor Jelks Papers.

94. C. F. Seviers, "Immigration Address of the Commissioners of Immigration to the Citizens of Alabama," 1876, Agriculture and Industry, Annual Reports.

95. *Memphis Daily Appeal,* February 17, 1870.

96. *Manufacturers Record* to Gov. Jelks, July 20, 1905, reel 24, Governor Jelks Papers.

97. "An Appeal on Behalf of Free Transportation," undated, but likely around 1910, box 36, folder 5, Underwood Papers, ADAH.

98. Office of the Chairman, Tennessee Coal, Iron and Railroad Company to Oscar Underwood, February 22, 1906, box 9, folder 3, Underwood Papers. Of 985 men employed in the Chapin mine, the nationalities reportedly comprised the following numbers and percentages: Italy: 314 (32%); Scandinavia: 291 (30%); England: 154 (16%); Austria: 79 (8%); Germany: 78 (8%); Canada: 24 (2.4%); Finland: 19 (2%); Ireland: 15 (2%); other: 11 (1.1). See Office of the Chairman, Tennessee Coal, Iron, and Railroad Company to Oscar Underwood, February 22, 1906, box 9, folder 3, Underwood Papers.

99. Frank V. Evans to Oscar Underwood, April 26, 1906, box 9, folder 7, Underwood Papers.

100. *Birmingham News,* July 22, 1905.

101. Mrs. Jac. "Perle" Smith to Oscar Underwood, April 28, 1906, box 9, folder 7, Underwood Papers.

2. "JOHN CHINAMAN" IN NEW SOUTH ALABAMA

1. *Tuskaloosa Gazette,* August 10, 1893. See also *Daily News* (Birmingham), August 5, 1893.

2. "Jerry Haley," U.S. Federal Census of 1900, Ancestry.com; *Tuskaloosa Gazette,* September 7, 1893.

3. *Tuskaloosa Gazette,* November 9, 16, 1893.

4. *Birmingham News,* April 23, 1897. See also *Tuskegee News,* April 29, 1897.

5. The Alabama miscegenation statute written in 1866 essentially stayed in force with little change, and it gained institutionalization in the 1901 constitution, which prohibited the state legislature from enacting any law recognizing interracial unions. A U.S. Supreme Court decision in 1883, *Pace v. Alabama,* upheld the criminalization of interracial sex and marriage. See Julie Novkov, "Racial Constructions: The Legal Regulation of Miscegenation in Alabama, 1890–1934," *Law and History Review* 20, no. 2 (Summer 2002), 225–232. Jackson, *Dixie's Italians,* notes the role of bureaucrats such as licensing agents as "racial gatekeepers" building and applying racial definitions and proscribing access to "informal citizenship" rights such as marriage (121–125, 143–144).

6. In cities with much larger Chinese populations, Chinese laundrymen provoked suspicions rooted in gendered and racialized stereotypes among both U.S.-born and European immigrant residents. Americans blamed the Chinese, not British or American merchants, for the presence of opium in urban areas. Chinese businesses risked being targeted by locals and officials as sites of immoral, drug-oriented, and licentious activities. Chinese laundries ran wholly masculine spaces, according to one scholar, but were devoted to a "feminized" occupation, creating an "ambiguously gendered" image of footloose men who were difficult to pigeonhole by race or sex. A similar dynamic regarding U.S.-born southerners' responses to Chinese men appears in local and regional newspapers in the New South; however, the vastly smaller presence of the

Chinese may also have reduced the perceived threat. See Mary Ting Lui, *The Chinatown Trunk Mystery: Murder, Miscegenation, and Other Dangerous Encounters in Turn-of-the-Century New York City* (Princeton, NJ: Princeton University Press, 2005), 67–72.

7. The number of immigrants the census documented should always be considered a minimum, since it only provided a very imperfect snapshot of an often itinerant and mobile population in any given year. The numbers of Chinese thus recorded were 1 (1870); 5 (1880); 1890 unavailable; 55 (1900); 49 (1910); 58 (1920); 61 (1930); and 58 (1940). U.S. Federal Census, Ancestry.com.

8. For other examples of Chinese victims calling on their connections to white patrons or customers for support, see Lui, *Chinatown Trunk Mystery,* 61, 73.

9. Arnold Shankman notes that African American views of the Chinese "waxed and waned" with the degree to which they were competitors in agriculture or in the laundry business. He also found that the Black press generally stopped short of explicitly backing anti-Chinese legislation, including the Exclusion Act of 1882. Shankman, *Ambivalent Friends: Afro-Americans View the Immigrant* (Greenwood, CT: Greenwood Press, 1982). Nor did Black editors advocate for discrimination or violence against the Chinese, though both sides viewed the other through the racial stereotypes prevalent at the time. Daniel Bronstein identifies African American women as primary competitors to Chinese laundrymen in Georgia's cities and towns and notes that some Chinese laundry proprietors hired Black female hands. Bronstein, "The Formation and Development of Chinese Communities in Atlanta, Augusta, and Savannah, Georgia: From Sojourners to Settlers, 1880–1965" (PhD diss., Georgia State University, 2008), 44, 49. For more on African American washerwomen and Chinese laundries, see Tera W. Hunter, *To 'Joy My Freedom: Southern Black Women's Lives and Labors after the Civil War* (Cambridge, MA: Harvard University Press, 1997), 78–79, 81.

10. Indeed, in the West, producing "'dead Chinamen' became a natural consequence of American progress, no different than boring a tunnel or felling a tree," according to Dearinger, *Filth of Progress,* 161–167. White, *Railroaded* points out that "coolies emerged as the most dangerous subset of contract labor—virtual slaves, racially inferior, and inalterably alien. What the Chinese were—free immigrant labor—became submerged beneath the inverted and immigrant coolie." Thus, in the West, the Chinese were especially deeply hated by other laboring classes, yet they also "occupied a strange place where they were both essential and exotic" (297). Jung, *Coolies and Cane* offers an opposite conclusion, identifying how the 1862 Coolie Labor Act and its subsequent applications replaced the notion of the unfree "coolie" with that of the "voluntary migrant," thereby giving southern planters access to Chinese bodies for agricultural exploitation.

11. Although this labor action failed, the Chinese had "demonstrated their wherewithal, tenacity, and ability to defend their rights and claim dignity as builders of American progress." Dearinger, *Filth of Progress,* 169.

12. Historiography of Chinese immigrant and sojourn laborers in the United States may be categorized, roughly, as studies emphasizing the exploitation and wholesale victimization of the Chinese, studies emphasizing successful Chinese participation in the conventional "achieving the American dream" and "striving toward whiteness" narratives, and those highlighting the actual agency of Chinese immigrants within the often challenging and unequal circumstances

that defined their lives. Though the first two categories each offer elements important to understanding the case of Alabama's Chinese, the third category more aptly captures the distinct experience of Chinese immigrants in the New South, including in Alabama. Examples of the victimization literature include Sylvia Krebs, "John Chinaman and Reconstruction Alabama: The Debate and the Experience," *Southern Studies* 21, no. 4 (Winter 1982): 369–384; Erika Lee, *At America's Gates: Chinese Immigration during the Exclusion Era, 1882–1943* (Chapel Hill: University of North Carolina, 2003); Ngai, *Impossible Subjects;* Jung, *Coolies and Cane;* Scott Reynolds Nelson, "After Slavery: Forced Drafts of Irish and Chinese Labor in the American Civil War, or The Search for Liquid Labor," in *Many Middle Passages: Forced Migration and the Making of the Modern World,* ed. Emma Christopher, Cassandra Pybus, and Marcus Rediker (Berkeley: University of California Press, 2007); and Karuka, *Empire's Tracks.* Examples of the "American dream" and "Chinese push for whiteness" category include James Loewen, *The Mississippi Chinese: Between Black and White* (Cambridge, MA: Harvard University Press, 1971); Bronstein, "Formation and Development of Chinese Communities"; and Daniel Bronstein, "Segregation, Exclusion, and the Chinese Communities in Georgia, 1880s–1940," in *Asian Americans in Dixie: Race and Migration in the South,* ed. Khyati J. Joshi and Jigna Deshai (Urbana: University of Illinois, 2013). Examples of the "agency" and "racial fluidity" category include Peck, *Reinventing Free Labor;* Vivek Bald, "Selling the East in the American South: Bengali Muslim Peddlers in New Orleans and Beyond, 1880–1920"; and Leslie Bow, "Racial Interstitiality and the Anxieties of the 'Partly Colored': Representations of Asians under Jim Crow," both in *Asian Americans in Dixie;* and Dearinger, *Filth of Progress.*

13. My discussion of Chinese railroad laborers who came to Alabama in 1870 borrows heavily from the excellent work of Lucy M. Cohen, *Chinese in the Post–Civil War South: A People without a History* (Baton Rouge: Louisiana State University Press, 1984), as well as from Krebs, "John Chinaman and Reconstruction Alabama."

14. For a relevant overview, see Lisa Yun and Ricardo Rene Laremont, "Chinese Coolies and African Slaves in Cuba, 1847–74," *Journal of Asian-American Studies* 4, no. 2 (June 2001).

15. Guterl, "After Slavery," 213, 225, 228, 230.

16. See Jung, *Coolies and Cane,* 5–7, 13, 37, 40, 72. Zach Sell notes that "the vision . . . of coolies moving across the British Empire providing cheap labor free from exploitation while facilitating indigenous dispossession was part of a broader cynical white imagination of free labor after the abolition of slavery." Thus, as southern white planters envisioned it, "African Americans would either 'work or starve' in a new society that whites would create through the mass importation of coolie, Pacific Islander, or European labor." Sell, "Asian Indentured Labor in the Age of African American Emancipation," *International Labor and Working-Class History* 91 (Spring 2017): 20–22. The term "coolie" stands today as a racially derogatory term; however, the term commonly occurs throughout primary sources from the era in reference to laborers originating from Asia. The term, when quoted here, reflects specific usage in documents from this historical period.

17. Cindy Hahamovitch, "Slavery's Stale Soil: Indentured Labor, Guestworkers, and the End of Empire," in *Making the Empire Work: Labor and United States Imperialism,* ed. Jana Lipman and Daniel Bender (New York: New York University Press, 2015), 227–263.

18. See Andrew Gyory, *Closing the Gate: Race, Politics, and the Chinese Exclusion Act* (Chapel Hill: University of North Carolina Press, 1998), 32–33; Cohen, *Chinese in the Post–Civil War South;* Peck, *Reinventing Free Labor,* 50–52; White, *Railroaded,* 296–297; and Jung, *Coolies and Cane,* 5–7, 13, 37, 40, 72, 86. Yun and Laremont, "Chinese Coolies and African Slaves," 107, note that as the prices of enslaved laborers steeply increased in the nineteenth century, Cuban planters tried using European immigrants on their plantations, but these workers were unwilling to do the labor, prompting a switch to importing "coolies" from outposts of the British Empire.

19. Hahamovitch, "Slavery's Stale Soil," 229.

20. Around 1840, the British Empire "effectively 'opened' a valuable labor market of displaced or impoverished peasantry in southern China while actively suppressing the African slave trade." Yun and Laremont, "Chinese Coolies and African Slaves," 103–107.

21. For decades after the Taiping defeat in 1865, travelers to China still described a devastated countryside. One estimate puts the total loss across the five most war-ravaged provinces at 87 million, with around 57 million people dead because of the war and the rest a projected loss due to births that never happened. In 1913, the Chinese population had not yet rebounded to its pre-Taiping levels. See Stephen R. Platt, *Autumn in the Heavenly Kingdom: China, the West, and the Epic Story of the Taiping Civil War* (New York: Alfred A. Knopf, 2012), xxiii, 358. In the wake of the war, a drought-produced famine struck northern China, particularly in the Beijing region, in 1867–1868. Mike Davis, *Late Victorian Holocausts: El Niño Famines and the Making of the Third World* (New York: Verso, 2001), 64–65.

22. Judy Yung, *The Chinese Exclusion Act and Angel Island: A Brief History with Documents* (New York: Bedford/St. Martin's, 2019), 2. As one scholar concluded, "Whether they were peasants, experienced miners, merchants, or day laborers, the Guangdong immigrants sought a life in America free from the turmoil of their native land." Dearinger, *Filth of Progress,* 153. Other related factors compelling out-migration of the Chinese from southeastern China included rapid population growth as well as inflationary food prices in the mid-nineteenth century. See Scott Alan Carson, "The Biological Living Conditions of Nineteenth-Century Chinese Males in America," *Journal of Interdisciplinary History* 37, no. 2 (Autumn 2006), 201.

23. For more on the Chinese laborers on the infrastructural projects of the West, see Dearinger, *Filth of Progress;* and Karuka, *Empire's Tracks.*

24. Merchants in San Francisco dominated these associations, operating essentially as import/export businesses specializing in migrant labor and contracting with the railroad, mining, and timber interests of the West. Through their individual agents, the Six Companies directed thousands of Chinese laborers to the Central Pacific Railroad. Dearinger, *Filth of Progress,* 154, 160; Peck, *Reinventing Free Labor,* 52. See also Karuka, *Empire's Tracks,* 83–85.

25. Cohen, *Chinese in the Post–Civil War South,* 40–44, 60–63, 72–75, explains the vicissitudes on the part of American consular officials in China over how to apply the 1862 act when labor agents tried to contract with Chinese migrants for southern planters and entrepreneurs, particularly regarding whether any Chinese migrant could be "certified" as "free or voluntary." On the Burlingame Treaty of 1868, see Dearinger, *Filth of Progress,* 155.

26. Jung, *Coolies and Cane,* 118–124, 157–158, details the struggles of southern recruiting agents to fit into this system, highlighting especially the struggles of labor agent and Louisiana

planter John Williams and labor agent George Gift to procure laborers in China for Louisiana plantations.

27. Cohen, *Chinese in the Post–Civil War South,* 52–58; and Jung, *Coolies and Cane,* 40, 72, 86. One article, originally published in the Louisiana *Plantation Banner,* ran in numerous southern papers in 1869. The author was a visitor to a Louisiana plantation in 1869 who remarked upon the planters having brought in a group of Chinese laborers for fieldwork. When he first encountered them in 1867, "they had just been brought over from Cuba." *Alabama Daily State Journal,* October 1, 1869.

28. *Weekly Clarion* (Jackson, MS), July 21, 1870.

29. Quoted in Jung, *Coolies and Cane,* 107.

30. The Central Pacific Railway released its Chinese laborers, numbering around ten thousand by that point, in April 1869. See Najia Aarim Heriot, *Chinese Immigrants, African Americans, and Racial Anxiety in the United States, 1848–1882* (Urbana: University of Illinois Press, 2003), 80, 112.

31. A Montgomery editor called for an immigration convention to be attended by the "most prominent businessmen and planters of this city and county," noting that local hotels and railway lines would offer half fares and rates for those delegates attending. *New York Times,* May 14, 1869.

32. Cohen, *Chinese in the Post–Civil War South,* 63. Jung, *Coolies and Cane* finds that attendees were mostly southern employers "struggling to cope with emancipation, Radical Reconstruction, and global competition" (106).

33. Cohen, *Chinese in the Post–Civil War South,* 65–66.

34. While his global counterparts focused on recruiting laborers for plantations in the Caribbean, Australia, and New Zealand, and for the gold mines of South Africa, Cornelius Koopmanschap focused on the United States. For more on the Chinese and Indian sojourners recruited into the plantation economies of the British Empire, see Marjory Harper and Stephen Constantine, *Migration and Empire* (Oxford: Oxford University Press, 2010), 149, 154, 158–159, 294, 296.

35. Cohen, *Chinese in the Post–Civil War South,* 67–71, and generally, offers the most details on Koopmanschap's background and activities as a labor agent.

36. Cohen, *Chinese in the Post–Civil War South,* 69. As Jung describes them, together they represented "the old South, imperial Europe, and colonized Asia." Jung notes how this tripartite collaboration "attested to the complex links that slavery, coolieism, and capitalism had forged. In the summer of 1869, these men from the Old South, imperial Europe, and colonized Asia shared a hope of making money by cultivating and catering to the postemancipation demand for coolies." This served as "a testament to slavery's resiliency and an instrument to welcome the age of capital." Jung, *Coolies and Cane,* 106.

37. In a spurt of excited good faith, convention delegates formed the Mississippi Valley Emigration Company, a joint stock venture charged with gathering subscriptions from southern planters and entrepreneurs to fund the importation of "as many Chinese immigrant laborers as possible in the shortest time." The chairman of the finance committee, Gideon Pillow, a planter and former Confederate officer, told delegates of plans to place agents in New York City and San Francisco to recruit both European and Chinese laborers. Capital investors in the scheme

included Koopmanschap himself ($5,000) and General Forrest, "who pledged $5,000 to employ one thousand Chinese laborers, as president of New Selma, Marion, and Memphis Railroad." Forrest apparently acted on the assurances of an acquaintance serving as an immigration commissioner in Hawaii, who pointed to his own experience "importing Chinese and Japanese to the islands of Hawaii." Planter schemes to obtain such labor on the best (cheapest) terms possible could get elaborate. A California newspaper reported a plan to take the Chinese workers laid off with the completion of the transcontinental railroad, send them "back to China," and then bring them back "directly to the South," in a vague scheme to evade the contract labor law. See *Weekly Clarion Ledger* (Jackson, MS), July 22, October 7, 1869; *New York Times,* July 16, 18, 21, 1869; *Memphis Daily Appeal,* July 15, 1869; Cohen, *Chinese in the Post–Civil War South,* 67–68, 71; Jung, *Coolies and Cane,* 102–103; Gyory, *Closing the Gate,* 33. Chinese laborers apparently did arrive on other railroad projects in the New South, including in Alabama, though the record is even scarcer for these men. A Tennessee newspaper reported in the fall of 1870, for example, that "the latest arrival noted in the South is that of about 200, who reached Selma, Ala., having been sent from San Francisco by Koopmanschap and Co. They are to be employed as laborers in the construction of the Selma and Gulf Railroad, and have contracted to work for the period of three years." *Nashville Union and American,* September 4, 1870.

38. On the dizzying array of complicated financial and political maneuverings that produced and surrounded the Alabama and Chattanooga Railroad project, and on the Stanton brothers, see Fitzgerald, *Reconstruction in Alabama,* 101, 209–210, 213–214, 223–228, 248–249, 253–256, 273–276, 321; and Moore, "Railroad Building in Alabama," 216, 429–430. The Stantons also appear in Cohen, *Chinese in the Post–Civil War South,* 89–90, 94–95; and Jung, *Coolies and Cane,* 196.

39. Fitzgerald, *Reconstruction in Alabama,* 101, 209–210, 213–214, 223–228, 248–249, 253–256, 273–276, 321; Moore, "Railroad Building in Alabama," 216, 429–430; Cohen, *Chinese in the Postwar South,* 89–90, 94–95; and Jung, *Coolies and Cane,* 196.

40. Fitzgerald, *Reconstruction in Alabama,* 101, 209–210, 213–214, 223–228, 248–249, 253–256, 273–276.

41. Largely inexperienced as a labor manager, and saddled with his own racial blinders, Nimrod Bell often found it difficult to handle his recalcitrant African American crews. In one instance, for example, he attempted to break up a fight between two men. When he hit one combatant with a shovel, drawing blood and knocking him unconscious, several other men who witnessed the incident threatened to kill him. Bell immediately armed himself with a knife and pistol, but it took the intercession of "a large black man" who was the "leader of my gang" to prevent further violence. This man "jumped up in front of me and told them all that he would kill the first man that attempted to hurt me. They all then went to work." Bell was certain that had it not been for this man's intervention, "no doubt they would have killed me, as all of the white men nearby were scared almost to death." See James A. Ward, ed., *Southern Railroad Man: Conductor N. J. Bell's Recollections of the Civil War Era* (DeKalb: Northern Illinois University Press, 1994), 51.

42. Ward, *Southern Railroad Man,* 55.

43. *Memphis Daily Appeal,* June 22, 1870; Krebs, "John Chinaman and Reconstruction Alabama," 379; Cohen, *Chinese in the Post–Civil War South,* 68. A. B. Moore describes the Stantons

as "thrifty and shifty promoters" aiming for "the largest profits possible" as explanation for the shift to Chinese labor. They wanted to import "Chinese laborers from California and the Central Pacific to help cheap Negro labor construct the road." Moore, "Railroad Building in Alabama," 428.

44. On antebellum accounts of Chinese laborers, typically focusing on the British Caribbean, see Jung, *Coolies and Cane,* 5, 11–38; and Sell, "Asian Indentured Labor," 8–27.

45. Jung, *Coolies and Cane,* 106, 100. Also see Cohen, *Chinese in the Post–Civil War South,* 46.

46. Krebs, "John Chinaman and Reconstruction Alabama," 379.

47. Cohen, *Chinese in the Post–Civil War South,* 68, 90; Gyory, *Closing the Gate,* 47.

48. *Memphis Daily Appeal,* July 15, 1869; *New York Times,* July 18, 1869; *Weekly Clarion Ledger* (Jackson, MS) October 7, December 30, 1869; *Memphis Daily Appeal,* June 22, July 13, 1870; *New York Times,* July 19, 1870; *Knoxville Weekly Chronicle,* July 20, 1870.

49. *Weekly Clarion Ledger,* December 30, 1869. Williams also appears in Cohen, *Chinese in the Post–Civil War South,* 71–74, 77–78, 105, 107–113; and Jung, *Coolies and Cane,* 51, 123–124, 126, 154, 178, 185, 188–189.

50. See Jung, *Coolies and Cane,* 118–120.

51. Published in *Newberry Herald* (South Carolina), January 5, 1870; and *Abbeville Press Banner* (South Carolina), January 7, 1870.

52. While there was "in reality free and voluntary emigration . . . it was so surrounded, confused, and tainted with the virus of the trade of Chinese laborers as to require the utmost vigilance and scrutiny to separate legitimate and illegitimate emigration." Sing-Wu Wang, *The Organization of Chinese Emigration, 1848–1888: With Special Reference to Chinese Emigration to Australia* (San Francisco: Chinese Materials, 1978), 107.

53. Ward, *Southern Railroad Man,* 56. Koopmanschap had procured the New South's "single largest shipment" of contracted Chinese imported at one time to the New South. Jung, *Coolies and Cane,* 196. Jung, 154, citing Cohen, *Chinese in the Post–Civil War South,* 89–91, places the number at 960. Each laborer reportedly paid sixty-five dollars in gold to cover his fare to Chattanooga. See *Memphis Daily Appeal,* July 13, 16, 1870. Given the different schemes and proposals to procure Chinese labor, it remains difficult to clarify the exact origins of these Chinese men. Evidence points to their departure from the California railroad project and travel across the country to Alabama. But equally compelling evidence points to their origins in Hong Kong or the Caribbean, prior to their arrival in California. See *Daily Alta California,* July 13, August 1, 4, 1869; *Sacramento Daily Union,* June 2, 1869.

54. A reporter in Chattanooga described the men as "rough-looking and dirty," though that was to be expected after a long trip. "Otherwise," he remarked, they appeared to be "healthy, active, and cheerful." *New York Times,* July 19, 1870. Earlier, in Vicksburg, they made a "very odd and singular appearance" and "crowds of spectators followed them with the most spirited curiosity." *Vicksburg Weekly Herald* (Mississippi), July 23, 1870. General Forrest also obtained Chinese laborers from Koopmanschap to help build his Selma and Gulf Railroad. However, they seem to have left far fewer records than even the Chinese who worked on the Alabama and Chattanooga (AL-CH) Railroad. According to one newspaper report, Koopmanschap sent about two hundred laborers to Forrest. See *Nashville Union and American* (Tennessee), September 4, 1870.

55. Krebs, "John Chinaman and Reconstruction Alabama," 379. The Black press viewed such recruiting efforts with a jaundiced eye, correctly identifying the intent to use the Chinese to control or displace Black laborers. See David J. Helliwig, "Black Attitudes towards Immigrant Labor in the South, 1865–1910, *Filson Club Historical Quarterly* 54, no. 2 (April 1908): 154.

56. Cohen, *Chinese in the Post–Civil War South,* 89–91. Also see accounts in the *New York Times,* July 19, 1870; *Chattanooga Times,* July 15, 1870; and *Sweetwater Enterprise* (Tennessee), July 21, 1870.

57. James E. Webb to Zemma Webb, Greensboro, Alabama, August 4, 1870, Webb Letters, 1869–1873, SPR 206, Alabama Department of Archives and History, Montgomery.

58. *Alabama Daily State Journal,* March 15, 1871; *Memphis Daily Appeal,* March 15, 1871.

59. Cohen, *Chinese in the Post–Civil War South,* 91.

60. *Alabama Daily State Journal,* March 15, 1871. See also *Memphis Daily Appeal,* March 15, 1871.

61. The Stanton brothers were backed by financial houses in the U.S. Northeast as well as in Paris and Germany, and bonds issued by Alabama state government for the project ultimately made their way into the European bond market. See Moore, "Railroad Building in Alabama," 430, 432.

62. See *Alabama Daily State Journal,* January 6–11, 19–21, 27, 1871; *Mobile Daily Register* (Alabama), June 9, 10, 1871. Also see Krebs, "John Chinaman and Reconstruction Alabama," 380.

63. *Alabama Daily State Journal,* January 27, 1871.

64. See editorials in *Alabama Daily State Journal,* February 1–3, 8, 14, 1871. Such negligence was not confined to railroad builders, apparently. In testifying before a congressional committee investigating Chinese immigration, A. Vernon Seaman remarked that, in his experience observing the use of Chinese labor, "in all the cases I became cognizant of" that involved "some trouble between the Chinese and the planters," the conflict arose from "the non-payment of wages." See A. Vernon Seaman, Oliphant and Co., San Francisco, *Report of the Special Joint Committee to Investigate Chinese Immigration,* February 27, 1877, U.S. Congressional Serial Set, vol. 1734, Session vol. 3, 44th Congress, 2nd session, S. Rpt. 689, Ralph Draughon Brown Library, Auburn University, Auburn, Alabama (hereinafter cited as Special Joint Committee report).

65. The Chinese were still being recruited by a labor agent from Louisiana who was seeking workers for sugar plantations. At least some of the men appeared to have departed the railroad for Louisiana, even before the project collapsed into bankruptcy. See *Alabama Daily State Journal,* March 15, June 16, 1871.

66. Bell accompanied Stanton by rail down to the end of the constructed line. Stanton then proceeded on by hack to the site of the trouble, where the Chinese laborers were supposed to be engaged in grading work. Ward, *Southern Railroad Man,* 56. The African American trackliners possibly defended Stanton because they had been placed in overseer positions to help manage the Chinese workers. A local newspaper condemned the practice of Black "bosses" in any context, including on the AL-CH project. See *Livington Journal,* March 17, 1871.

67. Ward, *Southern Railroad Man,* 56.

68. Special Joint Committee report. In March, the *Mobile Register* reported the arrival of the steamer *Jennie Rogers* from Tuscaloosa, carrying about five hundred "heathen Chinee" fresh

from working on the AL-CH and bound for Louisiana. Another group that had left the railroad reportedly ended up not cutting sugarcane but working the swing shift in a cotton mill in the Louisiana state penitentiary in Baton Rouge. See Cohen, *Chinese in the Post–Civil War South,* 92–94, 141–142; Krebs, "John Chinaman and Reconstruction Alabama," 380. Stanton reportedly sued a labor agent for enticing his Chinese railroad workers for plantation work in Louisiana. Jung claimed that labor agent W. A. Kissam, who had procured Chinese laborers for the Merrill plantation in Louisiana, "shifted his field of operation to Alabama in 1871 and transported former railroad workers to employers in Louisiana." He is likely the agent sued by Stanton. Kissam also delivered some of Stanton's Chinese laborers to the cotton mill in the Louisiana state prison. Jung, *Coolies and Cane,* 196–199, 259 note 36. Still others landed temporarily in Memphis by rail, where, a journalist reported, "They made their way to the levee like a lot of ducks, one after another." Having been employed on Stanton's road "for over a year," the men "bore the marks of toil on their faces and clothing." *Memphis Daily Appeal,* July 23, 1871. Guterl, "After Slavery," 235, argues that the men chose Louisiana because of their prior experience on sugar plantations in Cuba. Without knowing the men's actual origins prior to arriving in Alabama, however, such conclusions remain speculative.

69. John H. Gindrat, *Receiver of the Alabama and Chattanooga Railroad, to the Governor* (Montgomery, AL: W. W. Screws, 1871).

70. Cohen, *Chinese in the Post–Civil War South,* 94; *Memphis Daily Appeal,* June 16, 1871; Ward, *Southern Railroad Man,* xviii, 56; Moore, "Railroad Building in Alabama," 433–434. A few scholars mention strikes by the Chinese in the South. Peck notes that the Chinese surprised many observers with a "remarkable militance against their employers" in the United States, citing a strike in Utah in 1868 and conflicts in the South. See Peck, *Reinventing Free Labor,* 52.

71. *Memphis Daily Appeal,* June 15, 16, 1871. The chaos on the Alabama and Chattanooga Railroad continued for years, including under a period of state ownership, until a London-based capitalist purchased the road in 1877 and renamed it the Alabama Great Southern Railroad. See Ward, *Southern Railroad Man,* xviii. In 1880, J. C. Stanton still lived in Chattanooga, with his wife, three sons, and a daughter. They all lived as boarders in a hotel, most likely the Stanton Hotel that J. C. built with the subsidy money from the state of Alabama. His occupation in the 1880 census appears as "capitalist." U.S. Federal Census, 1880, Ancestry.com. After a very long career on many of the southern railroads, Nimrod Bell died in 1902. He is buried in Cleveland, Tennessee.

72. Special Joint Committee report, 550–551; *Memphis Daily Appeal,* June 16, 1871; *Charleston Daily News* (South Carolina), July 29, 1871; and Cohen, *Chinese in the Post–Civil War South,* 95.

73. *Memphis Daily Appeal,* June 15, 1871.

74. As they waited around Tuscaloosa, some of the Chinese men found alternative employment as fruit peddlers, field hands, or domestic servants. Desperate planters created a high demand for their labor, however, and they were quick to contract with those who left the Alabama and Chattanooga and other railroads. According to Cohen, most of the AL-CH Chinese laborers ultimately ended up working on Louisiana sugar plantations, recruited by labor agents W. A. Kissam, "Ah Joe," "Say You," and Chin Poo. Krebs, "John Chinaman and Reconstruction Alabama," 381; Cohen, *Chinese in the Post–Civil War South,* 95, 105; Jung, *Coolies and Cane,* 198.

75. Jung, *Coolies and Cane,* 120, details some of the problems U.S.-based labor agents encountered when trying to procure Chinese laborers in Hong Kong, Macao, or Canton (Guangzhou).

76. Jung notes, among other obstacles to the success of the Chinese labor experiment in Louisiana, the tendency of the men to rebel "against their captors and employers" everywhere they went, including in Louisiana. However, "'coolie' fever" persisted because "the daily struggles between planters and black laborers kept it alive" in other locales, including Alabama. Jung, *Coolies and Cane,* 126–127.

77. *Memphis Daily Appeal,* February 23, 1871.

78. *Alabama Daily State Journal,* October 1, 1879.

79. Ward, *Southern Railroad Man,* 56. Having struck alongside their Black and white coworkers in Meridian, the Chinese workers who fled the AL-CH Railroad project for Louisiana were no more inclined to acquiesce to another unjust labor regime. Some refused to submit to the task system in Louisiana when their written contracts guaranteed that they would work together as gangs under their own Chinese "headman." Others ran away to nearby towns and cities (or farther away) to work as domestics, merchants, cooks, or in laundries. Others reportedly remained on plantations to labor as individual sharecroppers or tenants. See Cohen, *Chinese in the Post–Civil War South,* 110–111, 132.

80. Krebs, "John Chinaman and Reconstruction Alabama," 381.

81. *Charleston Daily News* (South Carolina), January 25, 1871.

82. Jung, *Coolies and Cane,* 197, 259 note 31.

83. In the end, the brief experiment with Chinese labor "for plantations and large-scale works such as building railroads in the lower South did not succeed . . . because the employees and employers had nearly opposite views of the meaning of the contract and of social relations between worker and employer." Cohen, *Chinese in the Post–Civil War South,* 132.

84. On the Chinese in Mississippi, see Loewen, *Mississippi Chinese;* on the Chinese in Louisiana, see Jung, *Coolies and Cane.* Chinese men finding Western communities increasingly inhospitable amid a swell of anti-Chinese sentiment nationally during the fallout of the 1870s recession looked eastward for new opportunities. Established Chinese communities in larger urban areas in the Midwest and the Northeast proved most appealing. See Dearinger, *Filth of Progress,* 155, 170–171; Peck, *Reinventing Free Labor,* 53, 57, 90–91, 169–170, 206, 210.

85. Elliot Young, *Alien Nation: Chinese Migration in the Americas from the Coolie Era through World War II* (Chapel Hill: University of North Carolina Press, 2014), 10.

86. Yung, *Chinese Exclusion Act,* 1. In the context of rising nativism against the Chinese, along with intensive lobbying from labor organizations amid the economic downturns of the 1870s, 1880s, and 1890s, the 1882 act inaugurated an era of expanding immigration restrictions aimed at "closing the gate" for open immigration to the United States. See Gyory, *Closing the Gate.*

87. Yung, *Chinese Exclusion Act,* 1–2, 10–18.

88. For more on the complicated development, application, and historical legacy of the U.S. Chinese Exclusion Acts, see Ngai, *Impossible Subjects;* Gyory, *Closing the Gate;* Guterl, "After Slavery"; and Matthew Pratt Guterl, *American Mediterranean: Southern Slaveholders in the Age of Emancipation* (Cambridge, MA: Harvard University Press, 2008). Also see Anna Pegler-

Gordon, "Chinese Exclusion, Photography, and the Development of U.S. Immigration Policy," *American Quarterly* 58, no. 1 (2006): 51–77.

89. In fact, despite the Exclusion Acts, the Chinese were able to keep replenishing their American population with young men, even as older Chinese people retired back to China. See Kenneth Chew, Marck Leach, and John Liu, "The Revolving Door to Gold Mountain: How Chinese Immigrants Got around U.S. Exclusion and Replenished the Chinese Labor Pool, 1900–1910," *International Migration Review* 43, no. 2 (Summer 2002): 410–430.

90. An 1885 amendment, for example, stated that a U.S. consul had to endorse certificates issued by the Chinese government that were supposed to validate one's exempt status. Three years later, an additional amendment prohibited the return of Chinese laborers who had previously gained legal entry to the United States but then had left, "unless he had family or assets and debts due him worth at least $1,000 in the United States." Yung, *Chinese Exclusion Act,* 13.

91. Bronstein, "Formation and Development of Chinese Communities," 110.

92. Federal customhouse agents in the Alabama port of Mobile recorded vessels moving in and out of Mobile Bay and registered information about passengers disembarking in the city. They identified several Chinese men who entered Mobile either to proceed by train to San Francisco on their way to China or to request permission to resume their residency in Mobile itself. If they had no local claim to residency, the documents suggest, they were sent on to California for deportation, with their arrival in San Francisco (or the arrival of someone with their papers) and subsequent departure on a vessel headed to China verified by a customhouse agent there. Those who sought to remain in Mobile offered documents that included statements signed by "upstanding white Mobilians" verifying that they were not laborers but were in fact merchants with businesses and a long residency in Mobile. See the records in 36.3.1, Federal Customs Service, RG 36, Collection District of Mobile, Alabama. National Archives and Records Administration, Atlanta, Georgia.

93. With the decline of slavery in the age of emancipation, planters in the Caribbean, Central America, and South America turned to other sources of labor, including indentured Chinese workers. The first Chinese laborers arrived in Cuba in 1847. They labored in exceedingly harsh conditions in Cuba, including being auctioned off in a manner much like a slave auction, for work on sugar plantations. According to one source, a "Cuban historian calculated that the suicide rate among the Chinese 'coolies' was some 500 per 100,000." Chinese laborers were also auctioned elsewhere in Latin America, including Costa Rica and Peru, for work on railroads and cotton plantations. Richard Dana, "The Trade in Chinese Laborers," in *The Cuba Reader: History, Culture, Politics,* ed. Aviva Chomsky, Barry Carr, and Pamela M. Smorkaloff (Durham, NC: Duke University Press, 2003), 79–82; and Lawrence Clayton and Michael Conniff, *A History of Modern Latin America,* 2nd ed. (New York: Thomson-Wadsworth, 2005), 139. For more on the recruitment of Chinese immigrants by the Mexican government, see Lee, *At America's Gates,* 157–158.

94. Petition by Chew Chan, July 25, 1900, Folder: Descriptive List of Chinese Laborer in Transition, C-K, Box 1, Customs House Records. Ah Chin assured the customs inspector that his occupation was merchant and that he was ultimately destined for Hong Kong. The deputy collector of customs, named Houston, scribbled across his certification documents that having

made careful inspection of any "physical peculiarities" of Ah Chin, he was "satisfied" of his "BONA FIDE intention to pass through out of the United States." Thus, he allowed Ah Chin, as well as the other Chinese people traveling under the auspices of the United Fruit Company, to land in Mobile. See "Know All Men by These Present," United Fruit Company, December 6, 1902, Box 1, Customs House Records.

95. Other reasons to leave and return included visiting family or finding a wife in China, among several. On the many complexities of traveling back and forth between the U.S. South and China during the exclusion era, see Bronstein, "Segregation, Exclusion, and the Chinese Communities in Georgia," 107–130.

96. Examples may be found among the various documents in box 1 of the customhouse records.

97. The types of information collected in the federal census differed across decades, and definitions of categories such as occupation, race, and naturalization status could be especially fluid, depending upon how Congress or the Bureau of the Census chose to define them and upon the skills, prejudices, and inclinations of an individual enumerator. Other obstacles to formulating an exact understanding of Chinese immigration in Alabama across time include the varied spellings of Chinese names, the undue pressures exerted by the threat of deportation under the Exclusion Laws, and the care (or carelessness) with which an individual enumerator collected family information. Nonetheless, given the scarcity of records, the census does provide a glimpse of who is recorded as living in a state and, to some extent, who they were.

98. U.S. Federal Census, 1870, Ancestry.com.

99. Fire destroyed most of the records of the 1890 population census. However, Ancestry.com also provides city directories, which serve as a useful way to document the existence of Chinese immigrants living in Alabama communities from 1890 to 1900 or so. See U.S. City Directories, Mobile, 1822–1995, Ancestry.com.

100. U.S. Federal Census, 1870, 1880, 1900, 1910, Ancestry.com.

101. Chinese women had joined the Alabama immigrant communities by 1920, though still in far fewer numbers than the men. U.S. Federal Census, 1920, 1930, Ancestry.com. The most detailed treatments of the Chinese experience in the South, in addition to Cohen's *Chinese in the Post–Civil War South,* are Loewen, *Mississippi Chinese;* Bronstein, "Formation and Development of Chinese Communities"; and Robert Seto Quan, *Lotus among the Magnolias: The Mississippi Chinese* (Jackson: University Press of Mississippi, 1982). Also see the useful and interesting memoir, John Jung, *Southern Fried Rice: Life in a Chinese Laundry in the Deep South* (Yin and Yang Press, 2005).

102. On census enumerators in the New South, see Jackson, *Dixie's Italians,* 126–128, 198 note 45. For a discussion of the issue of nonbinary racial categorization in the Jim Crow South, see Bow, "Racial Interstitiality."

103. Relying on Ancestry.com adds an additional wrinkle to the use of population schedules. In the transcriptions of individual records, users can submit alternative racial definitions that are added parenthetically to the transcription. For example, a person might be enumerated as "Chinese" by the original census taker but someone using Ancestry can, for instance, submit a "clarification" of "white" or "Black" for that individual. One can, however, still read the orig-

inal population schedule for each person in order to document what the enumerator actually recorded. In determining a racial categorization for an individual for these records, I use the actual schedule whenever possible, instead of relying on the transcription.

104. Bronstein, "Formation and Development of Chinese Communities," 44–45; Jung, *Southern Fried Rice;* Lui, *Chinatown Trunk Mystery,* 54.

105. In 1915, an Alabama newspaper reported the sad case of "one of the Luverne Chinamen" who had "lost his mind" and had to be placed by his comrades on a train back to San Francisco. *Luverne Journal* (Alabama), February 11, 1915. Bronstein, "Formation and Development of Chinese Communities," 91, found a similar case of a man who went "insane" when immigration authorities denied his request to bring his family from China to Georgia.

106. Bronstein, "Formation and Development of Chinese Communities," 47–49; Renqiu Yu, *To Save China, to Save Ourselves: The Chinese Hand Laundry Alliance of New York* (Philadelphia: Temple University Press, 1992), 25.

107. According to one estimate, around $75 to $200 would provide the capital to open a one-man laundry operation in the 1880s. Yu, *To Save China,* 9–11.

108. Bronstein, "Formation and Development of Chinese Communities," 49–50.

109. *Greenville Advocate,* July 18, 1918.

110. Bronstein, "Formation and Development of Chinese Communities," 44, 52–53.

111. *Birmingham News,* October 28, 1909.

112. *Montgomery Advertiser,* October 18, 1900. For more on such challenges, see Yu, *To Save China,* 25–27.

113. *Florence Herald,* March 14, 1895; *Andalusia Star,* November 9, 1920.

114. Jacobsen, *Barbarian Virtues,* 75–82; Lui, *Chinatown Trunk Mystery,* 53–55, 67–72.

115. Joshi and Desai, *Asian Americans in Dixie* emphasize the importance of Asians in the South alongside the popular notion of unfree "coolie" labor, despite their small overall numbers. Bronstein, "Formation and Development of Chinese Communities" notes that the small size of Chinese communities allowed a level of white "tolerance" and eventual acceptance as "honorary whites" in Georgia that otherwise might not have occurred.

116. Bronstein, "Formation and Development of Chinese Communities," 62, notes that discrimination kept Chinese immigrants in Georgia essentially locked out of most other occupations until after World War II. Nonetheless, the Chinese and other immigrants were able to exploit the racial hierarchies and industrial-commercial growth of the New South to locate an economic niche.

117. Lui, *Chinatown Trunk Mystery,* 54–56, describes the movement of Chinese men in and out of white public and private spaces in New York City through the service work they provided.

118. Bronstein, "Formation and Development of Chinese Communities," 103–107, 109–110, argues that the Chinese in Georgia were in such small numbers that state and local officials exerted little energy policing them in relation to Jim Crow laws, including laws on miscegenation. He found little anti-Chinese legislation in Georgia, and the few bills that did emerge typically met defeat, including school segregation efforts, until after 1927. Moreover, based on the failure to find that white rioters targeted Chinese businesses during the Atlanta Race Riot of 1906, Bronstein concludes that little anti-Chinese violence occurred in Georgia, though he does

mention an incident here and there. However, Bronstein misses several cases of Black versus Chinese violent conflict, including the murder of a Chinese laundryman in Rome, Georgia, in 1889, which resulted in a public execution of the African American man charged with the crime, an event that drew several Chinese people from Atlanta, as well as around five thousand white and Black spectators. See *Atlanta Constitution,* April 4, 7, June 20, 1889; *Macon Telegraph,* April 4, June 20, 1889.

119. "Tip Chung" and "Emily Pearl Spradling," Alabama, U.S. Naturalization Records, 1888–1891, Anniston and Birmingham, Ancestry.com.

120. *Franklin County Times,* October 20, December 21, 1916; "Joe Jung," U.S. Federal Census of 1920; "Emily Pearl Spradling," U.S. Federal Census of 1900; "Pearl Bradford," Alabama, U.S., Select Marriages Indexes, 1816–1942, Ancestry.com.

121. *Franklin County Times,* November 16, 1916; "Joe Jung," U.S. Federal Census of 1920; "Emily Pearl Spradling," U.S. Federal Census of 1900; "Pearl Bradford," Alabama, U.S., Select Marriages Indexes, 1816–1942. Emily Pearl Spradling first married J. T. Bradford, a thirty-two-year-old white man, in Jefferson County, Alabama, in 1912, but four years later married Joe Jung. No record indicates whether she divorced Bradford or was a widow by 1916. See "Pearl Spradling," Alabama, U.S., Select Marriages Indexes, 1816–1942; and "Pearl Bradford," Alabama, U.S., Select Marriages Indexes, 1816–1942, Ancestry.com. Emily Pearl Jung died in 1952, at age sixty-one, in Birmingham, followed by her husband, Joe Jung, in 1954. Both are buried in Elmwood Cemetery in Birmingham. See *Birmingham News,* August 4, 1952; and "Joe Jung" and "Emily Pearl Jung" in U.S., Find a Grave Index, 1600s–Current, Ancestry.com.

122. *Birmingham News,* February 21, 1916. Ben's friend, S. Y. Hampton, a forty-three-year-old white man and Spanish-American War veteran, worked in Birmingham in 1916 as a messenger for a service managed by his sister. See "S. Y. Hampton," U.S. City Directories, 1822–1945, Alabama, Birmingham, 1903, 1917, 1934, Ancestry.com; "Syd Hampton," U.S. Federal Census of 1930, Ancestry.com; Hampton obituary in the *Birmingham News,* August 6, 1934; "Chin Moon Ben," Index to Probate Estate Files, 1868–1936 (Jefferson County), in Alabama, U.S., Wills and Probate Records, 1753–1999, Ancestry.com.

123. *Birmingham News,* February 21, 22, 1916.

124. *Birmingham News,* February 21, 22, 25, 26, March 1, April 5, 1916; *Montgomery Advertiser,* February 25, 1916.

125. *Birmingham News,* March 10, 11, 15, 26, 1917; "Sam Loo" and "Charlie Loo Soe," in Alabama, U.S., Wills and Probate Records, 1753–1999, Ancestry.com.

126. *Birmingham News,* April 13, 14, 1917.

127. Mutual aid associations, which could be local, statewide, regional, or tied to the Six Companies of California, were essential institutions for Chinese immigrants in the United States (and elsewhere in the diaspora). One of the most important of these were *fongs,* organized as a sort of synthesis between clan/family associations and business/labor interests. Fongs provided much-needed social services to Chinese immigrant laborers as well as succor for unemployed or retired men who could not afford to return to China. The second most common organization were the *huiguans,* essentially businessmen's associations that linked merchants across Chinese communities into a loose federation networked under the Six Com-

panies of California. Huiguans also functioned as mutual aid associations and first appeared in the United States in San Francisco in the mid-nineteenth century. The Six Companies also worked to protect Chinese immigrants from anti-Chinese discrimination and violence, lobbying against the Exclusion Acts and posting reward money in cases of murder. Although huiguans began as benevolent associations, they also held a more authoritarian role in the lives of Chinese immigrants. Membership in a huiguan essentially was mandatory, because return tickets to China could only be purchased through the organizations. Huiguans also profited from the traffic in Chinese laborers and sometimes imposed repressive measures, such as licensing fees for Chinese laundries. A third institution was the *tongs,* secret societies of young men with a militaristic bent, sometimes tied to illegal activities such as prostitution, gambling, or opium peddling. "Tong fighters" also sometimes served as a defensive arm or enforcer for particularly powerful huiguans.

Huiguans, as well as other fraternal and benevolent organizations, including the Chinese Freemasons, existed among southern Chinese communities. However, little evidence exists that any authentic "tong war" occurred among the Chinese in the South, including in Alabama. The suspicion that tong wars explained the spate of killings of Chinese laundrymen in New South Alabama reflected the nationwide negative publicity about huiguan and tong conflicts in California, as well as the widespread racism and xenophobia that interpreted Chinese activities as suspicious, subversive, and inherently criminal. On these organizations in other parts of the South and the United States, see Bronstein, "Formation and Development of Chinese Communities," 132, 152–157; Lee, *At America's Gates,* 233–234, 237; Yu, *To Save China,* 12–17; and Scott Zesch, "Chinese Los Angeles in 1870–1871: The Makings of a Massacre," *Southern California Quarterly* 90, no. 2 (Summer 2008): 109–158.

128. *Birmingham News,* April 28, 1917.

129. *Gadsden Daily Times,* July 7, 20, 1921. On July 22, either police or Howell's Chinese kinsmen opened his safe and cataloged "$90 in gold, $110 in greenback and a $100 Libery bond." *Gadsden Daily Times,* July 22, 1921.

130. *Albany-Decatur Daily* (Alabama), July 20, 1921; *Gadsden Daily Times,* July 21, 1921.

131. *Gadsden Daily Times,* July 21, 26, 1921.

132. *Montgomery Advertiser,* July 31, August 1, 1921.

133. *Gadsden Daily Times,* August 4, 1921.

134. *Gadsden Daily Times,* August 31, 1921; *Birmingham News,* September 1, 1921.

135. *Gadsden Daily Times,* October 17, 19, November 5, 1921; "George Whatley," U.S. World War I Draft Registration Cards, 1917–1918; "G. C. Whatley," U.S Federal Census of 1920; "George C. Whatley," Headstone Applications for Military Veterans, 1925–1970, Ancestry.com.

136. *Gadsden Daily Times,* November 7, 1921; *Birmingham News,* November 8, 1921.

137. *Florence Herald,* March 14, 1895; *Birmingham News,* June 20, 1898; *Prattville Progress,* March 4, 1904; *Selma Times-Journal,* May 15, 1908.

138. See, of course, the path-breaking work on Black washerwomen in Hunter, *To 'Joy My Freedom.*

139. Quoted in Hunter, *To 'Joy My Freedom,* 78–81. Arwen Mohun notes that around 90 percent of the workforce in urban laundries in the South comprised African American women.

White working-class women refused to work in occupations labeled as "negro" work, or alongside Black women. Mohun, *Steam Laundries: Gender, Technology, and Work in the United States and Great Britain, 1880–1940* (Baltimore: Johns Hopkins University Press, 1999), 172.

140. *Atlanta Constitution,* December 17, 1882.

141. *Progressive Age* (Scottsboro, AL), October 12, 1889.

142. Bronstein, "Formation and Development of Chinese Communities," 44, 52–53.

143. *Evergreen Courant,* April 23, 1942. Census records identify Carolina Crosby as "laundress" in Evergreen from at least 1870 through 1910, though by 1920 she had moved to Dead Fall, in Butler County, Alabama, to live with her tenant farmer son. See "Caroline Crosby," U.S. Federal Census of 1870, 1880, 1910, 1920, Ancestry.com.

144. *Florence Herald,* October 12, 1916. The census records only two washerwomen working in Florence in 1910, both of whom were African Americans who took washing into their own homes. By 1920, using the same occupational label of "laundress," the census lists more than two hundred washerwomen, with 155 listed as Black and 33 as "mulatto." Chinese launderers do not appear in either census; however, they could have appeared and departed between the decennial years. See U.S. Federal Census of 1910, 1920, Ancestry.com.

145. *Birmingham News,* May 25, 1918.

146. Montgomery, *Fall of the House of Labor,* 67–68; Peck, *Reinventing Free Labor,* 52.

147. In the end, and as the proprietors of the Alabama and Chattanooga Railroad discovered, Chinese workers—whether in the deep South or in Cuba—"knew their rights under the law . . . seemed acutely aware of the value of their labor, and . . . expressed a confounding familiarity with both organized and disorganized resistance." Guterl notes that both Cuba and the American South had "steamy" climates and "awful" reputations that "encouraged European immigrants to settle elsewhere." Moreover, with "coolie" labor prohibited under the 1862 law, "Southerners were never able to bind the Chinese . . . to contracts as ruthlessly as had their Cuban counterparts." Guterl, "After Slavery," 232–233.

148. *Charleston Daily News* (South Carolina), August 19, 1869.

3. "ITALIANS . . . IN THE COLORED QUARTERS": IMMIGRANT AND AFRICAN AMERICAN ENCOUNTERS IN NEW SOUTH ALABAMA

1. *Herald-Journal* (Bessemer, AL), September 24, October 1, 1891.

2. Shankman, *Ambivalent Friends,* 98.

3. Jessica Jackson defines this instability as "racial transciency" or an "indeterminate racial status of Italians," which allowed movement "back and forth" across the color line. See Jackson, *Dixie's Italians,* 6–7, 10, 119, 125, 127, 129, 143.

4. See, for example, Jacobsen, *Barbarian Virtues.*

5. The best explanation of the shifting nature of immigrant racial identity in the New South is given in Jackson, *Dixie's Italians.*

6. Jackson, "Reconsidering the Experience of Italians," 314–315 note 39, citing Thomas Guglielmo, "No Color Barrier: Italians, Race, and Rumor in the United States," in *Are Italians White?: How Race Is Made in America,* ed. Jennifer Guglielmo and Salvatore Salerno (New York: Routledge, 2003).

7. Charlie LaRocca interview, Birmingfind. During the late nineteenth century, in particular, Italians who went abroad were primarily "unskilled peasants and workers, the pettiest of street traders, or owners of the tiniest parcels of land." Gabaccia, *"Gil italiani nel mondo,"* 12–16.

8. Jackson, *Dixie's Italians,* 5, notes that while Sicilians only numbered about one-fourth of the Italians who went to the United States, up to 90 percent of those who went to the South were Sicilians.

9. Gabaccia, *"Gil italiani nel Mondo,"* 12–16; Gabaccia, *Italy's Many Diasporas,* 75.

10. Italian Immigrants, Research Notes, Birmingfind. See also Jackson, "Reconsidering the Experience of Italians," 326–328.

11. Rose Maenza interview, Birmingfind.

12. Paul Lorina interview, Birmingfind.

13. Charlie LaRocca interview, Birmingfind.

14. Francis and Nellie Saia interview, Birmingfind.

15. On the Italian field workers of Louisiana, see Scarpaci, *Italian Immigrants in Louisiana's Sugar Parishes;* Luconi, "Lynching of Southern Europeans"; and Jackson, *Dixie's Italians.*

16. Although it clearly did exist, notes Letwin, "racial separation was not so pervasive at the mines themselves . . . to a remarkable degree, black and white miners worked in the same mines on equal terms," though not necessarily in the same occupations or at the same wage levels. Still, "this proximity below ground stood in marked contrast to the racial separation that characterized community life above ground." Letwin, *Challenge of Interracial Unionism,* 40.

17. For episodes of prejudice and discrimination recounted by Birmingham's Italian immigrants, see Francis Oddo, Rose Maenza, Paul Lorina, and Charlie LaRocca interviews, Birmingfind.

18. Mrs. Argentina Morganti interview, Birmingfind.

19. Paul Lorina interview, Birmingfind.

20. According to Nystrom, *Creole Italian,* 136–137, Sicilians who came to New Orleans in the nineteenth and early twentieth centuries often worked as fruit peddlers on the street to accumulate savings sufficient to open brick-and-mortar groceries. Bald, *Bengali Harlem,* 49–93, notes a similar role played by Bengali peddlers in New Orleans. Although Italians appear in the newspapers more frequently, other immigrant peddlers in the Birmingham District and other communities in Alabama included Greeks, Syrians, and Eastern Europeans/Russians. See, for example, Nancy Faires Conklin and Nora Faires, "'Colored' and Catholic: The Lebanese in Birmingham, Alabama," in *Crossing the Waters: Arabic-Speaking Immigrants to the United States before 1940,* ed. Eric J. Hooglund (Washington, DC: Smithsonian Institution Press, 1987), 69–73, 77–80.

21. See *Birmingham News,* November 4, 8, December 5, 1899; January 6, 16, December 20, 1902; January 13, 1903; December 28, 1906; October 29, 1908; and June 24, 1909. Such conflicts continued in the district throughout the New South era.

22. Francis Odda, Charlie LaRocca interviews, Birmingfind.

23. *Memphis Daily Appeal,* January 1, 1865.

24. Moreover, he added, "I am glad to say that the Negro has never joined anarchy and I hope he never will." *Marion Herald* (Alabama), October 16, 1886.

25. *Marion Herald* (Alabama), October 16, 1886.

26. T. G. Fowler to Oscar Underwood, undated but in with documents from 1906, box 36, folder 5, Underwood Papers.

27. Booker T. Washington to Oswald Garrison Villard, August 7, 1910, in *Booker T. Washington Papers,* vol. 3, ed. Louis R. Harlan (Urbana: University of Illinois Press, 1974), 363–364; Booker T. Washington to editor of *New York World,* January 2, 1915, in Harlan, *Booker T. Washington Papers,* 209–210. See also Shankman, *Ambivalent Friends,* 89–91.

28. *Birmingham News,* April 16, 1897. Vincenza Scarpaci found that some Italians who managed to leave fieldwork obtained "colored" saloon licenses, operating them with an Italian and Black customer base. Scarpaci, "Walking the Color Line: Italian-Americans in Rural Louisiana, 1880–1910," in *Are Italians White? How Race Is Made in America,* ed. Jennifer Guglielmo and Salvatore Salerno (New York: Routledge, 2003), 70–71.

29. *Birmingham News,* March 8, 1901.

30. *Birmingham News,* December 28, 1906.

31. *Union-Banner* (Clanton, AL), December 18, 1902.

32. In rural Black Belt Alabama, concludes Mary Ellen Curtin, "the most bitter economic conflicts centered around access to markets, particularly informal stores known as 'deadfalls.'" Curtin, *Black Prisoners and Their World,* 8, 40, 45, 49, 50–55.

33. The appearance of immigrant peddlers, and eventually groceries, competing with U.S.-born proprietors also provoked reactions from established business owners. As the commercial sector developed in the Birmingham industrial district, for example, so too did conflict between immigrant and American proprietors over spotty enforcement of blue laws, prohibition, and so forth. See, for example, the documents in the folder entitled "Fruit Stand Controversy," 809.2.2.1.26, Birmingfind. Also see *Birmingham News,* July 23, 1906.

34. *Montgomery Advertiser,* September 23, 1910. A similar incident took place in Montgomery a few years later, this time involving a Russian-Polish immigrant and an African American man, both driving wagons along Court and Coosa Streets. Robert Wilson's wagon accidentally collided with Isadore Meyer Bauman's fruit wagon, knocking a "small chunk of wood" from Bauman's wagon and reportedly enraging the vendor. "Infuriated at having his wagon hurt," reported the *Montgomery Times,* Bauman then "ran three squares to summon Officer Norman" in order to "have Wilson arrested." Officer Norman complied, but arrested and charged both men with "a case of collision." *Montgomery Times,* July 7, 1914. The record does not indicate how this turned out for Wilson, though Bauman remained a longtime fruit peddler in Montgomery until his death in 1946. Census records for Bauman identify him as a Russian-Polish immigrant, not Italian as was claimed in the newspaper article. He arrived in the United States in 1901 and was married to Austrian Rosie Schwartz Bauman. In census records, city directories, and the U.S. World War I draft registration records, Bauman is listed as a self-employed fruit peddler. See "Isadore M. Bauman," U.S. City Directories, 1822–1995; "Isidore Meyer Bauman," U.S. World War I Draft Registration Cards, 1917–1918; "Isadore M. Bauman," U.S. Federal Census, 1920, Ancestry.com.

35. Richard Straw locates the largest Italian presence in Birmingham in the mining communities of Ensley, where about five thousand Italian miners and their families lived, and in

Pratt City. By the early twentieth century, Italians constituted the third largest immigrant group across the district, according to Straw. The 1910 census, however, shows Italians as the single largest foreign-born nationality residing in each of Bibb, Jefferson, Shelby, Sinclair, and Walker counties. Straw, "This Is Not a Strike, It Is Simply a Revolution": Birmingham Miners Struggle for Power, 1894–1908" (PhD diss., University of Missouri–Columbia, 1980), 175; U.S. Federal Census, 1910, Ancestry.com.

36. *Dothan Eagle,* February 2, 1912; *Gadsden Daily Times* (Alabama), January 29, 1912; *Tuscaloosa News* (Alabama), January 29, 1912. On the history of Bessemer, see Lewis, *Sloss Furnaces,* 141–143.

37. *Tuscaloosa News* (Alabama), January 30, 1912.

38. *Gadsden Daily Times* (Alabama), January 29, 1912; *Tuscaloosa News* (Alabama), January 29, 1912.

39. *Tuscaloosa News* (Alabama), January 30, 1912.

40. *Montgomery Advertiser,* January 31, 1912.

41. *Montgomery Times,* February 8, 1912.

42. *Greene County Democrat* (Eutaw, AL), February 16, 1912.

43. *Montgomery Times,* March 12, 1912; *Montgomery Advertiser,* March 17, 1912.

44. A few other such incidents, albeit on a much smaller scale, occurred against Italians in other southern communities, including in Mississippi. The most recent interpretation of these lynchings notes that extreme racialization of Italian immigrants occurred *after* these events rather than preceding them. Even as xenophobic stereotypes of southern Italians as an "undesirable" sort of immigrant circulated throughout the United States, including in New South communities, their value as agricultural labor also could temper those sentiments. However, with a "transient" racial identity, Italians also lived in a state of racial instability that proved highly unpredictable. Thus, "Sicilians and other Italians passed among and between racial communities; they moved (and were moved) across as both 'white southerners' and 'people of color' back and forth across the color line." They could be "lynched in defense of 'white supremacy' but also possessed 'unconquerable white blood.'" They could exercise voting rights "as 'good citizens,' and 'foreign whites,' but were still. . . . a 'colony of vicious murderers and assassins.'" See Jackson, *Dixie's Italians,* 8.

45. Operators passed that reduction on to the miners in the form of a wage cut, from eighty cents to seventy or even sixty-five cents per ton. See *Montgomery Advertiser,* May 17, 1884; Letwin, *Challenge of Interracial Unionism,* 73.

46. Warrior was one of the three most significant coalfields in the Birmingham District, and "the largest and most heavily prized." Warrior grew quickly into one of the larger mining towns in Jefferson County in the boom years of the 1880s, comprising several thousand inhabitants. Warrior also had an early union presence through the organization of locals for the Greenback Labor Party, the Knights of Labor, and eventually the United Mine Workers. Letwin interprets the Warrior Coal incident as evidence of the growing solidarity among U.S.-born Black and white miners, who worked together to protest the Italian presence. He cites the Warrior strike as an unusual occurrence in which, at least in the Birmingham coal district, Black and white miners in the Knights of Labor drew a clear distinction between *their* type of labor and that

of the *other* type. What was notable in this case, Letwin argues, is that this line was drawn not between Black and white but between Alabama's U.S.-born miners and immigrant laborers. See Letwin, *Challenge of Interracial Unionism,* 10, 32, 69, 73–75, 206 note 2. Also see Matthew Hild, *Greenbackers, Knights of Labor, and Populists: Farmer-Labor Insurgency in the Late-Nineteenth-Century South* (Athens: University of Georgia Press, 2007), 53; Day, *Diamonds in the Rough;* Lewis, *Sloss Furnaces.*

47. *Montgomery Advertiser,* May 22, August 24, 1884.

48. Letwin, *Challenge of Interracial Unionism* describes these men as arriving from New York and being "virtually all unattached, inexperienced in mining, and unfamiliar with English" (73).

49. *Montgomery Advertiser,* August 28, 1884.

50. *Anniston Hot Blast* (Alabama), August 30, 1884.

51. *Montgomery Advertiser,* August 31, 1884.

52. *Montgomery Advertiser,* September 2, 1884.

53. *Montgomery Advertiser,* September 2, 1884. Straw and Letwin each note the ongoing presence of both French and German immigrants in the district, along with Italians and others. The African American *Huntsville Gazette,* September 13, 1884, typically unsympathetic to strikes or organized labor, blamed this strike on a company "composed of Northern capitalists," whereas the "old companies," rooted in southern tradition, "refused to join this war on the laborers." See Straw, "This Is Not a Strike," 17, 173; and Letwin, *Challenge of Interracial Unionism,* 23–25.

54. *Montgomery Advertiser,* September 11, 1884. Also cited in Letwin, *Challenge of Interracial Unionism,* 73–74.

55. A passing farmer noticed the support timbers of the trestle burning and alerted authorities, who extinguished the fire before significant damage occurred. *Montgomery Advertiser,* September 11, 1884.

56. *Columbia Recorder* (Alabama), October 10, 1884.

57. At least some Italians "who were sent up from the Warrior coal mines" still resided in Decatur in mid-October, now truly "destitute" and left to their own devices. *Troy Messenger* (Alabama), October 16, 1884.

58. *Montgomery Advertiser,* January 1, 1885; *Times and News* (Alabama), January 13, 1885.

59. *Shelby Chronicle* (Columbiana, AL), August 20, 1885. Letwin, *Challenge of Interracial Unionism,* 73–75, states that these men came directly to Warrior from Italy, with their passage paid by the Warrior Coal Company. However, accounts conflict as to their origins.

60. *Huntsville Gazette,* August 22, 1885.

61. Letwin argues that the strikers somehow "prevailed" on local officials to arrest the men on weapons charges, but he does not explain why they would choose to do so. See Letwin, *Challenge of Interracial Unionism,* 74, 146–147. Most accounts of southern labor conflicts in this era assign much of the responsibility for strike violence to county sheriffs and their deputies, either through instigating incidents with strikers in order to arrest them or through turning a blind eye to violence perpetrated by the coal operators' hired thugs or by Pinkerton "detectives." Certainly, that perspective is often validated in union sources, such as the *United Mine Workers Journal,* which reported on violence against striking miners and conflict with deputies in great detail. See, for example, *United Mine Workers Journal,* July 30, August 15, 20, 1908.

62. *Weekly Advertiser* (Montgomery, AL), August 25, 1885.

63. *Huntsville Gazette,* August 22, 1885.

64. *Montgomery Advertiser,* September 3, 1885.

65. *Morning Mercury* (Hunstville, AL), September 11, 1885; *Gadsden Times-News* (Alabama), September 18, 1885.

66. See, for example, Letwin, *Challenge of Interracial Unionism,* 23–26, 143; Kelly, *Race, Class, and Power in the Alabama Coal Fields,* 38–43; and Straw, "This Is Not a Strike," 172–181.

67. Italian, Hungarian, and Irish immigrants, for example, are mentioned in Green, *Devil Is Here in These Hills,* 28–29, 38–39, 78. Also see William P. Jones, *The Tribe of Black Ulysses: American Lumber Workers in the Jim Crow South* (Urbana: University of Illinois Press, 2005), 23–24.

4. "A FEW DEPRAVED WHITE MEN AND THE WORST ELEMENT OF NEGROES": IMMIGRANTS, AFRICAN AMERICANS, AND THE BIRMINGHAM STRIKES

1. "Jean Rien (Rieu)," New York, U.S. Arriving Passenger and Crew Lists (including Castle Garden and Ellis Island), 1820–1957, Ancestry.com; *New York Tribune,* December 22, 1888, 8; *Birmingham News,* February 14, 1896.

2. *Daily News* (Birmingham), July 26, 1894.

3. *Herald-Journal* (Bessemer), April 19, 26, May 3, 1894.

4. Letwin, *Challenge of Interracial Unionism,* 23–26, 143; Straw "This Is Not a Strike," 172–181. As shown in newspaper accounts and in Letwin, immigrants clearly were in the district during the 1894 strike; however, Letwin does not engage with their presence in relation to his exploration of interracialism. Letwin, *Challenge of Interracial Unionism,* 114. Straw mentions immigrants involved in the 1890s labor conflicts but not in significant detail. Straw, "This Is Not a Strike," 13, 17–18, 22.

5. *Herald-Journal,* May 3, 1894. Also see Straw, "This Is Not a Strike," 189; Letwin, *Challenge of Interracial Unionism,* 116, 135.

6. Robert D. Ward and William Warren Rogers, *Labor Revolt in Alabama: The Great Strike of 1894* (Tuscaloosa: University of Alabama Press, 1965), 68–69, 73, 88–89.

7. Ward and Rogers, *Labor Revolt in Alabama,* 69, 76, 78, 82–83, 89–90, 95–96, 103.

8. The sympathetic editor of Bessemer, Alabama's, *Herald-Journal* remarked on the miners' "starvation" wages, blamed the operators for attempting to reduce them further, and concluded, "If there ever was a justifiable excuse for men refusing to work and starve at the same time, then these miners have good reasons for their action, even though they may lose in the end." *Herald-Journal,* April 19, 26, 1894.

9. *Montgomery Advertiser,* July 17, 1894; Ward and Rogers, *Labor Revolt in Alabama,* 103–117.

10. *Montgomery Advertiser,* July 17, 19, 1894; *Daily News* (Birmingham), July 17, 1894.

11. *Daily News* (Birmingham), July 17, 1894; *Citizen-Examiner* (Hayneville, AL), July 26, 1894.

12. *Daily News* (Birmingham), July 17, 1894.

13. *Times and News* (Eufaula), July 26, 1894; *Jacksonville Republican,* July 21, 1894. Also cited in Ward and Rogers, *Labor Revolt in Alabama,* 112.

14. *Daily News* (Birmingham), July 26, 1894.

15. Jacobsen, *Barbarian Virtues,* 88–97.

16. *Daily News* (Birmingham), July 26, 1894.

17. *Daily News* (Birmingham), July 26, 1894.

18. Ward and Rogers, *Labor Revolt in Alabama,* 136.

19. *Birmingham News,* September 23, 1894; January 13, 1895; February 3, 4, 1895.

20. *Daily News* (Birmingham), August 23, 1894.

21. *Birmingham News,* September 23, 1894.

22. *Birmingham News,* February 4, 5, 7, November 9, 1895; February 14, 15, 1896.

23. The county coroner concluded that Regis ultimately died of an enlarged brain. See *Birmingham News,* February 14, 15, 1896.

24. Clark et al., *Who Built America?,* 130–134.

25. Straw, "This Is Not a Strike," 58–59, 174–175, mentions the importation of immigrant laborers by operators as one reason for the UMW's failed strike of 1904 to 1906. He also notes operators' complaints of labor scarcity in the "boom times" of the early 1900s and the push to recruit immigrants as a result.

26. Kelly, *Race, Class, and Power,* 38–40, citing *Birmingham Herald,* January 28, 1907.

27. Immigrant laborers moved around within the United States, back and forth to their home countries, and sometimes between the United States and Mexico and South American countries. Such mobility, as with African Americans in the New South, renders pinning down exact numbers residing in Alabama a difficult, if not impossible, task. The *Birmingham News* reported in 1908, for example, "the departure from the Birmingham district of forty-five Greeks and as many Italians en route to their old countries" as well as the arrival of "200 hundred Italians" aiming to reside at Ensley. "Half of the Italians coming back were once residents of that section, but when the financial depression came on several months ago went back to their home." Now, however, "it is their intention to take up permanent homes in the South, and many new immigrants will arrive here in the next few months with some of the former residents." *Birmingham News,* March 5, 1908. Also see "Italians Are Coming Back," *Jones Valley Times,* March 5, 1908; *Birmingham News,* February 4, 1908.

28. Letwin, *Challenge of Interracial Unionism,* 23–25, 201–202 note 33.

29. Letwin, *Challenge of Interracial Unionism,* 23

30. Letwin, *Challenge of Interracial Unionism,* 23–25, 201–202 note 33. Straw, "This Is Not a Strike," 173, argues that the 1910 census indicated that first- or second-generation immigrants made up about 25 percent of white workers in the district's manufacturing and mechanical industries and 50 percent in the iron and steel industries.

31. In every labor conflict in the district, "time . . . was on the operators' side. A steady flow of strikebreakers, primarily black although increasingly of southern and eastern European extraction as well, arrived from around the country and abroad." Letwin, *Challenge of Interracial Unionism,* 143.

32. *Birmingham Times,* August 28, 1903. For an overall account of the 1904–1906 United Mine Workers strike, see Letwin, *Challenge of Interracial Unionism,* 140–145.

33. *Mountain Eagle* (Jasper, AL), June 8, 1904; *Montgomery Advertiser,* June 11, July 2, 6, 10, 1904.

34. *Montgomery Advertiser,* July 13, 17, 19, July 26, 1904.

35. The 1900 federal population census, for example, listed for Jefferson County alone almost 2,000 Italians, more than 800 Germans, more than 1,000 English, 688 Scots, 254 Turks (or Syrians), and so on. U.S. Federal Census, 1900, Ancestry.com. Also see Kelly, *Race, Class, and Power,* 38–40; Straw, "This Is Not a Strike," 58–59, 174–175; Letwin, *Challenge of Interracial Unionism,* 23–27, 73–75, 143, 145.

36. The difficulty of pinning down the exact numbers of each immigrant group at work in the Birmingham District's communities over time makes it impossible to definitively establish the demographics of immigrant populations with precision. Rough census figures as well as other evidence suggest that the immigrant population shifted over time, from mostly northwestern European and British Isles immigrants to Southern and Eastern Europeans. A much greater diversity of immigrants, drawn from multiple continents, resided in the district, however. As some of the larger groups working in the district in the late nineteenth and early twentieth centuries, Italian, Slavic, and Austro-Hungarian nationalities appear most often in newspaper accounts and other records documenting Alabama's labor conflicts. For a sense of how immigrant groups clustered together throughout the district, see White, *Birmingham District.*

37. *Birmingham News,* August 8, 1904; *Montgomery Advertiser,* August 8, 10–11, 1904.

38. *Montgomery Advertiser,* August 11, 1904.

39. Steve Slovensky interview, Birmingfind.

40. *Montgomery Advertiser,* August 17, 1904; *Birmingham News,* August 16, 1904; *Birmingham Times,* September 16, 1904.

41. *Montgomery Advertiser,* September 15, 1904.

42. By the end of the month, however, the UMW's District 20 leader, Ed Flynn, was forced to argue that striking miners were *not* returning to work, in the belief that the strike was lost. See *Montgomery Advertiser,* October 2, 26, 1904. The national identities of these men are not apparent in the records.

43. *Montgomery Advertiser,* October 27, 1904; Letwin, *Challenge of Interracial Unionism,* 143.

44. *Mountain Eagle* (Jasper, AL), November 23, 1904; *Birmingham Times,* December 9, 1904; Letwin, *Challenge of Interracial Unionism,* 143–145.

45. Letwin interprets the 1904–1906 strike largely in the context of the strength of interracialism within the union and in the strikers' ranks that enabled them to withstand operators' assaults and the broader pressures of the Jim Crow context. He notes, though, that the UMW lost the strike, and in the aftermath the "miners' situation looked grim," with blacklistings and outmigrations. Moreover, "the mines now were worked largely by newcomers, many freshly arrived from other lands, who had come as strikebreakers." Letwin, *Challenge of Interracial Unionism,* 145.

46. *Monroe Journal* (Claiborne, AL), May 11, 1905.

47. *Jones Valley Times* (Birmingham, AL), December 7, 1905.

48. *Jones Valley Times* (Birmingham, AL), July 19, 1906.

49. *Pine Belt News* (Brewton, AL), August 16, 1906.

50. *Elba Clipper* (Alabama), July 2, 1907; *Coosa River News* (Centre, AL), July 5, 1907.

51. *Birmingham News,* September 20, 1906.

52. *Birmingham News,* August 15, 1907. Sometimes immigrant Christians attended Catholic, Greek Orthodox, or Russian Orthodox congregations together, despite nationality and religious divisions, since their smaller numbers often prevented erecting multiple buildings and so on. Over time, communities established their own institutions, such as Saint Joseph's Catholic Church in Birmingham's "Little Italy" and Saint Nicolas Russian Orthodox Church of Brookside. See White, *Birmingham District,* 278–279.

53. *Birmingham News,* December 18, 1907.

54. See, for example, Stephen Norwood, *Strikebreaking and Intimidation: Mercenaries and Masculinity in Twentieth-Century America* (Chapel Hill: University of North Carolina Press, 2002), 82, 87, 91–92, 109, 114–115, 118–119, 129–130, 136, 145–149.

55. *Montgomery Advertiser,* July 7, 1908; *United Miner Workers Journal,* July 9, 16, 1908. Letwin, *Challenge of Interracial Unionism,* 148–151, spends surprisingly little time on the 1908 conflict. Kelly, *Race, Class, and Power,* 17–25, devotes more pages and analysis to the strike but does not consider in any detail the pivotal role of immigrants prior to or during the 1908 strike. He argues that operators did not turn significantly toward importing foreign-born labor until *after* the UMW defeat in 1908 (37–39).

56. *Birmingham News,* July 13, 1908.

57. Straw, "This Is Not a Strike," 13, 17, 22, 58–60, 74, 113–114, 128, identifies imported foreign-born laborers on both sides of the district's labor conflicts in 1908.

58. *United Mine Workers Journal,* July 25, 1908; *Montgomery Advertiser,* July 7, 19, 1908; Letwin, *Challenge of Interracial Unionism,* 145–146, describes the 1908 strike as the UMW's "last stand" in the district.

59. *Birmingham News,* July 14, 1908.

60. On local law enforcement and the 1908 strike, see, for example, Letwin, *Challenge of Interracial Unionism,* 146–147.

61. Chief Deputy Sheriff Lucien Brown to Adjutant General Bibb Graves, Birmingham, July 15, 1908, folder: July 15–31, 1908, Adjutant General Papers, Administrative Files, 1905–1908, SG15234, ADAH (hereinafter cited as Adjutant General Papers). *Montgomery Advertiser,* July 19, 1908, reported that Tennessee Coal, Iron and Railroad brought in a Gatling gun and aimed it at strikers' camps at Blossburg.

62. *United Mine Workers Journal,* July 30, 1908.

63. *Montgomery Advertiser,* July 21, 1908.

64. Straw, "This Is Not a Strike," 119, citing *Birmingham News,* August 14, 1908.

65. *Montgomery Advertiser,* July 21, 1908. *United Mine Workers Journal* ran prominent advertisements warning union members to "Stay Away from Alabama." See *United Mine Workers Journal,* August 15, 1908.

66. *Montgomery Advertiser,* July 21, 1908.

67. Slovak resident Steve Slovensky recalled Republic as "a big mining town," where "some of the fellows around Brookside, when they were out of strike . . . would go to these towns and try to get them on strike. They had several gunfights and battles. Several of them got killed." Slovensky was unsure of the exact year, suggesting it might have been 1912; however, he more

likely remembered hearing about the events of the dramatic strike year of 1908. Slovensky interview, Birmingfind.

68. At least one Black miner, a man named Allen Dennis, died. Several deputy sheriffs were arrested on July 20, 1908, for Dennis's murder. *Montgomery Advertiser,* July 20, 1908.

69. In October 1908, the Jefferson County grand jury returned four indictments for the "alleged murder [that] is said to have taken place during the coal miners strike," including for two men named Fra[nk] and Sam Tombrella. See *Birmingham News,* July 17, 21, October 9, 1908. According to available records, Mitno Baratka was born in 1889 in Hewig, Austria-Hungary, and identified as Slovak. He arrived in the United States in the fall of 1907 at New York but lived in Birmingham by the time of the strike of 1908, where he was working in the coal mines. His World War I draft registration card of 1917 lists him as still a coal miner in Republic in the Birmingham District, though now married with four children. See "Metra Baratka," Alabama, Naturalization Records, 1888–1941; and "Metra Baratka, [Mintro Brathka]," U.S., World War I Draft Registration Cards, 1917–18; "Mitno Baratka," U.S. Federal Census, 1920, Ancestry.com.

70. *Montgomery Advertiser,* July 19, 1908.

71. Straw, "This Is Not a Strike," 128, citing a letter to the editor from organizer Duncan McDonald in *United Mine Workers Journal,* September 3, 1908.

72. *United Mine Workers Journal,* July 30, 1908.

73. *Elba Clipper* (Alabama), July 24, 1908.

74. *Montgomery Advertiser,* July 21, 1908.

75. *Union-Banner,* July 23, 1908.

76. *Montgomery Advertiser,* July 24, 1908.

77. *Montgomery Advertiser,* July 28, 1908.

78. During the 1904–1906 strike, operators put numerous immigrants into the Blocton mines. See for example, "Miro Curovich," manuscript schedule, Bibb County, Alabama, U.S. Federal Census, 1910, sheet 5, Ancestry.com, which lists as coal miners multiple Montenegrins and Bulgarians, among other nationalities.

79. *United Mine Workers Journal,* July 30, 1908.

80. The account names a Geo. Mancon as the interpreter. See *Blocton Enterprise* (Alabama), July 30, 1908.

81. *Blocton Enterprise* (Alabama), July 30, 1908.

82. *United Mine Workers Journal,* August 15, 1908.

83. *Montgomery Advertiser,* August 3, 1908.

84. Eventually, officials arrested for the crime two men who were reported to be either special deputies or on the company payroll, or both. *Birmingham News,* August 5, 1908; *Montgomery Advertiser,* August 6, 1908; Kelly, *Race, Class, and Power,* 23, 126.

85. *Montgomery Advertiser,* August 6, 1908.

86. *Birmingham News,* August 5, 1908. John Hughico appears to have been born in Hungary around 1869, and he arrived in New York City in the spring of 1905. By the spring of 1908, Hughico was married and living in Birmingham, where he declared for naturalization. In 1914, he applied for a U.S. passport from Birmingham. See "John Huhko," Alabama, Naturalization Records, 1888–1991; and "John Huhko," U.S. Passport Applications, 1725–1925, Ancestry.com.

87. *Montgomery Advertiser*, August 6, 1908. Also cited in Straw, "This Is Not a Strike," 119, 143. Jackson, *Dixie's Italians*, 5, identifies New Orleans as the main poin of entry for Italians who ended up in the Gulf South.

88. Straw, "This Is Not a Strike," 116–117, notes that strikers routinely packed the train depots throughout the district to prevent replacement workers from traveling to the mining communities. Multiple newspapers reported the same, as train cars and wagons brought these men for dispersal to key points in the district's mines and furnaces. See, for example, *Birmingham News*, August 3, 1908.

89. *Gadsden Daily Times*, August 10, 1908. Straw, "This Is Not a Strike" concludes that the train ambushes "accounted for the most dramatic scenes of violence during the strike" (122), although he does not examine either in much detail. These events are scarcely mentioned at all in other accounts of the 1908 strike. Letwin, *Challenge of Interracial Unionism* does not address the Blocton train ambush. It does get passing mention in Kelly, *Race, Class, and Power*, 20, who gives it precisely one sentence. Other sources that mention the event without describing it or interpreting it include Day, *Diamonds in the Rough*, 143, 193; Charles Edward Adams, *Blocton: The History of an Alabama Coal Mining Town* (Brierfield, AL: Cahaba Trace Commission, 2001), 99–100; Rhonda Coleman Ellison, *Bibb County, Alabama: The First Hundred Years, 1818–1918* (Tuscaloosa: University of Alabama Press, 1984), 176–177; Wayne Flynt, *Poor but Proud: Alabama's Poor Whites* (Tuscaloosa: University of Alabama Press, 1989), 140–141.

90. *Morning Mercury* (Huntsville, AL), August 11, 1908.

91. *Blocton Enterprise* (Alabama), August 13, 1908.

92. *Gadsden Daily Times* (Alabama), August 10, 1908.

93. *Centreville Press* (Alabama), August 13, 1908.

94. *Morning Mercury* (Huntsville, AL), August 11, 1908; *Blocton Enterprise* (Alabama), August, 13, 1908; *Gadsden Daily Times* (Alabama), August 10, 1908; *Centreville Press* (Alabama), August 13, 1908. Also see William H. Worger, "Industrialists and the State in the U.S. South and South Africa, 1870–1930," *Journal of Southern African Studies* 30, no. 1 (March 2004): 63–86.

95. The writer also claimed that "the native miners and the better class of negroes deplore the tragedy." *Birmingham News*, August 10, 1908.

96. *Blocton Enterprise* (Alabama), August 13, 1908.

97. *Gadsden Daily Times* (Alabama), August 10, 1908. Nor were these the first "Slavs" arrested for actions against mine operations. Local police arrested three men in 1907 for "soaping" railroad tracks, but later released them as wrongly charged. See *Birmingham News*, June 3, 1907.

98. Both the prosecuting and defense attorneys at Wasilije Wainovich's trial agreed with Bose Durkovich's account of being struck by Bibb County Sheriff Oakley when being arrested and of having several revolvers placed against his head to extract his information. *Montgomery Advertiser*, September 10, 1908; *Blocton Enterprise* (Alabama), August 13, 1908.

99. Gov. B. B. Comer to W. E. Fort, private secretary, Birmingham, August 10, 1908, folder: July–August 1908, reel 10, SG028325, Governor Comer Papers, Administrative Files, ADAH (hereinafter cited as Governor Comer Papers).

100. *Blocton Enterprise* (Alabama), August 13, 1908; *Gadsden Daily Times* (Alabama), August 10, 1908.

101. *Montgomery Advertiser,* August 15, 1908.

102. *Montgomery Advertiser,* August 14, 1908. Eventually, union officials such as Fairley floated the notion that operators and their allies actually had set up the ambush to discredit the strikers and the UWM. UMW vice president John P. White, who took over leadership of the strike from Fairley after the ambush occurred, claimed in the *Journal* that operators had known an ambush by strikers had been planned and had changed the train's route into Blocton accordingly. That the train ended up ambushed anyway raised questions for White, who wondered how the strikers would have known of the change in plans. His inference, of course, was that operators had set up the strikers who were arrested for the ambush. What White fails to acknowledge is the likelihood that *both* sides in the strike appear to have had informants who passed along information to their respective allies. One informant reported to the strikers that a train full of replacement laborers was headed to Blocton on the night of August 9. Another informant then reported to the operators, deputies, or the state militia that strikers were planning to ambush the train. Operators changed the route into Blocton, and the first informant likely reported back to the strikers that change of plans. The strikers then altered their own ambush plans so they were still able to carry out the assault. That scenario, although uncomfortable for the UMW and District 20 officials, makes much more sense than the operators planning an ambush on their own train, which was carrying not only strikebreakers, deputies, and national guardsmen but also several TCI officials. See *United Mine Workers Journal,* August 27, 1908.

103. *Blocton Enterprise* (Alabama), August 13, 1908.

104. *Montgomery Advertiser,* August 15, 1908.

105. *Montgomery Advertiser,* August 15, 1908. Also see *State v. Popovich,* fall 1908 term, Order Book 230; *State v. Wasile Wogonovich* (Wainovich); September 5, 1908, Order Book 232, 235; *State v. Mileto Popovich,* set for September 10, 1908, and *State v. Mihailo Lazarovich,* set for September 11, 1908, both in Order Book 232; *State v. Miloslav Kriracherich,* fall 1908 Term, and *State v. Karairch,* set for September 15, 1908, both in Order Book 233; *State v. Blagoyich,* set for September 17, 1908; Order Book 234, all in Bibb County Circuit Court Order Books, Administrative Offices of Courts, Montgomery, Alabama.

106. *Montgomery Advertiser,* August 13, 1908. John E. Morris, along with two other men, became an appointed trustee of the Southern Steel Company in the spring of 1908, when the operation went into receivership. See "Industrial," *Engineering and Mining Journal* 85, index, January–June 1908: 518.

107. *Crenshaw County News* (Luverne, AL), August 20, 1908.

108. *Centreville Press* (Alabama), August 13, 1908.

109. Because few accounts mention any details about the African Americans arrested for complicity in the assault, their origins in Birmingham are hard, if not impossible, to discern.

110. *Montgomery Advertiser,* July 19, 20, 22, 31, 1908; *Troy Messenger* (Alabama), July 22, 1908; *Union Banner* (Clanton, AL), July 23, 1908.

111. Adj. Gen. Bibb Graves to Gov. Comer, July 15, 1908, reel 12, Governor Comer Papers.

112. Sheriff J. O. Long, Walker County, to Gov. Comer, July 19, 1908, reel 12, SG028325, Governor Comer Papers.

113. Dep. Sheriff Lucien Brown to Adj. Gen. Bibb Graves, folder: Correspondence, July 1–14, 1908, Adjutant General Papers.

114. *Gadsden Daily Times* (Alabama), August 10, 1908.

115. "The Governor's Proclamation," *Canebrake Herald* (Uniontown, AL), August 13, 1908. Letwin, *Challenge of Interracial Unionism,* 150–152, identifies the "volatile racial climate of 1908" as enabling Governor Comer and local officials to more effectively race-bait the strike into defeat. However, he leaves out the perceived (or actual) immigrant–Black ambush of the train at Blocton as a factor shaping the efficacy of the governor's and the operators' racial strategy.

116. *Montgomery Advertiser,* August 17, 1908.

117. *Montgomery Advertiser,* September 1, 1908; Letwin, *Challenge of Interracial Unionism,* 150–152.

118. *Crenshaw County News* (Luverne, AL), September 10, 1908.

5. "THE LAND OF SNAKES, CROCODILES, NEGROES, YELLOW FEVER, AND DEATH": THE IMMIGRANT EXPERIENCE IN NEW SOUTH ALABAMA

1. The Slavonians so referenced were likely from Slavonia in Croatia. Occupying one of the three historical regions of Croatia, Slavonians had lived under multiple regimes, including the Roman Empire, the Croatian Kingdom, the Ottoman Empire, the Habsburg Empire, and the Kingdom of Hungary. In the wake of World War I, Slavonia was part of the newly formed Yugoslavia.

2. *Selma Times,* June 7, 1903.

3. For a discussion of such arrangements, see Peck, *Reinventing Free Labor.*

4. *Selma Times,* June 7, 9, 1903; *Montgomery Advertiser,* June 9, 1903; *Birmingham News,* June 8, 10, 1903; *Herald-Journal* (Bessemer, AL), June 11, 1903; *South Alabamian* (Jackson), June 13, 1903.

5. Harper and Constantine, *Migration and Empire,* 294, note the importance of local recruiting agents, who competed with one another in China, Europe, and India, among other places, to attract prospective laborers to the colonies of the British Empire. Among their many frustrations was the constant stream of "disinformation" circulated by their rivals.

6. F. S. Mount to Governor Patton, August 10, 1867, reel 25, Governor Patton Papers. Mount also reported that an association of German citizens in Montgomery had been incorporated by the state legislature "for the promotion and protection of German immigrants," which might, he speculated, be willing to "procure and publish an address which would not only be an answer to the article's evilness but contain a succinct summary of the advantages offered by our state to the German people to settle among us." Mount opined that "by printing this in German" and circulating it with other promotional materials, it would be "extensively circulated."

7. J. Watson to Governor Smith, April 27, 1867, folders 4–8, reel 6, Governor Smith Papers.

8. *Memphis Appeal,* June 3, 1871.

9. Paul Stevens to Gov. Smith, October 17, 1870, reel 10, Governor Smith Papers. Stevens, having relocated from the North, found that after three years in Alabama, "we must say that . . . we have never lived among a more peaceful, law-abiding people, a people more chivalrous, generous, and hospitable to strangers, no matter where their birthplace, than this very people,

of much abused and wickedly slandered, Alabama. . . . Again and again, times without number, they extended to us the most cordial welcome, to all genuine *bona fide* settlers, whether of Northern or European birth."

10. G. A. Park to A. R. Smith, December 20, 1905, folder 15, reel 24, Governor Jelks Papers. Park paid a German to get him a copy of one of these maps. He believed a "young" or commissioned person, "zealous" to get his passage to the northwestern United States covered, "may have adopted that means of misrepresentation" because "such unprincipled action would not be condoned, I do not think, by any railroad in the Northwest."

11. C. B. Carter to Underwood, December 29, 1905, folder 3: November 1903, box 8, Underwood Papers.

12. Eliot Norton to Gov. Jelks, 1905, reel 24, Governor Jelks Papers.

13. "Application for Labor," reel 24, Governor Jelks Papers.

14. Ross Smith, "Alabama and Immigration," report of chair of Immigration Committee of Birmingham Commercial Club, to the club, June 11, 1906, Agriculture and Industry records.

15. Frank Evans to Gov. Jelks, September 23, 1906, reel 24, Governor Jelks Papers.

16. In the summer of 1870, for example, Jasper J. Jones of Scottsboro reported that a George N. Steeley had murdered in premeditation a Scottish tanner named Wallace "by knocking him in the head with a billet of wood" and then absconding "as fast as his heels could carry him." Jasper J. Jones, July 22, 1870, reel 9, Governor Smith Papers. A few years later, an "armed white Democrat" threatened a German immigrant at a Fourth of July rally near Huntsville, showing off a concealed pistol and yelling, "This is a white man's country, and we don't want none of these radical Dutchmen to talk here." According to one historian, this was enough to scare "many Germans in northern Alabama" away from the polls "out of fear of Democratic reprisals." Cited in Matthew O'Neal, "'The Newspapers Will Invade Their Fireplaces': Politics, the Press, and the End of Reconstruction in Alabama" (master's thesis, Auburn University, 2016), 81. The state commissioner of immigration reported to the governor in 1878, "It is well known that statements prejudicial to the introduction of immigrants into Alabama are prevalent, and it is equally well known that Alabama has never taken any measure to remove this unfounded prejudice." See "To His Excellency, October 1, 1878," Report of the Commissioner of Immigration of the State of Alabama, November 1878, Agriculture and Industry records, 7. In another report to the state legislature, in 1886, the commissioner noted that despite distributing five thousand pamphlets on the state's agricultural and industrial resources and answering "extensive correspondence with individuals," he still had not received the response anticipated, "the parties seeming to be repelled by the absence of good roads, and of a more generously supported system of Public Schools." Report of the Commissioner of Agriculture of the State of Alabama, September 1, 1883–September 1, 1886, Agriculture and Industry records. The *Cullman Immigrant,* the local daily for the small German immigrant colony established in north Alabama in 1873, indignantly denied a "big cock and bull story" in a Kentucky newspaper in 1881 about a fight between "Germans and Americans" that disrupted the local court session. However, the daily had to admit that a fight *did* occur, although it was allegedly confined to only two Germans and an "American from Morgan County," and "no pistols or knives" were used and "no serious damage was done." *Shelby Sentinel* (Calera and Columbiana, AL), December 8, 1881, reprinted

from *Cullman Immigrant* (Alabama); Lauren Wiygul, "Cullman," *Encyclopedia of Alabama,* https://encyclopediaofalabama.org/article/h-2122.

17. Gridland actually sent this inquiry after he apparently received no response to his earlier message to the governor seeking information regarding Bailey's case. Mr. Gridland, British Consul, Mobile, to Gov. William Smith, June 1, 17, 1870, both in reel 9, folder 24, Governor Smith Papers.

18. "Henry Bailey," U.S. Federal Census, 1870, Ancestry.com.

19. In the spring of 1869, Secretary of State Hamilton Fish found himself addressing Alabama Governor Smith regarding "outrages" against a British citizen: "This department has received a communication from Mr. Thornton, the British minister here, complaining of outrages committed by an illegal organization known as the 'Ku Klux Klan' upon one James D. Weir, a British subject temporarily residing at Stevenson, Alabama." Fish never specified exactly what happened to Weir. He did explain, however, that "upon an investigation being made by the local United States Military Authorities, it is found that the outrages were actually committed" due to no known provocation on Weir's part beyond the simple fact that he "was a foreigner, and not identified with the people of the particular class represented by those engaged in this unlawful proceeding." Since Alabama no longer fell under U.S. "military jurisdiction," Fish had therefore contacted Governor Smith, as "it is hoped that your Excellency will cause proper steps to be taken to bring the offenders to justice," and especially "to protect Mr. Weir and others who may be similarly situated against injuries of the character complained of." See Secretary of State Hamilton Fish to Governor William Smith, April 22, 1869, folders 4–8, reel 6, Governor Smith Papers.

20. H. C. Bailey to F. J. Gridland, British Consul, Mobile, May 26, 1870; and F. J. Gridland to Gov. Smith, June 1, 1870, both in reel 9, folder 24, Governor Smith Papers.

21. "Robert Wiederkehr," Passenger Lists, 1812–1963, M259, New Orleans, 1820–1962; and "Robert Wiederkehr," U.S. Passport Applications, 1795–1925, both at Ancestry.com.

22. On immigration to the United States from Switzerland, see Clive H. Church and Randolph C. Head, *A Concise History of Switzerland* (Cambridge: Cambridge University Press, 2013), 175.

23. Although John Dahm is described initially in the *Mobile Daily Register* at the time of the murder as an "industrious and upright man," he is later described as having maintained a household that was remarkably unchurched in Protestant Christianity, or even in Christianity—or in any religion at all. Thus, it is hard to say for sure how Mobile's white and Black citizenry regarded him. See *Mobile Daily Register,* July 3, 1877.

24. *Mobile Daily Register,* June 3, 1877.

25. *Piedmont Post* (Alabama), May 21, 1886; *Montgomery Advertiser,* May 12, 1886.

26. *Mobile Daily Register,* June 3, July 3, 1877; Records of June Term, 1877, case books, Mobile County Circuit Court Books, The Doy Leale McCall Rare Book and Manuscript Library.

27. *Mobile Daily Register,* June 3, 1877.

28. Legal Notices, Swiss Ambassador's Office, A. C. Hueguenin, Swiss Ambassador in Mobile, May 19, 1879; and A. C. Hueguenin et al. to Governor Rufus W. Cobb, August 1879, both in folder

15: Pardon, Parole, and Clemency Files, ALA V88-A745/SG, 6453, reel 26, Governor Cobb Papers, ADAH (hereinafter cited as Governor Cobb papers).

29. A. C. Hueguenin to Gov. Rufus W. Cobb, June 18, 1880, Governor Cobb papers.

30. Robert Wiederkehr to A. C. Huguenin, first letter, Helena, Shelby County, Alabama, April 18, 1880, Governor Cobb papers.

31. *Piedmont Post* (Alabama), May 21, 1886; *Montgomery Advertiser,* May 12, 1886; Blackmon, *Slavery by Another Name,* 52, 56, 70–71, 73, 75–78, 94; Curtin, *Black Prisoners and Their World,* 20, 22, 68–69, 75, 85, 88, 90, 122.

32. Robert Wiederkehr to A. C. Huguenin, second letter, Helena, Shelby County, Alabama, April 18, 1880, Governor Cobb papers.

33. A. C. Huguenin, Mobile, Alabama, to Messrs. Comer and McCurdy, Helena, Shelby County, Alabama, April 20, 1880; and J. W. Comer, Helena, Shelby County, Alabama, to A. C. Huguenin, Mobile, Alabama, May 5, 1880, both in Governor Cobb papers.

34. *Montgomery Advertiser,* May 12, 1886. It is difficult to determine for certain the prevalence of the practice of granting parole or clemency to Alabama's convicts without quantifying such instances via an exhaustive review of thousands of convict records. Such data is beyond the scope of this study. However, both prisons and the convict mines were dangerous placements, due to disease, overwork, the brutal treatment of guards or other prisoners, and the ever-present threat and reality of violence. These conditions are well documented in Curtin, *Black Prisoners and Their World,* for example. Wiederkehr survived his sentence and ended up gaining early release. Hence, he found a luckier outcome, in the end, than many other Alabama convicts.

35. "Robert Joseph Wiederkehr," U.S. Passport Applications, 1725–1925, Ancestry.com. The federal census of 1930 lists a Robert Wiederkehr of Switzerland with the same birth date and birthplace, and as arriving in the United States in 1877, living in Dallas, Texas, in 1930, working as a restaurant dishwasher. U.S. Federal Census, 1930, Ancestry.com.

36. On the reborn "Black codes," see Cohen, *At Freedom's Edge;* Ayers, *Promise of the New South,* 154; and Hahn, *Nation under Our Feet,* 441.

37. Milfred C. Fierce, *Slavery Revisited: Blacks and the Southern Convict Lease System, 1865–1933* (New York: Africana Studies Research Center, Brooklyn College, City University of New York, 1994), 43; Blackmon, *Slavery by Another Name,* 53–54; Curtin, *Black Prisoners and Their World,* 42–62.

38. Pete Daniel, *In the Shadow of Slavery: Peonage in the South* (Urbana: University of Illinois Press, 1972), ix–xi, 10–17, 21–26, 30, 33, 35, 38–41, 43–45, 65–68, 77–80.

39. Daniel, *Shadow of Slavery* notes the increased numbers of immigrant laborers in Alabama in turpentining and railroad construction, though he identifies that trend as only beginning in 1906, when in fact immigrant laborers appeared far earlier. Daniel emphasizes peonage cases that drew national attention, primarily those involving African Americans; however, he does describe a few cases involving immigrant laborers, including the Lockhart timber case, which is also highlighted in Aaron Reynolds, "Inside the Jackson Tract: The Battle over Peonage Labor Camps in Southern Alabama, 1906," *Southern Spaces,* January 21, 2013, https://

southernspaces.org/2013/inside-jackson-tract-battle-over-peonage-labor-camps-southern-alabama-1906.

40. David M. Oshinsky, *"Worse Than Slavery": Parchman Farm and the Ordeal of American Justice* (New York: Free Press, 1996), 76. In this context, southern state governments, both before and after Radical Reconstruction, enacted discriminatory laws, known as the Black codes, to fill jails and prisons with what southern whites defined as a Black "criminal" class. A white man could walk down a country road or along a railroad track unimpeded and uncontested, for example, but a Black man doing the same thing risked arrest under vagrancy statutes. Thus, around 85 percent to 95 percent of the convicts leased in Alabama were African Americans who became embroiled in the New South system of "justice" for a variety of misdemeanor or felony offenses that ranged from petty to serious. See Edward L. Ayers, *Vengeance and Justice: Crime and Punishment in the 19th-Century American South* (New York: Oxford University Press, 1984), 197; and Lewis, *Sloss Furnaces,* 152–153. Scores of historians have explained this criminalization of African Americans, which began with the Reconstruction-era Black codes and then became recodified under the Redeemers and the eventual emergence of Jim Crow. See, for example, Foner, *Reconstruction,* 199–201, 208–209, 215, 225, 244, 257, 372, 519, 593; Nelson, *Steel Drivin' Man,* 41, 52–56, 61–63; Cohen, *At Freedom's Edge,* generally; and Curtin, *Black Prisoners and Their World.*

41. Oshinsky, *"Worse Than Slavery,"* 80.

42. Curtin, *Black Prisoners and Their World,* 67.

43. Curtin, *Black Prisoners and Their World,* 1–2, 6–7, 68, 71, 156, 167.

44. An excellent account of turpentine workers is Catherine Gyllerstom, "2,000 Trees a Day: Work and Life in the American Naval Stores Industry, 1877 to 1940" (PhD diss., Auburn University, 2014).

45. See Lewis, *Sloss Furnaces,* 36, 61–63; Curtin, *Black Prisoners and Their World,* 11, 20, 67–68; Blackmon, *Slavery by Another Name,* 70; Oshinsky, *"Worse Than Slavery,"* 80. B. B. Comer and William McCurdy apparently operated mines on Pratt land, but critics charged in 1883 that they did not operate independently from Pratt Consolidated Coal. See Robert David Ward and William Warren Rogers, *Convicts, Coal, and the Banner Mine Tragedy* (Tuscaloosa: University of Alabama Press, 1987), 36.

46. Curtin, *Black Prisoners and Their World,* 2, 156, 168.

47. Historian Matthew Mancini grimly notes this in his excellent history of the southern convict lease system, *One Dies, Get Another: Convict Leasing in the American South, 1866–1928* (Columbia: University of South Carolina Press, 1996). Also see Lichtenstein, *Twice the Work of Free Labor;* and Talitha Leflouria, *Chained in Silence: Black Women and Convict Labor in the New South* (Chapel Hill: University of North Carolina Press, 2015).

48. Blackmon, *Slavery by Another Name,* 75–78, 94, 135, 271–272. According to Curtin, *Black Prisoners and Their World,* 20–21, 68–69, 84, 91, 166, Alabama convict Ezekiel Archey wrote to Alabama prison inspector Reginald Dawson about the "horrific conditions" in the Eureka mines. For a discussion about Dawson supplying prisoners with paper, pens, and postage, and the literacy level of convicts, see Ward and Rogers, *Convicts, Coal, and the Banner Mine Tragedy;* and Oshinsky, *"Worse Than Slavery,"* 79.

49. Ward and Rogers, *Convicts, Coal, and the Banner Mine Tragedy.*

50. Blackmon, *Slavery by Another Name,* 70–71; Curtin, *Black Prisoners and Their World,* 68–69, and generally.

51. H. H. Hart, *Social Problems in Alabama,* 29, quoted in Frank Tannenbaum, *Darker Phases of the South* (New York: G.P. Putnam's Sons, 1924), 103.

52. Tannenbaum, *Darker Phases of the South,* 83.

53. Ayers, *Vengeance and Justice,* 197; Lewis, *Sloss Furnaces,* 152. In fact, a Polish prisoner named Harman Camiskie murdered Alabama prison warden Ambrose Burrows in 1862 with an ax to the back of the neck. See Brett Derbes, "The Production of Military Supplies at the Alabama State Penitentiary during the Civil War," *Alabama Review* 67, no. 2 (April 2014), 131–160.

54. Curtin, *Black Prisoners and Their World,* 63.

55. S. D. Morgan to Gov. Robert Patton, Montgomery, November 28, 1866, reel 23.

56. Curtin, *Black Prisoners and Their World,* 2.

57. *United Mine Workers Journal,* September 24, 1908.

58. The information on specific immigrant convicts in this section is derived mainly from Alabama Convict Records, 1886–1952; and U.S. Federal Census, 1870, 1880, 1900, 1910, 1920, both accessed via Ancestry.com. Individuals committing felony crimes ended up in the state prison. Misdemeanor crimes ended up in county jails. Both populations supplied the convict lease system. Digitized convict records for Alabama include both state and county records; however, only the state records cover the period of the 1880s through 1920. My sampling uses the state convict records. To glean from these records cases of immigrants imprisoned and leased, I reviewed each digitized volume, choosing to sample by reading every fifth page in each volume and noting whether that page included a convict record of an immigrant prisoner. Even this bare sampling turned up dozens of cases of immigrants incarcerated throughout the period, many of whom ended up leased to the TCI mining operations in Birmingham.

59. "Octo Vogel, white, is charged with horse stealing at Birmingham. He hired a horse from a livery stable in Birmingham and sold it to a negro at Green Pond." *Blount County News Dispatch* (Blountsville, AL), June 30, 1892.

60. Alabama State Convict Records, vol. 1: 1885–1889, 699; and vol. 3: 1889–1895, 1212, 1375, Ancestry.com.

61. Alabama State Convict Records, vol. 6: 1903–1908, 740; and vol. 4: 1895–1899, 575, Ancestry.com.

62. Alabama State Convict Records, vol. 1: 1885–1889, record 952; and vol. 4: 1895–1899, record 235, Ancestry.com.

63. U.S. Federal Census, 1900, Ancestry.com.

64. Marie Laurence Flahaux and Bruno Schoumaker, *Democratic Republic of the Congo: A Migration History Marked by Crises and Restrictions* (Washington, DC: Migration Policy Institute, 2016); Guy Vanthemsche, *Belgium and the Congo, 1885–1980* (Cambridge: Cambridge University Press, 2012), 65.

65. For another example of retaliation by southern white employers against an immigrant labor agent, see the case of an Italian, S. A. Guarina, in Ensley in the Birmingham District. *Birmingham News,* December 5, 1908. Parallel to the story of Richard Strickland is that of "Prince"

Fumu Chechechi, a West African missionary who toured the United States lecturing on the "heathenisms" of his home continent at the time of Strickland's incarceration and thereafter. Their stories intersected when Chechechi included Alabama churches on his tour in 1898. Chechechi ended up visiting Strickland in the Jefferson County jail, likely at the behest of local white sponsors. The ensuing encounter, reported in the *Birmingham News,* allegedly "proved" that Strickland was no native African but rather a scam artist. However, the actual newspaper account casts as much doubt on the writer and on Chechechi's motives as it does on Strickland's claims of being Congolese. Moreover, at the time of his later parole, state newspapers conceded that Strickland appeared to have been telling the truth about his nativity all along. Moreover, Chechechi, who married an Alabama woman around 1901 and lived in Autauga County, Alabama, for several years thereafter, ended up being sued in 1917 by his wife, Pearl Chechechi, for failure to support and for absconding from his marriage and from Alabama. See *Citizens Journal* (Troy, AL), February 26, 1898; *Birmingham News,* June 27, 28, 1898; *Xenia Daily Gazette* (Ohio), September 24, 1903; *Prattville Progress* (Alabama), July 25, 1912, May 24, 1917. Both Chechechis appear in the 1910 Federal Census as residents of Autauga County, with Fumu and both of his parents registered as born in West Africa and his wife's parents listed as Alabama natives. U.S. Federal Census, 1910, Ancestry.com.

66. *Athens Post,* February 5, 1875; *Opelika Times,* January 15, 1880.

67. *Daily News* (Birmingham), February 10, 1892.

68. *Birmingham News,* September 10, 1903.

69. *Montgomery Advertiser,* May 19, 1898. Also see *Roanoke Times,* November 27, 1898, which reported on an anonymous Black man successfully recruiting African Americans in Georgia and Tennessee for emigration to the Congo.

70. *Prattville Progress* (Alabama), June 3, 1898; *Montgomery Advertiser,* May 19, 1898.

71. "Richard Strickland," Alabama State Convict Records, vol. 4: 1895–1899, Ancestry.com.

72. *Weekly Advertiser* (Montgomery, AL), September 28, 1900.

73. David Van Reybrouck, *Congo: The Epic History of a People* (New York: Harper Collins, 2014), 79–96; U.S. Federal Census, 1900, Ancestry.com. Since Richard arrived in the United States in 1893, he may have joined the American missionaries in order to flee the rubber trade, or perhaps the missionaries adopted him as an orphaned child. However, he also may actually have been a labor recruiter for the rubber barons and accompanied the missionaries to the United States as a pretext. Either way, he appears to have avoided the horrific human rights abuses that accompanied the burgeoning rubber trade as it erupted in the 1890s. See John Reader, *Africa: A Biography of the Continent* (New York: Vintage Books, 1999), 543–546.

74. The most notorious and well-known case involved the operators of the Jackson Lumber Company, headquartered in Lockhart, Alabama. See Daniel, *In the Shadow of Slavery,* 87–88, 90; Reynolds, "Inside the Jackson Tract"; Alexander Irvine, "My Life in Peonage, I," *Appleton Magazine* 10 (July 1907): 3–15; *Tuscaloosa News* (Alabama), July 28, 1906; and *Elba Clipper* (Alabama), July 31, 1906.

75. I found no evidence that intervention by a consular official on behalf of an immigrant laborer ever achieved his or her release. State convict records do document frequent evidence

of Black and white prisoners receiving early release (known as "short time") for good behavior, pardons, or clemency, often associated with a prisoner nearing the end of a sentence and/or being too ill to any longer be of much use as a lessee. See Curtin, *Black Prisoners,* 43, 46, 94–95, 109, 153–154, 157.

76. Steve Slovensky interview, Birmingfind.

77. Jung, *Coolies and Cane,* 120.

78. G. A. Park to A. R. Smith, December 20, 1905, folder 15, reel 24, Governor Jelks Papers.

6. "THE SCUM OF THE FOREIGN ELEMENT": THE TRIALS OF THE BLOCTON FOUR

1. Curiously, the same seems to be true of the few historians who mention this episode in the 1908 strike. Those who do note the event offer a similar, brief accounting of the incident, mentioning that "Slavic" immigrants were arrested alongside Black workers in the case. However, few other details of the incident—and no analysis of the role of immigrants in this incident, in the strike generally, or in the trials, or of their apparent cooperation with Black union miners—are addressed. See, for example, Wayne Flynt, *Poor but Proud,* 140–141; Ellison, *Bibb County,* 176–177; and Day, *Diamonds in the Rough,* 141–143. The Blocton ambush and trial may also have gained so much press attention at the time because it came on the heels of other cases involving the maltreatment of immigrant laborers in the deep South, which had gained even more national and international publicity. A federal investigation into peonage practices in southern turpentine and timber camps, for example, occupied headlines in 1906 and eventually resulted in the trial and conviction of the proprietors and foremen of the Jackson Lumber Company, headquartered in Lockhart, Alabama, with operations spread across Alabama, Florida, and Georgia. Several other studies have examined the cases of peonage involving African Americans and European immigrants in the Jackson case, as well as in others, so I have not explored those here. See, for example, Daniel, *In the Shadow of Slavery;* and Reynolds, "Inside the Jackson Tract."

2. *Montgomery Advertiser,* September 10, 1908.

3. Few records of these cases exist aside from what appeared in state and local newspapers. The diligence of curator and researcher Hall Copeland at the Alabama Supreme Court and State Law Library in Montgomery uncovered a docket of cases in Bibb County that listed the Blocton cases, along with the names of the defendants, defense and prosecuting attorneys, and witnesses. Much of this is handwritten, however, rendering it difficult to be certain about the spelling of surnames. See Bibb County Circuit Court Order Books: *State v. Popovich,* fall 1908 term, Order Book 230; *State v. Wasile Wogonovich* (Wainovich); September 5, 1908, Order Book 232, 235; *State v. Mileto Popovich,* set for September 10, 1908, and *State v. Mihailo Lazarovich,* set for September 11, 1908, both in Order Book 232; *State v. Miloslav Kriracherich,* fall 1908 Term, and *State v. Karairch,* set for September 15, 1908, both in Order Book 233; *State v. Blagoyich,* set for September 17, 1908; Order Book 234.

4. *Montgomery Advertiser,* September 4, 1908. Solicitor Thompson ultimately dismissed the cases against the Italian immigrants. See *Montgomery Advertiser,* March 5, 1909

5. *Tuscaloosa News* (Alabama), September 10, 13, 1908; *Montgomery Advertiser,* September 10, 11, 13, 16, 1908; *Centreville Press* (Alabama), September 17, 1908; *Canebrake Herald* (Uniontown, AL), September 24, 1908.

6. The editor saw no irony in concluding, the day after the ambush, that "the best feature of the (strike) situation and the one which is most encouraging, is the fact that no white American has been charged with any of the foul crimes which have been perpetrated." The arrest of United Mine Workers Blocton local president Robert Hayes, the editor explained, was simply due "to the fact that he is an official of the union to which some of the murderers belong." *Gadsden Daily Times* (Alabama), August 11, 1908. Another article claimed that Hayes, who was born and raised in Bibb County, actually entered the Blocton mines in 1904 as a strikebreaker and remained "loyal" to Tennessee Coal, Iron and Railroad right up to the outbreak of the 1908 strike. At that time, TCI operators discovered that a UMW local led by Hayes had organized secretly in the Blocton mines. See *Montgomery Advertiser,* August 15, 1908.

7. *Blocton Enterprise* (Alabama), September 3, 1908; *Montgomery Advertiser,* September 4, 1908. Dabetich, Lazarovich, Popovich, and Wainovich were the only men convicted in the train ambush case and the only ones identifiable as participants in the strike of 1908 who also appear in the Alabama state convict records. See Alabama State Convict Records, vol. 7: 1908–1913, Ancestry.com.

8. Newspapers sympathetic to either side in the strike reported on the trials of Wainovich and Lazaraovich in similar detail. Little record exists of the trial, apart from these media reports, in either the records of the United Mine Workers District 20 or among the records of coal operators involved in the strike. Nor do the actual trial records appear to have survived. On the verdict, see *Birmingham News,* March 5, 1909.

9. The bloody sock apparently proved particularly compelling, as jurors later cited it as the key piece of evidence discussed in their deliberations. *Centreville Press* (Alabama), August 13, 1908; *Blocton Enterprise* (Alabama), August 13, 1908; *Montgomery Advertiser,* August 10, 1908.

10. *Montgomery Advertiser,* September 10, 1908.

11. Unless otherwise noted, this and subsequent details of the case, as given here, are from *Montgomery Advertiser,* September 9, 10, 11, 12, 13, 1908.

12. Catrina's father or husband wrote to "the State of Alabama" in the months following the strike to request the return of his shotgun, which apparently had been confiscated by state militia in the wake of the train ambush: "Dear Sir," he wrote, "On Alabama last strike you send the soldier and they take my shotgun and they never have return. So I am here in business and I have no gun for my protection. So I write you this letter for you investigate for my shot gun and return to me please." Governor Comer's secretary seems to have forwarded the request to the Alabama National Guard's Major Vaiden, who oversaw the militia's role in the strike, who passed it on to Bibb County deputy sheriff Henry C. Cole. Cole eventually returned the shotgun to Maria: "Dear Sir, G. Maria's gun, inquired of within, has been delivered to him." This series of exchanges is found in reel 13, Governor Comer Papers.

13. *Montgomery Advertiser,* September 11, 1908. The defense also called Hughey Hughes to testify, because he was in the commissary on the Saturday evening prior to the ambush. Hughes, a strike leader and "commissary man," denied that Hayes ever received any message while meet-

ing at the store. He also "denied all knowledge of guns or cartridges being distributed at Maria's store" and claimed to have heard about the train shooting only the next morning.

14. *Montgomery Advertiser,* September 11, 1908.

15. *Tuscaloosa News* (Alabama), September 13, 1908.

16. *Montgomery Advertiser,* September 13, 1908.

17. *Coosa River News* (Centre, AL), September 25, 1908.

18. *Montgomery Advertiser,* September 13, 16, 1908; *Centreville Press* (Alabama), September 17, 1908; *Tuscaloosa News* (Alabama), September 13, 1908.

19. *Centreville Press* (Alabama), September 24, 1908.

20. *Montgomery Advertiser,* September 16, 1908.

21. The most significant new evidence consisted of the "bloody clothes" from train conductor Joe Collins's body, provided by the undertaker. Although the defense objected to its introduction, Judge Miller allowed the new evidence to be entered. As one reporter noted of Lazarovich's trial, "Attorneys for the defense are making a world of objection to the introduction of testimony, thereby consuming much time." But their efforts were to no avail. *Centreville Press* (Alabama), September 17, 24, 1908; *Montgomery Advertiser,* September 16, 1908.

22. *Montgomery Advertiser,* March 2, 1909.

23. *Montgomery Advertiser,* March 5, 1908; "Borisa Dabetich," Alabama State Convict Records, vol. 7: 1908–1913, Ancestry.com.

24. The *Montgomery Advertiser* reported that two of the defendants appealed their cases to the state Supreme Court. However, no available evidence indicates what happened to the appeals. On the news of the appeal, see *Montgomery Advertiser,* September 21, 1908.

25. Will Battle, interview, May 21, 1981, Birmingfind.

26. In 1910, Durkovich was still working as a coal miner in the district, most likely in Bibb County. See "Bisse Durkiv (Bozo Durkovich)," District 012, Precinct 10, Bibb County, Alabama, U.S. Federal Census, 1910, Ancestry.com.

27. The best treatment of both the solidarity and tensions between Black and white miners in the Birmingham District is still Letwin, *Challenge of Interracial Unionism,* 31–54. Also see Kelly, *Race, Class, and Power.*

28. *United Mine Workers Journal,* August 15, 20, 1908.

29. "A Few Words about the Miners' Strike," to the editor, *Blocton Enterprise* (Alabama), July 30, 1908. The writer was most likely an Italian, given the syntax and religious references in the letter.

30. *Blocton Enterprise* (Alabama), July 30, 1908.

31. The most sensational case of Black miners during the 1908 strike involved the lynching of Black union miner Will Millen, allegedly by deputies, after his arrest for the dynamiting of the home of Finley Fuller, another Black miner. Millen denied the charge. See chapter 3, as well as *Montgomery Advertiser,* August 6, 1908; and Kelly, *Race, Class, and Power,* 23, 126.

32. *Birmingham News,* August 10, 1908.

33. As numerous scholars have established, Americans perceived immigrants in highly racialized terms. See, for example, Roediger, *Wages of Whiteness;* Jacobsen, *Whiteness of a Different Color;* Jacobsen, *Barbarian Virtues,* 85–89; Sanchez, "Race, Nation, and Culture";

Ngai, *Impossible Subjects;* Jung, *Coolies and Cane;* Gualtieri, *Between Arab and White;* and Bukowczyk, "Racial Turn."

34. *Montgomery Advertiser,* September 11, 1908.

35. For examples of Montenegrins in Bibb County, Alabama, see "Miro Curovich," in the U.S. Federal Census, 1910, Ancestry.com, where he is listed along with several other Montenegrins living in the same boardinghouse, all of whom have occupations listed as "miner."

36. For more on the history of Montenegro, see Barbara Jelavich, *History of the Balkans: The Eighteenth and Nineteenth Centuries,* vol. 1 (Cambridge: Cambridge University Press, 1983), 240, 247, 253, 260–261.

37. On such linguistic challenges in the Balkan countries, both past and present, see Jaako Kolhi, "Language and Identity in Montenegro: A Study among University Students," in *Balkan Encounters: Old and New Identities in South-Eastern Europe,* vol. 1, *Slavica Helsingiensia,* ed. Jouko Lindstedt and Max Wahlstrom, 80–86 (Helsinki: University of Helsinki, 2012). Also see Jelavich, *History of the Balkans,* 247–248, 253, 260–261.

38. *Montgomery Advertiser,* September 11, 1908.

39. *Birmingham News,* September 7, 1908.

40. Jackson, *Dixie's Italians* notes that the judgment of southern white juries derived, in part, from "appearance, performance, association, and 'common sense,' [along with] community testimony, rumor, and reputation" (123).

41. For the list of the jurors' names, see *Birmingham News,* September 9, 1908; for census details, see U.S. Federal Census, 1910, Ancestry.com. R. L. Foley and D. R. Smitherman were the only two jurors I could not identify in the 1910 census for Bibb County, Alabama.

42. *Montgomery Advertiser,* September 12, 1908. Leon Czolgosz, convicted of assassinating President William McKinley, actually was neither a very "devoted anarchist" nor a resident alien. However, according to Jacobsen, *Barbarian Virtues,* given his decidedly non-English surname and his apparent role as a presidential assassin, even his rather "vague association with the anarchist movement reignited the antiradical nativism that had smoldered in American political thought since the Haymarket bombing" (94–95). Thus, the new U.S. immigration act of 1903 excluded immigrants on the basis of political beliefs, and the immigration act of 1906 essentially required immigrants applying for naturalization to swear a loyalty oath to "organized government" and the preservation of the principles of the U.S. Constitution.

43. See, for example, the treatment of Chinese laborers detailed in Jung, *Coolies and Cane;* and attacks on immigrant anarchists described in James Green, *Death in the Haymarket: A Story of Chicago, the First Labor Movement and the Bombing that Divided Gilded Age America* (New York: Pantheon Books, 2006); and Jacobsen, *Barbarian Virtues.*

44. On the racial typologies of the "black Austrians," see LaVigne, "'Black Fellows' of the Mesabi Iron Range," 18–19.

45. *Montgomery Advertiser,* September 13, 1908.

46. *Centreville Press* (Alabama), August 13, 1908.

47. *Blocton Enterprise* (Alabama), September 3, 1908.

48. *United Mine Workers Journal,* August 15, 1908.

49. *United Mine Workers Journal,* August 15, 1908.

50. *United Mine Workers Journal,* September 5, 1908.

51. *Montgomery Advertiser,* December 9, 1910. No indication is given regarding what the family and friends of the men killed during the train ambush thought about Governor Comer's decision to commute the sentences of the men.

52. "Proceedings of the Fourteenth Annual Convention of District 20," Birmingham, Alabama, June 12, 1911, folder 37, box 88, United Mine Workers of America, President's Office Correspondence with Districts, HCLA 1822, Special Collections Library, Pennsylvania State University. The consideration of governors Comer and O'Neal in commuting these sentences and finally paroling the Blocton Four could reflect an element of white privilege that the four possessed as Europeans. However, such commutations of sentences to "short time," as well as paroles, appeared to be relatively common after 1883, including for African American prisoners. See Curtin, *Black Prisoners and Their World,* 23, 92–93.

53. Partly in response to criticisms over the horrific conditions at its Coalburg prison mine, Sloss-Sheffield officials restructured the relatively new Flat Top mines by separating state convicts from county prisoners. Regardless, the Flat Top mines still constituted a "black Hell" of close quarters and hard labor, almost all of which was done by hand, often while lying prone along the coal seams. In 1906, one inspector found that guards whipped prisoners at Flat Top "on the slightest provocation." Such conditions help to explain why prisoners at Flat Top rioted in 1916. See Lewis, *Sloss Furnaces,* 310–311; Kelly, *Race, Class, and Power,* 91–93; and Curtin, *Black Prisoners and their World,* 165.

54. "Proceedings of the Fourteenth Annual Convention of District 20."

55. *Centreville Press* (Alabama), June 15, 1911.

56. "Annual Report of Secretary-Treasurer J. L. Clemo," Birmingham, Alabama, June 10, 1912, folder 38, box 88, United Mine Workers of America, President's Office Correspondence with Districts, HCLA 1822, Special Collections Library, Pennsylvania State University.

57. *United Mine Workers Journal,* September 24, 1908.

58. *United Mine Workers Journal,* September 24, 1908.

59. *United Mine Workers Journal,* September 24, 1908.

CONCLUSION

1. *Blount County News and Dispatch* (Blountsville, AL), January 14, 1892; Robin Sterling, ed., *Cullman County, Alabama Confederate Soldiers* (self-published), 524; biographical information, Willoughby-Jones Papers, PR 434, Alabama Department of Archives and History, Montgomery, Alabama (hereinafter cited as Willoughby-Jones Papers).

2. On the Know Nothing Party, see Michael F. Holt, *The Political Crisis of the 1850s* (New York: John Wiley and Sons, 1978); and Tyler Anbinder, *Nativism and Slavery: The Northern Know Nothings and the Politics of the 1850s* (New York: Oxford University Press, 1992). On this party in Alabama, see Jeff Frederick, "Unintended Consequences: The Rise and Fall of the Know-Nothing Party in Alabama," *Alabama Review* 55, no. 1 (January 2002): 3–33.

3. J. H. Willoughby to editor, Gaynesville, AL, July 3, 1855, Willoughby-Jones Papers.

4. U.S. Federal Census, 1850, Ancestry.com.

5. The population of Alabama in the U.S. Federal Census, 1850, stood at 771,623, with 426,514 whites and 345,109 African Americans. "1801–1860," *Alabama History Timeline: From Prehistory to Modern Day,* Alabama Department of Archives and History, https://archives.alabama.gov/timeline/al1801.html.

6. For the final draft of this bill as enacted, see "Alabama Immigration Law (Act No. 2011-535)," Alabama Immigration Information Center, http://immigration.alabama.gov/Immigration-Act-No-2011-535-Text.aspx. See also Joseph Weber, "Statehouse Wins Put GOP in Redistricting Driver's Seat," *Washington Times,* November 3, 2011, http://www.washingtontimes.com/news/2010/nov/3/the-republican-midterm-wave-swept-through-state-ca/print; David White, "Alabama GOP Lawmakers Begin Their Work on Their 'Handshake with Alabama' List of Priorities," *Birmingham News,* March 2, 2011, http://blog.al.com/spotnews/2011/03/post_631.html.

7. "Benedictine Nuns Oppose Immigration Bill," *Montgomery Advertiser,* reader opinion, August 16, 2011; Nicola Menzie, "Church Leaders: Alabama Anti-Immigration Law 'Merciless,'" *Christian Post,* August 2, 1011, http://www.christianpost.com/news/church-leaders-alabama-anti-immigration-law-merciless-53216; Daniel Altschuler, "Not Just Unconstitutional, but Un-American," *Chronicle of Higher Education,* September 11, 2011, http://chronicle.com/article/Not-Just-Unconstitutional-but/128932/; Peggy Gargis, "Alabama Sets Nation's Toughest Immigration Law," Reuters, June 9, 2011, https://www.reuters.com/article/instant-article/idUSTRE7584C920110609.

8. Specifically, the identified Hispanic/Latino population in Alabama, as counted by the U.S. census of 2010, totaled 185,602 people, or 3.9 percent of the state's total population of 4,779,736. The real point, of course, was that this relatively small number represented a 144 percent increase of the Hispanic/Latino population in the state since 2000. That rate of increase was much higher in some small rural communities that targeted employment to that population, such as the north Alabama poultry industry or the central Alabama peach production agribusiness. See CensusViewer, "Population of Alabama, Census 2010 and 2000, Interactive Map, Demographics, Statistics, Quick Facts," http://censusviewer.com/state/AL.

9. Quoted in Nick Banaszak, "Fellow Congressman Blasts Brooks over Immigration 'Shooting' Statement," WHNT News 19, July 14, 2011; Brian Lyman, "U.S. Rep. Mo Brooks Jumps Into Alabama Senate Race," *Montgomery Advertiser,* May, 15, 2017. I am, fortunately, not related to Representative Brooks.

10. See Watson, "Immigration to Alabama," 18, 63.

11. Several pragmatic southern congressmen formed an alliance with western representatives to enact the Chinese Exclusion Act in 1882. In return, the southern states received western votes against further civil rights legislation, effectively granting to the South "local control" of African American populations. See Young, *Chinese Exclusion Act,* 11; Guterl, "After Slavery," 231–233, 237.

12. C. F. Seviers, "Report of the Commissioner of Immigration," November 1878, Agriculture and Industry, Annual Reports, ADAH.

13. Jacobson, *Barbarian Virtues,* 69–73; Sam Erman, *Almost Citizens: Puerto Rico, the U.S. Constitution, and Empire* (Cambridge: Cambridge University Press, 2019), 76; Peck, *Reinventing Free Labor,* 18; Karuka, *Empire's Tracks,* 82–83; Ngai, *Impossible Subjects.*

14. The most well-known opponent of immigration in Alabama came to be U.S. Representative Oscar Underwood of the Birmingham District, who elevated his own national political ambitions by decrying against the Southern and Eastern European "flood" into the United States in the early twentieth century. Underwood came to the Birmingham District to practice law in its years of early development. See Elbert L. Watson, "Oscar Underwood," *Encyclopedia of Alabama,* http://www.encyclopediaofalabama.org/article/h-2961; and Evans C. Johnson, *Oscar W. Underwood: A Political Biography* (Baton Rouge: Louisiana State University Press, 1980). First as a congressional representative and then as a U.S. senator, Underwood received a great deal of constituent correspondence applauding the distinctions he made between "desirable" and "undesirable" immigrants. For instance, dozens of machinist and mechanic labor organizations, typically clustered in the Birmingham area, frequently forwarded to Underwood's offices preprinted circulars from national anti-immigration organizations. See, for example, Jason B. Draper to Underwood, November 9, 1905, box 8, folder 2, Underwood Papers.

15. Watson, "Immigration to Alabama," 4.

16. *Birmingham News,* November 29, 1907.

17. For a discussion of the national phenomenon of anti-immigrant reactions, see Jacobsen, *Barbarian Virtues.*

18. *Birmingham News,* September 26, 1907.

19. U.S. Federal Census, 1910, Ancestry.com.

20. Watson, "Immigration in Alabama," 65–67, 69.

21. U.S. Federal Census, 1910, Ancestry.com.

22. James Martin, President of the Loyal League, et al., to Gov. William Smith, May 25, 1869, folders 4–8, Governor Smith Papers, Administrative Files, 1868–1870, SG023108, ADAH.

23. All data here derived from the U.S. Federal Census, 1910, Ancestry.com.

BIBLIOGRAPHY

PRIMARY SOURCE COLLECTIONS

Online Databases

Alabama, Deaths and Burials Index, 1881–1974. Provo, UT: Ancestry.com Operations, 2011.

Alabama, Naturalization Records, 1888–1991. Provo, UT: Ancestry.com Operations, 2013.

Alabama, Select Marriages Indexes, 1816–1942. Provo, UT: Ancestry.com Operations, 2013.

Alabama, U.S. Wills and Probate Records, 1753–1999. Provo, UT: Ancestry.com Operations, 2013.

Passenger Lists, 1812–1963, M259, New Orleans, 1820–1962. Provo, UT: Ancestry.com Operations, 2009.

United States Federal Census, 1850, 1860, 1870, 1880, 1890, 1900, 1910, 1920, 1930. Provo, UT: Ancestry.com Operations, 2009.

United States Federal Census, Population, Alabama, 2000, 2010. Interactive Map, Demographics, Statistics, Quick Map, http://censusviewer.com/state/AL.

U.S., City Directories, 1822–1995. Provo, UT: Ancestry.com Operations, 2011.

U.S., Find A Grave Index, 1600s–Current. Provo, UT: Ancestry.com Operations, 2012.

U.S., Headstone Applications for Military Veterans, 1925–1970. Provo, UT: Ancestry.com Operations, 2013.

U.S. Passport Applications, 1795–1925. Lehi, UT: Ancestry.com Operations, 2007.

U.S., World War I Draft Registration Cards, 1917–1918. Provo, UT: Ancestry.com Operations, 2005.

Manuscript Collections

Alabama Department of Archives and History, Montgomery, Alabama

Adjutant General Papers, Administrative Files, 1905–1908.

Alabama Commissioner of Agriculture and Industry records, 1888–1914.

Alabama Department of Corrections, State Publications, 1845–2011.

Department of Agriculture and Industries, Annual Reports, 1883–1926.

Johnston, Joseph F. Papers, LPR64.

McKee, Robert. Papers, LPR26.

Underwood, Oscar R. Papers, Administrative Files.

United States, District of Alabama, Administrative Files, 1865–1868, Government Records Collection.

Webb, James E. Letters. SPR 206.

Wheeler, Joseph. Family Papers, LPR 50.

Willoughby-Jones. Family Papers, PR 434.

Alabama Governor, Government Records Collections

Cobb, Gov. Rufus W. Papers, Pardon, Parole, and Clemency Files.

Comer, Gov. Braxton Bragg. Papers, Administrative Files.

Jelks, Gov. Robert. Papers, Administrative Files.

Jones, Gov. Thomas Goode. Papers, Administrative Files.

Lewis, Gov. David P. Papers, Administrative Files.

Lindsay, Gov. Robert B. Papers, Administrative Files.

Oates, Gov. William C. Papers, Administrative Files.white

O'Neal, Gov. Edward A. Papers, Administrative Files.

O'Neal, Gov. Emmett. Papers, Administrative Files.

Patton, Gov. Robert. Papers, Administrative Files.

Smith, Gov. William Hugh. Papers, Administrative Files.

Birmingham Public Library

Birmingfind Papers. Interviews and Research Notes.

Mobile County Circuit Court Records, The Doy Leale McCall Rare Book and Manuscript Library.

Montgomery, Alabama, Administrative Offices of Courts

Bibb County Order Books, Circuit Court, Montgomery, Alabama.

Records of Customhouses and Collection Districts.

36.3.1, Federal Customs Service, RG 36, Collection District of Mobile, Alabama. National Archives and Records Administration, Atlanta, Georgia.

Records of the Assistant Commissioner for the State of Alabama, Bureau of Refugees, Freedmen, and Abandoned Lands, 1865–1870. Microform. Na-

tional Archives and Records Administration, 1969. Ralph Brown Draughon Library, Auburn University.

United Mine Workers of America.
President's Office Correspondence with Districts, HCLA 1822, Special Collections Library, Pennsylvania State University.

Interviews
(from transcriptions and notes from Birmingfind Papers)

Battle, Will
Bensko, John
Cameau, Annie
Ducek, Katie
Harmon, Alice Slovensky
LaRocca, Charlie
Lorina, Paul
Maenza, Rose
Morganti, Argentina
Oddo, Francis
Patchen, Annie Latenosky
Saia, Francis and Nellie
Slovensky, Steve
Tallent, Father

Newspapers

Abbeville Press Banner (SC)
The Advance (Saint John, KS)
Alabama Daily State Journal (Montgomery)
Albany-Decatur Daily (Albany, AL)
Andalusia Star (AL)
Anniston Hot Blast (AL)
Asheville Daily Citizen (NC)
Birmingham Iron Age (AL)
Birmingham News (AL)
Birmingham Times (AL)
Blocton Enterprise (West Blocton, AL)
Blount County News-Dispatch (Blountsville, AL)
Canebrake Herald (Uniontown, AL)
Centreville Press (AL)

Chattanooga Times (TN)

Charleston Daily News (SC)

Christian Post

Citizen Examiner (AL)

Columbia Recorder (AL)

Coosa River News (Centre, AL)

Crawford Avalanche (MI)

Crenshaw County News (Luverne, AL)

Cullman Immigrant (AL)

Daily Alta California (San Francisco)

Daily Gazette (Fort Worth, TX)

Dalles Times-Mountaineer (OR)

Dothan Eagle (AL)

Elba Clipper (AL)

Eufaula Daily Times (AL)

Eutaw Whig and Observer (AL)

Evergreen Courant (AL)

Florence Herald (AL)

Fort Worth Gazette (Texas)

Franklin County Times (Russellville, AL)

Gadsden Daily Times (AL)

Gadsden Times-News (AL)

Greene County Democrat (Eutaw, AL)

Grenada Sentinel (MS)

Herald-Journal (Bessemer, AL)

Honolulu Republican (HI)

Honolulu Star-Bulletin (HI)

Huntsville Gazette (AL)

Indianapolis Journal (IN)

Jones Valley Times (Birmingham, AL)

Journal-Tribune (Gadsden, AL)

Knoxville Weekly Chronicle (TN)

Lineville Headlight (AL)

Luverne Journal (AL)

Macon Telegraph (GA)

Marion Herald (Hamilton, AL)

Memphis Daily Appeal (TN)

The Messenger (Troy, AL)

Mississippi Clarion Ledger (Jackson)

The Mitchell Capital (Dakota Territory)
Mobile Daily Register (AL)
Monroe Journal (Claiborne, AL)
Montgomery Advertiser (AL)
Montgomery Herald (AL)
Montgomery Times (AL)
Morning Mercury (Huntsville, AL)
Mountain Eagle (Jasper, AL)
Nashville Union and American (TN)
New Orleans Times-Picayune (LA)
Newberry Herald (SC)
New York Times
New York Tribune
Ozark Star (AL)
Pacific Commercial Advertiser (Honolulu, HI)
Piedmont Post (AL)
Pine Belt News (Brewton, AL)
Prattville Progress (AL)
Progressive Age (Scottsboro, AL)
Russell Register (Seale, AL)
Sacramento Daily Union (CA)
Selma Times (AL)
Shelby Chronicle (Columbiana, AL)
Shelby Sentinel (Calera, AL)
South Alabamian (Geneva, AL)
St. Louis Globe-Democrat (MO)
The Sun (New York)
Sweetwater Enterprise (TN)
Times and News (Eufaula, AL)
Tuscaloosa News (AL)
Tuskaloosa Gazette (Tuscaloosa, AL)
Tuskegee News (Tuskegee, AL)
Troy Messenger (AL)
Union Banner (Clanton, AL)
Union Springs Herald (AL)
United Miner Workers Journal
Vicksburg Weekly Herald (MS)
Washington Times (DC)
Waterbury Evening Democrat (CT)

Weekly Advertiser (Montgomery, AL)
Weekly Clarion Ledger (Jackson, MS)
Xenia Daily Gazette (OH)

Web Pages

Encyclopedia of Alabama, www.encyclopediaofalabama.org.
JewishGen, www.jewishgen.org.
"World Culture Encyclopedia," Countries and Their Cultures, www.everyculture.com.

Printed Primary Sources

Gindrat, John H. *Receiver of the Alabama and Chattanooga Railroad, to the Governor.* W. W. Screws, 1871.

Hart, Hastings H. *Social Problems of Alabama, Study of the Social Institutions and Agencies of the State of Alabama as Related to its War Activities.* Montgomery, AL, 1918.

"Industrial." Engineering and Mining Journal, index, vol. 85 (January–June 1908).

Ledyard, Erwin. "An American Italy." *The Southern States: An Illustrated Monthly Magazine Devoted to the South* (March 1894). Available at http://www.gutenberg.org/files/53231/53231-h/53231-h.htm.

Seaman, A. Vernon, and Oliphant and Co., San Francisco, *Report of the Special Joint Committee to Investigate Chinese Immigration,* February 27, 1877.

Testimony Taken by the Select Committee of the House to Inquire into the Alleged Violation of the Laws Prohibiting the Importation of Contract Laborers, Paupers, Convicts, and Other Classes. 50th Congress, First Session, 1888, No. 572. U.S. Congress, Washington, DC.

SECONDARY SOURCES

Adams, Charles Edward. *Blocton: The History of an Alabama Coal Mining Town.* Brierfield, AL: Cahaba Trace Commission, 2001.

Altschuler, Daniel. "Not Just Un-Constitutional, But Un-American." *Chronicle of Higher Education,* September 11, 2011.

Althern, Robert G. *In Search of Canaan: Black Migration to Kansas, 1879–80.* Lawrence: Regents Press of Kansas, 1978.

Anbinder, Tyler. *Nativism and Slavery: The Northern Know Nothings and the Politics of the 1850s.* New York: Oxford University Press, 1992.

Armes, Ethel. *The Story of Coal and Iron in Alabama.* Birmingham, AL: Book-Keepers Press, 1972.

Arnesen, Eric. "Whiteness and the Historians' Imagination." *International Labor and Working-Class History* 60 (Fall 2001): 3–32.

Ayers, Edward L. *The Promise of the New South: Life after Reconstruction.* Oxford: Oxford University Press, 1992.

———. *Vengeance and Justice: Crime and Punishment in the 19th-Century American South.* New York: Oxford University Press, 1984.

Baker, William D. *Minority Settlement in the Mississippi River Counties of the Arkansas Delta, 1870–1930.* Little Rock: Arkansas Historic Preservation Program, 1991.

Bald, Vivek. *Bengali Harlem and the Lost Histories of South Asian America.* Boston: Harvard University Press, 2013.

———. "Selling the East in the American South: Bengali Muslim Peddlers in New Orleans and Beyond, 1880–1920." In *Asian Americans in Dixie: Race and Migration in the South,* ed. Khyati Y. Joshi and Jigna Desai. Urbana: University of Illinois Press, 2013.

Banaszak, Nick. "Fellow Congressman Blasts Brooks Over Immigration 'Shooting' Statement." WHNT News 19, July 14, 2011.

Bankston, Carl L. "New People in the New South: An Overview of Southern Immigration." Special *Global South* issue, *Southern Cultures* 13, no. 4 (Winter 2007): 24–44.

Barrett, James R., and David Roediger. "Inbetween Peoples: Race, Nationality, and the 'New Immigrant Working Class.'" *Journal of American Ethnic History* 16, no. 3 (Spring 1997): 3–44.

Bederman, Gail. *Manliness and Civilization: A Cultural History of Gender and Race in the United States, 1880–1917.* Chicago: University of Chicago Press, 1995.

Bender, Daniel E., and Jana Lipman. *Making the Empire Work: Labor and United States Imperialism.* New York: New York University Press, 2015.

Bender, Thomas. *A Nation Among Nations: America's Place in World History.* New York: Hill and Wang, 2006.

"Benedictine Nuns Oppose Immigration Bill." *Montgomery Advertiser,* August 10, 2011.

Berthoff, Rowland T. "Southern Attitudes toward Immigration, 1865–1914." *Journal of Southern History* 17, no. 3 (August 1951): 328–360.

Birmingfind. *Birmingham's Lebanese: "The Earth Turned to Gold."* Birmingham, AL: Birmingfind, 1981.

———. *The New Patrida: The Story of Birmingham's Greeks.* Birmingham, AL: Birmingfind, 1981.

Blackmon, Douglas. *Slavery by Another Name: The Re-Enslavement of Black Americans from the Civil War to World War II.* New York: Anchor Books, 2008.

Bodnar, John. *The Transplanted: A History of Immigrants in Urban America.* Bloomington: Indiana University Press, 1985.

Bow, Leslie. "Racial Interstitiality and the Anxieties of the 'Partly Colored': Representations of Asians under Jim Crow." In *Asian Americans in Dixie: Race and*

Migration in the South, ed. Khyati Y. Joshi and Jigna Desai. Urbana: University of Illinois Press, 2013.

Brandfon, Robert. "The End of Immigration to the Cotton Fields." *Mississippi Valley Historical Review* 50, no. 4 (March 1964): 591–611.

Bronstein, Daniel. "The Formation and Development of Chinese Communities in Atlanta, Augusta, and Savannah, Georgia: From Sojourners to Settlers, 1880–1965. PhD diss., Georgia State University, 2008.

———. "Segregation, Exclusion, and the Chinese Communities in Georgia, 1880s–1940." In *Asian Americans in Dixie: Race and Migration in the South,* ed. Khyati J. Joshi and Jigna Deshai. Urbana: University of Illinois Press, 2013.

Brooks, Jennifer E. "'No Juan Crow!': Documenting the Immigration Debate in Alabama Today." *Southern Cultures* 18, no. 3 (Fall 2012): 49–56.

Bukowczyk, John J. "The Racial Turn." *Journal of American Ethnic History* 36, no. 2 (Winter 2017): 5–10.

Carson, Scott Alan. "The Biological Living Conditions of Nineteenth-Century Chinese Males in America." *Journal of Interdisciplinary History* 37, no. 2 (Autumn 2006): 201–217.

Chew, Kenneth, Mark Leach, and John Liu. "The Revolving Door to Gold Mountain: How Chinese Immigrants Got around U.S. Exclusion and Replenished the Chinese Labor Pool, 1900–1910." *International Migration Review* 43, no. 2 (Summer 2002): 410–430.

Church, Clive H., and Randolph C. Head. *A Concise History of Switzerland.* Cambridge: Cambridge University Press, 2013.

Clark, Christopher, Nancy A. Hewitt, Roy Rosenzweig, Nelson Lichtenstein, Joshua Brown, and David Jaffree. *Who Built America? Working People and the Nation's History.* Vol. 1, *To 1877.* 3rd ed. New York: Bedford/St. Martin's, 2008.

Clayton, Lawrence, and Michael Conniff. *A History of Modern Latin America.* 2nd ed. New York: Thomson-Wadsworth, 2005.

Clune, Elizabeth. "Black Workers, White Immigrants, and the Postemancipation Problem of Labor." In *Global Perspectives on Industrial Transformation in the American South,* ed. Susanna Delfino and Michael Gillespie. Columbia: University of Missouri Press, 2005.

———. "From Light Copper to the Blackest and Lowest Type: Daniel Tompkins and the Racial Order of the Global New South." *Journal of Southern History* 76, no. 2 (May 2010): 275–314.

Cobb, James C. "Beyond Planters and Industrialists: A New Perspective on the New South." *Journal of Southern History* 54, no. 1 (February 1988): 45–68.

———. *The Most Southern Place on Earth: The Mississippi Delta and the Roots of Regional Identity.* Oxford: Oxford University Press, 1992.

Cohen, Lucy M. *Chinese in the Post–Civil War South: A People without a History.* Baton Rouge: Louisiana State University Press, 1984.

Cohen, William. *At Freedom's Edge: Black Mobility and the Southern White Quest for Racial Control, 1861–1915.* Baton Rouge: Louisiana State University Press, 1991.

Colby, Jason M. "Progressive Empire: Race and Tropicality in United Fruit's Central America." In *Making the Empire Work: Labor and United States Imperialism,* ed. Jana Lipman and Daniel Bender. New York: New York University Press, 2015.

Cole, Stephanie, and Alison Parker, eds. *Beyond Black and White: Race, Ethnicity, and Gender in the U.S. South and Southwest.* College Station: Texas A&M University Press, 2004.

Collins, William J. "When the Tide Turned: Immigration and the Delay of the Great Black Migration." *Journal of Economic History* 57, no. 3 (September 1997): 607–632.

Conklin, Nancy Faires, and Nora Faires. "'Colored' and Catholic: The Lebanese in Birmingham, Alabama." In *Crossing the Waters: Arabic-Speaking Immigrants to the United States before 1940,* ed. Eric J. Hooglund. Washington, DC: Smithsonian Institution Press, 1987.

Cooper, Frederick, Thomas C. Holt, and Rebecca J. Scott, eds. *Beyond Slavery: Explorations of Race, Labor, and Citizenship in Postemancipation Societies.* Chapel Hill: University of North Carolina Press, 2000.

Cribbs, Lennie Austin. "The Memphis Chinese Labor Convention, 1869." *West Tennessee Historical Society Papers* (1983): 74–81.

Crowell, Jackson. "The United States and a Central American Canal, 1869–1877." *Hispanic American Historical Review* 49, no. 1 (February 1969): 27–52.

Curtin, Mary Ellen. *Black Prisoners and Their World, Alabama, 1865–1900.* Charlottesville: University Press of Virginia, 2000.

Dana, Richard. "The Trade in Chinese Laborers." In *The Cuba Reader: History, Culture, Politics,* ed. Aviva Chomsky, Barry Carr, and Pamela M. Smorkaloff. Durham, NC: Duke University Press, 2003.

Daniel, Pete. *In the Shadow of Slavery: Peonage in the South, 1901–1906.* Urbana: University of Illinois Press, 1972.

Daniels, Roger. *Asian America: Chinese and Japanese in the United States since 1850.* Seattle: University of Washington Press, 1988.

———. *Coming to America: A History of Immigration and Ethnicity in American Life.* New York: Perennial, 2002.

Davis, David Brion. *The Problem of Slavery in the Age of Emancipation.* New York: Vintage Books, 2016.

Davis, Mike. *Late Victorian Holocausts: El Niño Famines and the Making of the Third World.* New York: Verso, 2001.

Davis, Robert S. "The Old World in the New South: Entrepreneurial Ventures and the Agricultural History of Cullman County, Alabama." *Agricultural History* 79, no. 4 (Autumn 2005): 439–461.

Day, James Sanders. *Diamonds in the Rough: A History of Alabama's Cahaba Coal Field.* Tuscaloosa: University of Alabama Press, 2013.

Dearinger, Ryan. *The Filth of Progress: Immigrants, Americans, and the Building of Canals and Railroads in the West.* Oakland: University of California Press, 2016.

Delfino, Susanna, and Michael Gillespie, eds. *Global Perspectives on Industrial Transformation in the American South.* Columbia: University of Missouri Press, 2005.

Derbes, Brett. "The Production of Military Supplies at the Alabama State Penitentiary during the Civil War." *Alabama Review* 67, no. 2 (April 2014): 131–160.

Deutsch, Sarah. "Being American in Boley, Oklahoma." In *Beyond Black and White: Race, Ethnicity, and Gender in the U.S. South and Southwest,* ed. Stephanie Cole and Alison Parker. College Station: Texas A&M University Press, 2004.

Dinnerstein, Leonard, Roger L. Nichols, and David M. Reimers. *Natives and Strangers: A History of Ethnic Americans.* 6th ed. New York: Oxford University Press, 2015.

Dykema, Frank E. "An Effort to Attract Dutch Colonists to Alabama, 1869." *Journal of Southern History* 12, no. 2 (May 1948): 247–261.

Egerton, Douglas. *Wars of Reconstruction: The Brief, Violent History of America's Most Progressive Era.* New York: Bloomsbury, 2014.

Ellison, Rhonda Coleman. *Bibb County, Alabama: The First Hundred Years, 1818–1918.* Tuscaloosa: University of Alabama Press, 1984.

Erman, Sam. *Almost Citizens: Puerto Rico, the U.S. Constitution, and Empire.* Cambridge: Cambridge University Press, 2019.

Fede, Frank Joseph. *Italians in the Deep South: Their Impact on Birmingham and the American Heritage.* Montgomery, AL: Black Belt Press, 1994.

Fields, Barbara J. "Whiteness, Racism, and Identity." *International Labor and Working-Class History* 60 (Fall 2001): 48–56.

Fierce, Milfred C. *Slavery Revisited: Blacks and the Southern Convict Lease System, 1865–1933.* New York: Africana Studies Research Center, Brooklyn College, City University of New York, 1994.

Fink, Leon. *The Maya of Morganton: Work and Community in the Nuevo New South.* Chapel Hill: University of North Carolina Press, 2003.

———. *Workers across the Americas: The Transnational Turn in Labor History.* Oxford: Oxford University Press, 2011.

Fitzgerald, Michael. *Reconstruction in Alabama: From Civil War to Redemption in the Cotton South.* Baton Rouge: Louisiana State University Press, 2017.

Flahaux, Marie Laurence, and Bruno Schoumaker. *Democratic Republic of the Congo: A Migration History Marked by Crises and Restrictions.* Washington, DC: Migration Policy Institute, 2016.

Fleming, Walter L. "Immigration to the Southern States." *Political Science Quarterly* 20, no. 2 (June 1905): 276–297.

Floyd, Ryan. "Looking Over the Horizon: The Birmingham Iron and Coal Industry's Interest in American Imperialism during the 1890s." *Alabama Review* 63, no. 1 (January 2010): 30–61.

Flynt, Wayne. *Poor but Proud: Alabama's Poor Whites.* Tuscaloosa: University of Alabama Press, 1989.

Frederick, Jeff. "Unintended Consequences: The Rise and Fall of the Know-Nothing Party in Alabama." *Alabama Review* 55, no. 1 (January 2002): 3–33.

Friedman, Max Paul. "Voting with Their Feet: Toward a Conceptual History of 'America' in European Migrant Sending Communities, 1860s–1914." *Journal of Social History* 40, no. 3 (Spring 2007): 552–575.

Foner, Eric. *Nothing but Freedom: Emancipation and Its Legacy.* Baton Rouge: Louisiana State University Press, 1983.

———. *Reconstruction: America's Unfinished Revolution, 1863–1877.* New York: Harper and Row, 1988.

Gabaccia, Donna. *Foreign Relations: American Immigration in Global Perspective.* Princeton, NJ: Princeton University Press, 2012.

———. "*Gli italiani nel mondo:* Italy's Workers around the World." *OAH Magazine of History* 14, no. 1 (Fall 1999): 12–16.

———. *Italy's Many Diasporas.* Seattle: University of Washington Press, 2000.

———. *Militants and Migrants: Rural Sicilians Become American Workers.* New Brunswick, NJ: Rutgers University Press, 1988.

Gargis, Peggy. "Alabama Sets Nation's Toughest Immigration Law." Reuters, June 9, 2011.

Gilmour, Robert Arthur. "The Other Emancipation: Studies in Society and Economy of Alabama Whites during Reconstruction." PhD diss., Johns Hopkins University, 1973.

Goldfield, David. "Unmelting the Ethnic South: Changing Boundaries of Race and Ethnicity in the Modern South." In *The American South in the Twentieth Century,* ed. Craig Pascoe and Karen Trahan. Athens: University of Georgia Press, 2005.

Grafton, Carl, and Anne Permaloff. *Big Mules and Branchheads: James E. Folsom and Political Power in Alabama.* Athens: University of Georgia Press, 1985.

Green, James. *Death in the Haymarket: A Story of Chicago, the First Labor Movement and the Bombing that Divided Gilded Age America.* New York: Pantheon Books, 2006.

——. *The Devil Is Here in These Hills: West Virginia's Coal Miners and Their Battle for Freedom.* New York: Atlantic Monthly Press, 2015.

Green, Nancy L., and Roger Waldinger. *A Century of Transnationalism: Immigrants and Their Homeland Connections.* Urbana: University of Illinois Press, 2016.

Greene, Julie. *The Canal Builders: Making America's Empire at the Panama Canal.* New York: Penguin Books, 2009.

Grossman, Jonathan. "Toward a Definition of Diaspora." *Ethic and Racial Studies* 42, no. 3 (2019): 1263–1282.

Gualtieri, Sarah M. A. *Between Arab and White: Race and Ethnicity in the Early Syrian American Diaspora.* Berkeley, CA: University of California Press, 2009.

Guglielmo, Jennifer, and Salvatore Salerno, eds. *Are Italians White?: How Race Is Made in America.* New York: Routledge, 2003.

Guglielmo, Thomas. "No Color Barrier: Italians, Race, and Rumor in the United States." In *Are Italians White?: How Race Is Made in America,* ed. Jennifer Guglielmo and Salvatore Salerno. New York: Routledge, 2003.

——. *White on Arrival: Italians, Race, Color, and Power in Chicago, 1890–1945.* New York: Oxford University Press, 2003.

Guterl, Matthew Pratt. "After Slavery: Asian Labor, the American South, and the Age of Emancipation." *Journal of World History* 14, no. 2 (June 2003): 209–241.

——. *American Mediterranean: Southern Slaveholders in the Age of Emancipation.* Cambridge, MA: Harvard University Press, 2008.

——. *The Color of Race in America, 1900–1940.* New Brunswick, NJ: Rutgers University Press, 2001.

Gyllerstom, Catherine. "2,000 Trees a Day: Work and Life in the American Naval Stores Industry, 1877 to 1940." PhD diss., Auburn University, 2014.

Gyory, Andrew. *Closing the Gate: Race, Politics, and the Chinese Exclusion Act.* Chapel Hill: University of North Carolina Press, 1998.

Hahamovitch, Cindy. *Fruits of Their Labor: Atlantic Coast Farmworkers and the Making of Migrant Poverty, 1870–1945.* Chapel Hill: University of North Carolina Press, 1997.

——. *No Man's Land: Jamaican Guestworkers in America and the Global History of Deportable Labor.* Princeton, NJ: Princeton University Press, 2011.

——. "Slavery's Stale Soil: Indentured Labor, Guestworkers, and the End of Empire." In *Making the Empire Work: Labor and United States Imperialism,* ed. Jana Lipman and Daniel Bender. New York: New York University Press, 2015.

Hahn, Stephen. *A Nation under Our Feet: Black Political Struggles in the Rural South from Slavery to the Great Migration.* Cambridge, MA: Belknap Press of Harvard University Press, 2003.

Hale, Grace Elizabeth. *Making Whiteness: The Culture of Segregation in the South, 1890–1940.* New York: Vintage Books, 1999.

Harlan, Louis T., ed. *The Booker T. Washington Papers.* Vol. 3. Urbana: University of Illinois Press, 1974.

Harper, Marjory, and Stephen Constantine. *Migration and Empire.* Oxford: Oxford University Press, 2010.

Helliwig, David J. "Black Attitudes toward Immigrant Labor in the South, 1865–1910." *Filson Club Historical Quarterly* 54, no. 2 (April 1980): 151–168.

Heriot, Najia Aarim. *Chinese Immigrants, African Americans, and Racial Anxiety in the United States, 1848–1882.* Urbana: University of Illinois Press, 2003.

Higham, John. *Strangers in the Land: Patterns of American Nativism, 1860–1925.* New Brunswick, NJ: Rutgers University Press, 1955.

Hild, Matthew. *Greenbackers, Knights of Labor, and Populists: Farmer-Labor Insurgency in the Late-Nineteenth-Century South.* Athens: University of Georgia Press, 2007.

Holt, Michael F. *The Political Crisis of the 1850s.* New York: John Wiley and Sons, 1978.

Holt, Thomas C. "The Essences of the Contract: The Articulation of Race, Gender, and Political Economy in British Emancipation Policy, 1838–1866." In *Beyond Slavery: Explorations of Race, Labor, and Citizenship in Postemancipation Societies,* ed. Frederick Cooper, Thomas C. Holt, and Rebecca J. Scott. Chapel Hill: University of North Carolina Press, 2000.

Hooglund, Eric J., ed. *Crossing the Waters: Arabic-Speaking Immigrants to the United States Before 1940.* Washington, DC: Smithsonian Institution Press, 1987.

Hunter, Tera W. *To 'Joy My Freedom: Southern Black Women's Lives and Labors after the Civil War.* Cambridge, MA: Harvard University Press, 1997.

Irvine, Alexander. "My Life in Peonage, I." *Appleton Magazine* 10 (July 1907): 3–15.

Jackson, Jessica Barbata. *Dixie's Italians: Sicilians, Race, and Citizenship in the Jim Crow Gulf South.* Baton Rouge: Louisiana State University Press, 2020.

———. "Reconsidering the Experience of Italians and Sicilians in Louisiana, 1870s–1890s." *Journal of the Louisiana Historical Association* 58, no. 3 (Summer 2017): 300–338.

Jacobson, Matthew Frye. *Barbarian Virtues: The United States Encounters Foreign Peoples at Home and Abroad, 1876–1917.* New York: Hill and Wang, 2000.

———. *Whiteness of a Different Color: European Immigrants and the Alchemy of Race.* Cambridge, MA: Harvard University Press, 1998.

Jelavich, Barbara. *History of the Balkans: The Eighteen and Nineteenth Centuries.* Vol. 1. Cambridge: Cambridge University Press, 1983.

Johnson, Evans C. *Oscar W. Underwood: A Political Biography.* Baton Rouge, LA: Louisiana State University Press, 1980.

Jones, William P. *The Tribe of Black Ulysses: American Lumber Workers in the Jim Crow South.* Urbana: University of Illinois Press, 2005.

Joshi, Khyati Y., and Jigna Desai, eds. *Asian Americans in Dixie: Race and Migration in the South.* Urbana: University of Illinois Press, 2013.

Jung, John. *Southern Fried Rice: Life in a Chinese Laundry in the Deep South.* Yin and Yang Press, 2005.

Jung, Moon-Ho. *Coolies and Cane: Race, Labor, and Sugar in the Age of Emancipation.* Baltimore, MD: Johns Hopkins University Press, 2006.

Karuka, Manu. *Empire's Tracks: Indigenous Nations, Chinese Workers, and the Transcontinental Railroad.* Oakland: University of California Press, 2019.

Kelly, Brian. *Race, Class, and Power in the Alabama Coalfields, 1908–1921.* Urbana: University of Illinois Press, 2001.

Kolhi, Jaako. "Language and Identity in Montenegro: A Study among University Students." In *Balkan Encounters: Old and New Identities in South-Eastern Europe.* Vol. 41, *Slavica Helsingiensia,* ed. Jouko Lindstedt and Max Wahlstrom, 80–86. Helsinki: University of Helsinki, 2012.

Kramer, Paul. "Power and Connection: Imperial Histories of the United States in the World." *American Historical Review* 116, no. 5 (December 2011): 1348–1391.

Krebs, Sylvia. "John Chinaman and Reconstruction Alabama: The Debate and the Experience," *Southern Studies* 21, no.4 (Winter 1982): 369–384.

LaVigne, David. "The 'Black Fellows' of the Mesabi Iron Range: European Immigrants and Racial Differentiation during the Early Twentieth Century." *Journal of American Ethnic History* 36, no. 2 (Winter 2017): 11–39.

Lee, Erika. *At America's Gates: Chinese Immigration during the Exclusion Era, 1882–1943.* Chapel Hill: University of North Carolina, 2003.

———. "Enforcing the Borders: Chinese Exclusion along the U.S. Borders with Canada and Mexico, 1882–1924." *Journal of American History* 89, no. 1 (June 2002): 54–86.

———. "A Part and Apart: Asian American and Immigration History." *Journal of American Ethnic History* 34, no. 4 (Summer 2015): 28–42.

Leflouria, Talitha. *Chained in Silence: Black Women and Convict Labor in the New South.* Chapel Hill, NC: University of North Carolina Press, 2015.

Letwin, Daniel. *The Challenge of Interracial Unionism: Alabama Coal Miners, 1878–1921.* Chapel Hill: University of North Carolina Press, 1998.

Lewis, Ronald L. "From Peasant to Proletarian: The Migration of Southern Blacks to the Central Appalachian Coalfields." *Journal of Southern History* 55, no. 1 (February 1989): 77–102.

Lewis, W. David. *Sloss Furnaces and the Rise of the Birmingham Industrial District: An Industrial Epic.* Tuscaloosa: University of Alabama Press, 1994.

Lichtenstein, Alex. *Twice the Work of Free Labor: The Political Economy of Convict Labor in the New South.* New York: Verso, 1996.

Link, William A. *Southern Crucible: The Making of an American Region.* New York: Oxford University Press, 2015.

Lipman, Jana, and Daniel Bender. *Making the Empire Work: Labor and U.S. Imperialism.* New York: New York University Press, 2015.

Loewen, James. *The Mississippi Chinese: Between Black and White.* Cambridge, MA: Harvard University Press, 1971.

Lowenberg, Bert J. "Efforts of the South to Encourage Immigration, 1865–1900." *South Atlantic Quarterly* 33 (October 1934): 363–385.

Lowery, J. Vincent. "'Another Species of Racial Discord': Race, Desirability, and the North Carolina Immigration Movement of the Early Twentieth Century." *Journal of American Ethnic History* 36, no. 2 (Winter 2017): 32–59.

Luconi, Stefano. "The Lynching of Southern Europeans in the Southern United States: The Plight of Italian Immigrants in Dixie." In *The U.S. South and Europe: Transatlantic Relations in the Nineteenth and Twentieth Centuries,* ed. Cornelis A. van Minnen and Manfred Berg. Lexington: University Press of Kentucky, 2013.

Lui, Mary Ting. *The Chinatown Trunk Mystery: Murder, Miscegenation, and Other Dangerous Encounters in Turn-of-the-Century New York City.* Princeton, NJ: Princeton University Press, 2005, 67–72.

Lyman, Brian. "U.S. Rep. Mo Brooks Jumps Into Alabama Senate Race." *Montgomery Advertiser,* May 15, 2017.

Magnaghi, Russell Mario. *Italians in Alabama.* New York: Heritage Press, 2018.

Mancini, Matthew. *One Dies, Get Another: Convict Leasing in the American South, 1866–1928.* Columbia: University of South Carolina Press, 1996.

McKiven, Henry M. Jr. *Iron and Steel: Race, Class, and Community in Birmingham, Alabama, 1875–1920.* Chapel Hill: University of North Carolina Press, 1995.

Menzie, Nicola. "Church Leaders: Alabama Anti-Immigration Law 'Merciless.'" *Christian Post,* August 2, 2011.

Mohun, Arwen. *Steam Laundries: Gender, Technology, and Work in the United States and Great Britain, 1880–1940.* Baltimore: John Hopkins University Press, 1999.

Montgomery, David. *The Fall of the House of Labor: The Workplace, the State, and American Labor Activism, 1865–1925.* Cambridge: Cambridge University Press, 1987.

Moore, A. B. "Railroad Building in Alabama during the Reconstruction Period." *Journal of Southern History* 1, no. 4 (November 1935): 421–441.

Moran, Jeffrey. "Chinese Labor for the New South." *Southern Studies: An Interdisciplinary Journal of the South* 3, no. 4 (Winter 1992): 277–304.

Murphy, Arthur D., et al. *Latino Workers in the Contemporary South.* Athens: University of Georgia Press, 2001.

Myers, John B. "Black Human Capital: The Freedmen and the Reconstruction of Labor in Alabama, 1860–1880." PhD diss., Florida State University, 1974.

Nelson, Scott Reynolds. "After Slavery: Forced Drafts of Irish and Chinese Labor in the American Civil War, or The Search for Liquid Labor." In *Many Middle Passages: Forced Migration and the Making of the Modern World,* ed. Emma Christopher, Cassandra Pybus, and Marcus Rediker. Berkeley: University of California Press, 2007.

———. *Iron Confederacies: Southern Railways, Klan Violence, and Reconstruction.* Chapel Hill: University of North Carolina Press, 1999.

———. *A Nation of Deadbeats: An Uncommon History of America's Financial Disasters.* New York: Alfred A. Knopf, 2012.

———. *Steel Drivin' Man: John Henry, The Untold Story of an American Legend.* Oxford: Oxford University Press, 2006.

Ngai, Mae M. "The Architecture of Race in American Immigration Law: A Reexamination of the Immigration Act of 1924." *Journal of American History* 86, no. 1 (June 1999): 67–92.

———. *Impossible Subjects: Illegal Aliens and the Making of Modern America.* Princeton, NJ: Princeton University Press, 2004.

Noe, Kenneth. *Southwest Virginia's Railroad: Modernization, and the Sectional Crisis in the Civil War Era.* Urbana: University of Illinois Press, 1994.

———, ed. *The Yellowhammer War: The Civil War and Reconstruction in Alabama.* Tuscaloosa: University of Alabama Press, 2013.

Norrell, Robert J. "Caste in Steel: Jim Crow Careers in Birmingham, Alabama. *Journal of American History* 73, no. 3 (December 1986): 669–694.

Norwood, Stephen. *Strikebreaking and Intimidation: Mercenaries and Masculinity in Twentieth-Century America.* Chapel Hill: University of North Carolina Press, 2002.

Novkov, Julie. "Racial Constructions: The Legal Regulation of Miscegenation in Alabama, 1890–1934." *Law and History Review* 20, no. 2 (Summer 2002): 225–232.

———. *Racial Union: Law, Intimacy, and the White State in Alabama, 1865–1954.* Ann Arbor: University of Michigan, 2008.

Nystrom, Justin. *Creole Italian: Sicilian Immigrants and the Shaping of New Orleans Food Culture.* Athens: University of Georgia Press, 2018.

Odom, Mary E., and Elaine Lacy, eds. *Latino Immigrants and the Transformation of the U.S. South.* Athens: University of Georgia Press, 2009.

O'Neal, Matthew. "The Newspapers Will Invade Their Fireplaces": Politics, the Press, and the End of Reconstruction in Alabama." Master's thesis, Auburn University, 2016.

Oshinsky, David M. *"Worse Than Slavery": Parchman Farm and the Ordeal of American Justice.* New York: Free Press, 1996.

Painter, Nell Irvin. *Exodusters: Black Migration to Kansas after Reconstruction.* New York, Knopf, 1977.

Paoni, Matthew Carl. "'Dixie's Arms Are Open': The Promotion of Settlement in the Postbellum-Era South." PhD diss., Johns Hopkins University, 2010.

Peacock, James L., Harry L. Watson, and Carrie R. Matthews. *The American South in a Global World.* Chapel Hill: University of North Carolina Press, 2005.

Peck, Gunther. *Reinventing Free Labor: Padrones and Immigrant Workers in the North American West, 1880–1930.* Cambridge: Cambridge University Press, 2000.

Pegler-Gordon, Anna. "Chinese Exclusion, Photography, and the Development of U.S. Immigration Policy." *American Quarterly* 58, no. 1 (2006): 51–77.

Platt, Stephen R. *Autumn in the Heavenly Kingdom: China, the West, and the Epic Story of the Taiping Civil War.* New York: Alfred A. Knopf, 2012.

Pruett, Katharine M., and John D. Fair. "Promoting a New South: Immigration, Racism, and 'Alabama on Wheels.'" *Agricultural History* 66, no. 1 (January 1992): 19–41.

Quan, Robert Seto. *Lotus among the Magnolias: The Mississippi Chinese.* Jackson: University Press of Mississippi, 1982.

Reader, John. *Africa: A Biography of the Continent.* New York: Vintage Books, 1999.

Reynolds, Aaron. "Inside the Jackson Tract: The Battle over Peonage Labor Camps in Southern Alabama, 1906." *Southern Spaces,* January 21, 2013, https://southernspaces.org/2013/inside-jackson-tract-battle-over-peonage-labor-camps-southern-alabama-1906.

Reynolds, Alfred Wade. "The Alabama Negro Colony in Mexico, 1894–1896." *Alabama Review* 6 (January 1953): 31–58.

Ring, Natalie. "Inventing the Tropical South: Race, Region, and the Colonial Model." *Mississippi Quarterly* 56, no. 4 (Fall 2003): 619–631.

———. *The Problem South: Region, Empire, and the New Liberal State, 1880–1930.* Athens: University of Georgia Press, 2012.

Rippy, J. Fred. "A Negro Colonization Project in Mexico, 1895." *Journal of Negro History* 6, no. 1 (January 1921): 66–73.

Roediger, David R. *The Wages of Whiteness: Race and the Making of the American Working Class.* New York: Verso, 1991.

———. *Working toward Whiteness: How America's Immigrants Became White.* New York: Basic Books, 2005.

Rogers, William Warren. *One-Gallused Rebellion: Agrarianism in Alabama, 1865–1896.* Baton Rouge: Louisiana State University Press, 1970.

Rogers, William Warren, and Jeneane Kaiser. "From the Rhine to the Alabama: Hugo Lehmann Lures the Germans." *Alabama Review* 35 (January 1982): 14–29.

Rogers, William Warren, Robert David Ward, Leah Rawls Atkins, and Wayne Flynt. *Alabama: The History of a Deep South State.* Tuscaloosa: University of Alabama Press, 1994.

Sanchez, George. "Race, Nation, and Culture in Recent Immigration Studies." *Journal of American Ethnic History* 18, no. 4 (Summer 1999): 66–84.

Scarpaci, Jean Ann. *Italian Immigrants in Louisiana's Sugar Parishes: Recruitment, Labor Conditions, and Community Relations, 1880–1910.* New York: Arno Press, 1980.

Scarpaci, J. Vincenza. "Labor for Lousiana's Sugar Cane Fields: An Experiment in Immigrant Recruitment." *Journal of American Ethnic History* 36, no. 2 (Winter 2017): 19–41.

———. "Walking the Color Line: Italian Americans in Rural Louisiana, 1880–1910." In *Are Italians White?: How Race Is Made in America,* ed. Jennifer Guglielmo and Salvatore Salerno. New York: Routledge, 2003.

Scott, Rebecca J. "Fault Lines, Color Lines, and Party Lines: Race, Labor, and Collective Action in Louisiana and Cuba, 1862–1912." In *Beyond Slavery: Explorations of Race, Labor, and Citizenship in Postemancipation Societies,* ed. Frederick Cooper, Thomas C. Holt, and Rebecca J. Scott. Chapel Hill: University of North Carolina Press, 2000.

Sell, Zach. "Asian Indentured Labor in the Age of African American Emancipation." *International Labor and Working-Class History* 91 (Spring 2017): 8–27.

Shankman, Arnold. *Ambivalent Friends: Afro-Americans View the Immigrant.* Greenwood, CT: Greenwood Press, 1982.

Shapiro, Karin A. *A New South Rebellion: The Battle against Convict Labor in the Tennessee Coalfields, 1871–1896.* Chapel Hill: University of North Carolina Press, 1998.

Shifflett, Crandall A. *Coal Towns: Life, Work, and Culture in Company Towns of Southern Appalachia, 1880–1960.* Knoxville: University of Tennessee Press, 1991.

Smith, Claudia Sadowski. "Unskilled Labor and the Illegality Spiral: Chinese, European, and Mexican Indocumentados in the United States, 1882–2007." *American Quarterly* 60, no. 3 (September 2008): 779–804.

Somers, Robert. *The Southern States since the War, 1870–71.* Tuscaloosa: University of Alabama, 1965.

Sterling, Robin, ed. *Cullman County, Alabama Confederate Soldiers.* Self-published.

Straw, Richard A. "'This Is Not a Strike, It Is Simply a Revolution': Birmingham Miners Struggle for Power, 1894–1908." PhD diss., University of Missouri–Columbia, 1980.

Strickland, Jeffrey G. "Ethnicity and Race in the Urban South: German Immigrants and African-Americans in Charleston, South Carolina during Reconstruction." PhD diss., Florida State University, 2003.

Summers, Mark. *Railroads, Reconstruction, and the Gospel of Prosperity Aid under the Radical Republicans, 1865–1877.* Princeton, NJ: Princeton University Press, 2014.

Tannenbaum, Frank. *Darker Phases of the South.* New York: G. P. Putnam's Sons, 1924.

Vance, Rupert B. *All These People: The Nation's Resources in the South.* Chapel Hill: University of North Carolina Press, 1945.

Van Reybrouck, David. *Congo: The Epic History of a People.* New York: Harper Collins, 2014.

Vanthemsche, Guy. *Belgium and the Congo, 1885–1980.* Cambridge: Cambridge University Press, 2012.

Vasquez, Irene A. "The *Longue Durée* of Africans in Mexico: The Historiography of Racialization, Acculturation, and Afro-Mexican Subjectivity." *Journal of African American History* 95, no. 2 (Spring 2010): 183–201.

Wang, Sing-Wu. *The Organization of Chinese Emigration, 1848–1888: With Special Reference to Chinese Emigration to Australia.* San Francisco: Chinese Materials, 1978.

Ward, James A., ed. *Southern Railroad Man: Conductor N. J. Bell's Recollections of the Civil War Era.* DeKalb: Northern Illinois University Press, 1994.

Ward, Robert D., and William Warren Rogers. *Convicts, Coal, and the Banner Mine Tragedy.* Tuscaloosa: University of Alabama Press, 1987.

———. *The Great Strike of 1894.* Tuscaloosa: University of Alabama Press, 1965.

———. *It Is Union and Liberty: Alabama Coal Miners and the UMW.* Tuscaloosa: University of Alabama Press, 1999.

———. *Labor Revolt in Alabama: The Great Strike of 1894.* Tuscaloosa: University of Alabama Press, 1965.

Watson, Carolyn Laverne. "Immigration to Alabama, 1865–1890." Master's thesis, Auburn University, 1963.

Weber, Joseph. "Statehouse Wins Put GOP in Redistricting Driver's Seat." *Washington Times,* November 3, 2010, http://www.washingtontimes.com/news/2010/nov/3/the-republican-midterm-wave-swept-through-state-ca/print.

Weise, Julie. *Corazon de Dixie: Mexicans in the U.S. South since 1910.* Chapel Hill: University of North Carolina Press, 2015.

Whayne, Jeannie. *Shadows over Sunnyside: Evolution of a Plantation in Arkansas, 1830–1945.* Fayetteville: University of Arkansas Press, 1993.

White, David. "Alabama GOP Lawmakers Begin Their Work on Their 'Handshake with Alabama' List of Priorities." *Birmingham News,* March 2, 2011, http://blog.al.com/spotnews/2011/03/post_631.html.

White, Marjorie Longnecker. *The Birmingham District: An Industrial History and Guide.* Birmingham, AL: Birmingham Historical Society, 1981.

White, Richard. "Information, Markets, and Corruption: Transcontinental Railroads in the Gilded Age." *Journal of American History* 90, no. 1 (June 2003): 19–43.

———. *Railroaded: The Transcontinentals and the Making of Modern America.* New York: W. W. Norton, 2011.

Wilkerson, Isabel. *The Warmth of Other Suns: The Epic Story of America's Great Migration.* New York: Random House, 2010.

Wilson, Bobby M. *America's Johannesburg.* New York: Rowan and Littlefield, 2000.

Woodward, C. Vann. *Origins of the New South, 1877–1913.* Baton Rouge: Louisiana State University Press, 1951.

Worger, William H. "Industrialists and the State in the U.S. South and South Africa, 1870–1930." *Journal of Southern African Studies* 30, no. 1 (March 2004): 63–86.

Worthman, Paul B. "Black Workers and Labor Unions in Birmingham, Alabama, 1897–1904." *Labor History* 10, no. 3 (Summer 1969): 375–407.

Wright, Gavin. *Old South, New South: Revolutions in the Southern Economy since the Civil War.* New York: Basic Books, 1986.

Young, Elliot. *Alien Nation: Chinese Migration in the Americas from the Coolie Era through World War II.* Chapel Hill: University of North Carolina Press, 2014.

Yu, Renqiu. *To Save China, to Save Ourselves: The Chinese Hand Laundry Alliance of New York.* Philadelphia: Temple University Press, 1992.

Yun, Lisa, and Ricardo Rene Laremont. "Chinese Coolies and African Slaves in Cuba, 1847–74." *Journal of Asian-American Studies* 4, no. 2 (June 2001).

Yung, Judy. *The Chinese Exclusion Act and Angel Island: A Brief History with Documents.* New York: Bedford/St. Martin's, 2019.

Zahra, Tara. *The Great Departure: Mass Migration from Eastern Europe and the Making of the Free World.* New York: W. W. Norton, 2016.

———. "Travel Agents on Trial: Policing Mobility in East Central Europe, 1889–1989." *Past and Present* 223 (May 2014): 161–193.

Zecker, Robert. "'Let Each Reader Judge': Lynching, Race, and Immigrants' Newspapers." In *Swift to Wrath,* ed. William D. Carrigan and Christopher Waldrep. Charlottesville: University of Virginia Press, 2013.

Zesch, Scott. "Chinese Los Angeles in 1870–1871: The Makings of a Massacre." *Southern California Quarterly* 90, no. 2 (Summer 2008): 109–158.

Zimmerman, Andrew. *Alabama in Africa: Booker T. Washington, the German Empire, and the Globalization of the New South.* Princeton, NJ: Princeton University Press, 2010.

INDEX

Note: Page numbers followed by "f" and "n" indicate figures and endnotes, respectively.